D1354515

5 109 218 2

A Critic Writes

ESSAYS by REYNER BANHAM

Reyner Banham in the 1980s. Photo by Bud Jacobs.

A Critic Writes

ESSAYS by REYNER BANHAM

SELECTED BY   Mary Banham

Paul Barker

Sutherland Lyall

Cedric Price

Foreword by   *Peter Hall*

UNIVERSITY OF CALIFORNIA PRESS

Berkeley   Los Angeles   London

Published with the assistance of
a grant from the Graham Foundation
for Advanced Studies in the Fine Arts

University of California Press
Berkeley and Los Angeles, California

University of California Press
London, England

First Paperback Printing 1999

Library of Congress Cataloging-in-Publication Data

Banham, Reyner.
    A critic writes : essays by Reyner Banham / selected by Mary Banham
. . . [et al.].
     p.   cm.
    Includes bibliographical references and index.
    ISBN 0-520-21944-9 (pbk. : alk. paper)
    1. Design—History—20th century.   2. Modernism (Art)
3. Architecture.   4. Art.   I. Banham, Mary.   II. Title.
NK1390.B28   1996
745.2—dc20   96-14255
                                          CIP

Printed in the United States of America

1 2 3 4 5 6 7 8 9

The paper used in this publication meets the minimum requirements of American National Standard for Information Sciences—Permanence of Paper for Printed Library Materials, ANSI Z39.48-1984

Contents

Acknowledgments

To: Edward Dimendberg of the University of Califormia Press, whose idea this book was and who pursued it determinedly across time and continents.

To: Peter Hall, Cedric Price, Paul Barker, and Sutherland Lyall, who devoted many voluntary hours to the Introduction and the reading and selection of fifty-odd articles from over one thousand.

To: Fiona Walmesley for her precise and timely work on the bibliography.

And to: Ben Banham for his reliable memory, ongoing support, and technical expertise.

Mary Banham
London, May 1996

Foreword

Peter Hall

An introduction to the works of Reyner Banham is almost superfluous. He introduces himself. Within the first half page, those who knew him will hear that plain-speaking, matter-of-fact, no-nonsense Norwich voice; those who did not will immediately be seized by the startlingly new insights, the striking discovery of significance in something everyone else thought banal, the deadly destruction of platitudes, that were the weekly Banham stock-in-trade. They will know, within a paragraph, that here was one of Nature's originals.

So why waste the time, why defer this special gratification? (After all, he would have hated being fussed over.) Because Banham really demands a moment of our attention. He was a most unusual person; one of the most unusual that many of us have had the privilege of knowing. He was a brilliant polemical journalist, a meticulous scholar, and a sociologist /anthropologist of twentieth-century design. In each of these, he exalted, and, unusually, all were uniquely combined. The resulting cocktail, shaken and delivered week by week in the public prints, was a devastatingly heady concoction.

So it is worth making some points about him. The first is that though he spent a good part of his life studying architecture, he was not an architect. He was trained as an aeroengineer, and in an important sense an engineer he remained. (Paul Barker recalls a last glimpse of him: fast-fading in the Royal Free Hospital, he was fascinated by the medical technologies that were keeping him and his fellow patients alive.) Engineers by and large are not noted for lateral thinking, for feats of imagination. But when they do achieve this, they are true geniuses.

The engineer in Banham explains his early work on theory and design in the first machine age. The result was his Ph.D. dissertation, which made his reputation; he could understand machinery and how people related to it. It was a true work of scholarship, produced under Sir Nikolaus Pevsner's supervision at the Courtauld Institute.

Banham was already writing for the *Architectural Review;* he was a journalistic natural. Early in his career, he had worked as art critic for the *Eastern Daily Press.* Now, already seasoned—his first essay in this collection was published when he was 33— he brought to his journalism his extraordinary interest in the minutiae of everyday life, and in turn the job honed his skills. To the end, all his writing had the immediacy, the vitality, the concreteness of the best journalism. It causes one to ponder: if other academics had come to research and teaching that way, would not academic writing be immeasurably better than it is, on average, and would not the academy be an infinitely richer and more interesting place? But perhaps not; the world produces very few Banhams.

Banham then made his move back into academe, where he supremely belonged. Richard Llewelyn Davies recognised his genius and brought him to University College London, first as senior lecturer, then reader, finally as professor of the history of architecture. No one present that night in 1970, in the UCL Darwin Theatre, will forget his inaugural. 'At Shoe Fly Landing.' What could the title mean? The massed ranks of Britain's architecture and planning establishment, of the UCL professorate, sat there intrigued. Like the good journalist he was, Banham did not keep them waiting long: the title had been one of those placard headlines that compel you to buy the paper. Shoe Fly Landing, it turned out, was the place on Santa Monica Bay where Europeans had first set foot in the Los Angeles basin; we were on Banham's favorite ground.

But further bafflement followed. The site had been close to the present Santa Monica Pier. And this led Banham, by a sudden intellectual leap, into an extraordinary scholarly disquisition on the archaeology of the pier and its predecessor. For it turned out that there had been not one but two. Painstakingly, illustrated by a wealth of slides, Banham traced in meticulous detail the way in which one had archaeologically succeeded another; then, with equal loving care, he analyzed the architecture and land uses of the present structure, the bars and amusement arcades and other banal delights. Half the audience clearly thought they were being elaborately sent up. Almost another half didn't know what to think at all. A small minority, Banham's friends and intellectual confidants, found it a tour de force. It is reproduced here, in truncated form.

The inaugural was in many ways archetypal Banham, for it illustrated in supreme measure the qualities he brought together in all his best work. First was the extraordinarily penetrating quality of his eye: his capacity, which he shared with great visual art-

ists, to see things that everyone else missed, to find significance in the apparently banal. Second was his meticulous, almost Teutonic, scholarship; not for nothing did
he worship at the feet of Pevsner, his Courtauld master, and of Henry Russell Hitchcock. (In a late piece, he pays Hitchcock the supreme compliment: 'He knew his buildings.') And third was his historicosociological insight, his extraordinary intellectual
capacity to explain buildings in terms of a particular society and culture in a particular
place and at a particular time.

The inaugural was a turning point, of course. For now Banham was free as air, free
to do what he did incomparably best: to speculate, to turn his huge gifts of insight
and observation to subjects completely of his choosing. He had found an ideal vehicle
in *New Society,* the weekly magazine of the social sciences, which Tim Raison had
founded in 1962 and Paul Barker had edited from 1965. His first major piece there
was a review published in August 1965 of a totally unknown but quite brilliant first
book by a totally unknown American writer, *The Kandy-Kolored Tangerine-Flake Streamlined Baby* by Tom Wolfe. Barker shared his delight in exploring the byways of popular
sociology and popular design. (It was also the period when artists, both British and
American, were delving into popular culture: Lichtenstein, Warhol, and Oldenberg were
producing their most memorable work at just this time; Peter had been one of the be-
getters of the entire movement.) Barker gave him virtual carte blanche in his monthly
column, 'Society and Design.' Most of his best writings outside the big books, certainly the most perceptive, appeared there between 1965 and his death in 1988;
they form the solid core of this collection.

They show his particular genius. There was the eye—his ability to see things fresh
and unencumbered by preconception. He thus saw again and again what others failed
to see: the importance of a bike shed as well as of a cathedral or of an Eames house.
He praised Hitchcock and Pevsner for that quality; neither, however, was as catholic,
as all-seeing as he. That came with another feature, his refusal to put a boundary line
around architecture; it merged into the design of everyday objects, from bolo ties to
cars to sheriff stars, from ice cream vans to bricolage to the buildings in the Ironbridge
Gorge. Some of these pieces (Ironbridge, bricolage) show his impatience with his fellow academics; unlike them, he started from his absolute engineer's knowledge of
what things were like and how they really worked, which made him impatient with—
and contemptuous of—any theory that did not spring from the deep soil of experience.

Less evident, perhaps, was the scholarship; that comes out more clearly in work
for fellow scholars, such as reviews. He was a very generous person, but on the rare
times that he was rude it was occasioned by what he saw as shoddy scholarship,
which he could not abide. (Compare his tribute to Hitchcock with his blistering attack
on Watkin.)

There was another feature, and this may seem odd: his worship of modernism. As
he was at pains to point out in one of his last essays, he was an unrepentant chroni-
cler and worshiper of the modern movement, and one cannot understand much else—

his refusal to delimit architecture from industrial design, for instance—without understanding that basic fact. He really believed, as many thinking people of his generation did but few of their children seem to do, that technology was a liberating and beneficent force. Notice how, in an early piece, he argues that the problem with the housing drive of the late 1950s was that at vast public cost it produced substandard caravans, and how, a little later, he extols the virtues of airplanes. For him, as you can see in his appreciative early essay on Stirling and Gowan's celebrated Leicester engineering block, form truly followed function. He believed that engineering could be applied to solve problems. Consider his celebrated article on Gizmos, or his article on *Barbarella* and his belief that technology can help us escape from the nineteenth-century city, or—perhaps most significant, because one of his fiercest pieces—his article on the Tennessee Valley dams, in which he admires engineering for its capacity to do good deeds.

It may seem odd, because much of what he found interesting, because most quirky, can hardly be called modern except in a very special and obscure sense. He liked the same buildings that a postmodernist guru like Robert Venturi did (and indeed he liked them much earlier), but for subtly different reasons—Venturi because they suggested a new architectural order, Banham because they were manifestations of popular culture. (In an early *New Society* piece he effectively identifies Bolsover Castle as the first postmodernist building, though of course in 1969 he does not use the term; his description of its columns precisely describes what Venturi would do on the National Gallery extension, over twenty years later.) He was one of the first to appreciate the significance of Portman's huge hotel atria, in an article of 1979; but the point is that he characteristically finds they derive from the style of the 1935 H. G. Wells–derived movie *Things to Come.* When he admires a specific postmodern building, like Stirling's Staatsgalerie—which, in his last piece, he puts at the end of a European mainstream that started with Stonehenge—he labels it modern; perverse, perhaps, but perhaps after all the Stuttgart building is modern with jokes. To the end he remained uncompromisingly opposed to postmodernism as such, which in that wonderful final piece of 1990, posthumously published, he describes as having 'the same relationship to architecture as female impersonation to femininity. It is not architecture, but building in drag.'

The inaugural, and much that came after, illustrates another theme, his love of America and above all of the American West. His early *New Society* article that extolls the virtues of Frank Lloyd Wright's Broadacre City, in which he speaks of Wright's 'alternative vision of civilization that no European could ever know,' perfectly encapsulates his twin and entirely congruent beliefs in America and in technology. And when he rhapsodizes on the virtues of the taco chip, it is as an example of American engineering. He became a regular and much-loved presence at the Aspen (Colorado) Design Conference, where he found himself with other free spirits. It was just, somehow, that he should have migrated to the University of California at Santa Cruz, a campus that was a living embodiment of western design of the 1960s and 1970s and one that for a while seemed the quintessence of the spirit of 1967. There he found the freshness, the freedom to experiment, the refusal to be limited by conventional notions of what was right and good that he had failed to find in old Europe or on the East Coast.

What he particularly found and particularly valued in the American West was ordinary people, designing the way they wanted, untrammelled by the self-appointed thought-arbiters of good taste. Notice the characteristically iconoclastic piece in which he compares ice cream vans with medieval cathedrals. And notice too a piece, not included in this collection, that conferred on a group of us—he, Paul Barker, Cedric Price, and me—a certain collective notoriety: 'Nonplan: An Experiment in Freedom,' published in *New Society* in 1969, in which we called for an American-style experimental approach to the development of selected bits of Britain.

The posthumous 1990 piece is particularly significant, not simply because it was his swan song, but because he knew it was and wrote it that way. In it he makes the statement—which I find extraordinary for him, but perhaps *nothing* was too extraordinary for him—that there is such a thing as an absolute quality of architecture, which Hawksmoor possessed but which Wren did not, and to which all architects must subscribe. Architecture, he insists, is distinguished from other perfectly good ways of making perfectly good buildings (like builders building bike sheds, or all the wonderful mad things that people did and do in the American West) by the fact that it *does drawings;* doing drawings is what architecture is about. He tells the wonderful story of the apocryphal architect who, asked to produce a pencil as a tourniquet to save a dying man on the street, asks, 'Will a 2B do?'

It sounds almost like a deathbed attempt to become reconciled with the church that he had questioned and even devastatingly undermined for so long. But of course it is not: he insists he is looking at architecture as he always had, as an anthropologist. (It is not a casual remark when he describes architects as inhabiting a tribal longhouse.) He ends this piece, and his creative life, on a quintessential Banham note by calling for an anthropological inquiry into the profession. That perhaps was supremely unnecessary; it is what he had been doing, single-handedly, for the best years of his life. For it, and for so much else, we owe him a debt that can never be repaid, and we salute him in sorrow and with love, as a friend, colleague, and intellect of a kind we shall not expect to find again.

University College London
October 1993

» The 1950s

BY 1950 REYNER BANHAM had spent a year at the Courtauld Institute, University of London, studying art history.

After leaving school in 1939, he had embarked on a management training course at the Bristol Aeroplane Company in the west of England . . . aeroplanes being a Banham family passion. When war came in September of that year, the course was terminated, and after the war he decided he would prefer to do something else with his life.

When the opportunity came to study at the prestigious Courtauld Institute in 1949, he left his hometown of Norwich in eastern England where he had, for three years, been writing art exhibition reviews for two major local newspapers.

On arriving in London he continued to review art exhibitions for London magazines while pursuing his studies as a late entrant undergraduate and as a central organising member and recorder for the Independent Group at the Institute of Contemporary Art, where he met artists, architects, writers, designers, musicians who were excitedly gathering in London after frustrating years away from their developing interests during the war.

In 1952 he joined the staff of the *Architectural Review,* which since its inception had been a campaigning architectural magazine of international importance. Here he wrote about another passion, contemporary architecture. At the same time he worked with Sir Nikolaus Pevsner on his Ph.D. dissertation, which was rewritten for publication under the title *Theory and Design in the First Machine Age.* This book was to make his reputation.

While at the *Architectural Review* he met most of the world's best-known architects, who would not pass through London without visiting the 'Bride of Denmark,' the famous pub in the basement at Queen Anne's Gate, and signing their names on the big mirror behind the bar.

During this decade Banham began to lecture at the Courtauld, the ICA, and the Tate Gallery and to broadcast for the BBC. By the end of the 1950s he was writing regularly for other magazines as well as *Architectural Review* and *Architects Journal,* including the left-wing *New Statesman.* His reputation as a writer and a speaker was growing apace.—M.B.

1

Vehicles of Desire

The New Brutalists, pace-makers and phrase-makers of the Anti-Academic line-up, having delivered a smart KO to the Land-Rover some months back, have now followed it with a pop-eyed OK for the Cadillac convertible, and automobile aesthetics are back on the table for the first time since the 'Twenties. The next time an open "Caddy" wambles past you, its front chrome-hung like a pearl-roped dowager, its long top level with the ground at a steady thirty inches save where the two tail-fins cock up to carry the rear lights, reflect what a change has been wrought since the last time any architect expressed himself forcibly on the subject of the automobile.

That was in the 'Twenties when Le Corbusier confronted the Parthenon and the Bignan-Sport, and from then to the New Brutalists the Greek Doric motor-car with its upright lines, square styling, mahogany fascia and yellowing nickel trim has remained the *beau ideal* of world aesthetes from Chicago to Chelsea Polytechnic. So great has been the aesthetic self-aggrandisement of architects, so great the public's Ruskin-powered terror of them that when Le Corbusier spoke, no-one dared to argue, and it has been placidly assumed ever since that all artefacts should be designed architect-

Originally appeared in *Art,* 1 September 1955, p. 3.

wise, and that later automobiles, which deviated from the Doric norm of the 'Twenties were badly designed. But what nonsense this is. Far from being *uomini universali* architects are by training, aesthetics and psychological predisposition narrowly committed to the design of big permanent single structures, and their efforts are directed merely to focussing big, permanent human values on unrepeatable works of unique art.

The automobile is not big—few are even mantel-piece high—it is not permanent—the average world scrapping period has lately risen, repeat risen, to fifteen years—and they certainly are not unique. The effective time-base against which the impermanence of the automobile should be reckoned is less than even fifteen years, because the average re-sale period—the measure of social obsolescence—is only three to six years, while technical obsolescence is already acute after eight to ten years. And as to uniqueness, even relatively unpopular cars have a bigger annual output than all but the most sought-after pre-fabricated, serially-produced buildings. This is a field where the architect is rarely qualified to work, or to pass judgment, and automobiles designed by architects are notoriously old-fashioned, even where—like Walter Gropius's *Adler* coupés—they introduce marginal novelties such as reclining seats.

The technical history of the automobile in a free market is a rugged rat-race of detail modifications and improvements, many of them irrelevant, but any of the essential ones lethal enough to kill off a manufacturer who misses it by more than a couple of years. The "classic" automobiles whose "timeless" qualities are admired by aesthetes are nowadays the product of abnormal sales conditions—the slump-crazy market on which Citroen's *traction-avant* was launched was as freakish as the commercially and ideologically protected one on which Dr. Porsche launched the *Volkswagen*. On the open market, where competition is real, it is the cunningly-programmed minor changes that give one manufacturer an edge over another, and the aesthetics of body-styling are an integral part of the battle for margins. Under these circumstances we should be neither surprised nor shocked to find that styling runs the same way as engineering development, and in any case there can be no norms of formal composition while
the automobile remains an artefact in evolution, even though particular models are stabilised.

In fact it is a great deal more than an artefact in evolution as a concept while standardised in any passing type; it is also numerous as a possession while expendable as an individual example, a vehicle of popular desire and a dream that money can just about buy. This is a situation with which no pre-industrial aesthetic ever had to cope; even Plato's side-swipe at the ceramic trade in the *Philebus* falls a long way short of our current interpretative needs, for the Greek pot, though numerous and standardized, had long given up evolving and was not conspicuously expendable. But we are still making do with Plato because in aesthetics, as in most other things, we still have no formulated intellectual attitudes for living in a throwaway economy. We eagerly consume noisy ephemeridae, here with a bang today, gone without a whimper tomorrow—movies, beach-wear, pulp magazines, this morning's headlines and tomorrow's TV programmes—yet we insist on aesthetic and moral standards hitched to permanency, durability and perennity.

The repertoire of hooded headlamps, bumper-bombs, sporty nave-plates, ventilators, intakes, incipient tail-fins, speed-streaks and chromium spears, protruding exhaust-pipes, cineramic wind-screens—these give tone and social connotation to the body envelope; the profiling of wheel-arches, the humping of mudguards, the angling of roof-posts—these control the sense of speed; the grouping of the main masses, the quality of the main curves of the panels—these balance the sense of masculine power and feminine luxury. It is a thick ripe stream of loaded symbols—that are apt to go off in the face of those who don't know how to handle them.

The stylist knows how, because he is continually sampling the public response to dream-car prototypes, fantasy vehicles like Ford's fabulous *Futura,* but other people must be more careful. As the New York magazine *Industrial Design* said, when reviewing the 1954 cars, "The most successful company in the history of the world makes automobiles; in 1953 General Motors' sales totalled $10,028,000,000, an unheard of sum. Under the circumstances, passing judgment on a new crop of cars is like passing judgment on a Nation's soul."

But coupled with this admirable caution, *Industrial Design* also possesses a shame-faced, but invaluable, ability to write automobile-critique of almost Berensonian sensibility. In its pages, fenced about with routine kow-tows to the big permanent values, one will find passages like "the Buick . . . is perpetually floating on currents that are permanently built into the design. The designers put the greatest weight over the front wheels, where the engine is, which is natural enough. The heavy bumper helps to pull the weight forward; the dip in the body and the chrome spear express how the thrust is dissipated in turbulence toward the rear. Just behind the strong shoulder of the car a sturdy post lifts up the roof, which trails off like a banner in the air. The driver sits in the dead calm at the centre of all this motion—hers is a lush situation."

This is the stuff of which the aesthetics of expendability will eventually be made. It carries the sense and the dynamism of that extraordinary continuum of emotional-engineering-by-public-consent which enables the automobile industry to create vehicles of palpably fulfilled desire. Can architecture or any other Twentieth Century art claim to have done as much? and, if not, have they any real right to carp?

All right then, *hypocrite lecteur,* where are you now with the automobile? As an expendable, replaceable vehicle of the popular desires it clearly belongs with the other dreams that money can buy, with *Galaxy, The Seven Year Itch, Rock Rattle 'n' Roll* and *Midweek Reveille,* the world of expendable art so brilliantly characterised by Leslie Fiedler in the August issue of *Encounter.* The motor car is not as expendable as they are, but it clearly belongs nearer to them than to the Parthenon, and it exhibits the same creative thumb-prints—finish, fantasy, punch, professionalism, swagger. A good job of body styling should come across like a good musical—no fussing after big, timeless abstract virtues, but maximum glitter and maximum impact.

The top body stylists—they are the anonymous heads of anonymous teams—aim to give their creations qualities of apparent speed, power, brutalism, luxury, snob-appeal, exoticism and plain common-or-garden sex. The means at their disposal are symbolic iconographies, whose ultimate power lies in their firm grounding in popular taste and the innate traditions of the product, while the actual symbols are drawn from Science Fiction, movies, earth-moving equipment, supersonic aircraft, racing cars, heraldry and certain deep-seated mental dispositions about the great outdoors and the kinship between technology and sex. Arbiter and interpreter between the industry and the consumer, the body-stylist deploys, not a farrage of meaningless ornament, as fine art critics insist, but a means of saying something of breathless, but unverbalisable, consequence to the live culture of the Technological Century.

2

The New Brutalism

'L'Architecture, c'est avec des matieres bruts, établir des rapports émouvants. '
—Le Corbusier, *Vers une Architecture*

Introduce an observer into any field of forces, influences or communications and that field becomes distorted. It is common opinion that *Das Kapital* has played old harry with capitalism, so that Marxists can hardly recognize it when they see it, and the widespread diffusion of Freud's ideas has wrought such havoc with clinical psychology that any intelligent patient can make a nervous wreck of his analyst. What has been the influence of contemporary architectural historians on the history of contemporary architecture?

They have created the idea of a Modern Movement—this was known even before Basil Taylor took up arms against false historicism—and beyond that they have offered a rough classification of the 'isms' which are the thumb-print of Modernity into two main types: One, like *Cubism,* is a label, a recognition tag, applied by critics and historians

---

Originally appeared in *The Architectural Review* 118 (December 1955): 354–361.

to a body of work which appears to have certain consistent principles running through it, whatever the relationship of the artists; the other, like *Futurism,* is a banner, a slogan, a policy consciously adopted by a group of artists, whatever the apparent similarity or dissimilarity of their products. And it is entirely characteristic of the New Brutalism—our first native art-movement since the New Art-History arrived here—that it should confound these categories and belong to both at once.

Is Art-History to blame for this? Not in any obvious way, but in practically every other way. One cannot begin to study the New Brutalism without realizing how deeply the New Art-History has bitten into progressive English architectural thought, into teaching methods, into the common language of communication between architects and between architectural critics. What is interesting about R. Furneaux Jordan's parthian footnote on the New Brutalism—'. . . Lubetkin talks across time to the great masters, the Smithsons talk only to each other'—is not the fact that it is nearly true, and thus ruins his argument, but that its terms of valuation are historical. The New Brutalism has to be seen against the background of the recent history of history, and, in particular, the growing sense of the inner history of the Modern Movement itself.

The history of the phrase itself is revealing. Its form is clearly derived from *The Archi tectural Review's* post-war *trouvaille* 'The New Empiricism,' a term which was intended to describe visible tendencies in Scandinavian architecture to diverge from another historical concept 'The International Style.' This usage, like any involving the word *new,* opens up an historical perspective. It postulates that an old empiricism can be identified by the historian, and that the new one can be distinguished from it by methods of historical comparison, which will also distinguish it from a mere 'Empirical Revival.' The ability to deal with such fine shades of historical meaning is in itself a measure of our handiness with the historical method today, and the use of phrases of the form 'The New X-ism'—where X equals any adjectival root—became commonplace in the early nineteen-fifties in fourth-year studios and other places where architecture is discussed, rather than practised.

The passion of such discussion has been greatly enhanced by the clarity of its polarization—Communists versus the Rest—and it was somewhere in this vigorous polemic that the term 'The New Brutalism' was first coined.[1] It was, in the beginning, a term of Communist abuse, and it was intended to signify the normal vocabulary of Modern Architecture—flat roofs, glass, exposed structure—considered as morally reprehensible deviations from 'The New Humanism,' a phrase which means something different in Marxist hands to the meaning which might be expected. The New Humanism meant, in architecture at that time, brickwork, segmental arches, pitched roofs, small windows (or small panes at any rate)—picturesque detailing without picturesque planning. It was, in fact, the so-called 'William Morris Revival,' now happily defunct, since Kruschev's reversal of the Party's architectural line, though this reversal has, of course, taken the guts out of subsequent polemics. But it will be observed that The New Humanism was again a quasi-historical concept, oriented, however spuriously, toward that mid-nineteenth century epoch which was Marxism's Golden Age, when you could recognize a capitalist when you met him.

However, London architectural circles are a small field in which to conduct a polemic of any kind, and abuse must be directed at specific persons, rather than classes of persons, since there was rarely enough unanimity (except among Marxists) to allow a class to coalesce. The New Brutalists at whom Marxist spite was directed could be named and recognized—and so could their friends in other arts. The term had no sooner got into public circulation than its meaning began to narrow. Among the non-Marxist grouping there was no particular unity of programme or intention, but there was a certain community of interests, a tendency to look toward Le Corbusier, and to be aware of something called *le beton brut,* to know the quotation which appears at the head of this article and, in the case of the more sophisticated and aesthetically literate, to know of the *Art Brut* of Jean Dubuffet and his connection in Paris. Words and ideas, personalities and discontents chimed together and in a matter of weeks— long before the Third Programme and the monthlies had got hold of the phrase—it had been appropriated as their own, by their own desire and public consent, by two young architects, Alison and Peter Smithson.

The phrase had thus changed both its meaning and its usage. Adopted as something between a slogan and a brick-bat flung in the public's face, The New Brutalism ceased to be a label descriptive of a tendency common to most modern architecture, and became instead a programme, a banner, while retaining some—rather restricted— sense as a descriptive label. It is because it is both kinds of -ism at once that The New Brutalism eludes precise description, while remaining a living force in contemporary British architecture.

As a descriptive label it has two overlapping, but not identical, senses. Non-architecturally it describes the art of Dubuffet, some aspects of Jackson Pollock and of Appel, and the burlap paintings of Alberto Burri—among foreign artists—and, say, Magda Cordell or Edouardo Paolozzi and Nigel Henderson among English artists. With these last two, the Smithsons collected and hung the I.C.A. exhibition *Parallel of Life and Art,* which, though it probably preceded the coining of the phrase, is nevertheless regarded as a *locus classicus* of the movement. The more instructive aspects of this exhibition will be considered later: for the moment let us observe that many critics (and students at the Architectural Association) complained of the deliberate flouting of the traditional concepts of photographic beauty, of a cult of ugliness, and 'denying the spiritual in Man.' The tone of response to The New Brutalism existed even before hostile critics knew what to call it, and there was an awareness that the Smithsons were headed in a different direction to most other younger architects in London.

Alison Smithson first claimed the words in public as her own in a description of a project for a small house in Soho (*Architectural Design,* November, 1953) designed before the phrase existed, and previously tagged 'The warehouse aesthetic'—a very fair description of what The New Brutalism stood for in its first phase. Of this house, she wrote: '. . . had this been built, it would have been the first exponent of the New Brutalism in England, as the preamble to the specification shows: "It is our intention in this building to have the structure exposed entirely, without interior finishes wherever practicable. The contractor should aim at a high standard of basic construction, as in a small warehouse".' The publication of this project led to an extensive and often hilarious correspondence in various periodicals through the summer of 1954, a correspondence which wandered further and further from its original point because most writers were in fact discussing either the exhibition *Parallel of Life and Art,* or the (as yet) unpublished school at Hunstanton. When this was finally published (AR, September, 1954) the discussion took a sharper and less humorous tone, for here in three-dimensional and photographic reality, and in the classic Modern Movement materials of concrete, steel and glass, was the Smithsons' only completed building. The phrase The New Brutalism was immediately applied to it, though it had been designed in the spring of 1950, long before even the house in Soho, but the Brutalists themselves have accepted this appellation, and it has become the tag for Hunstanton wherever the building has been discussed.

Hunstanton, and the house in Soho, can serve as the points of architectural reference by which The New Brutalism in architecture may be defined. What are the visible and identifiable characteristics of these two structures? Both have formal, axial plans—Hunstanton, in fact, has something like true bi-axial symmetry, and the small Gymnasium block alongside the school is a kind of exemplar in little of just how formal the complete scheme was to have been—and this formality is immediately legible from without. Both exhibit their basic structure, and both make a point of exhibiting their materials—in fact, this emphasis on basic structure is so obsessive that many superficial critics have taken this to be the whole of New Brutalist Architecture. Admittedly, this emphasis on basic structure is important, even if it is not the whole story, and what has caused Hunstanton to lodge in the public's gullet is the fact that it is almost unique among modern buildings in being made of what it appears to be made of. Whatever has been said about honest use of materials, most modern buildings *appear* to be made of whitewash or patent glazing, even when they are made of concrete or steel. Hunstanton *appears* to be made of glass, brick, steel and concrete, and is in fact made of glass, brick, steel and concrete. Water and electricity do not come out of unexplained holes in the wall, but are delivered to the point of use by visible pipes and manifest conduits. One can see what Hunstanton is made of, and how it works, and there is not another thing to see except the play of spaces.

This ruthless adherence to one of the basic moral imperatives of the Modern Movement—honesty in structure and material—has precipitated a situation to which only the pen of Ibsen could do justice. The mass of moderate architects, *hommes moyens sensuels,* have found their accepted practices for waiving the requirements of the conscience-code suddenly called in question; they have been put rudely on the spot, and they have not liked the experience. Of course, it is not just the building itself which has precipitated this situation, it is the things the Brutalists have said and done as well, but, as with the infected Spa in *An Enemy of the People,* the play of personalities focuses around a physical object.

The qualities of that object may be summarized as follows: 1, Formal legibility of plan; 2, clear exhibition of structure; and 3, valuation of materials for their inherent qualities 'as found.' This summary can be used to answer the question: Are there other New Brutalist buildings besides Hunstanton? It is interesting to note that such a summary of qualities could be made to describe Marseilles, Promontory and Lake-shore apartments, General Motors Technical Centre, much recent Dutch work and several projects by younger English architects affiliated to CIAM. But, with the possible exception of Marseilles, the Brutalists would probably reject most of these buildings from the canon, and so must we, for all of these structures exhibit an excess of *suaviter in modo,* even if there is plenty of *fortiter in re* about them. In the last resort what characterizes the New Brutalism in architecture as in painting is precisely its brutality, its *je-m'en-foutisme,* its bloody-mindedness. Only one other building conspicuously carries these qualities in the way that Hunstanton does, and that is Louis Kahn's Yale Art Centre. Here is a building which is uncompromisingly frank about its materials, which is inconceivable apart from its boldly exhibited structural method which—being a concrete space-frame—is as revolutionary and unconventional as the use of the Plastic Theory in stressing Hunstanton's steel H-frames. Furthermore, the plan is very formal in the disposition of its main elements, and makes a kind of symmetry about two clearly defined axes at right angles to one another. And this is a building which some Brutalists can apparently accept as a constituent New Brutalist structure.

But, with all due diffidence, the present author submits that it still does not quite answer to the standard set by Hunstanton. For one thing, the Smithsons' work is characterized by an abstemious under-designing of the details, and much of the impact of the building comes from the ineloquence, but absolute consistency, of such components as the stairs and handrails. By comparison, Kahn's detailing is arty, and the stair-rail and balustrading (if that is the word for stainless netting) is jarringly out of key with the rough-shuttered concrete of the main structure. This may be 'only a matter of detailing' but there is another short-fall about Yale Art Centre which could not be brushed off so easily. Every Smithson design has been, obviously or subtly, a coherent and apprehensible visual entity, but this Louis Kahn's design narrowly fails to be. The internal spaces will be cluttered with display screens which, in the nature of his programme and his solution of it, must be susceptible of being moved, so that formal clarity is always threatened. But beyond this the relation of interior to exterior fails to validate the axes which govern the plan. Available viewpoints, the placing of the entrances, the handling of the exterior walls—all tend to lose or play down the presence of planning axes. No doubt there are excellent functional reasons for the doors being where they are, and excellent structural reasons for the walls being treated in the way they are—but if these reasons were so compelling, why bother with an axial plan anyhow?

This is a hard thing to have to say about a seriously considered building by a reputable architect of some standing, but contact with Brutalist architecture tends to drive one to hard judgements, and the one thing of which the Smithsons have never been accused is a lack of logic or consistency in thinking through a design. In fact it is the ruthless logic more than anything else which most hostile critics find distressing about Hunstanton—or perhaps it is the fact that this logic is worn on the sleeve. One of the reasons for this obtrusive logic is that it contributes to the apprehensibility and coherence of the building as a visual entity, because it contributes to the building as 'an image.'

An Image—with the utterance of these two words we bridge the gap between the possible use of The New Brutalism as a descriptive label covering, in varying degrees of accuracy, two or more buildings, and The New Brutalism as a slogan, and we also go some way to bridge the gap between the meaning of the term as applied to architecture and its meaning as applied to painting and sculpture. The word *image* in this sense is one of the most intractable and the most useful terms in contemporary aesthetics, and some attempt to explain it must be made.

A great many things have been called 'an image'—S. M. della Consolazione at Todi, a painting by Jackson Pollock, the Lever Building, the 1954 Cadillac convertible, the roofscape of the *Unité* at Marseilles, any of the hundred photographs in *Parallel of Life and Art.* 'Image' seems to be a word that describes anything or nothing. Ultimately, however, it means something which is visually valuable, but not necessarily by the standards of classical aesthetics. Where Thomas Aquinas supposed beauty to be *quod visum placet* (that which seen, pleases),[2] image may be defined as *quod visum perturbat*—that which seen, affects the emotions, a situation which could subsume the pleasure caused by beauty, but is not normally taken to do so, for the New Brutalists' interests in image are commonly regarded, by many of themselves as well as their critics, as being anti-art, or at any rate anti-beauty in the classical aesthetic sense of the word. But what is equally as important as the specific kind of response, is the nature of its cause. What pleased St. Thomas was an abstract quality, beauty—what moves a New Brutalist is the thing itself, in its totality, and with all its overtones of human association. These ideas of course lie close to the general body of anti-Academic aesthetics currently in circulation, though they are not to be identified exactly with Michel Tapié's concept of *un Art Autre,*[3] even though that concept covers many Continental Brutalists as well as Edouardo Paolozzi.

Nevertheless this concept of *Image* is common to all aspects of The New Brutalism in England, but the manner in which it works out in architectural practice has some surprising twists to it. Basically, it requires that the building should be an immediately apprehensible visual entity, and that the form grasped by the eye should be confirmed by experience of the building in use. Further, that this form should be entirely proper to the functions and materials of the building, in their entirety. Such a relationship between structure, function and form is the basic commonplace of all good building of course, the demand that this form should be apprehensible and memorable is the apical uncommonplace which makes good building into great architecture. The fact that this form-giving obligation has been so far forgotten that a great deal of good building can be spoken of as if it were architecture, is a mark of a seriously decayed condition in English architectural standards. It has become too easy to get away with the assumption that if structure and function are served then the result must be architecture—so easy that the meaningless phrase 'the conceptual building' has been coined to defend the substandard architectural practices of the routine-functionalists, as if 'conceptual buildings' were something new, and something faintly reprehensible in modern architecture.

All great architecture has been 'conceptual,' has been image-making—and the idea that any great buildings, such as the Gothic Cathedrals, grew unconsciously through anonymous collaborative attention to structure and function is one of the most insidious myths with which the Modern Movement is saddled. Every great building of the Modern Movement has been a conceptual design, especially those like the Bauhaus, which go out of their way to look as if they were the products of 'pure' functionalism, whose aformal compositions are commonly advanced by routine-functionalists in defence of their own abdication of architectural responsibility. But a conceptual building is as likely to be aformal as it is to be formal, as a study of the Smithsons' post-Hunstanton projects will show.

Hunstanton's formality is unmistakably Miesian, as Philip Johnson pointed out, possibly because IIT was one of the few recent examples of conceptual, form-giving design to which a young architect could turn at the time of its conception, and the formality of their Coventry Cathedral competition entry is equally marked, but here one can safely posit the interference of historical studies again, for, though the exact priority of date as between the Smithsons' design and the publication of Professor Wittkower's *Architectural Principles of the Age of Humanism* is disputed (by the Smithsons) it cannot be denied that they were in touch with Wittkowerian studies at the time, and were as excited by them as anybody else.

The general impact of Professor Wittkower's book on a whole generation of post-war architectural students is one of the phenomena of our time. Its exposition of a body of architectural theory in which function and form were significantly linked by the objective laws governing the Cosmos (as Alberti and Palladio understood them) suddenly offered a way out of the doldrum of routine-functionalist abdications, and neo-Palladianism became the order of the day. The effect of *Architectural Principles* has made it by far the most important contribution—for evil as well as good—by any historian to English Architecture since *Pioneers of the Modern Movement,* and it precipitated a nice disputation on the proper uses of history. The question became: Humanist principles to be followed? or Humanist principles as an example of the kind of principles to look for?

Many students opted for the former alternative, and Routine-Palladians soon became as thick on the ground as Routine-Functionalists. The Brutalists, observing the inherent risk of a return to pure academicism—more pronounced at Liverpool than at the AA—sheered off abruptly in the other direction and were soon involved in the organization of *Parallel of Life and Art*.

Introducing this exhibition to an AA student debate Peter Smithson declared: 'We are not going to talk about proportion and symmetry' and this was his declaration of war on the inherent academicism of the neo-Palladians, and the anti-Brutalist section of the house made it clear how justified was this suspicion of crypto-academicism by taking their stand not only on Palladio and Alberti but also on Plato and the Absolute. The new direction in Brutalist architectural invention showed at once in the Smithsons' Golden Lane and Sheffield University competition entries. The former, only remembered for having put the idea of the street-deck back in circulation in England, is notable for its determination to create a coherent visual image by non-formal means, emphasizing visible circulation, identifiable units of habitation, and fully validating the presence of human beings as part of the total image—the perspectives had photographs of people pasted on to the drawings, so that the human presence almost overwhelmed the architecture.

But the Sheffield design went further even than this—and aformalism becomes as positive a force in its composition as it does in a painting by Burri or Pollock. *Composition* might seem pretty strong language for so apparently casual a layout, but this is clearly not an 'unconceptual' design, and on examination it can be shown to have a composition, but based not on the elementary rule-and-compass geometry which underlies most architectural composition, so much as an intuitive sense of topology. As a discipline of architecture topology has always been present in a subordinate and unrecognized way—qualities of penetration, circulation, inside and out, have always been important, but elementary Platonic geometry has been the master discipline. Now, in the Smithsons' Sheffield project the roles are reversed, topology becomes the dominant and geometry becomes the subordinate discipline. The 'connectivity' of the circulation routes is flourished on the exterior and no attempt is made to give a geometrical form to the total scheme; large blocks of topologically similar spaces stand about the site with the same graceless memorability as martello towers or pit-head gear.

Such a dominance accorded to topology—in whose classifications a brick is the same 'shape' as a billiard ball (unpenetrated solid) and a teacup is the same 'shape' as a gramophone record (continuous surface with one hole) is clearly analogous to the displacement of Tomistic 'beauty' by Brutalist 'Image,'[4] and Sheffield remains the most consistent and extreme point reached by any Brutalists in their search for *Une Architecture Autre*. It is not likely to displace Hunstanton in architectural discussions as the prime exemplar of The New Brutalism, but it is the only building-design which fully matches up to the threat and promise of *Parallel of Life and Art*.

And it shows that the formal axiality of Hunstanton is not integral to New Brutalist architecture. Miesian or Wittkowerian geometry was only an *ad hoc* device for the realization of 'Images,' and when *Parallel of Life and Art* had enabled Brutalists to define their relationship to the visual world in terms of something other than geometry, then formality was discarded. The definition of a New Brutalist building derived from Hunstanton and Yale Art Centre, above, must be modified so as to exclude formality as a basic quality if it is to cover future developments and should more properly read: 1, Memorability as an Image; 2, Clear exhibition of Structure; and 3, Valuation of Materials 'as found.' Remembering that an Image is what affects the emotions, that structure, in its fullest sense, is the relationship of parts, and that materials 'as found' are raw materials, we have worked our way back to the quotation which headed this article 'L'Architecture, c'est, avec des Matières Bruts, établir des rapports émouvants,' but we have worked our way to this point through such an awareness of history and its uses that we see that The New Brutalism, if it is architecture in the grand sense of Le Corbusier's definition, is also architecture of our time and not of his, nor of Lubetkin's, nor of the times of the Masters of the past. Even if it were true that the Brutalists speak only to one another, the fact that they have stopped speaking to Mansart, to Palladio and to Alberti would make The New Brutalism, even in its more private sense, a major contribution to the architecture of today.

NOTES   1. There is a persistent belief that the word *Brutalism* (or something like it) had appeared in the English Summaries in an issue of *Bygg-Mastaren* published late in 1950. The reference cannot now be traced, and the story must be relegated to that limbo of Modern Movement demonology where Swedes, Communists and the Town and Country Planning Association are bracketed together as different isotopes of the common 'Adversary.'

2. Paraphrasing *Summa Theologica* II (i) xxvii, I. The passage is normally rendered into English as 'but that whose very apprehension pleases is called beautiful.'

3. *See* his book of the same name, published in 1952. A closely analogous development is that of *musique concrete,* which uses 'real sounds,' manipulated in a manner which resembles the manipulation of some of the photographs in *Parallel,* and does not concern itself with harmony or melody in any recognizable way.

4. This analogy could probably be rendered epistemologically strict—both beauty and geometry, hitherto regarded as ultimate properties of the *cosmos,* now appear as linguistically refined special cases of more generalized concepts—image and topology—which, though essentially primitive, have been reached only through immense sophistication. Once this state of sophistication has been achieved, and the new concept digested, it suddenly appears so simple that it can be vulgarized without serious distortion, and for a handy back-entrance to topology without using the highly complex mathematics involved, the reader could not do better than acquire a copy of *Astounding Science Fiction* for July, 1954.

Ornament and Crime

The Decisive Contribution of Adolf Loos

Everyone knows that Modern Architecture is undecorated. This concept is the layman's recognition check: flat roof, big windows, no decoration. It is also one of the great seminal half-truths that have now become rules of design morality. But how did this state of affairs come about? Did the spirit of the times command? Did the *Zeitgeist*, like a baroque angel, swoop down to stay a thousand pencils as they held poised above the beginning of an Ionic volute or an Art Nouveau lily?

In this particular case we can put these art-historical miasmas back where they belong, and recognize that they are the cloaks of ignorance. Ideas do not bumble about in the abstract, looking for somewhere to settle. They are formulated in the minds of men, and communicated from man to man. The *Zeitgeist* is primarily a record of our ignorance of the communications that took place in any particular epoch—grandiose statements of the order of 'Perspective was not the discovery of any one person, it was the expression of the whole era,' are simply a roundabout way of admitting that we don't know to whom Brunelleschi talked before he talked to Manetti, and that we would

---

Originally appeared in *The Architectural Review* 121 (February 1957): 85–88.

rather not go to the labour of drawing up the family tree of personal contacts that runs from Brunelleschi to all the great perspectivists of the Quattrocento.

We are a bit too glib in presupposing diffuse cultural forces that act upon creative minds like the weather or the common cold, and a little too chary of conceding that some one specific person at some determined (if no longer determinable) moment must have been the first to conceive of central perspective, the undulating facade, architecture without ornament.

To us, now, the idea of an undecorated architecture has so nearly the status of a Mosaic commandment, to be flouted in practice but never queried in theory, that it is difficult to conceive of it as the thought of one man, and much easier to refer it back to the collective unconscious of the pioneers of Modern design. But the surviving literary evidence from the first twenty years of this century does not reveal any widely diffused hostility to decoration. There were ideas like Significant Form that were later to reinforce such a hostility when it had taken hold; there was a certain suspicion of past styles of decoration; there was even a certain indifference to ornament, articulated by Geoffrey Scott and earlier by Auguste Choisy, as the feeling that ornament was something that one might do without if one's command of formal composition was sufficiently sure. But only in the writings of one man, the Viennese architect Adolf Loos, will one find a positive anathema on ornament.

Did Adolf Loos, then, beat ornament single-handed? He certainly thought so himself, for he wrote in the introduction to his book *Trotzdem,* published in 1930, 'I have emerged victorious from my thirty years of struggle. I have freed mankind from superfluous ornament.' This is an uncommonly big claim even for a big-talking movement like Modern Architecture, and it needs scrutiny. But scrutiny will be facilitated if we look first at the weapons with which he fought. The example of his buildings was not decisive—their exteriors are sometimes, but not always, plain; the interiors, though devoid of decorative objects for the most part, exhibit almost a milliner's sense of the decorative qualities of wood and marble, fairface brick, turkey carpets, glass and metal. His doughtiest blows at ornament were struck in print, and the doughtiest of all in one single essay, published in 1908.

Its title is an eye-blacker for a start, *Ornament und Verbrechen:* Ornament and Crime. It brings the reader up with a jerk and sets his stock responses jangling. It is probably the first appearance of that pugnacious moral tone that was to characterize the writings of the Twenties and Thirties, and the opening paragraphs fully sustain this bourgeois-blasting, damn-your-delicate-feelings attitude:

> The human embryo goes through the whole history of animal evolution in its mother's womb, and when a child is born his sensory impressions are those of a puppy. His childhood takes him through the stages of human progress; at the age of two he is a Papuan savage, at four he has caught up with the Teutonic tribesmen. At six he is level with Socrates, and at eight with Voltaire. At this age he learns to distinguish violet, the colour that the eighteenth century

discovered—before then violets were blue and tyrian was red. Physicists can already point out colours that they have named, but that only later generations will be able to distinguish.

Children are amoral, and so, for us, are Papuans. If a Papuan slaughters his enemies and eats them, that doesn't make him a criminal. But if a modern man kills someone and eats him, he must be either a criminal or a degenerate. Papuans tattoo their skins, decorate their boats, their oars—everything they can get their hands on. But a modern man who tattoos himself is either a criminal or a degenerate. Why, there are prisons where eighty per cent of the convicts are tattooed, and tattooed men who are not in prison are either latent criminals or degenerate aristocrats. When a tattoed man dies at liberty, it simply means that he hasn't had time to commit his crime.

The urge to ornament oneself, and everything else within reach, is the father of pictorial art. It is the baby-talk of painting. All art is erotic.

The first ornament born, the cross, is of erotic origin. The earliest art-work, the first creative active of the earliest artist, was smudged on the cave wall to let off emotional steam. A horizontal stroke, the reclining woman; a vertical stroke, the man who transfixes her. The man who did this felt the same impulse as Beethoven, was in the same heaven of delight as Beethoven composing the Ninth.

But the man of our own times who smudges erotic symbols on walls is either a criminal or a degenerate. It is clear that this violent impulse might seize degenerate individuals in even the most advanced cultures, but in general one can grade the cultures of different peoples by the extent to which lavatory walls are drawn upon. With children this is a natural condition, their first artistic expressions are erotic scribblings on the nursery wall. But what is natural to children and Papuan savages is a symptom of degeneracy in modern man. I have evolved the following maxim, and present it to the world: The evolution of culture marches with the elimination of ornament from useful objects.

This is still a tremendous performance nearly a half-century after its composition. . . . But it won't stand re-reading. This is *Schlagobers-Philosophie,* that whisks up into an exciting dish on the café table, and then collapses as you look at it, like a cooling soufflé. It is not a reasoned argument but a succession of fast-spieling double-takes and non-sequiturs holding together a precarious rally of clouds of witness—café-Freudianism, café-anthropology, café-criminology. The testimonies of these various witnesses don't really support one another, but they must have appeared convincing at the time, partly because they were all new and hot, but more especially for an overriding reason that will be discussed later. But Loos has no intention of giving the reader time to pick the argument to pieces, he wants to detail the poor response that the world made when presented with his 'maxim.'

I had thought with this rule to bring a new joy into the world, but no-one has thanked me for it. Rather, people have pulled a long face and hung their heads. What oppressed them in my discovery was the proposition that no new ornament could be invented. Were we, men of the nineteenth century, to be incapable of doing what the simplest negro, the men of every previous age or nation, had been able to do?

'Men of the nineteenth century'—this must mean that the maxim had been enunciated in the Nineties originally, and at that time, with Viennese Art Nouveau flourishing like a rain-forest, it must have sounded more mad than sad. Loos, however, followed it up with Old Testament rhetoric.

> Then I said: Weep not. Behold the true greatness of our age, that it can no longer bring forth ornament. We have vanquished decoration and broken through into an ornamentless world.
> Behold. The time is at hand and fulfilment awaits us. Soon the pavements of our cities shall glisten like marble; Like Zion, the holy city, the Capital of Heaven.[1]

But no-one thanked him. What had gone wrong? Almost inevitably, he alleges an Imperialist plot: Certain reactionaries rejected his prophecies, the Austrian state continued to support and subsidize a reign of ornamental terror, retarding progress, making people wear felt boots instead of rational footwear, because it had found that a backward people was easier to govern. Some citizens of the Austro-Hungarian Empire were so backward that they had not yet been converted to Christianity, would have been looked down on by the Goths and Visigoths. Happy the country that has no such stragglers! Happy America!

America for Loos, as for so many of the pioneers, was the promised land of technology. Not a word about the Indian reservations or the hookworm belt, nor the coloured slums of the Northern cities, which he must have seen on his visit to the U.S. Americans were his ideal Twentieth Century men and

> When two men live side by side, all things else being equal, the twentieth-century man gets richer, the eighteenth-century man gets poorer, assuming that each lives according to his inclinations, for the man of the twentieth century can cover his needs with smaller outlay, and thus make savings.
> The vegetable that tastes good to him when simply boiled in water and glazed with butter, is only palatable to the other when served with honey and nuts, after the cook has slaved over it for hours. Decorated plates are expensive, whereas the plain white crocks that modern man prefers are cheap. One saves, the other overspends, and it is the same with nations. Woe to a people that hangs back from cultural progress. The English get richer, and we get poorer.

What would he have made of a Cadillac economy, where undecorated goods are apt to be in an inaccessible luxury price-bracket, while ornamental products are within the reach of all but the most depressed strata of society? One can guess, for a few paragraphs later he sketches in a satirical draft of a high-obsolescence economy, where everything is highly decorated and thrown away almost as soon as it is made, and everyone swims in wealth and well-being. But it is only a satirical view of a vulgar 'Land of Cockayne.' He is not envisaging it as a way of life that need be taken seriously, nor one that he wants any part in. He exhibits here that peasant streak so common in reformist aesthetes, and can see objects of use only as possessions whose market value must be maintained, not as equipment to be discarded when technically obsolete. Not for him the scrapping economy implicit in Futurism's 'Every generation its own house,' or

Le Corbusier's 'On jette, on remplace.' In fairness one should note that he could accept expendability in trashy materials: 'I can accept papier maché in an artists' club, run up in a couple of days, torn down when the exhibition is over. But to play ducks and drakes with golden sovereigns, to use banknotes to light cigars, to crush pearls and drink them—*das wirkt unästhetisch.*'

But in skipping on thus far we have overpassed the vital paragraph that holds the historical key to 'Ornament and Crime,' and explains the instance of its writing and the immediate power of conviction that it undoubtedly possessed.

> Now that ornament is no longer organically integrated into our culture, it has ceased to be a valid expression of that culture. The ornament that is designed to-day has no relevance to ourselves, to mankind at large, nor to the ordering of the cosmos. It is unprogressive and uncreative.
>
> What has happened to the ornamental work of Otto Eckmann? What has happened to van de Velde? The artist used to stand for health and strength, at the pinnacle of humanity, but the modern ornamentalist is either a cultural laggard or a pathological case. He himself is forced to disown his own work after three years. His products are already unbearable to cultured persons now, and will become so to others in a little time. Where are now the works of Eckmann, and where will those of Olbrich be ten years from now? Modern ornament has neither forbears nor descendants, no past and no future. It may be received with joy by uncultured folk, to whom the true greatness of our time is a book with seven seals, but even by them in a short time forgot.

That fixes him in time. Where other men of his day may have had an uneasy feeling that Art Nouveau was losing its impetus, he had a personal quarrel with Hoffmann and the *Wiener Sezession,* and any stick would serve to beat the *Wiener Werkstätte.* For all that, it took courage—truculence even—to launch these personal attacks at a time when the world reputation of both *Sezession* and *Werkstätte* were at their height, and had made Vienna a centre of artistic pilgrimage. On the other hand, the crack-up was already signalled. Long-witted operators like Peter Behrens were quietly sloughing off Art Nouveau, and that symptomatic young person Charles Edouard Jeanneret was, in the very year of 'Ornament and Crime,' telling Josef Hoffmann he could keep his *Werkstätte,* recognizing that it was no longer creative. In articulating his quarrel with the *Sezession,* Loos was polarizing the attitude of a generation to decoration, as surely as Marinetti in the next few months was to polarize its attitude to machinery. In a time of decision his was a decisive gesture.

The decision taken, his position was clear: all forms of cultural regression are crime and waste; ornament is cultural regression and must therefore be a waste and a crime; worse than that, sex-crime. With his position so clearly given, and in such forthright terms, it comes as a further shock to find him hedging the issue with soft options.

> I address myself particularly to those natural aristocrats who stand at the summit of human progress, and yet have the deepest understanding of the needs and impulses of lesser men—the Kaffir who weaves an ornament into his cloth after a receipt so subtle that it is

only seen when the whole is unpicked; the Persian knotting his rugs; the Slovak peasant working her lace; the grannie who works wonders with crochet-hook, beads and silk—he understands them and lets them alone, for these are consecrated hours in which they work. A vulgar revolutionary might burst in on them and say 'that's a lot of rubbish,' just as he might shout to old ladies performing their Stations of the Cross 'There is no God.' But under an aristocracy even an atheist takes off his hat when passing a church.

Then he goes on to relate a touching parable of the dismay of his shoemaker on being asked to make a pair of utterly plain shoes, even at a third over the price of the normally-ornamented model. Ornament, he says, is the culture of the poor, and we—aristocrats who have Beethoven and Wagner—have no right to deprive them of it. But a cultured man who goes to hear the Ninth Symphony and sits down to design a sampler is either a show-off or a degenerate.

> The death of ornament has brought the other arts to unbelievable heights. The symphonies of Beethoven could never have been written by a man who had to wear velvet, silk and lace. Anyone who goes around to-day in a velvet coat is no artist, but a clown or a housepainter. Wandering tribesmen wore bright colours to distinguish themselves from one another, but we have grown subtler and more refined—we moderns wear our clothes as a mask.
>
> So unbelievably powerful is a modern personality that it can no longer be expressed through clothing. Freedom from ornament is a sign of mental strength, and modern man may use the ornament of historic and exotic cultures at his discretion, but his own inventive talents are reserved and concentrated on other things.

In spite of the slight crescendo for the coda this is still a stingless tail, all passion spent. Nevertheless, 'Ornament and Crime' is still good fighting talk. In its author's own eyes it ranks with *Architektur,* written a year later, as one of his two prime writings, but not necessarily as his unique blow against ornament. To revert to the introduction to *Trotzdem,* we find that it continues 'Ornament was once synonymous with beautiful, but thanks to my life's work it now means inferior.' Life's work, he says, and on the narrow stage of Austria this might be true, but on the wider screen of the Modern Movement at large much of his writing after 1900 went by default for lack of republication on foreign presses. It is on the reprinting history of 'Ornament and Crime' that his claim to have liberated mankind must rest.

But it rests securely. Already in the Nineteen-teens it had attracted enough notice outside Vienna to earn republication, first in Herwarth Walden's expressionist magazine, *der Sturm,* in 1912, and then in Georges Besson's sprightly translation in *Les Cahiers d'Aujourdhui* in 1913.

These reprints brought Loos—and the essay—to the notice of an interested if restricted international readership. They also presumably brought Loos's ideas to the notice of the Futurist Sant'Elia, the first writer outside Vienna to be visibly influenced by them—Marinetti, the leader of the Futurists, had contacts with *der Sturm* as well as Parisian circles.

The French version was once more reprinted, unaltered, in No. 2 of *l'Esprit Nouveau*. One should remember that at this early date (March, 1920) *l'Esprit Nouveau* still had a third director beside Ozenfant and Le Corbusier, and while its appeal to those two for its relevance to architecture and design is obvious enough, its appeal to the third director, Paul Dermée, would be equally strong. For though he was a poet, he was also close in with the Dadaists, and one can imagine how gratefully any attempt to equate Beethoven with a cave artist, and a comfort-station muralist, would fall upon the ears of those who were trying to get the Morgue accepted as an object of sentimental interest and had already moustached the Mona Lisa. The reappearance of 'Ornament and Crime' while Dada was still going full blast was uncommonly timely, and guaranteed it a favourable hearing at another moment of decision.

For this reprint appeared after Le Corbusier had finished with his flower-box-smothered house-projects of the war years, but before the Villa at Vaucresson that ushered in his new style. It was read, and of this we can be certain, by Erich Mendelsohn, between his first and second Dutch visits; after the decorated Luckenwald factory, and before the undecorated Sternefeld house. It appeared after Gropius's decorated Sommerfeld House had been designed, but before the 'reformed' projects and the undecorated Jena theatre, and again we can safely posit communication between Paris and Germany. Riding hard behind this timely reappearance came the publication of Loos's first book of collected essays, *Ins Leere Gesprochen,* which covers the years 1897–1900 only, but shows him in his Plumbing-before-Art-work mood, and remains to this day better known and more widely read than *Trotzdem.*

For, by the time *Trotzdem* appeared, Loos had ceased to be timely. He caught no mood of disgust with *Art Nouveau,* nor any Dadaist mood of disgust with art in general. Not only had the mood changed, but the ideas he had pushed had now been so thoroughly absorbed and understood that they looked more like Laws of Nature than the Works of Man.

All his best ideas had been pirated by younger men. His advocacy of Thonet chairs and *Fauteuils Grandconfort 'Maple'* had been so thoroughly taken over by Le Corbusier that Loos began to deride Thonet as *eine falsches Modell* in order to maintain some show of independence. But even the anti-ornament campaign had been plagiarized without acknowledgment, and in the introduction to *Trotzdem* he says, following what has been quoted already,

> But even the echo as it answers believes the note to be its own, and that perfidious book *Die Form ohne Ornament,* published in Stuttgart in 1924, conceals my efforts even while it falsifies them.

He might well complain. *Form without Ornament* was the catalogue *de luxe* of a Werkbund exhibition that toured Germany in 1924–25. Its illustrations make a brisk start with Jena glass and Stuttgart soap, but then trail off through such objects as Breuer's early Bauhaus furniture until they wind up with products so arty that they can only be described as *Sezession ohne Ornament.* The impossible, as Loos had seen it, had taken place, and the fine art designers had climbed on the anti-ornamental band-waggon. Wolfgang Pfliederer says, in his introduction to this 'perfidious' book, 'If we survey the field of artistic handicraft today we find that it is not unified, but draws . . . from two sources . . . Technical form and Primitive form.'

Technical Form and Primitive Form. Engineers and peasants had been identified by Loos in that other prime essay, *Architektur,* as the two good, clean form-givers who did not commit the crimes of architects and artists, and to suggest that they might be tributary to the artistic handicrafts was to turn his arguments upside down and inside out. Within three years he was dead anyhow, and rapidly passing into that special limbo of oblivion that is reserved for those who have ideas that are too good to belong to one man alone. He had settled the problem of ornament as Alexander settled the Gordian knot, shockingly but effectively, and his ideas had gained an empire wider than the Macedonian's wildest dream. It is impossible now to imagine how the Modern Movement might have looked as a decorated style, but it might have been just that, had not its creators had ringing in their ears Adolf Loos's challenging equation: Ornament equals Crime.

NOTE   1. Depressingly enough, Loos's views on clothing were entirely consistent with his views on architecture. His ideal was *der Mann im Overall,* so his Holy City would have looked rather like a set for *1984.*

4

Ungrab That Gondola

Once upon a *dreadful* day, a tall, dark neo-Palladian yawned at the mention of "Divina Proporzione," and the panic was on. It had been a terrible season: a ranking Brutalist had been rude about Alberti, a man at the ICA had described *Bicycle Thieves* as "creep," *Vogue* had spoken up for ordinary coffee, and old Astragal had treated an exhibition of Italian Industrial Design with what sounded like tolerant amusement, instead of the loutish self-abasement required by protocol. In other words, the bright boys had eased the skids under the Italian influence just when it was building up nicely, and it has now slipped so far that an Espresso bar is a place where you have Devonshire teas in Cuban décor to the strains of a skiffle group, and a copy of *Domus* lasts forever, instead of getting shredded in a fortnight.

At this point, the weekend egg-heads—always prompt to flog the dead horse of a stationary band-waggon—have begun to take it up (as a lost cause, presumably) and at the Café Royal one dull evening recently a team of middle-essayists, lady film-critics and Establishment art-pundits wagged their heads gravely over the influence of *espresso*, scooters and Italian films on the English way of life. It was the kind of discussion that

Originally appeared in *The Architect's Journal* 126 (15 August 1957): 233–235.

makes the average symposium on elemental bills sound like dialogue by Oscar Wilde, but it left a question uppermost in one's mind—what made the Italian influence tick?

Leaving aside the purely trade reasons operative on architecture students, *viz.,* the refusal of their elders and betters to teach them anything about architecture, and the permanent manic-depressive influences like Venetian honeymoons, lady water-colourists, Ruskin, Norman Douglas and Our Gracie, what was it hit the English about 1950 and left them spin-dizzy for over half a decade? The answer was briefly sighted by Paul Reilly in the course of the Café Royal forum, when he observed that *espresso* machines as such seemed to be designed to fit into chromium, American-style bars, not the Espresso bar as it is understood in the Brompton Road.

That was the first clue to the answer, and the rest followed by checking what had occupied the vacuum left by the fading of Italian influence—Jayne where Lollo had been, Plymouth where Ferrari had been, Mies where Ernesto had been, Aspen Congress where the Triennale had been, Norbert Wiener where Croce had been, and so on all down the cultural line. Italy, in fact, had been a "clean" substitute for America in the panic years when the onset of the Cold War had forced puzzled pinks, tweedsmen and do-gooders generally to face the fact that F.D.R. was dead, and that you couldn't incline to the gusto and busto of the American Way of Life while leaning to the Left.

Italy, undergoing a maximum wave of American influence (the first post-war Italian car I saw on Italian soil was an imitation Studebaker crammed on a *Topolin* chassis in 1950) and in many ways outdoing the U.S. at its own game (remember those side elevations of Silvana Mangano?), but rendered respectable to the veterans of the Pink Decades by virtue of the biggest Communist Party and the worst social problems in Europe, was the perfect let-out. Add the traditional connections mentioned earlier, and a modicum of guilt for having won the War, and we didn't stand a chance, did we?

Those days look as if they have gone forever. Give it a decade, and someone will make a fortune by reviving *Grab me a Gondola* as a period musical.

5

Machine Aesthetes

You don't have to be very clever to find a link between the New Brutalists and the Angry Young literaries, but you don't do yourself much good in the process. Unlike Angries Unanimous, who are as English and as dated as last week's pools coupons, the Brutalists are not parochial. Their name came from Scandinavia in the first instance, and although it is claimed particularly by an English team of Redbrick extraction—Alison and Peter Smithson—the ideas they deploy are of live international currency, and have been effective in wrecking modern architecture's first world-wide organisation of father-figures, *les Congrès Internationaux d'Architecture Moderne*—CIAM for short.

A more instructive comparison would be with that junior revolutionary movement in sculpture that has no name, but has been identifiable in England since the Paolozzi-Turnbull exhibition at the Hanover Gallery in 1950, and rather longer on the Continent. Aspects of this movement have been called *l'art brut,* and there have been phases of close collaboration between the Smithsons and Paolozzi, but there remains a vital difference. The aims of the young sculptors are, or were, 'to kick Henry Moore in the teeth'

Originally appeared in *New Statesman* 55 (16 August 1958): 192–193.

(I quote), and they have resolutely rejected that aesthetic of pure form and direct carving that has hung like a millstone about the neck of English sculptors ever since Wilenski first propounded it.

The young sculptors have rejected both the forms and the theory of the Thirties; the Brutalists have rejected only the forms, on the ground that they are false to the theory; and the theory they accept in its full moralistic, functional and rationalistic rigour, as it has been accepted, more or less, by progressive architects for over a century now. They believe in uncompromising truth to materials, structure and function, and they assert, by word and deed, that what James Stirling calls the 'white architecture of the Thirties' did not.

The White Architecture was largely produced by a piece of special pleading of basic functional-rationalist doctrine in terms of (a) the idea of living in a Machine Age and (b) the idea of reinforced concrete as a material symbolic of that age. Somewhere along the line a couple of crucial aesthetic prejudices were read into the equation with results that would have gone something like this, had it been possible, psychologically, to set them down in cold print:

> This is a Machine Age.
> Machine surfaces are smooth and plain.
> Machine forms are of rule-and-compass simplicity.
> Reinforced concrete is the Machine Age material.
> *Therefore*
> Reinforced concrete has a smooth surface and must be used in rule-and-compass shapes.

The second and third propositions have never been necessarily true of machine technology, though they may have appeared so in the early Twenties, but the myth was kept alive in the Thirties, when they were manifestly untrue, by aesthetic fumbletrumpets who were forever galloping into print with ill-drawn analogies between machinery and abstract art. In the upshot, a false aesthetic was imposed on concrete, whereas structural and material truth suggests that it should be used rough-textured in complex vault-forms.

Since the so-called Machine Aesthetic of the Thirties required it to be otherwise, the difference had to be smudged over with double-talk and white rendering. The epitome of this aesthetical nonsense was achieved at the opening of the Isokon Flats, in Lawn Road, Hampstead, one of the key monuments of the decade of white architecture and pink politics. On that celebrated occasion, the machine analogy was driven to the lengths of having a 'launching ceremony', but the bottle was not the only thing that broke, and the force of its impact dislodged a large area of the rendering, which fell on the photographers below.

Obviously this fakery could not survive, but the immediate effect of its demise was that cover-it-with-anything-you-fancy attitude manifests in a great deal of post-war design, and still visibly with us in the Espresso and Shoe-shop styles. The Brutalists and *Team Ten* connections have gone off on the opposite vector, however, and put surface coverings behind them, except where functionally indicated. Furthermore, they have been as honest about materials as one might hope an engineer would be, and they have been sufficiently courageous in their mechanistic convictions to build in brick, and to let the brick appear.

But the fact that they have rejected the Machine Aesthetic has caused certain established modern dead-heads to suppose they have rejected technological culture, and the fact that they have expressed an interest in certain movements, such as Futurism and Expressionism, that were current before the white plague paralysed architectural thought—this interest has caused other dead-heads to call the younger architects 'old-fashioned'.

Admittedly, the position is confusing for those who, on the basis of the ideas of the Thirties (which are all that you can find in the books so far), had come to think that they knew what modern architecture was all about and what it looked like. To find the junior *avant-garde* admiring with equal fervour peasant houses on Santorin, and the chrome-work on Detroit cars; the *Cutty Sark,* Chiswick house, *Camels* cigarette packs, and Le Corbusier's chapel at Ronchamp; Pollock, Paolozzi and Volkswagens—all this sounds like the complete abandonment of standards. In fact it is nothing of the sort—it is the abandonment of stylistic prejudice, and its replacement by the concept of 'the style for the job'. This abandonment opens the way for a more viable integration of design with practicalities of machine age existence.

6

Unesco House

After Galileo, the next most subversive thought of Western Man was Walter Gropius's proposal that Unesco headquarters should *not* be in Paris. But it was only a tactic to call town-planning authorities to heel, the basic unimaginative decision remained. This choice of location was a masterstroke of mental inertia on the part of the Men of Goodwill and Cold Feet, and they have got the building that they deserved. The half-dozen-or-so best architects in the world (Gropius included) they had safely tied up in an advisory committee so they couldn't design, only delegate responsibility to a second team to lay out the building—a second team that shows evidence of massive lobbying in the choice of members.

The disparate talents of Marcel Breuer (U.S.A.), Bernard Zehrfuss (France) and Pierluigi Nervi, the romantic Italian engineer, were expected to collaborate as equals among themselves, with interior designers, painters, sculptors and gardeners. The diplomatic talents of Breuer, in particular, saved this dated dream of *Gesamtkunstwerk* from utter failure, but there is visible evidence of hard horse-trading behind the scenes. There

Originally appeared in *New Statesman* 55 (6 December 1958): 802.

was an initial sell-out to the *Beaux-Arts* planning prejudices of the local authority, resulting in the main façade becoming a bent plane that only pretends to honour the quadrant of the other half of the Place de Fontenoy. Behind the central curve of this face, a third leg runs back, giving the main, seven-storey mass a lazy-Y sort of plan, and trapped under the end of this leg is the *pas-perdus* leading to the congress block, which stands clear of the main structure, as does the annexe known as the *Bâtiment Saxe* on the other side.

Apart from the congress block, and the *portes-cochères* of the main building, there is no external evidence of Nervi's contribution; these showpieces appear to have been given him as conscience-savers by the two architects, who elsewhere had to mess up his contribution pretty effectively. There is little to detain the visitor inside the big Y, an overcrowded office-warren. The modish splayed legs of the ground-floor structure (which make you feel like an incredible shrinking man under a *House and Garden* sideboard) only begin to register towards the back end of the back leg of this block, and, in general, the main interest of the scheme is all at this end.

The *pas-perdus* goes off to the right, and brings you to much the best interior space, the foyer of the congress halls. This occupies the space under the central low point of the pleated concrete butterfly roof, where it rests on a row of columns, and the halls lie on either side of it. Salle I occupies the whole of the right-hand half of the block, and the inner faces of the concrete pleats give it a stark *Caligari* quality that can, unfortunately, be killed by over-lighting.

The foyer is simply the space left over between the dead-wall of Salle I, with its storey-high overhangs, and a miscellany of walls and spaces, including another dead-wall, a balcony, a bar and a documentation centre on the other side, with slab-concrete balustrades to the stairs leading up to the balcony, and to a bridge that edges nervously across to the upper part of Salle I. Neither square nor anything else in plan or section, this foyer promises to become a first-class mess. It doesn't, because of three things. First, the effective dominance in every direction of coarse, bush-hammered concrete surfaces, on which the eye rests thankfully. Second, the columns, huge solids of linear transformation, circular at the base, rectangular at the roof, marching in a relentless file through the bustle and crowds on the floor, asserting structural order and heroic scale. Third, the Picasso mural.

Having no professional stake in Picasso's reputation, I can record my relief that this was not another piece of his political rhetoric, and my admiration for the magnificent way in which it functions on the end wall of the main space of the foyer. Picasso picked this site himself, the best in the building, and worked from a model of the interior, including the much-maligned bridge. The colours pick up, or set off, those of the surrounding surfaces, the forms are big enough to dominate the crowds and echo the scale of the columns, and—almost as a consequence of this—the iconography is sufficiently vacuous not to demand of the crowds an attention they aren't going to give it anyway. The bridge is put to work, as a mask that reveals successive layers of the composition as one approaches from the *pas-perdus,* and as a vantage point for high level views of the busier areas of the iconography.

This added art-work at least is visually and functionally related to the building—one cannot say as much for Miro's boring Guggenheim Prize ceramic murals, Moore's eroded dowager or Calder's droopy mobile on a base big enough to launch missiles. The only other place where added art-work has made a significant contribution is in Isamu Noguchi's 'Zen' garden on the other side of the back leg of the Y, under the shadow of the *Bâtiment Saxe.* This is in two parts, a sunken garden, and an upper terrace dotted with stone objects, some geometrically fine-hewn, others in a state of highly sophisticated nature, the abstract artefacts of the Thirties informed with a meaning that no Hepworth or Nicholson ever gave them.

The garden proper, surrounded by strip windows lighting basement work-rooms, is a heaving terrain-sculpture of mounds and pools, moss, grass, raked marble chips, ground-ivy, stepping stones, small conifers and stone 'lanterns'. How far this is really Zen, Japanese or only the fashionable ingenuity that has always marked Noguchi's work is hard to decipher—it is not even an absolute novelty in Paris, for there is, or was, a decidedly exquisite Zen garden at the side of the Japanese hostel in the *Cité Universitaire.* It is also overcrowded, but it strikes a note of freshness that isn't much to be found elsewhere, it unites the two buildings in a satisfactory and visually rewarding scene, and it plays up the superficial inter-cultural relevance of Zen in a witty manner—for instance, a double-curved surface in the centre of the garden has its paving-setts arranged in a pattern that recalls the abscissae of mathematical models.

Picasso, old, and Noguchi, unfamiliar, have managed to contribute something to the whole that the middle-aged and overfamiliar have failed to produce, in spite of the overall conception being phrased in their terms. The two artists who have had to pay greatest regard to functional and planning limitations have succeeded far better than those who were able to luxuriate in the phoney freedom of open sites and isolated plinths. There seems to be a lesson here that one could read back through the whole building to find that it was known before work began—give a good man a definite job, a watertight briefing, and let him get on with it. Had this principle been honoured from the start, Unesco might yet have had one of the best post-war buildings in the world, instead of one of the best post-war buildings in Paris.

7

The Glass Paradise

The public were less surprised by Lever House than was the architectural profession—
and this was logical, for had not a massive body of opinion-making machinery been
telling them, since the mid-Twenties, that modern architecture was just a lot of glass
boxes? Architects, on the other hand, knew that between the glass legend and the
concrete fact there was a great gulf fixed—a gulf forty years wide and as deep as
the building industry.

In spite of near-misses like Gropius's *Faguswerke,* and any number of exhibition
buildings, in spite of Mies van der Rohe, Lever House was still the first of the glass
towers to realize a seminal concept that has lurked in the mind of the Modern Movement since before the first World War. The reasons for this extraordinary lack of phas-
ing may be traced back to the Movement's own view of itself, and particularly to its
tendency to try and tidy up its own history as it goes along.

The respectable genealogy of the glass legend is primarily the work of two men: one
was Hermann Muthesius, father of the *Deutscher Werkbund,* who wrote in his *Stilarchi-
tektur und Baukunst* of 1902, of the beauties of the Crystal Palace and the Galérie des

---

Originally appeared in *The Architectural Review* 125 (February 1959): 87–89.

Machines, station halls, covered markets, and most of the totemic objects of the glass dream—a pioneer re-assessment of the nineteenth century. The other is Sigfried Giedion, whose *Bauen in Frankreich* of 1928, related the architecture of his contemporaries back to Muthesius's canon of nineteenth-century masterpieces, and interpolated, with great historical subtlety and erudition, a philosophy common to both. His contemporaries were, of course, delighted to find that they were following such distinguished precedents, most of which were unknown to them until they opened the book.

But if these precedents were, in practice, unknown to them, what precedents did they follow, what motives drove them? What, in fact, had been said and done to further the glass dream between 1902, when Muthesius pointed the way, and 1929, when Giedion's book was shortly followed by others by e.g. Artur Korn or Konrad Werner Schulz, which dealt specifically and exclusively with glass in building.

One can point first to two respectable contributions, Meyer's *Eisenbauten,* before the first World War, and the *Ingenieurbauten* of Lindner and Steinmetz after it, which both drew attention to buildings of the type originally praised by Muthesius, but were not particularly slanted toward glass. One sees also that Bauhaus teaching, and the example of the Bauhaus buildings in Dessau must have turned men's minds in the direction of transparent membranes, even though Le Corbusier's first *pans de verre* were still, so to speak, around the corner of a white rendered wall. But in all these there is no sign of the singing tones of prophecy, the incantatory repetitions that give a material those symbolic powers, over and above the recommendations of reason, that make it a live component of architecture.

It is to Germany, in the months immediately preceding and immediately following the first World War, that we have to turn to find that prophetic tone, to the period bracketed by the completion of the glass wall of the *Faguswerke,* late in 1913, and the second, 1920, glass-tower project of Mies van der Rohe. Both of these are accounted works of the party of reason, yet both, on examination, are found to have some curious cousins. Mies's glass-towers have been justly called Expressionist, while their contemporaries, from Gropius's side, include the first Bauhaus proclamation with its gushing rhetoric about buildings 'like crystal symbols,' and a three-spired gothic cathedral on its cover.

All this is commonly written off as an aberration due to 'Post-war Berlin.' But if it was, then it was an aberration that gripped a generation, and must have more in it than meets the eye. In fact, there is a great deal in it, a great deal of the Modern Movement's disreputable ancestry, but as far as the glass legend is concerned, there are two dominant strains, both traceable back to the Werkbund's exhibition in Cologne in 1914. The importance of that exhibition for the glass dream is known, and acknowledged in every history by an illustration of one of the staircases of Gropius's office block in its glass hemicylinder. But that is only half the story.

There was also at Cologne for that exhibition a pavilion devoted to the glory of glass exclusively, a pavilion that demonstrably had a far greater immediate effect on the imagination of German architects than Gropius's did, for sundry descendants of it can be identified in designs done after the war, including Mies's first, faceted design for the Friedrichstrasse skyscraper. This pavilion cannot be comfortably fitted into the history of the modern movement—particularly if that history, like Giedion's, is slanted for continuity—because it is so wrong for its time: a primitive geodesic dome of steel and glass, raised on a drum of glass bricks containing staircases with glass treads and glass risers, a design imbued with the homogeneity and visual certainty that Gropius's office block so conspicuously lacks, even allowing for differences in function and form.

The Glass Pavilion was the work of Bruno Taut, and so far exceeds every other design from his drawing board that one may properly enquire what lies behind it. The clue is given by Konrad Werner Schulz: it was *Paul Scheerbart gewidmet,* and this Paul Scheerbart was *der literarischer Vorläufer und Anreger moderner Glasarchitektur.* Now, the statement that the literary forerunner and instigator of modern glass architecture was Paul Scheerbart will probably come as a complete surprise to English-speaking readers and to many German-speakers as well. In German architectural literature his name is unknown outside the works of Schulz, Platz (two brief references in his *Baukunst der neuesten Zeit*) and some forgotten books by Bruno Taut. In English, there is a glancing reference in Giedion's *Walter Gropius: Work and Teamwork,* but not a word in *Space, Time and Architecture.*

The oblivion into which Scheerbart's name has fallen suggests—and how rightly— that he is not to be numbered among Modern Architecture's respectable ancestors. Handbooks of German literature, unanimously unaware of his architectural interests, record an almost spherical bohemian layabout—and Kokoschka's portrait confirms this—a fringe-member of the Futurist-Expressionist *Sturm* group, born in 1863 and dead in 1915, the author of fanticated novels, mostly short and decorated by his own hand in Yellow Book style. Many of these novels can best be described as contra-science-fiction, astral pantomimes, moon romances, astral novelettes and what-have-you. Beyond this, his output included appendices to the Munchausen legend, Harem romances, an *Eisenbahnroman* that appears to be the pioneer of that genre of literature whose chief ornament is the *Madonna of the Sleeping Cars,* a 'Hippopotamus' novel (of which more in due course), and a telegraphic romance called *The Mid-Ocean Hay-fever Sanatorium,* in whose very title one perceives something of the vein of practical logic that runs through his one work specifically devoted to the arts of building, *Glasarchitektur,* published in 1914.

Dedicated, as one might have guessed, to Bruno Taut, it is a slim, soberly-presented volume, quite unlike his novels in typography and format, and runs about a chapter to a page—some of the chapters no more than single thoughts noted in a couple of sentences—for 125 pages. These chapters are only loosely connected, though not much more loosely than those of Le Corbusier's *Vers Une Architecture,* and like that work they expound an unpredictable mixture of uninhibited vision and sharp practicality. Both the vision and the practicality draw their strength from the things that Scheerbart knew at first hand or had seen with his own eyes—glazed verandas, palm-houses, public halls, searchlights, zeppelins, sanatoria, mirror-panelled café interiors, theosophist publications, the Cologne pavilions of Taut (explicitly) and Gropius (by inference), and much more besides. The vision he offers is a compound of all these, torn from their contexts, and re-assembled by a mind unrestrained by conventional ideas and received opinions, but buttressed by a shrewd idea of what will, and what won't work.

> The vision of a glass world . . . as entirely delectable as the gardens of the Arabian Nights . . . a paradise on earth . . . we shall show no longing for the paradise of heaven

begins with something that was common knowledge to Scheerbart and most of his readers, the glazed conservatory. This he envisaged becoming ever larger and more important until it had to be emancipated from the house, and set up independently in the garden. The glass-world citizen then abandons his old house and moves into the conservatory, which is aesthetically linked to the garden (floodlit at night) by glass walls and screens that extend its structure into its surroundings. As a habitable environment, the conservatory-house, which Scheerbart seems to envisage as something like Taut's glass pavilion, has double walls of coloured glass carried in a reinforced concrete frame clad in mother of pearl or mosaic. Its floors were to be of coloured ceramic tiling, its furniture of glass with brightly enamelled steel legs and upholstery of glistening glass-fibre cloth. Artificial light was to enter the rooms from sources between the double-glazing, and from hanging lamps of oriental style, the heating under the floor.

The landscape in which the jewel-like house and its floodlit garden are situated is to be a diffuse metropolis, with air navigation beacons winking from the tops of its taller buildings. Illuminated trains, cars and motorboats, like blazing jewels traverse the night scene, while overhead, zeppelins, brightly-lit themselves, and shedding light over the land, cruise toward an air-terminal in a park of experimental glass buildings, one of which is a hangar whose roof-space is occupied by an exhibition of models of historic airships, all with their own miniature lights ablaze. The shore line of the Swiss lakes, the outlines of the smaller Alps are picked out in brilliantly lit glass hotels, the summits of the higher peaks are floodlit in colour. Venice—or a new movable Venice—is a cluster of huge pyramidal buildings, glazed and illuminated and doubled by their reflections in the calm sea. Tourists, no longer hurrying from distraction to distraction, move calmly from the contemplation of one glass wonder to another.

About this vision certain things need to be said. Its inspiration was certainly personal—Scheerbart, it appears, was often poor, cold and miserable in squalid surroundings, and had an acquired hatred of the ill-lit and oppressive atmosphere of congested masonry cities. Hence the diffuse planning of the glass dream-world, the gardens and the greenery. Hence, too, the dedicatory motto he pronounced at Taut's Cologne Pavilion

> Das Glas bringt uns die neue Zeit
> Backsteinkultur tut uns nur Leid
> (Glass brings us the new age
> Brick culture does us only harm)

and his insistence that the 'metropolis in our sense' must be dissolved. But Scheerbart, unlike some of the glass-enthusiasts of later generations, was under no illusion that glass was in itself a universal panacea. He had too much practical sense for that, and knew the weaknesses and side effects of its use. He knew that it was all too pervious to heat, and insists frequently on the need for double glazing. He knew also of the green-house effects it can produce, and insisted that glass architecture was for the temperate zones, and not the tropics nor the polar regions. He knew that his call for *Mehr Farbenlicht!*—More coloured light!—that runs through the whole book, could only reasonably be answered when electricity was more cheap and plentiful than at the time he wrote. When hydroelectric power came in, he prophesied, then even private persons will have floodlighting in their gardens. He knew from Taut that the making of convincing models of glass buildings awaited more tractable materials than the picture-glass and brass strip then in use, and looked forward to developments in transparent plastics (he names a forgotten proprietary product: *Tektorium*). Beyond that again, he looked forward to even better materials than glass for full-size buildings, and identified laminated glass (zwischen zwei Glasplatten eine Zelluloïdplatte) which had only just come in, as an example of what should be looked for from a lively and developing technology, for

> We stand at the beginning, not the end, of a culture-period.
> We await entirely new miracles of technology and chemistry.
> Let us never forget it.

This optimistic view of technology puts him at one with the Futurists, whose works he certainly knew, and in this, as in his long-range prophecies, he is clearly of the party of progress, a member of the mainstream of modern architectural thought. Where he is conspicuously outside that mainstream is in the detail aesthetics of his vision. Whether or not he knew any Tiffany interiors, he certainly knew and admired individual pieces of Tiffany glass, and its aesthetics, notably the nuanced colours that he calls *die Tiffany-Effekte,* inform many of his visualizations. To this must be added an insistence on ornament based on mineral forms and vegetation—perhaps like Louis Sullivan's—and a strong strain of conscious orientalism that directs his thoughts on light fittings, cloths and fabrics, floor coverings, tile-work and so forth.

Here, in fact, we see him headed against the supposed tide of Modern Movement ideas. As Charles Mitchell pointed out some time ago, the idea of good modern design for which we have settled is a profoundly classical idea, in opposition to the anti-classicism of much nineteenth-century thought. Scheerbart was no classicist, and for an entirely logical reason: *Hellas ohne Glas*—Greece without Glass. Equally logically he admired those cultures that delighted in coloured glass, in the Orient and in Gothic Europe. Equally logically again, he combated the classicist polemics of Adolf Loos (by implication if not by name) against ornament.

But—and still perfectly consistently—he also saw Gothic architecture as the true forerunner of the great glass and iron structures of the nineteenth century that he admired quite as much as Muthesius ever did, and in this linking back of the *Grands Constructeurs* to the Gothic spirit, he is at one with the French Rationalist tradition from Viollet-le-Duc to Auguste Choisy, the tradition that produced most of the buildings that were featured in *Bauen in Frankreich.* Again, his orientalisms, gothicisms, his interest in theosophy and light-mysticism, which all seem a mile away from mainstream Modern Movement ideas, are no distance at all away from the frame of mind in which Johannes Itten created one of the greatest glories of the Modern Movement, the Bauhaus preliminary course. The Bauhaus connection cuts even closer than this—much of the text of the first proclamation, where it deals with eliminating the barriers between brain-worker and artisan, directly echoes the apocalypse of Scheerbart's *Immer Mutig* (the Hippopotamus novel referred to above) where

Kings walk with beggarmen, artisans with men of learning

and the three-spired cathedral in Lyonel Feininger's woodcut on the cover is now seen to be topped, not—as has been supposed—by three stars of Bethlehem, but by three navigation lights for Zeppelins.

One could pursue the matter further, into the ever-ramifying but ever more attenuated influence of Scheerbart as it runs on into the Twenties—including perhaps the glass towers of Le Corbusier's *Plan Voisin de Paris,* for they are close cousins to Mies's Friedrichstrasse project, and their form with emphatic vertical accents was later written off by Le Corbusier as a mistake peculiar to German architecture. But the mere pursuit is not the point—it is the necessity and attractions of the pursuit that are the point. Why, in a word, do we have to re-write the history of the Modern Movement?

Not because that history is wrong; simply because it is less than lifesize. The official history of the Modern Movement, as laid out in the late Twenties and codified in the Thirties, is a view through the marrow-hole of a dry bone—the view is only possible because the living matter of architecture, the myths and symbols, the personalities and pressure-groups have been left out. The choice of a skeletal history of the movement with all the Futurists, Romantics, Expressionists, Elementarists and pure aesthetes omitted, though it is most fully expressed in Giedion's *Bauen in Frankreich,* is not to be laid to Giedion's charge, for it was the choice of the movement as a whole. Quite suddenly modern architects decided to cut off half their grandparents without a farthing.

In doing so, modern architecture became respectable and gutless; it entered on what Peter Smithson has justifiably called its Academic phase, when it became a style with books of rules, and could be exported to all parts of the Western world. But having set itself up as something more than a style, as a discipline of pure reason, it had to double-talk fast and frequently to explain its obsession with certain materials, particularly glass and that smooth white reinforced concrete that never existed outside architects' dreams and had to be faked in reality with white rendering. Clearly, these materials were symbolic, they were totemic signs of power in the tribe of architects. But while concrete has never lacked respectable medicine-men, from Auguste Perret to Pierluigi Nervi, to maintain its *mana,* the image of Gropius as the official witch-doctor of glass has never looked very convincing. On the other hand the fanaticism of a Bruno Taut possessed by the spirit of Paul Scheerbart, as by a voodoo deity, has much more the air.

This is not to say that we now throw away the history of glass in modern architecture as it has been established so far—the position of Muthesius and Gropius among its prophets is not demolished, only diminished. We have to find some space for Scheerbart, as Giedion now clearly recognizes. The problem, which is not to be settled by a single article, is—how much space? As to his right to that space there can be no further doubt, for if one applies to him the normal test for missing pioneers, that of prophecy uttered in the right ears at the right time, he scores more heavily than many other writers of his day. Not only were his architectural writings known and in varying degrees influential among the generation of Gropius and Mies van der Rohe, but at a time when many spoke of steel and glass, he also spoke of water as the natural complement of glass, of the need to temper the white glare of light through glass by the use of coloured tinting, he spoke of America as the country where the destinies of glass architecture would be fulfilled, and he spoke of the propriety of the 'Patina of bronze' as a surface. In other words, he stood closer to the Seagram Building than Mies did in 1914. To put him back into the history of modern architecture is to shed upon it precisely what he would have us shed upon it—*Mehr Farbenlicht!*

8

Primitives of a Mechanized Art

Early in September 1951, I found a bound volume of Futurist Manifestos on a bookstall outside the Brera, Milan. I picked it up, I looked at it, put it down again, and walked off without even inquiring the price. I must have been mad—or, rather, I should say that I cannot now possibly reconstruct the frame of mind in which I could do such a thing. A mere three years later I was cajoling and browbeating officials of the *Soprintendenza* in order to get into the Modern Gallery in Milan, which was temporarily closed, to see the Futurist paintings and sculptures there, having just come down from Como, where I had been making similar manoeuvres in order to see the drawings of the Futurist archi-tect, Antonio Sant'Elia.

THE ARRIVAL AT FUTURISM   I recount this fragment of autobiography in order to fix the point in time where Futurism suddenly became important for myself, and for the circle of friends on whom, at that time, I sharpened my wits and tried out my theories. We have arrived at Futurism by working backwards from the things we were interested in at that particular moment,

Originally appeared in *The Listener* 62 (3 December 1959): 974–976.

most notably the machine aesthetic, motion-studies in art, a-formal composition (as in action-painting) and what we then termed non-art, but is now called anti-art. We knew, because it was well-documented in all the books—we knew what the School of Paris and the Germans had contributed to these aspects of twentieth-century art, but again and again in lectures and discussions in which we participated at the Institute of Contemporary Arts we found that the trail led back to the Futurist movement. Clearly, someone had to do some research, and since I was the art-historian of the group they all pointed to me.

What emerged was a less confused and irrelevant picture than might be expected, considering that one was leap-frogging back fifty years in time, to a world that was separated from ours by two global disasters and the Russian revolution and the atom bomb. The apparent confusion is daunting enough, as one surveys the Futurist movement's programme of quasi-political demonstrations, leaflet raids, public brawls and obscure polemics, but the confusion is not difficult to resolve because the irrelevancies of Futurism can be pared away fairly easily.

The outstanding irrelevancy from our point of view is the irredentist strain, the patriotic ambition to redeem slices of Italian-speaking territory that were still under foreign rule. We are still accustomed to hear Italians generating heat and passion about marginal territories like Trieste, but before 1914 the territories involved were hardly marginal: the *Baedeker* I had with me on that second visit to Milan had been published in 1906 and it treated the whole of the Venezia as a separate country. The irredentist theme was far from irrelevant to the Marinetti connexion, and it produced a quantity of warlike noises and some genuine acts of heroism when Italy finally entered the war; and it led to the final submersion of Futurism in Fascism. But the hatred of foreign dominion was extended by Marinetti and his associates to cover the hordes of foreign art-lovers who came to browse among the monuments of Italy's glorious past.

SNEERS FROM MARINETTI Many members of this 'foetid gangrene of professors, archaeologists, cicerones and antiquarians', as Marinetti called them, were clearly open to hatred because they spoke German, the language of the Austrian oppressor; but Americans and Englishmen were not exempt, and some of Marinetti's sharpest sneers are at 'your deplorable Ruskin . . . with his sick dream of a primitive agrarian life, his nostalgia for Homeric cheeses and the spinning-wheels of legend. . .'. In the first place, then, the anti-art reaction of the Futurists was against the art of the past, and against culture as something inherited from the past: 'Set fire to the bookstacks of the libraries, divert canals to flood out the museums. Oh, the pleasure of seeing all the glorious old canvases borne away on the flood, torn and stained by the water', declares the foundation manifesto of 1909.

That pronouncement must have had a specifically Italian relevance for men to whom

Venice and Florence were 'running sores' on the face of the country; yet even here Marinetti touched a nerve that was to twitch for two more decades outside Italy. 'Must we burn the Louvre?' demanded the *Esprit Nouveau* circle in the 'twenties, 'would you defend the National Gallery?' inquired the Left poets of the 'thirties. The moment the Futurists set foot outside the narrow terms of purely Italian relevance, the moment they said something that could be generalized, they spoke a language that was international, and comprehensible long after other art jargons had become dead languages.

There are two fairly obvious reasons for this. First, the Italians did not invent that anti-art pitch. Their debts to outside sources, particularly France, were considerable. Futurism would not have been what it was without—for instance—the liberated typography of Mallarmé's *Un Coup de Dés,* without the example of Alfred Jarry, without the example of Walt Whitman: but chiefly, not without the example of the School of Paris as a kind of mass *avant-garde*. France had come to terms with the idea of revolutionaries in art, and had given them places, occasions, and organizations where they could function without upsetting the rest of the community too much. But in Italy even these restricted outlets were not available. The Futurists, and similar groups like the *Voce* circle in Florence, felt stifled by a situation where the small public tolerance for advanced art was being completely monopolized by Gabriele D'Annunzio. Political discontents increased the psychological pressure, and sooner or later something had to give. But when it did, and the Futurists launched their manifestos on the world, it was only the flaming language and the rough-house techniques (borrowed from politics) that were new and unfamiliar; the message had been heard before.

ATTACHMENT TO NEW ELEMENTS IN LIFE

That last statement was not altogether true. The second reason why the Futurists were understood was that when they rejected art they did not, as the Dadaists so often did, adopt a position of impregnable but vacuous nihilism. Detaching themselves from art, they attached themselves instead to the new elements in life whose very possibility the ancients could not have suspected, to paraphrase Sant'Elia. Bundled together, those new elements added up to life in the mechanized metropolises of the northern hemisphere. The Futurists did not merely accept the fact that they had to live in the twentieth century; they volunteered to join it.

Futurist painting and Futurist poetry have a characteristic landscape as certainly as Impressionist painting belongs to the Seine Valley, or poetry-'n'-jazz belongs to the Pacific Coast. The characteristic setting of Futurist thought is to be found in those aspects of Edwardian Milan and Turin that could have been duplicated at the same time in New York, Berlin, Manchester, and Barcelona—even in Paris or Vienna. In so far as trams, electric lighting, advertising, railways, motor-cars, factories, covered markets, aviation, and so forth were international, the Futurists were internationally understood; in so far as these things are still with us, the Futurists are still understood today.

Their achievement was to identify, with some accuracy, how people were going to live in the twentieth century; and to indicate, with some authority, certain basic ways of responding to it. It may not be too much to say that anti-art has become a characteristic twentieth-century attitude because the Futurists made it so. Certainly, the range and percipience of their anticipation of later anti-art manifestations are startling.

To take it at its longest range first: there is, I suppose, absolutely no direct connexion between the true 'Beat' generation and the Futurists, unless by a long détour through the poetry of Mayakowski, who at one time called himself a Futurist. It may simply be that one touch of protest makes the whole world kin. But, on the other hand, the *Foundation Manifesto* opens with a nocturnal discussion on philosophy and poetry in a consciously weird setting, and continues with an orgy of wild and irresponsible automobilism that is like nothing else in Western literature except parts of Kerouac's *On the Road,* ending with a car-crash that is the pretext for a kind of secular mystical experience and mock-gospelling that again is very like.

This was Marinetti on his own, and the particular strain found here is not repeated elsewhere in Futurist literature, but in much of the Futurist output one curious anticipation of hipsterism persists—the preoccupation with night people. The *Foundation Manifesto,* as I said, begins at night and its first major visual image is of a brightly lit tram plunging past in the darkness. Marinetti identifies himself and his friends as alone with the stokers of ships and trains and 'the gesturing drunks who flap uncertainly along the walls of the city': one thinks of the weirdies that Kerouac seems always to meet wandering and muttering in the small hours. The night people are in Boccioni, too, in his paintings of tarts under the lights of the Piazza del Duomo and incomprehensible scuffles in the Galleria, or in his writings—'we adore the waiter, and the playboy, geometricized by the black and white of their clothes, the glitter of a cocotte caught between the lights and the gleam of glasses . . .' or, in his railway-station triptych, the figures in 'These Who Stay' are seen sloping off (literally sloping) through the rain across the asphalt of some badly lit piazza, submissive and huddled in their sporty raincoats.

There is plenty more of this, without going to the works of the Futurist poets with their *vers-libre* apostrophes on great cities and the marvels of technology. But with Boccioni all this has a peculiar significance. He was—with the possible exception of Antonio Sant'Elia—the most formidable mind the movement produced, intelligent, well-read, systematic; a mind different in its complexion from, say, Marcel Duchamp's, but comparable in range and subtlety. Applying his mental equipment to the art of his time, he codified and sorted out many tendencies that Parisian and German writers could handle only at the poetic level of an Apollinaire, the emotional level of a Herwarth Walden.

He was easily the first European writer to propose method and justification for *collage,* and the use of new, anti-artistic materials such as synthetics and ignoble metals;

his analysis of the art of Picasso leads him to a merciless demonstration of how little in Cubism was truly revolutionary, and he sets up against the formal, centralized composition of Cubist painting a field-theory of composition and space that is spectacularly in advance of its time. The compositional theory is best seen at work in Balla's abstract paintings of 1912 and 1913, rather than his own—the picture-surface ripples with energetic faceting from one side to another, the motion marked off by vertical (or nearly vertical) interruptions from top to bottom; and the feeling of movement is directed by sinuous curves that pursue nearly horizontal courses across the canvas. The space theory comes out in Boccioni's own work in sculpture. The verbal statement is in the *Technical Manifesto of Futurist Sculpture* which he published in 1912: 'We must begin', he writes, 'from the central nucleus of the object as it strives for realization, in order to discover the new laws, that is, the new forms that relate it invisibly but mathematically to the plastic infinity within, and visible plastic infinity without . . . Thus sculpture must bring objects to life by rendering plastic, apprehensible and systematic their prolongations into space, since it cannot be doubted any longer that one object only finishes where another one begins, and there is not an object around us . . . that does not cut and section us with some arabesque of curved or straight lines'.

The visible sense of this is probably best seen as I saw it in 1954 when I finally got into that museum. The place was being cleaned, the exhibits were all on the floor, and suddenly I was looking down on Boccioni's famous still-life sculpture 'The Bottle Evolving in Space', seeing it as one never normally sees it, in plan; seeing how every solid and void started, one way or another, from the central axis of the bottle, suggesting its forms and spiralling out to engage other objects such as the plate on which the bottle stands.

DEAD ENDS But Balla's painting and Boccioni's sculpture were both dead ends: not to mince words, Boccioni—as a revolutionary artist—was the failure of the century and at the time of his death, in 1916, he was painting Cézannes, near enough. In fact, the whole movement—as a movement—was a dead end, as every responsible historian of twentieth-century art has pointed out, while offering various reasons. Sir Herbert Read, for instance, has lately proposed that the reasons for Futurism's failure lay in the fact that it 'was fundamentally a symbolic art, an attempt to illustrate conceptual notions in plastic form. A living art begins with feeling, proceeds to material and only *incidentally* acquires symbolic significance'. I disagree with Sir Herbert's view of symbolic art, but that is not what I want to argue about here. What I cannot accept is the proposition that Futurist art was not felt. It seems to me impossible to read the prologue to Marinetti's *Foundation Manifesto* and not be conscious of how acutely the experience of motoring was felt, at a kind of split level, simultaneously of minute observation and poetic exaltation. It is impossible to look at Boccioni's 'The Street Enters the House' and not see how intensely the dynamism of a mechanized city had been felt, or read Sant'Elia's views on architecture and not see how intensely he felt the surge of a new kind of building, the vision of a new kind of city.

Conceivably, these feelings are not, to Sir Herbert, the true voice of feeling. To me they are the true voice of twentieth-century feeling. Boccioni was right when he said: 'The era of great mechanized individualities has begun, and all the rest is archaeology . . . therefore we claim to be the primitives of a sensibility that has been completely over-hauled'. The type of feeling that is expressed in Futurist art, poetry, and philosophy is, for better or worse, the feeling of a mechanized sensibility such as did not exist before. Marinetti's tag-line, 'the man multiplied by the motor', is a fair identification of the char-acteristic type of inhabitant of contemporary culture. But when Boccioni used the word 'primitive' I think he put his finger on the source of both the splendours and the miser-ies of Futurism.

His generation stood on the very threshold of twentieth-century culture and they asked of it more than it could give them in its primitive state: to take one example that demands to be taken, Luigi Russolo's *Manifesto on the Art of Noise,* which appeared in 1913, lays down the programme for *musique concrète* in some detail. The mani-festo demands an enlargement of the repertoire of sound used in music by the inclu-sion of noises produced by mechanical sources, and in two of its propositions Russolo draws very close to what finally happened in *musique concrète.* Number 5 suggests that 'we can change the pitch of a noise . . . for instance, by reducing or increasing the speed of the noise-source if it has a rotatory movement', and number 6 that 'it will not be by means of a series of sounds imitating life, but by an imaginative combination of these various sounds and different rhythms that our new orchestra will attain new and complex emotional sonorities'. None of this could happen as technology then stood: Russolo's team of *bruiteurs* had to make do with cumbersome hand-operated devices like giant klaxons. Not until the early 'fifties did tape recorders and electronic tackle at last catch up with the Futurist dream. No man is likely to live out a forty-year gap be-tween desire and achievement and, in a sense, Futurism died—as a movement— of frustration and distraction by more easily soluble problems.

THE 'NEW
SENSIBILITY'

But if they were wrong in asking too much, they were historically right in asking. They saw, as no one else outside the realm of technology and science could see, what a mechanized civilization should be able to offer its inhabitants. I said earlier that the Futurists themselves may have made anti-art part of twentieth-century feeling: they certainly saw it as the common factor of the culture of our time. In a vital passage of his book, *Pittura Scultura Futurista,* Boccioni demands the abolition of the art of the past and then continues: 'We will put into the resulting vacuum all the germs of the power that are to be found in the example of primitives and barbarians of every race, and in the rudiments of that new sensibility emerging in all the anti-artistic manifestations of our epoch—café-chantant, gramophone, cinema, electric advertising, mechanistic architecture, skyscrapers . . . night-life . . . speed, automobiles, aeroplanes and so forth'.

Alter *café-chantant* just enough to mean espresso bar (or even popular music, which Boccioni praised elsewhere), the rest follows naturally—'hi-fi', cinemascope, the lights in Piccadilly Circus, curtain-walled office-blocks—indeed the last four terms, night-life, speed, automobiles, aeroplanes, need no altering at all—these images describe the London scene into which we stepped as we left the Institute of Contemporary Arts those evenings in 1953 and 1954. We were at home in the promised land that the Futurists had seen afar off but had been denied entry to, wandering for forty years in a wilderness of disregard, their tremendous efforts brushed off, as Basil Taylor said in the first of these talks[1], as 'unruly incidents'. No wonder we found in them long-lost ancestors of our own preoccupations, right down to the details. There is an extraordinary phrase of Boccioni's where he identified as his own the characteristics which we attributed to action painting: 'Gesture, for us . . . will decisively be dynamic sensation eternalized as such'.

The phrase accurately identifies the kinaesthetic quality of the paint-trails in a painting by Pollock or Mathieu; we recognized the fact, and saluted Boccioni as a great forerunner. What we did not recognize then, and has only occurred to me now, is that Boccioni also, probably, identified the subject we have all been talking about in this series, for the first time. I know of no earlier use of the word anti-artistic as a term of praise; in fact I know of no earlier use of the term at all than the half-dozen instances in the book by Boccioni I have quoted. He is the acknowledged father of art—anti-art.

NOTE   1. *The Listener*, November 12.

» The 1960s

IN THE 1960s BANHAM was invited by students at the Bartlett School of Architecture, University College, London, to give lectures for their own 'alternative' courses which they were running concurrently with the official degree programme. The success of this student protest resulted in the first architecture school revolution, bloodless but effective, in Britain. Out of it grew Richard Llewelyn-Davies's new School of Environmental Studies, for which Banham was asked to work full-time. In 1968 he became the first Professor of Architectural History in the United Kingdom.

He had left the *Architectural Review* in 1964 with regret and some misgivings about becoming a full-time academic, but the move allowed him a better opportunity to honour the increasing number of invitations to give lectures overseas, particularly in the United States.

Early in the '60s Philip Johnson asked him to go for a weekend to New York City—an exotic notion for Europeans in those days—in order to enter into public debate with him. This was the first time he had visited the shores of a country admired since childhood, and it was the realization of a longheld dream. Further invitations followed. This is when he began speaking on a regular basis at the annual Aspen Design Conference, where he met top designers and architects from all over the world. His worldwide travels increasingly informed his writing, and he became something of an 'overseas correspondent' for British readers and listeners.

He published *Architecture of the Well-Tempered Environment,* largely about American buildings (on a Graham Foundation Award) in 1969 and was working in Los Angeles on *Los Angeles: The Architecture of Four Ecologies* at the end of the decade.
—M.B.

9

1960—Stocktaking

TRADITION

Architecture, as the professional activity of a body of men, can only be defined in terms of its professional history—architects are recognized as architects by their performance of specific roles that have been assigned to the profession in previous generations. Any significant attempt to extend or alter those roles will be dismissed, by most of the profession and even more of the public, as something other than the business of architects as architects. As James Cubitt

TECHNOLOGY

Architecture, as a service to human societies, can only be defined as the provision of fit environments for human activities. The word 'fit' may be defined in the most generous terms imaginable, but it still does not necessarily imply the erection of buildings. Environments may be made fit for human beings by any number of means. A disease-ridden swamp may be rendered fit by inoculating all those who visit it against infection, a bathing beach may be rendered fit by

Originally appeared in *The Architectural Review* 127 (February 1960): 93–100.

rewrote recently 'Designing roundabouts or doorknobs is not architecture. The idea that it is arises from a misconception of the purposes of the Bauhaus, primarily a school of industrial design. Architecture is, and always will be concerned, roughly speaking, with "carefully balancing horizontal things on top of vertical things".'

In spite of the much-debated 'revolution' in architecture in our time, the roles of architects have not been significantly extended, and certain extensions of role—into product-design, for instance—seem to have been tacitly abandoned since the nineteen-thirties. There are probably a number of reasons for this, but most of them, including the legally enforced codes of conduct that architects have created for themselves, are traceable to a feeling that modification of the accepted roles beyond a certain point threatens the integrity, or even the identity, of the profession.

Quite apart from certain obvious worries about such marginally extra-professional activities as contracting, this self-stabilizing tendency operates also in a more generalized and diffuse manner to preserve the *status quo.* We have seen a notable example of this in the past decade, one that has done much to precipitate the present confused state of world architecture. Using student opinion—articulate but disengaged from the daily routine of business—as a barometer of opinion, one could distinguish, shortly after 1950, a strong feeling that architectural theory was leaning so far towards sociology and technology as determinants of architectural form that—in practice—architectural form was not being determined at all, or—alternatively—such form as was being determined was not architectural. There were demands to get *back to architecture*—a classic response, closely resembling that which Charles Eames described in his 1959 Discourse at the RIBA as a reliance on 'the lore of the operation.' Whether or not this situation brings with it the dangers to which he also referred—'The danger of this procedure is that operational lore, being an integration of experience rather than apparent intelligence (i.e. available information), sacrifices sensitivity in order to gain stability'—whether or not this is true, it has happened, and constitutes one of the two major pressures to which architecture has been subjected in the last decade.

The first phase of this return to operational lore was Anglo-Italian, an appeal to the Classical Tradition; not to the nearer end of that tradition as summed up in, say, the work of Auguste Perret, but to the beginnings of modern classicism in the Italian Renaissance. Its symbol was the Vitruvian Man, its slogan 'Divina Proporzione,' its hero Palladio, its prophet—quite coincidentally—Rudolf Wittkower. The appeal was not to the forms and details of Renaissance architecture, but to the underlying proportional mathematics, as set out in Professor Wittkower's *Architectural Principles of the Age of Humanism,* and echoed after a fashion—equally coincidentally—in Le Corbusier's *Modulor.* The upshot was not Neo-Georgian, but an aggressive axiality of plan, and a reliance on modular devices as planning tools. This particular moment has passed, moving land-mines left over from the last war, a natural amphitheatre may be rendered fit for drama by installing lights and a public address system, a snowy landscape may be rendered fit by means of a ski-suit, gloves, boots and a balaclava. Architecture, indeed, began with the first furs worn by our earliest ancestors, or with the discovery of fire—it shows a narrowly professional frame of mind to refer its beginnings solely to the cave or primitive hut.

The service that architects propose to perform for society can often be accomplished without calling in an architect in the sense discussed in the article that runs parallel to this, and the increasing range of technological alternatives to bricks and mortar may yet set a term to the custom-sanctioned monopoly of architects as environment-purveyors to the human race. These alternatives, whose justification is measurable performance rather than some cultural sanction, extend, however, beyond the provision of technological services, and include analytical techniques as well, so that it becomes possible to define 'home' without reference to hearth or roof, but simply as the integration of a complex of intrapersonal relationships and mains-services. To do so would, in fact, be to depart so far from the operational lore of the society which we inhabit as to provoke alarm and discomfort even among the scientists and technicians who, within their specialties, regularly employ these techniques. Nevertheless, a moment's reflections on such phrases as *TV Theatre* or *Radio Concert-hall* will show how far technological advance has made nonsense of concepts that were hitherto building-bound, and yet has gained popular social and cultural acceptance.

Under the impact of these intellectual and technical upheavals the solid reliance of architects, as a profession, on the traditions of that profession must eventually give way. Yet the Functionalist slogan 'a house is a machine for living in' gives nothing away because it begins by presupposing a house. Far more seditious to the established attitude of architects is the proposition that, far from caravans being sub-standard housing, housing is, for many functions, sub-standard caravans. Outside the context of architectural discussion this would be a pretty radical criticism of current architectural concepts, but within the profession it stands simply as a marginal criticism, of some aspects of housing that need improvement in detail.

This may be taken as typical of the profession's professional attitude to the impact of technological and scientific alternatives for the art of building. The profession tolerates a few peripheral radicals, whose ideas call the whole professional apparatus in question. Such a man is Buckminster Fuller, recently made a member of AIA, and thus accepted as relevant to architecture in the professional sense. But it is clear that Fuller is admired for his structures and accepted as a form-giver, while his elaborate body of theory and fundamental research into the shelter-needs of mankind is mostly and not left much behind—some projects for 'Palladian Power-stations,' some hotly-discussed Fifth-year student Thesis projects, now forgotten, and a slowly waning admiration for things Italian—of which the slowest-waning, perhaps, is the reputation of Luigi Moretti, whose *Casa del Girasole,* discovered by Anglo-Saxons in 1952, was for some years a test of taste.

But, in a more generalized sense this moment in the history of modern architecture has left much behind. It marks the beginning of the persistent belief in modular number patterns as disciplines inherently beneficial to architecture—a belief now institutionalized in the Modular Society, where, however, attempts are being made to give it a footing in something more solid than vague sentiments inspired by reliance on operational lore. Somewhere in this moment too lie the origins of the present addiction to formality of the middle and elder generation among U.S. architects—the use of classical pavilion forms by Ed Stone and Walter Gropius in their recent embassies in New Delhi and Athens, or by Mies van der Rohe in his Baccardi building, or the use of multi-axial symmetries and vaulted coverings by Philip Johnson, in such examples as his Shrine at New Harmony. In the case of Johnson—early a devout Wittkowerian—the apparent historicism is backed by the resounding proclamation of faith: 'Hurrah for History. Thank God for Hadrian, for Bernini, for Le Corbusier and Vince Scully.'

Scully, through his celebrated lectures at Yale, has—like Wittkower, Colin Rowe, Bruno Zevi, and others—done much to give history-teaching a new dynamic, and thus to add a richness to the traditions of operational lore that has not been there since the death of Soane and Schinkel. What is new in this situation is the way that the revived interest in history has not come about in countries whose great architecture is all in the past, and the future has nothing to offer, but in countries—like the U.S.—who appear to have a wave of great architecture ahead of them in the immediate future, and one of the effects of this new sense of history has been to produce a reassessment of the work of the masters who will set the style for that future. Thus, just before the 're-discovery' of history, there was a current of opinion that tended to evaluate Mies van der Rohe's architecture in 'technological' terms as a theoretically endless accretion of 'additive' units. After the rediscovery of history, this view, propagated by Richard Llewelyn-Davies and Gerhard Kallmann, was replaced by an emphasis on Mies as a classicist, on the axial symmetry, regularity and modular organization of his planning, and his debts to German Neo-Classicism.

Aside from these returns to the classical lore of the architectural operation, another, older stream of latent historicism has burst forth on the surface again, after a period when it was buried by classicist enthusiasms. This is the strain of historicist defeatism—entirely lacking in the intellectual exaltation of the classical revival—that was first manifest in a muted, self-effacing way as the new Empiricism of the dismissed unread. An extreme technologist more to the profession's taste is Konrad Wachsmann, whose work does not question the need for buildings but concentrates a fanatical watchmaker ingenuity on the solution of certain problems within the given context of built structure—and here it may be noted that while his celebrated joint for the space-frame roof of the B36 hangar was associated with a fairly radical structure, his equivalent work on the General Panel House was associated with a dwelling-concept of the utmost banality. Again, the research and teaching being undertaken by the *Hochschule für Gestaltung* at Ulm, while it asks some searching questions and produces some truly radical answers, does so within a mental concept that substantially accepts the limits that the architectural profession has set itself. In many ways, Le Corbusier's *Murondin* project for installing sophisticated mechanical services in mud-huts showed a greater radicalism of approach than either of these last two examples.

In any stocktaking of the present condition of architecture, then, it must be accepted that the human environments under consideration are constructed environments, static, more or less permanent and designed to operate without the consumption of too much mechanical energy. These last two provisos are both rather relative since no discussion of the present state of architecture could decently ignore the tented structures of Frei Otto and other semi-permanent exhibition environments, nor could it ignore the fact that some of the most permanent and static structures being built today—such as atom-proof command posts or office blocks in extreme climates—can only be kept fit for human activities at the cost of pouring vast quantities of mechanical energy into them in the form of air-conditioning and artificial light. Within these provisos, the mechanization of the total environment in which architects are called upon to work still acts as a powerful stimulus to their professional activities. Automobiles, the ever-present symbolic objects that typify the present epoch of technological culture, are the irritant that causes constant revision of a number of cherished concepts. These revisions are not always radical, but, nevertheless, it is no longer possible for architects to think of cities as collections of buildings with spaces between them, but as collections of buildings with streams of metallic objects flowing round them—a revision that requires them to think differently about the way the buildings touch the ground, differently about the relationship of building to street, differently about the relationship of building to those who look at it, since the viewers may now be passing it at sixty-plus mph on a gently rising curve or in an underpass whose sides may effectively blank off the whole of the lower storey when the viewer is on the axis of the main façade.

Conversely automobiles as the manifestation of a complex and agitated culture-within-a-culture producing discrete objects which are themselves environments for

Scandinavian North in the late 'Forties, and now reappears in a more aggressive and wilful form as *Neoliberty* in Italy. Both movements exhibit the same tendency to rely on purely *local* operational lore, one might almost say the lore of the local building industry, rather than the lore of architecture at large. Both also rely on the lore of materials, declining to use new ones because they are visually 'unreliable' under weathering and use. Both have been interpreted as relying also on the lore of public taste, not wishing to put up buildings that the average citizen cannot understand (i.e., not putting up buildings that he hasn't seen before). It is worth noting that most of these observations are also true of the architecture of the English New Towns, where the same frame of mind appears to have governed the town-planning as well.

Neoliberty also introduces another problem of acute interest in the present state of architecture, but this must be left over, for the moment, in order to consider the general import of these historicist trends. The blanket term most commonly in use to cover all the tendencies in modern architecture that deviate from the functionalist norms of geometrical purity and plan-wise asymmetry, is *Formalist.* The term is fair enough, provided limitations are placed around its usage. There is little sign at the moment of out-and-out formalism, of shape-making for the sake of shape-making. Even the paper-projects of an architect like Marcello d'Olivo keep within certain bounds, and those bounds are within the limits of the lore of the operation—nothing like Action-painting has happened to architecture yet. For this reason, the deviation from the canons of Functionalist form does not constitute *Une Architecture Autre,* as Odo Kulterman appears to believe (to judge from his article in *Baukunst und Werkform,* 8, 1958). If the concept of an Other architecture has any place in this survey, it is in the article that runs parallel to this one. New shapes notwithstanding, it is still the same old architecture, in the sense that the architects involved have relied on their inherited sense of primacy in the building team, and have insisted that they alone shall determine the forms to be employed. Formalism it may be, but it remains formalism within the limits of a professional tradition, albeit that tradition is now wide enough to span from the Neolibertarians to d'Olivo, from Mies van der Rohe to Bruce Goff.

But to return to the specific significance of Neoliberty. It is a revival, but not of an historical style in the sense that Doric or Gothic are historical styles. Art-historical niceties about the precise degree of modernity that Liberty (Art Nouveau) can claim do not affect that it is not a style enjoying long-ingrained cultural approbation, like the great styles of the remoter past, but a style of our own time, propagated through international magazines and exhibitions by men conscious of living in a machine age.

Its revival implies a recognition that the allegedly anti-traditional Modern Movement has a tradition of its own. Reliance on the traditional lore of the operation no longer necessarily means relying on a tradition older than oneself—the men who made the human activities, provide a standard of comparison for the activities of the architectural profession. They may ruefully compare the scale of the constructional work produced by the automobile culture with that entrusted to architects; they may enviously admire the apparently close communion that exists between users and producers, the direct way in which designers and stylists seem to be able to apprehend the needs of motorists and satisfy them, and they may also draw from the work of stylists some sobering conclusions about the possibility of tailoring aesthetics to fit the aspirations or social status of the clients. The concept of *the style for the job,* which was most recently enunciated in the *Architectural Review* by James Gowan in December 1959, has frequently been explained or criticized in terms of the gradations of automobile style for different parts of the market, always with the assumption (sometimes justified) that these gradations are the result of scientifically accurate market research.

However, there is no ambition to imitate automobile form—the only exception to this rule appears to be the 'styling' of the Smithson's *House of the Future* on the assumption that mass-produced houses would need as high a rate of obsolescence as any other class of mass-produced goods. Such a sentiment is rare, however, because the operational lore of architecture seems not to include the idea of expendability. On the other hand, the forms of the more permanent products of technology are liable to imitation—to cite a notorious example, the development of cooling towers for power stations has been paralleled by a series of pseudo-cooling towers from Eric Mendelsohn's hat factory of 1921, to Le Corbusier's Parliament House for Chandigarh.

This sincere flattery of technology is one facet of the almost fetishistic regard afforded to certain classes of engineers, an admiration that has undergone an important change in the last decade. The respects paid by the early masters of modern architecture to the engineers they admired was not paralleled by any attempt to mimic the forms of their work—where will you find Freyssinet echoed in early Corbusian design, or Maillart in Max Bill despite the latter being the great bridge-builder's devoted biographer? Yet nowadays the desire to incorporate engineering forms into architectural designs is so overwhelming that engineers like Nervi, Candela, Torroja and others enjoy a status both as collaborators with architects, and as the creators of imitable forms, that engineers have never had before.

Just how far this is merely the employment of engineers as alibis for fancy formalisms is difficult to assess, though Robin Boyd made some pertinent suggestions on this subject in *The Engineering of Excitement* (*Architectural Review*, November 1958). Over and above this is the possibility that the freeing of floor-space from intermediate supports which new vaulting techniques and space-frame trusses make possible, is being used in one way and explained in another. Great clear spans make possible a free and untrammelled functional disposition of interior spaces—this is one of the

tradition are, mostly, still alive. However, a further new factor, over and above the recognition of a new tradition, is the existence of two different ways of looking at that tradition. On the one hand, it may be accepted as a tradition of the sort we have known
before, passed from master to pupil, teacher to student, almost subliminally as a
succession of ever-mutating attitudes and preconceptions, constantly in process of
change as the needs and aspirations of successive generations came to bear upon
it. This, if it existed, would be the mainstream of Modern Architecture today. But the
stream has practically vanished, and consists of isolated individuals, like pools in a
drying torrent-bed—and the pools are drying out, too. Two years ago, one could have
pointed to Wells Coates and André Sive as mainstream modernists, in the sense of
men inhabiting a live modern tradition, but not any more. For the most part, this kind of
smoothly-developing modernism exists nowadays in the work of large offices such as
Skidmore, Owings and Merrill, or Yorke, Rosenberg and Mardall, or in solitary originals
like Bakema, Goldfinger or Denys Lasdun. It also exists, with pronounced local characteristics, in Brazil and other Latin American countries.

But what, then, of the men who ought to be the great mainstreamers, the four architects whom Henry-Russell Hitchcock identified as the masters of the Twenties and
Thirties? J. J. P. Oud long ago made his private retreat into local professional lore. Mies
van der Rohe has isolated himself in a bronze tower more pure than ivory, driven there
by a logic that would have worked equally well in a vacuum where modern architecture
did not exist. Gropius has become the Dean of the Formalists, Doric in Athens, Islamic
in Baghdad. And Le Corbusier?

While it is generally conceded that the apparent formalisms of a Frank Lloyd Wright
were a law unto themselves, justified by the dimensions of an almost Michelangelesque personality, there is clearly a widespread feeling that the apparent formalisms
of Le Corbusier answer to some law obscurely, but vitally, inherent in the business of
architecture. No sooner were the implications of Ronchamp apparent than a dozen
pens were at work explaining that its forms were not a wilful contradiction of everything
that Le Corbusier had done before, but the fulfilment of certain aspects of himself, or
modern architecture in general, that had lain dormant. It is clear that Ronchamp is not
Formalism in the commonly accepted sense, because it does not gain the one secure
advantage of formalizing within the tradition—that of communicability. No one doubts
that Ed Stone's Delhi Embassy, or Saarinen's in London, look like representational government buildings, but the argument over what Ronchamp looks like is still proceeding,
the only basis of agreement being that it does *not* look like a church.

The attempts to explain why Ronchamp is as it is, and how it is connected with the
true nature of modern architecture, bring out the other way of regarding the Modern

promises of Fuller's domes, for instance. But they also clear the floor for free and un-trammelled exercises in architectural sensibility—which seems to be what happened, in fact, inside the geodesic dome furnished by Roberto Mango at the 1954 *Triennale di Milano.*

Such situations are not as rare as might be supposed—Mies van der Rohe's proj-ect for a theatre in a giant aircraft hangar is another debatable case in point—and they represent the continuance of a trend that has been with us since the beginning of the century; the marriage of the logical objectivity of abstract aesthetics to the experimen-tal objectivity of advanced science. It goes back to Perret, it also has roots in *de Stijl* and Constructivism. In the guise of the 'logical formalism' of Mies van der Rohe it has served the important function of easing the acceptance of curtain walling and other additive prefabricating systems as 'architecture' in a sense that can be as-similated to the lore of the operation.

However, it should be noted that when prefabrication gets out of the direct control of architects, into the hands of engineers, it almost invariably ceases to be rectangular in its format. Fuller's work is again a case in point, so is that of Jean Prouvé, which has persistently relied on tapered portals, sloping walls and curved members. However, there is a division of mind here between architects and engineers that goes much deeper. The operational lore of the architectural profession has assimilated prefabrica-tion as a technique applied to fairly small repetitive components to be assembled on site. Such an arrangement leaves the determination of functional volumes still se-curely in the hands of architects, and the physical creation of those volumes securely in the hand of traditional-type site labour.

But prefabrication, for most of the creative minds in the plastics business, means something quite different. It means—as Michael Brawne has suggested (*Polyester Fi-breglass, Architectural Review*, December 1959)—the fabrication of components large enough to be effective determinants of functional volumes. Thus, the Monsanto House has only four large components to form the whole of one of its cantilevered rooms (bar the lateral windows) while some of the products envisaged by the French group around Coulon and Schein call for the off-site fabrication of complete functional volumes such as bathrooms and kitchens, a procedure which both has structural advantages and makes it possible to complete most of the fabricating work under controlled, laboratory conditions. The result seems likely to be a house put together from large non-repeating units—except for the joiners which, like railway corridors, must be universal fits. In larger structures room-units might be carried in an independent frame, but in either case the result should be that service-rooms, which need to be connected to the public mains, might be treated as expendable clip-on components, thus obviating some of tradition itself—not as a man-to-man communication of attitudes and concepts, but as an immutable and scientifically ascertainable succession of historical facts. Such an approach is in direct conflict with the 'traditional' view of the modern tradition, and has been described as 'using facts to pervert the history of modern architecture' by supporters of that view. It has also led to persistent allegations of modern eclecticism being levelled against younger architects who hold to the 'scientific' view of recent history. Very often this is true, particularly at student level where the formal vacuum of half-trained minds can as easily be filled with pickings from the Twentieth Century as from other centuries. But much of this alleged eclecticism has been the stimulus, mask, or vehicle of radical attempts to establish 'what really happened in modern architecture.'

The most important aspect of this view of the tradition is its all-inclusiveness. The other type of tradition proceeds by what might be called 'selective amnesia,' each generation forgetting anything that had ceased to be of interest in order to find room for new matters of interest that had come up in its own time. The new view, on the other hand, demands total recall—everything that wasn't positively old-fashioned at the time it was done is to be regarded as of equal value. The Futurists must be discussed in the same breath as the Deutscher Werkbund, de Klerk must be put alongside Rietveld, Maybeck alongside Wright. The guardians of the Modern tradition, such as Sigfried Giedion, have been called in question for forgetting too much, and—it is claimed—distorting the truth by over-selectivity. In revenge, every discarded formal and functional device that was dropped or ignored by the developing mainstream must now be re-examined and, wherever applicable, re-used.

Much of what results—projects and a few finished buildings—is, indeed, modern movement revivalism, the resurrection of usages (though rarely of total building forms) of the architecture of the Twenties, or even the Forties—David Gray's house at Lowestoft can serve as an example of the former, the Smithson's school at Hunstanton of the latter. But Hunstanton—the building by which the much-battered term 'New Brutalism' is commonly defined—immediately raises another problem altogether. Wherever the scientific and all-inclusive attitude to recent history is found, it is nearly always accompanied by a similar attitude to the use of materials. The mystique of materials 'as found' involves (*a*) a resolute honesty in their use (paralleling the refusal to allow a selective attitude to historical fact) and (*b*) an insistence that all the qualities of a material are equally relevant.

Thus, in the Hunstanton School, steel is given a far higher valuation than the rather abstract one implicit in Mies's work. Its visual quality as a rolled product with makers' trade marks embossed on it is given value, the nature of its ultimate performance under stress is acknowledged in the use of plastic theory by the engineer responsible the difficulties of the Appliance House project, which runs the risk of degenerating into a series of display-niches for an ever-changing array of domestic machinery.

However, such ideas have hardly touched the general body of architecture at all as yet. Much of the most painstaking and valuable research that can be shown has been undertaken in conditions that presuppose the existence of rectangular buildings. Much of this work has been structural, concerned chiefly with prefabrication techniques, a field in which, for instance, the Ministry of Education and independent commercial experimenters can be found advancing, from the other end, into territory already being prospected by the Modular mathematicians. Elsewhere, as with the Nuffield Trust, a great deal of solid, plodding work, that most architects would rather not undertake, has been accomplished in the fields of space-requirements and the physiological effects of daylighting and colour. The fruits of such work, because of the 'logical formalist' connection discussed above, often wear a characteristic air of grid-like simplicity which, it should be noted, derives more from the mental disposition of the men involved than from the findings of the research programmes.

Where research has been surprisingly thin has been in office-design, in spite of the large sums involved (although there has been some clever *ad hoc* rationalizing in this field) and in domestic work, in spite of the vast amount of housing still necessarily being built. Even clever *ad hoc* rationalization could show results in housing, but, as was said at the beginning of this article, the operational lore of our whole culture renders domestic architecture practically proof against scientific attitudes. On the other hand, it should be noted that via market and motivation research, and the long accumulation of sociological data, extensive scientific inroads into the 'sanctity of the home' have already been made, and when domestic designers can master their fairly long-standing distrust of sociologists and their new-found distrust of 'Hidden Persuaders' they may well find that a great deal of very suggestive research is already at their disposal.

In the meantime, science and technology touch architecture chiefly at the level of structural justification and organizational confusion. One specialist consultant makes the building stand up, six others render it largely useless by means of the services that are intended to make it usable. By and large, architects have established a peaceable and fruitful technique of working with their structural engineers. In England, engineers like Samuely, Arup and Jenkins, in France men like the late Bernard Laffaille and René Sarger, in the U.S.A. men like Fred Severud, Mario Salvadori and Paul Weidlinger or offices like Smith, Hynchman and Grylls, could claim to have played a dominant and valuable role in the architectural developments of the last ten years, but no other body of consultants could claim anything of the sort—though some architects might, nowadays, find a good word for the more enterprising type of quantity surveyor.

The fact remains that heating, lighting, ventilating, air-conditioning, acoustics, office for the structural calculations. Or, to take another work that has been abused for modern eclecticism, the development at Ham Common by Stirling and Gowan differs from its acknowledged sources (such as Le Corbusier's Jaoul houses) by using brickwork calculated to the limits of the load-bearing capacity—a decision that is more responsible than any Twenties-revivalism for the use of the dropped windows, with their inverted-L shape.

This, finally, brings us to the most significant aspect of the rigorous scrutiny of the history of the modern movement: the rediscovery of science as a dynamic force, rather than the humble servant of architecture. The original idea of the early years of the century, of science as an unavoidable directive to progress and development, has been reversed by those who cheer for history, and has been watered down to a limited partnership by the mainstream. Those who have re-explored the Twenties and read the Futurists for themselves feel, once more, the compulsions of science, the need to take a firm grip on it, and to stay with it whatever the consequences.

The consequence, in some cases, appears to be to whisk them straight out of formalism and modern historicism altogether, to make them abandon the lore of the operation, and make use of 'apparent intelligence' instead. But this may be only an appearance—certainly John Johansen's *Airform* house has the appearance of a radical reversal of attitude for a one-time Neo-Palladian of the strictest sort, but equally certainly, many of the most apparently liberated spirits of our time, the intellectual freebooters of the border-land between tradition and technology will not, in the last resort, renounce the lore of the operation. Thus Charles Eames, who has introduced the concept of operational lore into architectural thought, and made with it a plea for the acceptance of scientific attitudes of mind, could still say, toward the end of his Discourse 'Yet, in this circumstance I have described, and in these tools that I have described, I see and feel something which is a real continuity in the architectural tradition. . . . The real planning, the real architecture, and building of the future, is going to be built with something similar to these tools, and part of these circumstances. My plea is that it fall under the head of that great name, architecture, which embraces it.'

machinery and other more specialist services seem for the moment incapable of as-similation to the harmony established over the years between structural engineers and architects. The few breaks in this unpromising situation appear to derive from lighting engineers and acousticians with architectural training, and from a few liberated spirits, notably Lou Kahn with his 'topological' science blocks for the University of Pennsylva-nia, or Marco Zanuso with his integrated structure-and-air-conditioning schemes.

This may be a bull-dozer solution for a problem that Mies van der Rohe, for in-stance, believes should be solved in secret. But it is a solution that brings us to the point of fusion of the technological and traditional aspects in architecture today. Kahn is sympathetic to, and has been classed with, the Brutalists. On both sides, enterpris-ing and intensive scrutiny of tradition and science appears to suggest a way out of a dilemma, if not a solution to a problem. But it is a balancing feat that may prove to need acrobatic skill and expertise in brinkmanship as architects edge temeriously along the margin of the scientific disciplines and never quite put a foot over into the other camp. From the scientific side there is neither such caution nor such finesse. It appears always possible that at any unpredictable moment the unorganized hordes of uncoordinated specialists could flood over into the architects' preserves and, ignorant of the lore of the operation, create an Other Architecture by chance, as it were, out of apparent intelligence and the task of creating fit environments for human activities.

THE GAP-TOWN PLANNING

When all this has been said, and stock has been taken of the present situation, there remains one yawning and alarming chasm between technology and tradition, between operational lore and apparent intelligence—town planning. In a field too expensive for experiment, too full of practical minutiae for paper guesses or diagrammatic utopias to carry much conviction, the pull between the Two Cultures, as Sir Charles Snow has called them, results in a situation that would be tragic were it not more like the nihil-istic farce of Ionesco and the Other theatre.

The idea of cities is an ineradicable part of the operational lore of civilization—a word which implies cities anyhow. The concepts we have of cities are as old as philoso-phy, and are so rooted in the language of cultured discourse that to say 'Cities should be compact' is to commit a tautology—we cannot conceive of a diffuse city, and have invented other words, such as *conurbation, subtopia,* to underline our inability to conceive it.

Against this, the manifestations of apparent intelligence, in communications, traffic planning, services, industries, entertainment, sport, all dealing with the here and the

now, preoccupied with current information, news and statistics, have no regard for the inherited traditions of urbanism by which towns are defined.

Yet most citizens—including those called upon to plan—are determined to have the best of both worlds. They expect to be able to drive straight down an Autoroute de l'Ouest, straight through the Arc de Triomphe, and into a Champs Elysées that still has the urbanity of a sequence from *Gigi*. They demand suburban expansiveness, and urban compactness, ancient monuments and tomorrow's mechanical aids simultaneously and in the same place.

They get neither, because on one side is a tradition which cannot be expanded to deal with new developments without disintegrating, and on the other hand a disorderly pressure of new developments whose effect—because they are competitive and lack an integrating discipline—is disruptive anyhow.

There may be any number of logical solutions to this problem—but the only one we have so far is the relatively desperate solution of handing over responsibility to the will of a dictator—Le Corbusier at Chandigarh, Lucio Costa at Brasilia—and we are entitled to ask whether this is an adequate solution for our most pressing problem in design.

10

Alienation of Parts

The art-student who fell down the front steps was typical—it was probably her highly typical spike heel that tripped her. But the building from which she fell was far from typical, beginning with the double doors, which were hinged in the middle, not at the outside. But much more untypical than that . . . the second corollary to the fourth Law of Subtopia states 'In any given community, the ugliest building will be the school of art.'

Not in Glasgow. The art school there (1896) is an undoubted masterpiece—*the* masterpiece of its designer, Charles Rennie Mackintosh; one of the handful of really important buildings to emerge from *Art Nouveau*. It is also, I think, the weirdest building I have ever been in. Weird? Bent, twisted, real gone Mac. This is not to say that it is unfunctional, or wildly extravagant. Far from it; the materials used are homely and sparse, and it appears to work as well as any comparable building I have been in, Max Bill's *Hochschüle* at Ulm not excepted. But the effect is just manic-depressive—exhilaration at its boldness, cunning and untrammelled imagination, alternating with something like sick panic at the dripping decadence of most of its detailing.

Originally appeared in *New Statesman* 59 (5 March 1960): 331–332.

It isn't difficult to see why. The design is a triumph of absolute integrity—craftsmanly integrity in the use of materials, artistic integrity in honouring the demands of genius. The proof of genius is in the perfect synthesis of the two integrities in almost everything you see—only the synthesis is different for each material employed in its construction, and where an ordinary sane genius would evolve a single coherent aesthetic for the whole design, Mackintosh has an independent one for each major material.

In stone and brick he proceeds like an ideal Ruskinian master-mason, building a medieval castle—but a Castle Perilous since it has a low-arched Norman crypt *on the top floor.* Glass is to transmit light, or relieve the solidity of opaque materials—for the studios he puts up enormous windows with over-thin mullions, as if he were determined not to exclude one fraction of a lumen of usable daylight, and elsewhere he inserts tiny heart or bean-shaped jewels of coloured glass in the doors. Wood comes in trees or planks—vertical members shoot up like tapering, squared-off saplings, but the joists from which beams and short posts are made, he treats as if they were sacred timbers, never to be cut. They cross or overlap inviolate, without mortise or rabbet. Where a beam would normally pass through or over a post, he twins it, so that it passes on either side. In the tall two-storey library (the last part completed, in 1906) twinned beams grip the upright two-storey posts, and support a balcony whose edge-beam and balustrade stand back a clear two feet from the uprights, so that these fastidiously virginal and dissociated members add up the first great space-game of the Modern Movement, a generation ahead of its time.

But the metal-work is the manic-depressive limit. Ever one for paring down to ultimates, Mackintosh reduces metal *ad absurdum*—thin hammered sheets, fine twisted rails, balustrades like iron whalebone, safety-grilles so thin that they tremble under the hand, knotted turks'-heads of wiry inconsequence crowning willowy uprights. All honestly hand-wrought, but over-wrought to the point of dematerialization, so that little remains but a thin handwriting in space, a Mathieu painting in 3-D.

Space is the good word here. You are constantly made aware of it, and of Mackintosh's almost premature mastery of it, both in the Baroque sense of volumes made rhetorical by controlled light and shade, and in the Modernist sense of an empty continuum made eloquent and apprehensible by spidery structural gestures that define but never enclose the volumes. Mackintosh, in pursuit of his own neurotic vision, overran the frontier between traditional space concepts and modern ones, without knowing or caring—it took the rest of the *pietätvolle Architektentum* another twenty years to edge its way cautiously into the new world of space.

The mastery of space is one of the things that holds the design together, it is the master-aesthetic absorbing the disparate aesthetics of the parts. The other unifying concept becomes comprehensible only when, having grasped the spatiality of the whole, you see the parts in relation and context. Individually the works in different materials are such strangers to one another that a collection of them in an exhibition looks like a group exhibit, not a one-man show. But all together in the original building they add up to what one might call a system of graduated licence.

In masonry and glass there is practically no licence. I suspect these were not materials that could be wrought as Mackintosh would have liked, and he handles them expansively, but simply. In wood he is far more inventive—the roof of the main hall has fairly simple trusses, but he exaggerates the king-posts to braggart dimensions; the library is without precedent, and the roof structure of the studio above culminates in piles of crossed timbers that might, just, have come from Japan if they did not come from the recesses of his whisky-lashed imagination.

In iron, it is no holds barred, with one very revealing exception—in general the metal that brackets out from sober stone is much less frantic than where it grows out of the ever-friskier woodwork. It was this tempering of imaginative licence in the presence of masonry that first gave me the clue to the method—if I have got it right. I think I have, because it makes sense as you look at it. Not ordinary man-in-Sauchiehall Street sense, but the sort of sense that the choice of sick metaphors makes in the last scene of Ibsen's *Ghosts*—that terrifying moment when the images of 'soft' and 'velvety' force themselves insanely through the hard crust of flat-footed dialogue.

Mackintosh is like that—or as near to it as you can get in a building that will stand normal wear and tear. In uncomfortable truth it is astonishing how the last twists of Romantic Agony *in extremis* come through, and insofar as it survives and still convinces it is one of a very small company of masterpieces of that mood and period that have stood the erosion of time. What else is there? Munch's painting before his breakdown—neither Toorop nor Ensor is really comparable—some of Richard Strauss, some of *A Portrait of the Artist*. But nothing in architecture; continental *Art Nouveau* at its battiest was never like this, not even Gaudi. Mackintosh's combination of unity in the whole with alienation among the parts is unique, masterly, and profoundly disturbing.

Design by Choice

11

1951–1961

AN ALPHABETICAL CHRONICLE OF
LANDMARKS AND INFLUENCES

Alarmist Literature: In the 1950's the shortcomings of some aspects of product design became a subject for sensational journalism which—in some cases—contained an element of serious warning. The most prolific of these professional Jeremiahs was the American writer, Vance Packard, whose book *The Hidden Persuaders* drew attention to the social consequences of motivation research (q.v.). His subsequent works *The Status Seekers* and *The Waste Makers* continued variations of the same theme of social enquiry into design, but began to suggest that he had fallen victim to the very situation against which he was protesting: his elevation to the best-seller class involved him in the dynamics of the mass market and more or less committed him to bring out a 'new model' every other year. At a less sensational level, warnings to consumers were transmitted in Great Britain by way of the Editorials in *Which?* and *Shoppers' Guide.*

Appliance: The increasing mechanization of households in the Western world, and the beginning of

It is said that Industrial Design has altered out of recognition in the last ten years. Alternatively, it is said that only fashions have changed, and that Industrial Design is what it always was. It would be as well, therefore, to start by setting out what is unchanged, and what has been transformed. Firstly, the *subject matter* of Industrial Design has not changed; it is still concerned with (*a*) quality (materials and workmanship); (*b*) performance (functional and human) and (*c*) style (of appearance and use). Secondly, the *problem* of Industrial Design has not changed; it is still a problem of affluent democracy, where the purchasing power of the masses is in conflict with the preferences of the élite. In a subsistence economy there is no problem (though progressive Indians are just beginning to be aware of it) and in a controlled society there is no problem—a couple of jovial

---

Originally appeared in *The Architectural Review* 130 (July 1961): 43–48.

mechanization of households in other continents, gave a special status to electrical and other power-operated tools in the eyes of manufacturers, designers and consumers. The rise of 'do-it-yourself' acquainted many householders with small power tools for the first time, but also introduced a degree of mechanization into the creative work of painters, sculptors and designers, thus giving them an increased first-hand knowledge and sympathy for the world of appliance design—the whole output of Charles Eames (q.v.) can be related in one way or another to the mechanization of the designers' workshop, but appliances also claimed a widely recognized function as indicators of the social status of their owners. The diversification of different types of refrigerators and washing-machines, not to mention the almost annual increase in the screen size of television sets, became a recognized method of indicating or claiming improved social and financial status, and was duly damned by puritanical critics and sociologists. At the same time, however, certain less grandiose appliances became the accepted symbols of intellectual status—the possession of an Olivetti typewriter (q.v.) or a Braun gramophone or radio became one of the standard ploys in the world of intellectual snobbery.

Aspen Congress: One of the major international centres of discussion of industrial design was established at the mountain resort of Aspen, Colorado, which had been built up by the late Walter Paepke, President of Container Corporation of America, as a species of secular retreat for meditation and discussion among business executives. The Annual Design Congress there, of which there have been now twelve, confronted the leading opinion-makers of the American business world with designers, manufacturers, critics and theorists from Europe, South America and Japan. While the findings of these congresses don't constitute a body of literature comparable with that of CIAM, the reports made annually by speakers returning to their native countries and customary business, have provided a running survey of the preoccupation and troubles of thinking designers all over the world. Aspen has, to some extent, replaced the Triennale (q.v.) as a world centre of opinion and debate.

Brand Image (or House Style): During the 1950's it became the practice in all large industrial concerns to inculcate into the minds of the public a recognizable style to identify their products or services. In many cases this was a process of necessary rationalization where a large firm found itself with a number of different styles and a number of different designers. Where unification of style was undertaken as a form of rationalization and in good taste, this process was known as 'creating a house style,' but

interruptions, larded with Ukrainian proverbs, at the relevant annual congress will put things right.

But, in the affluent democracies where the problem exists, the whole manner of squaring up to the subject matter of Industrial Design has changed, because the foundation stone of the previous intellectual structure of Design Theory has crumbled—there is no longer universal acceptance of Architecture as the universal analogy of design. When the Modern Movement was young, there were obvious and valid reasons for giving architects hegemony over the training of designers and the formulation of theory: architects alone of arts men had any technical training even remotely applicable to product design; alone of tech-men they had a sufficiently liberal education to be able to relate their designs to the general environment of human life; they alone had been doing anything consciously to further the practice and theory of Industrial Design.

Almost everything of interest written, said or done in this field between 1900 and 1930 is the work of an architect or someone closely connected with architecture—Voysey, Lethaby, Muthesius, Gropius, Wright, Le Corbusier, Moholy-Nagy, all heirs of the polymath attitude of the Morris / Webb circle of the previous century. In the next twenty years to 1950 the architectural claim was accepted by writers like Edgar Kaufmann and Herbert Read as the natural basis for argument—the latter announcing in his *Art and Industry* of 1934 'I have no other desire in this book than to support and propagate the ideals . . . expressed by Doctor Gropius.' The only novelty of even apparent consequence in this line of thought did not appear until 1954, when G. C. Argan, at that year's *Triennale* Congress proposed that urbanism, rather than architecture, should be at the head of the design hierarchy.

But even at that date, alternative estimates of the nature and principles of Industrial Design had begun to appear. Paradoxically, while most of these favoured the kind of design associated with the architectural dispensation—spare, neat, unadorned, etc.—they defended it by arguments that could equally well have been used to where it was undertaken as part of an advertising campaign it was called 'fixing the brand image.' Examples of both processes can be seen in the stabilization of the design of filling-stations and filling-station equipment by such companies as Shell/BP or Esso, both of whom developed international styles in the period; in the restyling programmes undertaken by brewery companies like Courage in the earlier 1950's, and Watney towards the end of the decade; and in the restyling of chain stores.

British Railways: Though it is the largest industrial concern in Britain, and probably in Europe, British Railways did not set the universally high standards of design that were hoped for at the time of nationalization. Nevertheless, valiant efforts were made, in spite of the progressive dismemberment of British Railways into independent regions, and as nationalized concerns go, it has probably done as much as any, except the Post Office, to promote a lively attitude to design. The change-over to diesel traction has had industrial designers built into the contract as consultants almost from the beginning, and although there have been technical difficulties, the influence of Design Research Unit and of Jack Howe has been noticeably beneficial. Other British Railway adventures in design include experimental carriage interiors designed by various architects; the setting up of a Design Advisory Panel in an attempt to improve the style of station equipment; and the activities of Eastern Region's development group in improved ticket-office design; and in commissioning waiting-room furniture by Robin Day which should become standard for all regions.

Citroen: Like the Volkswagen (q.v.) the Citroen was one of the two fixed points in a world of rapidly changing car design—until 1957 when the familiar *Traction-avant* of 1934 vintage was dramatically replaced by the DS 19. Although few found it possible to admire the DS's apparent mixture of different automotive styles, brand-loyalty coupled with something like awe at its technical specification served to establish the DS, almost at once, in the same position of esteem as was enjoyed by the preceding model, and by the end of the decade its radical appearance no longer excited the same alarm as before.

Consumer Research: The formal recognition of a specific consumer viewpoint in relation to industrial design is one of the more important new factors that has emerged in the 1950's. Viewed broadly, it covers market research into consumer preferences and human engineering or ergonomics (q.v.) as well as what is more specifically regarded as the defence of consumers' interests. Organizations for

favour completely different styles of design. The classic instance is Hayakawa's essay, memorably entitled *Your Car Reveals your Sex Fears,* which assailed Detroit styling by means of semantic and ikonographic arguments that could equally well have been used to demonstrate, say, how the London taxi, acclaimed by Charles Eames as the best industrial design in the world, reveals the communal death-wish of the English ruling classes.

Eames must be saluted at this point as the last figure from the architectural side to make a significant contribution—with his Ahmedabad Report—to design thinking. Otherwise, architects have relinquished control of the mind of design to theorists and critics from practically any other field under the sun. The new men in the U.S.A., for instance, are, typically, liberal sociologists like David Reisman or Eric Larrabee; in Germany, the new men at Ulm are mathematicians, like Horst Rittel, or experimental psychologists like Mervyn Perrine; in Britain they tend to come from an industrial background, like Peter Sharp, John Chris Jones or Bruce Archer, or from the pop-art polemics at the ICA like Richard Hamilton. In most Western Countries, the appearance of consumer-defence organizations has added yet another voice, another viewpoint, though no very positive philosophy.

In these circumstances, where no single viewpoint is sufficiently widely held to make effective communication possible, arguments tend to be conducted in an eclectic framework of postulates gathered from a variety of disciplines; the basis of selection may be unscrupulously slanted to justify some point of view to which the speaker is committed (this is true of most arguments on aesthetics or styling) or, more honestly, to give directions through a field that needs to be explored—hence the preoccupation with information theory at Ulm, where it is felt that many pieces of equipment are insufficiently explicit about their functions and mode of use. Lash-up formulations of this sort are, of course, only *ad hoc* intellectual structures and should be neatly put away when they have done the job for which they were assembled. Thus, a narrowly Stalinist frame of reference, rigidly maintained beyond its last point of utility, has resulted in the sterility this latter purpose have emerged both at an official and unofficial level; thus most of the nationalized industries have some form of Consumers' Consultative Committee built into their administrative structure, and the British Standards Institute sponsors a Consumers' Advisory Council which publishes a periodical—*Shoppers' Guide.* However, there are also Consumer organizations whose attitude embodies an element of social protest, viz.: The Consumers' Councils in the U.S.A. and the Consumers' Association in England, which publishes a periodical called *Which?,* and whose leading figure, Michael Young, has even proposed the formation of a Consumers political party (see his pamphlet *The Chipped White Cups of Dover*).

Design Centre: The foundation of the Design Centre in the Haymarket, London, gave the Council of Industrial Design an opportunity to give tangible form to its views on design by placing on show a constantly changing selection of products, chosen by Committees appointed by the Council. Although the selections have constantly been a subject of dispute throughout the subsequent five years of the Centre's existence, they have undoubtedly performed an important function, if only in putting before the public alternatives to the normal commercial selections undertaken by buyers for even the most progressive shops. It was only towards the end of this five-year period that doubts began to be expressed that the Centre might be driving the Council of Industrial Design into something like a commercial position itself, when it was observed that the rents recovered from exhibitors at the Centre amounted to a sizeable proportion of the Council's income.

Detroit: If the most suspect aspects of commercial design were symbolized by any one object or class of objects in the 1950's it was by the American automobile industry—the phrase 'Detroit-Macchiavellismus' was coined in Germany to describe everything that was felt to be hateful about U.S. design. At the same time, there was a visible tendency to admire Detroit products for their unconventionality and boldness, and even in some circles serious attempts to discuss objectively their social and moral implications. In many ways Detroit was a symbol also for the War of the Generations, and the language of American automobile advertising became the language of revolt among the young. The hard core of any admiration for Detroit, however, was the belief that here was a language of visual design, no longer based on subjective standards like 'good taste,' but on objective research into consumers' preference and motivations. The phrase 'an objective aesthetic' could be taken to refer

and subsequent disappearance of radical left-wing design criticism in Western democracies, and leaves intelligent socialists, like Richard Hoggart, apparently sharing the opinions of an 'Establishment' that they otherwise despise.

For those who are not too rigid, however, the situation is, as the saying goes, manipulative—it is possible to discuss anything, even the validity of the architectural claim. Not on the basis of right or wrong—Industrial Design can use a short rest from exclusive moralities—but on the basis of what contribution architects could reasonably be expected to make, and the needs they might reasonably hope to see satisfied.

Looking back, one sees that in truth large parts of the architectural claim have never been seriously pressed—aircraft design, for instance, has cheerfully been left to aero-dynamicists, architects retaining only the right to criticize the results. There are other areas where architects have persistently intervened—pleasure boats are an example—without contributing anything very interesting to their design; clearly, architects have extra-curricular activities where they put their professional skills on one side. But, where, then, is the architect's real area of painful or profitable involvement with industrial design? It is easiest to define convincingly by considering questions of scale and propinquity—how big things are, and how near to buildings. A survey of architectural communications such as conversations, letters to editors, and other daily small-talk will show that architects are hypersensitive to the design of objects roughly comparable in scale to building components. Some of this sensitivity is simply an atavistic relic from the days when the architectural claim was universal in its coverage, but if it is trimmed down to include only objects in or near buildings, then it makes operational sense. Architects are clearly right to be concerned over the design of things like automobiles, lamp-posts, refrigerators and crockery, since these are classes of objects that commonly inhabit the same view, occupy the same space, supplement the functions of their buildings and no one in his right mind will deny their right to be heard on such subjects.

either to the absolute logic of pure form or to absolute subjection to market research statistics.

Eames, Charles: Although a number of substantial figures in the world of design emerged in or around the decade following the Festival of Britain, none has made so great an impact on the world, both by his products and his personality, as Charles Eames. By 1951 his first chairs in moulded plywood on steel frames were becoming known outside the United States of America, and were the inspiration of innumerable copies all over Europe, and in most other continents. It was generally recognized that the Eames Chair constituted the first major development in chair design since the Breuer chairs of 1928. After this there followed, in a bewildering succession, toys, films, scientific researches, lecture tours, special exhibits, three further generations of chairs, the celebrated Ahmedabad report on design in development countries, and a great number of awards and citations, culminating in the Kaufmann award to himself and his wife Ray in recognition of their work together for the progress of industrial design.

Ergonomics: The most important branch of design science by the end of the 1950's was undoubtedly Ergonomics, which seemed likely to push matters of taste and aesthetics well into the background. As the derivation of the word suggests, the earliest studies to receive the name were concerned with economy of human effort in the operation of mechanical equipment, notably complicated electronic and aeronautical equipment developed towards the end of the War, some of which taxed the mental and physical capacity of its operators beyond the limits of efficiency. By the end of the decade, however, the term had been expanded by thinkers and readers in many parts of the world to cover all forms of relationships between man and equipment, including purely physical studies of human engineering and the communicative studies of control systems and others, in which matters of mental capacity and perception of vision were involved. Unlike most words or phrases, which are promoted to the level of slogans or catchwords, Ergonomics has generated little facile optimism, except for a faith that by patient and painstaking research the relationship between men and their tools can be improved. At one level this has meant quite simply the reshaping of the handles of traditional tools, but at other levels it has meant exercises as abstract as the devising of new sets of symbols for the keys on the control panels of computers.

Festival of Britain: Great hopes were entertained for the influence that the Festival of Britain would have on the arts of design, and the level of public

To say this is not to revive inflationary or imperialistic claims that architects are 'total designers' or 'responsible for the whole human environment,' but simply to say that even if the practice of architecture is viewed in quite a narrow and conventional professional sense, there is a wide variety of equipment which is not structurally part of their buildings nor mentioned in the specification, but is, nevertheless, their concern.

It ought to be much more their concern than it is at present. Even if we no longer regard the architect as the universal analogy for the designer, a large area of the architectural claim is rightly his. But if this is an area where he has rights, then he also has responsibilities. If he is to be heard, then his utterance must carry weight— howls of 'I won't have that ugly trash in my building' will no longer serve, reasons must be given, improvements suggested.

But how? If architects have lost their original dominance over the field—a dominance always more *de jure* than *de facto*—what is their standing now? It is precisely at the level of objects comparable in scale to building components that the average architect's capacity as a designer begins to taper off, and this diminished capacity is due far less to technical ignorance of, say, electronics or gas technology, than to the training, experience and habits of mind that fit a man to be an architect. This combination of intellectual factors tends to make an architect not only unfit to design free-standing appliances, but even the interiors of his own buildings—as the *Architectural Review* pointed out in justification of its *Interior Design* features in April 1958.

As was also pointed out then, the fundamental difficulty is incompatible rates of obsolescence; architects, for entirely valid reasons, are habituated to think in terms of a time scale whose basic unit is about half a century. Industrial design works on a variety of time-scales, roughly proportional to the bulk of the objects being designed, and none of them phased in units one fifth the size of the architect's. This situation is not the product of an evil economic situation, as professional alarmists like Vance Packard maintain (though there is a constant taste. At first sight, the whole exercise was a failure in these terms: its influence, as Sir Gerald Barry (its Director) more or less admitted in a 10th Anniversary lecture, has been practically negligible in the field of design—the 'Festival Style' has practically disappeared from the face of the land and left only a few travesties behind. But it is clear that for reasons that are not altogether coincidental, the Festival marks a turning point in the history of public taste in Britain. Public taste may not have improved, but it has become infinitely more sophisticated in the ten years since the Festival. This development must be attributed to the influence of the mass media such as television and illustrated magazines, but the Festival played a vital part in setting before the public an image of a brighter, smarter and more colourful world of design. This may not have been what the originators of the Festival set out to do, but in this they undoubtedly secured a lasting success.

Italian Craze: One of the most remarkable developments of the 1950's was the craze for Italian design which galvanized the smarter elements of all classes of British Society. The Scooter, the Olivetti typewriter, furniture by Gio Ponti, hairstyling by Richard Henry, Espresso coffee and its attendant machinery, certain tricks of shape, design and display, and even certain type faces from the Nebiolo foundry, helped to stamp the image of Italy as the home of good design at all levels of consumption. The reasons for this development have baffled critics and sociologists from the time of its first appearance in 1953 to its waning around 1960. The Triennale (q.v.) was a major contributing influence at the level of conscious design. The cinema and motor-racing also played their part, but explanations based simply on good taste and engineering cannot explain the whole Italian mania. Espresso machines, as several critics pointed out, usually had a strong flavour of Detroit or 'Paris 1925.' There is little doubt that the rise of teenage affluence and the improved quality of inexpensive, fashionable clothes, had also a large part in the phenomenon.

Japan: In 1960 it was discovered that Italian manufacturers were plagiarizing Japanese designs for transistor radios—a situation that symbolized, as well as anything could, the change of exotic influences on Western design. Everything in the way of studied elegance and rare qualities in the handling of materials that had been true of Italian design, was found to be yet more true of Japanese, with the added incentives of the abstract power of Japanese calligraphy, the philosophical prestige of Zen Buddhism, and the technical aptitude of the Japanese for Miniaturization (q.v.). At the architectural level these developments were supported by the growing pressure towards hastened obsolescence in capitalist countries) but exists because industrial designers are creating objects in which the opposing forces of stabilized investment and technical improvement are in a different equilibrium to that governing the design of a building. A building-structure will not be disastrously out of date for some centuries in many cases, and there are lifts at work in London that saw the century in, but are still mechanically sound and have not been rendered noticeably obsolete by sixty years of technical improvement.

But a sixty year old car, even if in perfect mechanical condition, would nowadays cause traffic jams and invite accidents if it were let loose among the nimbler products of more recent decades—as witness the elaborate policing and marshalling required to isolate the carefully maintained veterans on the Brighton Run from real traffic. This is an extreme case of rapid mechanical obsolescence, no doubt (only by an architect's standards, by those of aeronautics or electronics, automotive technology has been sluggish) but it can easily be paralleled inside buildings—consider the history of electric lighting from carbon filament to colour corrected cathode, from the concentrated light source of a bare bulb in an exposed socket, that even Brutalists tolerate only as a gesture, to the even glow from a lumenated ceiling that psychologists and physiologists are already beginning to question for going too far the other way.

The design of light fittings is very much a case in point. On the basis of scale and propinquity, they lie firmly within the architectural area of concern. Over the years, a number of leading modern architects, from Rietveld to Utzon, have made forays into the field of lighting design, and—the product being mechanically simple—they have been able to produce equipment that was workable as well as handsome. But, reviewing the period covered by this development, one cannot help feeling that an excess of aesthetic and emotional capital has been squandered on ephemera. There is hardly any important modern-movement interior that is still lit as the architect originally designed it—not only the equipment but the whole installation has been rendered obsolete by later events.

reputation of men like Kenzo Tange and Maekawa, and the final seal of Western acceptance of Japanese dominance was set by the enthusiasm with which Western designers, critics and theorists participated in the World Design Congress in Tokyo in 1960.

Jet Liners: The successful establishment of the Jet Passenger Liner in air transportation marked the first major break-through in air-line operation since the introduction of the first Boeings and Douglases early in the 1930's. They also marked a phase of increasing sophistication in air travel, and nearly all had their interiors designed by well-known industrial design offices, rather than by the aircraft designers. Whether French, American or British, all tended towards a grey and tan international style with aluminum trim, except for the Russians who resolutely maintained their traditional Victorian Rococo with cut-glass and flowers even on the TU104.

Magazines: Late in the 1950's one of the pioneer industrial design magazines passed away in one of those fits of financial cannibalism which currently overtake the British Press. However, *Art and Industry* had been displaced long before its death by the CoID magazine *Design* which—though born before the beginning of the decade under review—had gone from strength to strength in circulation, in breadth of vision (under the editorship of Michael Farr) and in international prestige. It was in particular one of the organs that made known the science of ergonomics (q.v.) to working designers all over the world. Its most distinguished foreign contemporaries by the end of the decade, though of varying influence in Britain, were *Industrial Design* (New York), the most professional of design magazines under the editorship of Jane Fiske McCullough who finally retired from the paper in 1960, and the other was *Stile Industria,* an offshoot of the Domus publishing house, under the editorship of Alberto Rosselli, which consistently maintained the Italian viewpoint, both on matters of practice and theoretical approach.

Medals and Awards: It was justifiably observed by an Italian critic that the ever-increasing supply of medals, certificates, prizes and other awards for designers, were signs of an inflationary epoch in design. As far as Britain is concerned the most important awards were those given by the CoID under a variety of names, finally stabilized as the 'Design Centre Awards.' These were supplemented in 1959 by the 'Duke of Edinburgh's Award for Elegant Design,' a clear indication of the vastly increased prestige of industrial design in the eyes of British governing classes. Perhaps the most hotly discussed of all awards in the 1950's was the 'Compasso

In other fields, where their technical inadequacies are more obtrusive, architects can only do what they affect to despise in other designers—style up the outside of machinery that has been designed by somebody else. The polite name for this, of course, is 'built-in equipment' in which everything the architect is incapable of designing is bundled into cupboards that he *can* design. But this solution, too, is subject to the effects of technical obsolescence, as cookers, radios, and so forth, change their bulk, performance, power needs and relationship to the surrounding space, and entirely new equipment such as TV enters the domestic scene. Built-in equipment is little more than an attempt to impose a veneer of totalitarian order in a situation where something like democratic give and take may have been more to the point.

This, again, is not to ask the architect to abandon responsibility for the equipment in the buildings he is called upon to design, for it is possible to abandon the position of autocratic dominance implicit in Bauhaus theory without losing control of the over-all design. Very small powers of accommodation enable an architect to do what Le Corbusier anticipated as long ago as 1925, that is, to exercise creative choice. His *Pavillon de l'Esprit Nouveau* was entirely furnished and equipped from manufacturers' catalogues, without the architect himself having to design a thing.[1] Although the convincing unity of the total effect was doubtless helped by the fact that the rooms themselves had been designed in what he conceived to be the style of the objects that were to furnish them (and in this there is a lesson to be pondered), the whole operation was a triumph of disciplined and adventurous selection from what was at hand.

This, in practice, is how most architects and interior designers work anyhow. In the 1960's an architect knows he will be able to equip his interiors with Eames chairs, Noguchi lamps, Braun radios, Saarinen tables and so forth from stock, and the knowledge of their availability probably colours his designing, unconsciously, from the very beginning. Coloured, but not inhibited—the catalogues also offer him Bertoia chairs, Jacobsen chairs, Robin Day chairs; Utzon lamps, Rotaflex lamps, Atlas d'Oro,' sponsored by the Rinascente store in Milan as a kind of annual supplement to the Triennale. Awarded on an international basis by an international jury, the Compasso d'Oro reflected a growing crisis on design criticism by being awarded in 1960 and 1961 to the CoID, and to MIT, thus showing a clear lack of any confidence in the jury's ability to select an individual design or individual designer for a premiation; in contrast, the jury of the Kaufmann award (founded in 1960) clearly had no difficulty in awarding their substantial money prize to Charles and Ray Eames.

Miniaturization: The transistor radio has become the most obvious symbol of miniaturization in practice, and is the culminating development of a train of thinking in electronics which has been proceeding since the first airborne radar during the second World War. However, it is not the only trend in electronics, as witness the growing size of television screens, and it is not restricted to the electronic field. There has been a conspicuous and growing development of miniaturization in the world of personal transport, made possible by accumulated mechanical improvements over the previous 20 years. Italian motor-scooters at the beginning of the 1950's were succeeded by German bubble-cars in the middle of the decade, and by the BMC Ado 150 (Mimi-Minor or Austin 7) at the end of the decade. At the same time, Detroit reversed its own committed policy and introduced a flock of compact cars which, like the European miniatures, were distinguished by radical technical improvements as well as their diminished size.

Motivation Research: The branch of advertising regarded with the gravest suspicion in alarmist literature (q.v.) was Motivation Research, which formed the theme of Packard's first book *The Hidden Persuaders*. The object of this rather dubious science was to establish the 'real' or subconscious reasons for buying one product or another. It is thus, in a sense, a subbranch of ergonomics since it deals with a particular, though short-lived, relationship between man and equipment, and was cautiously welcomed by broad-minded ergonomists as an extension of our precise knowledge of man. Conversely, the manipulative intentions of its practitioners were clearly liable to anti-social perversion, but any mass take-over of consumers' minds seems to have been prevented by the imprecision of MR techniques of investigation. From the designer's point of view, MR was most suspect as yet another restriction on his freedom to design and his freedom to serve the public as he felt best. Yet it should be noted that one of the major triumphs of MR's High-Priest, Dr. Ernest Dichter, was to make a suggestion that any competent designer should have been able to make

lamps. . . . The range of choice is so broad that the equipment of the building by objects that were not designed by the architect may not diminish the value of the finished work by one material or aesthetic particular. Indeed, the prestige inherent in knowing that the chairs are by one of the world's greatest industrial designers and the radios by another adds a peculiar lustre to the whole operation.

However, the very breadth of choice increases the architect's responsibility—he must resist the temptation to hand over the interior to Jacobsen, Noguchi, Bertoia and Co. His choice must be disciplined by a clear idea of what the building has to do, and if there is nothing just right in the catalogues at hand, then he must go to other catalogues, his choice must be adventurous—*none* of the furniture in the Pavillon de l'Esprit Nouveau came from the catalogues of 'domestic' furniture manufacturers, it was all office and factory equipment.

Here, indeed, is one of the points where the architectural profession has a job to do in industrial design. By way of contract furnishing, architects are among the most articulate and most powerful sections of consumers, in some fields the most powerful absolutely. They have power economically in the market, they also have experience that far outstrips that of any domestic consumer who perhaps buys a dozen chairs in a lifetime, they are trained to study functional problems and human requirements. Simply by the exercise of their market influence, architects may find that they are in a position to kill a poor design, encourage a good one, and embolden a manufacturer to tool up for a new product. Further, by their experience and training they should be in a position to advise and assist manufacturers and designers to produce better goods, even where mechanical complexity puts them (as in the case of communications, ventilating systems, etc.) right outside their technical competence as architects.

This proposition may not be news, but it is worth saying again because it still needs to be acted upon; it is a field where positive action can be taken. However, there will be large fields of activity where the architect's careful before he appeared on the scene, that is, the fitting of rear-view mirrors to farm tractors so that those who set their hands to the plough need not look back.

Olivetti: The place of the Olivetti typewriter, both in the Italian craze and in the wider design sense, was best illustrated by the violent reaction to its threatened demise in 1960. The original design for the small portable (which has always been the hinge of the argument) was the work of Marcello Nizzoli, who is, of course, still the designer responsible for all Olivetti products. The neat, squarish case he devised was constantly being held up as an example of pure straightforward design in contrast to American 'styling,' but was in fact itself a styling job, since Nizzoli was in no way responsible for the machinery inside. This point was avoided in discussion until Diaspron, a larger typewriter, appeared in late 1959. This had faceted side and front panels, no doubt for quite sound constructional reasons, but immediately brought down the wrath of the critics on Nizzoli's head, because it was (apparently) 'irresponsible styling.' The reasons for the change of style, apart from any technical considerations, were clearly commercial, but Olivetti, probably because of his enlightened social policy, has always been treated as if he were nothing to do with commerce. What will happen under the new style and the new management, which has succeeded since Adriano Olivetti's early death, remains to be seen.

Organizations: The profession of designer became more heavily organized as well as more heavily bemedalled as the idea of design as an independent profession took hold and established itself. No longer content to proceed under the aegis of other professional bodies, such as those devoted to architecture, designers established or took control of new organizations in order to speak with their own voice. In Britain a major attempt was made to give the SIA (Society of Industrial Artists) a status and function equivalent almost to that of the RIBA, and, at a wider level, ICSID (International Council of Societies for Industrial Design) founded in 1957, began to assume functions broadly analogous to those of the IUA, though it has, so far, met more frequently. One of the major professional problems of both bodies has been the stabilization or establishment of effective copyright in design—a matter in which they are professionally ahead of architects.

Packaging: New ways of selling, summed up in the ambiguous phrase 'merchandising,' centred attention on the way in which goods were presented at the point of sale, but they also brought new classes of goods within the field covered by the package-

design will be filled with equipment not chosen by an architect or a sympathetic interior designer, but by an ordinary domestic occupier. Here is a classic instance of a conflict between mass taste and the preferences of an elite—or, in the form of words used to describe the situation when the *Unité* at Marseilles was ready for occupation, 'What will happen when the bourgeoisie move in with their inherited prejudices and imitation Louis Quinze wardrobes?' Le Corbusier's solution, to build in so much built-in furniture that there was no room for wardrobes and barely room to voice a prejudice, was, in fact, the result of unforeseeable circumstances,[2] and not even he would normally advocate so undemocratic a procedure.

For the architect simply to 'retire hurt' when faced with this situation, is no solution, and the idea of designing 'background architecture' of studied neutrality is an unconvincing attempt to make a thin virtue from a pressing necessity—there is no way of disposing a door and a window in a rectangular space without setting up a relationship that can be wrecked by an ill-placed TV set. The need is some sort of reasonably permissive architecture with built-in directions about where to put things. The so-called Appliance-House solution to this problem has tended, so far, either to take too much for granted, or to make heavy weather of the directions. Either it assumes too readily a community of taste between architect and occupier (Kikutake's 'Sky House' is occupied by Kikutake himself, so the problem disappears, but what happens when someone else moves in) or else—as in most of the Smithson projects in this genre—the whole house tends to degenerate into a series of display niches for ever-changing relays of hire-purchased status-symbols.

But there is no need for such elaborate controls, nor for hidden persuaders hopefully contrived out of plays of colour and lighting—though these have never yet proven sufficiently reliable to direct a Louis Quinze Wardrobe or seven cubic foot refrigerator to the point where the architect hopes to find it. On the contrary, the traditional location of a fifteen-amp plug next to the traditional British fireplace has done much to keep the TV set within the traditional area of focused attention in the traditional British designer's art. If frozen foods were the classic example of the new merchandising and the new packaging techniques, it should also be observed that long-playing gramophone records in their smartly designed sleeves, and reprints of best-sellers in exclamatory paper-back bindings, brought music and literature into the realm of general merchandising, both being sold through general stores, tobacconists and other non-specialist outlets. The actual design of such packages became one of the most flourishing departments of the graphic arts during this decade and like TV (q.v.) brought the latest and most sophisticated types of design into domestic environments which had hitherto been immune to them.

'Pop' Art: Alongside ergonomics (q.v.) one of the emergent concepts, though a bitterly disputed one, of the 1950's, was that of 'pop' art. This was distinguished from earlier vernacular arts by the professionalism and expertise of its practitioners (i.e. Rock 'n' Roll singers, TV stars, etc.). The concept was widely discussed in Europe and the United States, and impinges on industrial design at two points—two points which are not altogether independent of one another. Firstly, its visual manifestations, as in advertising or Detroit car-styling, were often endowed with a vitality (not always bogus) that seemed absent from the fine arts and from 'good' design. Secondly, the protagonists of 'pop' art at an intellectual level, i.e. those who insisted that it should be taken seriously and discussed rationally, maintained that there was no such thing as good and bad taste, but that each identifiable group or stratum of Society had it own characteristic taste and style of design—a proposition which clearly undermines the argument on which nearly all previous writing about taste in design had been based. This position was not adopted by any established authority in design, but was given serious discussion at some schools and was certainly accepted by a large part of the student body in *most* schools.

Television: The great increase in popular sophistication about all visual matters, including design, in the 1950's must be largely attributed to Television, even more than to magazines or educational bodies. For the first time, almost, in the history of man, a great part of the population was introduced to a constant stream of smart visual images, was shown new products and Old Masters, either in their own right or as the backgrounds to drama and discussion. In so far as well-designed products are smart in appearance, they have undoubtedly benefited from this trend whose influence had hardly been anticipated at the beginning of the 1950's. Television companies themselves seemed only

sitting room. With this approach, the architect no longer attempts to impersonate all the characters in the drama of design, as in the days of the universal analogy, but becomes the producer of the play, handling a mixed cast of metropolitan professionals and local talent.

This is a workable situation, provided the producer knows his players well enough to gauge the effect of ad-libbing and playing off the cuff—what happens in the architectural dialogue between dressing-table and light source, how far the eternal triangle of the three-piece suite can be expected to share the stage with a picture window opposite the fireplace. To handle these problems effectively—so effectively that he need not regret that the objects involved are not designed as he would have designed them—an architect needs to know just how, and how strongly, some desirable and visually fascinating piece of equipment like a tape recorder or a coffee-percolator focuses attention and thence organizes the visual and functional space around it. This must be known and thoroughly understood, if only at the intuitive level of knowing instinctively that a poster will always have a more galvanic effect than an abstract painting, that the real landmark in the length of the Grande Galérie of the Louvre is not the Mona Lisa but the view out of the window into the traffic of the Place du Carrousel.

It might appear, on the strength of a broad survey of present purely technical trends in design, that this problem is about to disappear. A really desirable and sophisticated (in the engineer's sense of the term) central heating system deals with the problem of the well-designed radiator by abolishing radiators and disappearing into the floor-slab or under the carpet. A man who looked at a TV set of *Britain Can Make It* vintage saw a lot of cabinet work as well as a small screen, but a head-on view of a modern twenty-one-incher is apt to consist simply of the screen itself. Nothing has shrunk faster than stereophonic gramophones, except sound radio, where transistors have produced such rapid miniaturization that there is a sort of regretful vacuum round the source of sound. And just when architects were despairing of ever making half aware of the genie they had conjured out of the electronic lamp, but programmes dealing specifically with design and visual arts, became a little more common as the 1960's began, on both the BBC and commercial networks.

Triennale: Four *Triennali di Milano* fall within the scope of this survey and of these, only the 11th in 1957 can be dismissed as trivial, partly because of the poor quality of the exhibits, and partly because of its failure to pull in an influential audience—neither the trend-setters nor their followers took much notice of it. The 9th and 10th (1951 and 1954), however, probably did more to establish the image of Italian design in the public mind than any other equivalent manifestation, and the 10th was followed by a Congress on industrial design that marks the beginning of a new self-consciousness among Italian designers, and sense of international solidarity amongst designers at large. The disappointing results of the 11th were to some extent a consequence of Italian self-satisfaction with the preceding two, and a degree of international boredom with Italian design that was already becoming apparent among the leaders of taste, if not among the mass followers. The 12th in 1960 was at cross-purposes with its audience. Intended as a serious revival of the best standards of the Triennale, it was unfortunately attended largely by those who had only now caught up with Italian design at a purely fashionable level, and its exhibits did not really receive the discussion that was their due. Among those exhibits was, of course, the complete Nottingham school which marks probably Britain's greatest impact on the international world of design.

Ulm: The Hochschule für Gestaltung at Ulm was certainly among the most important design organization to emerge in the last ten years. Originally founded in memorial piety as a successor to the Bauhaus at the time that most of the American descendants of the Bauhaus were going into decline, it had a functional plan in its buildings (designed by Max Bill) and a teaching programme (also directed by Max Bill) that both strongly recalled the original Bauhaus. In 1956 and 1957, however, there was something of a 'Palace Revolution' and a new order effectively headed by Tomas Maldonado took over the running of the school. An innovation of considerable importance made on this point was the disappearance of the Fine Art or Graphics department such as one normally finds in a school of this sort and their replacement by a division of verbal and visual communication. Ulm was thus the first school to withdraw completely and programmatically from the earlier dispensation dominated by architecture

much visual and spatial sense of domestic exteriors lumbered with *two* status-boasting, jet-styled Detroitniks, suddenly there were compacts and Mini-minors.

Miniaturization appears to be a consistent tendency at present, that must be agreed, but the chances are that the objects concerned will become more concentratedly desirable as they become smaller, or more functionally important as the systems they control vanish from sight. When the heat-source is invisible, its controls must be more visible than in the days when the tap accompanied a large, conspicuous radiator; when the radio becomes no bigger than an ashtray, then there is clearly a chance that it will become the equivalent of art-pottery—on a table in the office of the U.S. Ambassador to London there was recently a transistor radio in an elaborately hand-chased brass box, like an eighteenth-century clock mechanism.

The chances are, then, that the miniaturized product is going to demand attention with a hard, gem-like insistence, and focus attention as surely as the red button on which our atomic fate depends. And if it works by batteries, it may not be possible to fix its place on the domestic scene by a crafty location of power outlets. But the world of the miniaturized product is also the world of the visually sophisticated consumer, who may be susceptible to other forms of persuasion, may even, before long, be in a mental condition to seek architectural advice.

To sum up, the passing of the architect's claim to be the absolute master of the visual environment has not greatly reduced the area of his real responsibility at both the visual and functional levels. In fact, his responsibilities have increased—the stakes mark out a smaller claim, but he now has to dig all of it. The manner of implementing these responsibilities is not simply to assume control of the schools and expect everyone to accept architectural standards as the norm of judgment, as the theorists of the Thirties supposed, but to exercise choice and background control over the choice of others, to advise, suggest and demand on the basis of knowledge and understanding. Conceivably there may be less (here replaced by industrialized building) and by the Fine Arts. Although small, the school proved extremely influential in the world of design, at least at the level of ideas. Its manner of designing is best known through the cabinet work of Braun electrical appliances, but it has so far produced no characteristic style of design. Rather it has become a cool training ground for a technocratic élite.

Volkswagen: Since the end of the second World War, the design of motor-cars has been in constant revolution, but the standard against which most cars have been judged and found wanting (not always justifiably) has been the Volkswagen. Clearly it is a car that has meant different things to different men, but the points on which its reputation is based, are primarily these: That it had, until recently and with very few exceptions, a more advanced technical specification than any other vehicle produced in quantity, and that spares and after-sales service set a standard of practical involvement with users, and their problems, that few other manufacturers could equal. But the overwhelming virtue in the eyes of men of liberal conscience was that in a world of automotive flux its appearance remained constant and that in a period when cars grew larger year by year, it remained the same size. In other words, it was a symbol of protest against standards of Detroit, the mass media and the 'pop' arts.

glory involved than in being able to sign one's name to everything as 'designer' but there may be more useful work done and better service rendered to the public. If that is so, then ten years of uncertainty and dispute will not have been in vain.

NOTES

1. There was one exception only to this programme, the free-standing cupboard unit, which Le Corbusier had, in fact, designed as a prototype for manufacture by Thonet.

2. The *Unité* was originally designed to house the unfurnished proletariat.

12

Carbonorific

The recent destruction of the Euston Propylaeum and the forthcoming demolition of the London Coal Exchange have both aroused bad feelings—because they are/were buildings of too high a quality to be so lightly destroyed—and a great deal of bad blood—because the behaviour of Her Majesty's Ministers in both cases was high-handed, stupid, devious and disingenuous. But there the resemblances between the two cases end, for they are so dissimilar as to embody, as well as any two buildings could, the extreme polarities covered by the term Early Victorian Architecture.

Hardwick's Propylaeum, completed in 1839, is very Early Victorian, and represents an important, doomed branch of cultural earnestness—an attempt to express a progressive theme, the London-Birmingham railway, in the idiom of an accepted high style of architecture, Greek Doric. The dichotomy between theme and idiom could be hardly more complete, for the structure served no operational railway function but merely gave monumental form to an impressive sentiment in the only reliably impressive monumental style then known. Functionless, it called for what is termed (wrongly) pure architecture, an *exercice de style,* to which Hardwick responded with a true classicist's

Originally appeared in *New Statesman* 63 (4 May 1962): 655.

flourish of four giant columns *in antis:* i.e. the gable does not rest only on columns, but on two outer walls with the columns framed between them. As an exercise in style it was faultless, but it was more than accurate. Its giant scale—one-and-a-half times the size of the Doric of the Parthenon—gave it a classic *gravitas* that grew daily more austere, commanding, as the soot settled blacker on the stone.

One could say that it was more perfect even than the Parthenon: perfect in the strict sense of *perfectus,* completely finished or worked out, a mortuary perfection. The Coal Exchange, for all its plain errors of architectural taste, is a live birth. Lacking the unflappable classical authority of the Propylaeum it does not bring one up short with the spectacle of one of the great test-pieces of European civilization perfectly executed. It has the air of a grandiose fumble whose virtues impress only slowly and indirectly. In any case these virtues are concentrated in something that Hardwick was not called upon to provide—the interior. The outside is fairly routine Early Victorian sub-classical: the facades to Lower Thames Street and St Mary-at-Hill are relaxed, not to say flabby, in style. But the inside is a very different story.

The prime functional requirement that J. D. Bunning, the city's architect, had to answer was to provide a pit, or trading-floor, surrounded by tiers of dealers' offices. Such a requirement is, presumably, constituent to a high capitalist culture, but only two buildings of High Capitalism managed to make architecture by answering this problem honestly. At the end of the period, Berlage's *Beurs* in Amsterdam framed a rectangular floor in massive brick galleries of studied austerity, completed after 1900. The other is Bunning's Coal Exchange at the beginning of the period, and a more noteworthy building on practically every count, for all that Bunning was not half the architect that Berlage could be.

Bunning made his pit circular, with three galleries to serve the offices. At four equally spaced points around the circle the galleries are widened by breaking back through the line of the office wall, and these 'lay-bys' make the galleries something more useful and sociable than just circulation runs, as well as providing access to staircases and other ancillaries. But for structural and aesthetic reasons the line of the supporting columns is carried across these breaks, leaving two columns free-standing in each lay-by. And here one is brought hard up against the first sensational fact about the Coal Exchange. These columns are not masonry, and there is not a bit of masonry to be seen in the whole interior. The columns are of cast iron and the whole interior with its glazed dome is like an enormous cast-iron bird-cage.

The columns, which are flat and rectangular in section, rise uninterrupted to become the ribs of the dome, and just where they come out under the glass they bear the maker's name, Dewer, in a fine bold Ionic lettering, and the second sensational fact, the date—1848! Three years earlier than the Crystal Palace, the Coal Exchange will be, for the next few months, the oldest surviving metallic public space in Europe, as well as one of the handsomest. Professor Hitchcock was inspired to compare it to Labrouste's later, though larger, reading-room in the Bibliothèque Nationale, but in one way, at least, Bunning outdid Labrouste. Both the Bibliothèque and the Exchange are purely Iron Age buildings serving specifically Iron Age functions, so both have an edge over the split mind of the Euston Propylaeum. But whereas Labrouste used substantially traditional decorative motifs, somewhat jazzed up, Bunning has faced that fundamentally Early Victorian challenge, the idea of a new style for a new age, and come up triumphantly with a complete repertoire of ad hoc, invented decoration based on the history, extraction and transport of coal. The balustrades of the galleries are looped and knotted with cast-iron hawsers, and the main structural members are plaited with the same motif; the occasional blank panels between columns are enlivened with painted trophies of carboniferous plants and personages; the four desks on the trading floor stand on legs of giant cast-iron fossil plants; there are sundry views of carboniferous places like Sunderland, and the ring of blank panels under the edge of the dome originally had giant paintings of tree-ferns by Melhado.

Had. The whole place now breathes the had-it atmosphere of a building disowned. Not that it lacks admirers—in this I am at one with the most gaga Betjemanites—but no one in authority can be bothered with it any longer. The Ministry of Housing and Local Government off-handedly condemned it to demolition without even the elementary courtesy of informing the Victorian Society that all three schemes for preserving the Exchange from the depredations of the Ministry of Transport had been turned down. The City Corporation, who had it built in the first place, don't seem to care whether it stands or falls, but have stated that it will be open to the public some time before its demolition, and that the opening will be fully publicized.

Knowing how these things tend to go, keep a weather ear open for a blast of publicity not unlike a distant civil servant uttering a deprecatory cough, and then rush to see it while you have the chance. The echo is tremendous and makes it an ideal place for shouting 'God rot Keith Joseph and Henry Brooke!'

Big Doug, Small Piece

'Viscount,' said the flight-schedule, and for the first time it was wrong—both the four-motors on the tarmac at Perth had prehistoric-type dahlia-shaped piston engines, and both said DC-6B in foot-high letters on the fin. My anti-vintage hackles well-up, I boarded mine feeling that I had been swindled (*pistons* yet, in 1962!). Half an hour after takeoff I was adjusting to the idea of a major historical experience, like a posthumous conversation with Goethe, or some such. I missed flying in a big piston-powered Douglas while they were still alive, but—to quote a leading Aussie diplomat—'It's a real beaut kite, hey!' Aged, but not clapped out; repainted more than once, but not tatty; mechanically and structurally as sound as a bell; comfortable, not cramped; surprisingly quiet. It flew, with the sort of authority the Brighton Belle has lost, over an increasingly desert Westralian scrub-scape and finally turned out across the Bight.

We came in to Adelaide over suburbs rendered alien—to a British eye—by the tendency of Aussies to play footy on oval pitches with four goal-posts at each end, and there we changed, finally, to a Viscount. By the time we reached Sydney I knew just what was wrong with this Viscount, and right with the DC-6. The Doug was designed

---

Originally appeared in *The Architects' Journal* 136 (1 August 1962): 251–253.

with innate style by people who cared about designing airliners and built a good one: this Viscount seemed to have been designed with no thoughts beyond load-factors and paying seats. Cramped and badly finished as only a British aircraft can be, it vibrated a coffee-cup off the table (they *do* vibrate, after a certain age), the metal trim was adrift, the plastic surfaces were peeling, the seat-coverings were coming unstitched—it was the profit-motive with wings, and an uglier sight I hope never to see.

(You couldn't use the toilets either; there seems to be a grand old custom on Trans-Australia Airways, whereby the hostesses, having served the stingy meal with grudging haste, retire to powder their noses and stay there for most of the flight. I flew four legs of my trip with TAA, it happened every time.) After this, of course, I couldn't wait for the San Francisco/Seattle and Seattle/Chicago/New York legs, which were scheduled for jet Douglasses of United Airlines. The DC-8s did not disappoint—they are the aircraft that set the standard by which all other jets fail. Again, built like tanks with professionalism in every detail (you should see those patterns of rivet heads on the wing!); an interior plainer and better-detailed than that of a London bus; all ancillary services built into the backs of the simple leather-covered seats, no overhead clutter; no patterned surfaces and only a little veneer; and a gait as steady as a tea-trolley on a pile carpet. The Boeing 707, which is comparable in size, is a mass of neurotic twitches. Big Doug, by contrast, just trundles through the sky at mach-point-nine or so, with a lack of fuss that makes you realise, at last, that air-travel is just another form of transportation.

It can't happen here, of course. The discomforts of British airlines are now to be reinforced (if that is the word) by positive directives intended to make British aircraft aesthetically objectionable as well. The word has gone forth, apparently from the Lord High Small-Piece himself, Sir Basil Boac, that the interiors of the Super-VC10s shall contain no reference to aviation, shall resemble drawing rooms, and in no way remind the customers that they have actually left the ground. Any resemblance to the policy that made Cunarders the mausolea of the North Atlantic is coincidental; this particular attack of the tea-cosy aesthetic must antedate the merger proposals. Nevertheless it appears that the mistakes that were so persistently made in ship design of the pre-*Oriana* epoch are now to be repeated, by small-minded order, in the air as well.

If this BOAC's idea of how to design the inside of an aeroplane, why bother to hire, and waste, a designer of the quality of Robin Day? Why not go straight to Tottenham Court Road and have done with it?

Old Number One

Written into the script of every intelligent, car-owning English family is the following passage for children's voices:

> There it is! There's Stonehenge!
> But it's *tiny*!

For whereas British monuments are usually trailered by a hint of crenellation between Joe Lyons and Montague Burton, or a spire glimpsed over trees, Old Number One is not seen until it is seen entire, an event which is delayed partly by the landform of the approaches, but much more by the fact that it cannot be recognized until the visual *gestalt* has crystallized, and the sheer smallness of the image is not accepted by the mind as representing a monument that bulks so large in our national consciousness. Most ancient and most obtuse, Stonehenge is seen suddenly and minute under a vast dome of Wessex sky.

At every visit you brace against disappointment—nothing so small can be as im-

---

Originally appeared in *New Statesman* 64 (3 August 1962): 152.

pressive as you remembered—and at every visit Old Number One reasserts itself in bulk and meaning with every step nearer to the stones until, standing within the circle, oblivious to the kids playing tag, the clicking cameras, the mud underfoot, the horrible barbed-wire fences, you see Stonehenge once more as first among our monuments: first in age, foremost in impact. Not without reason is it the first illustration in the older histories of architecture—whatever the counter-attractions of Avebury's mysterious undressed sarsens, or the mind-withering vacuity of Warham's empty dish of grass, Old Number One has horizontal stones balanced on vertical stones, and is therefore Architecture.

Architecture in the historical and professional sense, but also in the true and functional sense of a place made fit for human activities. I allow that it is *just* possible that it was built at the whim of some Neolithic aesthete because it would look nice, but it is quite impossible to make this concept stay in your head in the face of these windswept stones. The aesthetic of Stonehenge is that of high engineering, of the Functional Tradition, and the fact that some of the stones were reused from an earlier henge seems to reinforce the Functionalist, not the Aesthetic presumption. Yet it is aesthetic refinements that make Stonehenge architecture. The weathered condition of the tumbled sarsens encourages us, sloppily, to think of it as a rude monument of primitive craftsmanship. We contrive to think thus, even while believing, vaguely, that the Slaughterstone (or something) is aligned accurately with the midsummer (or some other) sunrise. The alignments of Stonehenge are more numerous, subtle and meaningful than this, and suggest that—far from being rude or incompetent—the builders had a fair command of astronomy, geometry and surveying. An error of under point six per cent in setting out the 285-foot circle of the 'Aubrey Holes' is not to be sneezed at.

But it is the drawing of another circle that really confirms Number One's claim to be architecture. The lintels of the sarsen circle were sufficiently true in their cutting for their tongue-and-groove end-joints to clog together even as the holes in their underfaces dropped over the raised spigots on top of the uprights. But that the lintels were also cut on the curve to make a continuous circle is just too much, Man! The fact that you don't notice this for a long time shows how little it would have mattered if they had been cut straight—yet when you have noticed how the three lintels still in place on the north-east side (on stones 2, 1, 30 and 29) make a smooth curve on the radius of the circle, your attitude to the henge changes for good. Whether this was just gratuitous finesse, or a craftsman's determination to see a job properly done, Old Number One is in the class of monuments to which a true pro added the final flourish.

It conspicuously does not exhibit those amateurish lineaments of failed grand manner that make Saxon monuments like Wing or Bradford-on-Avon at once so heartbreaking and so contemptible. Old Number One is in full and confident command of the aesthetic proper to its technique, even if the technique was being worked near its limit, and when this is understood, Stonehenge can never be seen again in the traditional English sense, epitomized by Loggan's engravings, as a picturesque incident on

Salisbury plain. It becomes, instead, an object to be appreciated in and for itself, classical like the Parthenon.

This is a comfort, for the barbarities of the Ministry of Works's management of the site make the picturesque bit impossible. The MoW seem vaguely committed to the picturesque concept of fallen stones in a plain of grass, for they have not paved the mud puddle in the centre, and they have put the conveniences underground. But the foul militaristic barbed wire remains, like sundry sheds and notices on poles, too close to the stones to go unnoticed. The Ministry is simply trading on the fact that Old Number One is strong enough in character and architectural intent to withstand the kind of disrespect that works of feebler imagination, such as Westminster Abbey, could never tolerate.

Stonehenge can take it. Sheer strength of conception and certainty of execution enable it to triumph over the subtopia with which faceless men have chosen to insult it. But that is no reason in hell why it should have to. Graced with a monument that gives us a longer tradition of standing architecture (not mere Megalithic archaeology) than any other northern country, we could at least behave as if we valued it.

Kent and Capability

When I was a cub critic on that fine old Liberal paper, the *Eastern Daily Press*, I once went on record that the topographical watercolour was the only significant original British contribution to world art. By the next post came a stiff letter from a hyphenated art-loving lady pointing out that I had overlooked the greatest of all British contributions, the landscape park.

For a few minutes I felt genuinely chastened—I dig the landscape scene more than most art-forms. In spite of the fact that the 18th century is 'not my period,' I have actually read two of Repton's *Red Books* in the original handwriting, I know all the temples and pavilions at Stowe (even the Fane of Pastoral Poetry) and I could probably take a party on a convincing conducted tour of Chiswick Park. I make no claim to play in the same league as H. F. Clark, but I find some aspects of the landscape movement uncommonly sympathetic.

And yet, in spite of the manifest influence of the *Jardin Anglais* or *Parco Inglese* abroad (knock on any Schloss and ask for the *Englische Garten*) I find myself in increasing disagreement with my landed correspondent. For one thing, there are not

Originally appeared in *New Statesman* 64 (7 December 1962): 842–843.

enough masterpieces to add up to a contribution of significance—in fact, there is only one total and authoritative masterwork surviving, and that is Stourhead. For the rest, there are large areas of middling inspiration (most of Capability Brown) or fragments of genius, such as the orchestration of the tree-colours in the Grecian Vale at Stowe, or Kent's work at Rousham—which in no way deserves the panning it gets in Derek Clifford's patchily brilliant new book.[1] But, as works of high art in the accepted European sense, all but a very few landscape parks are compromised by the factor of use. Sheep may profitably graze, and all that . . . the average landscape park is an uncertain superimposition of a 3-D diorama after Claude on an acreage of agriculture. In this factor of use, of course, landscaping was close cousin to architecture, which is one of the things that recommends it to me, but at the same time it was removed thereby from the categories of Fine Art whose products, as four generations of English academic aesthetes have insisted, are great because they are no bloody use. Young Humphry Repton seems to have grasped this point at the very beginning of his career as a landscape architect. In a passage from the introduction to the Holkham *Red Book* which Dorothy Stroud[2] unaccountably fails to quote so that my version is only memory-perfect—in this passage which deals with the wooded bank beyond the lake, Repton characterizes the effect of the smoke from the chimney of a proposed cottage among the trees as having the 'air of industry with an affectation, rather than the reality, of penury.'

The reader may reflect on the Marie-Antoinette overtones of this observation at his leisure: the point here and now is the recognition that landscapes, as well as 'pompous buildings,' came within Alexander Pope's category of 'things of use.' But not at Stourhead. There, a crafty choice for the position of the dam that holds back the waters for the lake, and the landform of the valley whose floor the lake covers, combine to give a landscape composition focused inwards on itself. It is not a prospect that is commanded from the house. Colen Campbell's routine-Palladian villa stands outside the design; so does the cluster of houses commanding the approach-road. Only the transplanted Gothic 'Bristol Cross' is shared with any view from that side of the lake.

So, cupped in an irregular ring of hills, steered willy-nilly along a walk between the hanging woods and the shore, the visitor is conducted through a carefully composed sequence of views of trees, water and lakeside buildings. Each of these vignettes framed in green is, inevitably, *nature refaite d'après Poussin,* to invert the well-known Cézannism, only here it really is Poussin. In general, the movement's taste ran toward the soft options of Claude, rather than the tough architectonic disciplines of Poussin, and even where this was not the case, indifference and overgrowing have produced what the Knight of Glyn lately called such 'neglected and bebrambled vistas' that more precise designs are now lost in thickset obscurantism. But Stourhead's steep shores permit no fuzz of undergrowth, and the foreground is normally clear water, functioning visually with the clarity and precision of Poussin's broad and open forescenes, while the doubling reflections increase the impact of the simple architectural forms of such lakeside structures as the 'Pantheon.' The simplicity of the architectural incidents at Stourhead is almost as conspicuous as their lack of pseudo-poetic overtones. You don't have to read Thomson, Gay or Dyer, or even Pope, to get the full flavour from the Stourhead scene. The literary bit is concentrated in one single structure, the grotto, with its water-nymph and river-god presiding over the springs, and the necessary occasional quatrain by Pope is right there in front of you on the basin which the nymph damply supervises.

Yet right behind you as you read the lines is Stourhead's most stunning purely visual effect—the wall of the grotto is broached by a sizeable opening full of jagged teeth of rock and framing a view across to the Bristol Cross, a view that is almost too beautiful to look at. The purely visual aesthetic of Stourhead, free of sentimentality and allusion, is what puts it in the class of European masterpieces, plus a controlling sensibility that combined toughness of conception with tenderness toward the 'genius of the place' (Pope again, of course) in a manner that escaped Capability Brown for most of his life. The only thing that is even remotely comparable in purity and quality is Kent's management of the main lawn at Rousham, where I suspect Derek Clifford has missed the point completely. Kent called the arcaded traverse with its massive rustication a 'Praeneste'—thus inviting comparison with a unique antique scene, the heroic arches and ramps below the temple at Palestrina, architecture on the scale of landscape, architecture as equal partner with the landscape rather than as an incidental ornament on the face of the land. It may owe something to an earlier project by Bridgman, but this does not justify Mr Clifford in calling it 'neither one thing nor the other.' It is 'the other,' the kind of landscaping Kent might have done more often if left to himself, without noble improvers breathing down his neck.

Stourhead is equally 'other,' outside the tradition of conventional aristocratic aspirations and titled patronage. Its creator, Henry Colt Hoare, a banker, called in no fashionable consultant, but did it himself over some three decades. For this very reason, the creator of the only true masterpiece of the art surviving is unlikely to get his due in the present state of 18th-century studies, for the whole field seems to be infected to a greater or less degree with Nicolson Blight, a virus pest (named after the main focus of infection on the book page of the *Observer*) which afflicts the historical imagination much as Bushy Stunt affects tomato plants. In the output of affected writers, preoccupation with rank proliferates at the expense of the study of creative talent till it becomes impossible to distinguish between the defence of our artistic heritage and mere toadying to traditional privilege.

Few recent attacks have been as bad as the classic case of sickly aristophilia (a curiously pernicious French strain) exhibited by Cyril Connolly's introduction to *Les Pavillons,*[3] where the blight seems also to have spread to the 200 pages of illustrations of aristocratic rural retreats as well. In contrast to this, the prognosis for R. W. Ketton-Cremer is hopeful: the deep dynastic dreariness of his *Felbrigg*[4] seems to be due to a temporary attack of inbreeding—it is about his own forebears—and there is a fair chance that his next book will be back on his *Norfolk Worthies* form. But the most alarming case is that of James Lees-Milne whose latest production rejoices in the splendidly snobbish and aptly anticlimactic title of *Earls of Creation*.[5]

This study of Belted Patronage (in J. M. Richards's happy phrase) is a sorry descent from his earlier works of highbrow popularization, designed to make the architecture of Rome, Spain, Adam or Inigo Jones acceptable to those unfortunates who have suffered an Oxbridge education. This time he has fallen into the Nicolson trap of believing that the noble patrons who launched the landscape movement were more interesting than the creative minds who dreamed it up—like Addison and Pope—or the executants who made it real—like Kent and Brown. In fact, his introduction shoots down the rest of the book: Kent, he says, 'had all the imagination, fire and genius which . . . his noble patron lacked.' Why not a book about Kent, then? Admirably coarse personality, suitable for popularizing treatment, and Margaret Jourdain's book is now 14 years out of date.

Why not? He was a commoner, that's why! I don't suppose a decent, right-thinking publisher today would handle the book. Or any other serious work on the origins of the landscape movement that produced its masterpiece at Stourhead, for the awful truth is that it was invented and staffed by middle-class professionals. From Pope to Repton there isn't a creative nobleman in the business, except Lord Burlington, and he was only three generations away from trade. It would obviously be an over-simplification to try and assimilate Hoare too closely to these nonnoble pros, and equally unsafe to try and see him as wholly unlike the lordly improvers, for he clearly had tastes and admirations in common with them. But as his own designer and without pretensions to rank, he successfully avoided the condescensions—or, worse, the awful self-conscious anti-condescensions that were occasionally shewn towards Pope—and obsequiousnesses that contributed a strain of palsied intentions to so many lesser landscapes. At Stourhead there is an integration of conception and execution, a wholeness and vitality of one man's vision that puts the final product in an almost Michelangelesque class among landscapes.

NOTES
1. *A History of Garden Design*, Faber, 1962.
2. "Humphry Repton," *Country Life*.
3. Hamish Hamilton, 1962.
4. Hart-Davis, 1962.
5. Hamish Hamilton, 1962.

The Dymaxicrat

Buckminster Fuller needs no introduction—at last! It comes as a real relief to us foundation members of the Dymaxion Fan Club, who first got the message from *Mechanix Illustrated* about 1930, that it is no longer necessary to begin an article such as this with:

> See the clever Inventor
> See the pretty Dome
> Color the dome geodesic
> The inventor's name is Buck-min-ster Ful-ler
> Try not to color him eccentric.

It has been a long and thankless haul, the ultimate disproof of proverbs about better mousetraps—the world has now built a twelve-lane freeway through Fuller-land, but only after he has been in the magazines for thirty years. The curve of public acceptance did not finally intercept Bucky's orbit until about 1955; in the previous year the two paperboard domes at the Milan Triennale had forced world design-people to see

---

Originally appeared in *Arts Magazine* 38 (October 1963): 66–69.

him in the context of international architecture, and the famous photograph of a Marine Corps helicopter lifting another paperboard dome not only came to serve as a sort of certificate of proof of the objectivity of his ideas, but also became the most compulsive symbolic icon of far-out building technology the postwar world possessed.

But the world had been catching up on Fuller in any number of ways. His 1927 drawing of the 4D air-ocean town plan, with aircraft winging between tall towers of super-technology scattered over the globe, looked like Futurist revivalism at the time, but to anyone going Boeing between Hilton International hotels in 1963 it just looks like where we live. The pole-hung Dymaxion House project has been nearly put into production twice—once as the Wichita House by Beech Aircraft after the last war, and again by Bodiansky and the ATBAT design team to house a French antarctic expedition in IGY. Miniaturized editions, give or take very little, of the Dymaxion car project were built, twenty years later, by both Isetta and Heinkel (the latter still being produced in England), and in Bucky's recent forays into his synergetic universe of spherical closest-packing geometries, he has found himself face to face with protein biochemists who have got into the same territory from the other end and with quite other motives.

But few things really mark the present stage of public acceptance as sharply as the language of John McHale's new book on Fuller.[1] The mere publication of the book is no great wonder—George Braziller's determination to capsule all the big names of current architecture into five-dollar packets was bound to overrun Fuller sooner or later, but McHale's use of language in it is an achievement (though whether that achievement is to be credited to McHale or the *Zeitgeist* is difficult to assess). Like the rest of us, McHale has been growing middle-aged in a world increasingly rich in Fulleriana, increasingly receptive to the Dymaxion creed; but unlike the rest of us, McHale has himself been producing more Fulleriana than anyone else, and his writings have had a lot to do with the increasing acceptance of these ideas, especially among architectural students outside the U.S.

Now, writing about Bucky has its peculiar difficulties, of which the leading one is that it is almost impossible except in his own idiom. There is a very good reason for this—that his creative thinking does genuinely seem to be done in the grammar and syntax he uses when speaking. Problems are simultaneously bulldozed frontally, undermined termitically and outflanked by way of relative clauses lasting up to six weeks. All this is fine while Bucky is telling the tale himself, except possibly for people sitting at the back of large audiences who cannot follow his facial expressions or the subtleties of his hand-actions. Comprehensibility survives into print, if the text is Bucky's own, but if it is written by another hand . . . trouble! In Robert Mark's 1960 book on Bucky, the interference between his own manner of writing and Bucky's manner of thinking, produces a style that falls apart—ponderous and pedestrian on the maths, which it fails to illuminate, turgid when it turns to the narrative, which it fails to animate.

McHale, disciplined by six years' hard writing since his first Fuller article for the *Architectural Review,* and his understanding deepened by a great deal of close working with the Dymaxicrat himself, seems to have gone a long way toward thrashing this linguistic problem. He has eliminated some of the more angular and scholastic Scotticisms from his own style and opened its structure to the point where it can absorb Fullerisms without coming apart at the joints. As a result, he has a narrative tool and descriptive apparatus that are related to Fuller's thought patterns without being swamped by them. Only once in this book does the Master's rhetoric trap him into an overcapitalized metaphor, but it's a real bomb when it drops—"the upsurge of geodesic domes and their outward global explosion ten years later." (It sounds like a slow-motion commercial for a cosmic soap-powder.)

Fuller himself cannot lay a verbal egg like this, because he is himself the toughest critic of his own prose style. Talking to University College on his last visit to London, he involved himself in a twenty-minute relative clause about bird ecology, in the course of which he came up with ". . . and then the male birds fly off to sweep out areas of maximum anticipated metabolic advantage." At which point he paused just long enough to scrutinize what he had said and added "Worms," in a throwaway aside that got the biggest laugh of the afternoon. But in this, of course, he was also demonstrating his phenomenal ability to step from high-level abstraction to concrete example and back. It is like his famous bit where he observes that he has never known the Universe to let him down, and proves it by tossing up a coin and watching with justified satisfaction as it falls reliably back to earth instead of floating horizontally out of the window or turning into a winged serpent.

It is this side of him as much as anything else that endears him to children (McHale's, and my own, are among his most frantic fans) and to architectural students, whose teachers often have nothing to offer but airy theories and practical rules-of-thumb that never seem to cohere into any convincing professional discipline. On the other hand, very sophisticated people, especially with conventional dead-language European educations, tend to shy away from him—hence the bitter attacks on him by some British critics, and the campaign of snide witticisms that followed his European tour in 1958. But the boys and girls don't suffer these cultural inhibitions. They respond freely to a world view that can be reduced to the tetrahedron and the sphere, and even more eagerly (in an age when a mathematical model is apt to be a mile of punched tape) when the view is demonstrated by constructions that can be held in the hand or are made of table-tennis balls or drinking straws. Their reward is to be treated, for instance, to Bucky's unique nonmathematical demonstration of the theory of the gyroscope—a performance (why has it not been video-taped?) that gives some idea of what it must have been like to sit in while Pythagoras drew in the sand.

But in all this we should remember that his idiosyncratic and effective mathematical facility is a direct product of his preoccupation with human shelter and is fed back into the shelter situation as a structural discipline and a methodology of environmental control. His approach must be distinguished from that of the men with whom he is often compared, like Robert le Ricolais or Konrad Wachsmann. Neither begins with his impassioned estimate of the shelter-predicament, nor his radical concepts of its cure. Le Ricolais wings down from the heights of pure mathematics to propose structures which, he claims, can be made from a cubic meter of wood—but where can one buy wood by the cubic meter, square Maître?—while Wachsmann has done little more than pursue certain problems of structural jointing with the same fiendish narrow ingenuity that other typical German genii have applied to clockwork mice and magnetic mines.

Fuller, by contrast, tends to make simple joints between pieces of available lumber. Although he has talked a lot about waiting for lagging building technology to catch up with new design possibilities, he operationally demonstrates a true hot-rodder's faith that when he wants a component or adapter, one will pop out of the cornucopia of U.S. technology. Conversely, when he has to deal with less-abundant technologies, he hot-rods around for underexploited productive capacity—hence his protracted love-affair with the paper and printing industries, which seem to be present in countries where even Portland cement is not.

In this he sets himself apart from the architects of his generation, who have hardly done a thing to extend their technical resources, meekly accepting a few handouts from the structural engineers. Typically, Le Corbusier's reaction to a threatened break-down of technological abundance is to back down into primitivism, to mud walls and log roofs. Also, architects have tended to see the problem of shelter as one, simply, of creating more elegant spatial experiences, whereas Fuller has seen it as one of creating more and better-serviced volumes of habitation. That is why the Dymaxion House project of 1927 makes such a mockery of its architect-designed contemporaries, such as Mies van der Rohe's Lange House at Krefeld, Le Corbusier's Villa de Monzie at Garches, or Richard Neutra's Lowell House in Los Angeles. It was a design that could have delivered what the others promised but could not produce, a radically new environment for domestic living. As a technical proposition it proposed fully controlled and conditioned living space, and as an aesthetic proposition it offered what Corb alone (and five years later) was to promise and half-deliver—an idyllic prospect of the world from one story above the damp and dirt. In offering both, the Dymaxion House was—and still is—in a league where no one else is playing.

McHale scores here too; he gets Fuller out of the vacuum in which he is usually discussed and shows him in the context of the architecture of his time—which may be the most valuable and embarrassing thing the book has done. If it were left to the architects, and to the critics, pundits and historians who share their professional attitudes, Fuller would never get discussed at all; there is a real current of architectural opinion which does not want to know about him. Of course, it was the architects who pioneered his public acceptance, because they were captivated by the pretty domes and his ability to outtalk even Le Corbusier and Frank Lloyd Wright. But when they saw that his work, even more than his words, criticized their attitudes so sharply that they were left without a pilotis to stand on, the atmosphere chilled. For the front-runners who make opinion (if not the middle-runners who make the money), Fuller has now become a square, a nut, a Philistine, even—bless their tiny professional minds—a member of the Establishment.

Ultimately the laugh will be on them—and they probably know it. One reason why so many of them reject Fuller's root-and-branch rejection of the International Style and Bauhaus doctrine as they reached the U.S. after 1930, is that they have rejected them too, for different reasons, but don't want client-class to get wind of it. He damned both as superficial and tricky, cultural illusionism, and now, as "progressive" architects (not to mention *Progressive Architecture*) in the Eastern U.S. begin to head down the Gadarene slope toward a full-scale Beaux-Arts revival, it is clear that Gropius and his followers, in twenty years of teaching at Harvard and elsewhere, really did fail to put more than a veneer of functionalism and a lacquering of social responsibility over the academic and corrupt body of U.S. architecture—and in many cases it is Gropius's own students who are leading the downhill rush.

Unlike them, Fuller has something to offer the world, the real world out there where the U.S. and Europe are about to be assayed by fire and sword, hunger and newly educated millions. Not believing, like so many New England and European architects seem to do, that every millionaire has a right to his monument ("You could call me the Levitt of the museum-building industry," said one) before every man has a right to somewhere to live, Fuller offers the world the kind of design-concepts it needs. And if architects cannot offer the kind of service that the world needs, then architects will go the same way as rain makers and witch doctors and other pseudo-technicians who were preserved by cultural inertia in spite of declining evidence of performance—but were preserved only for so long. In a world where survival is a prime consideration, Dymaxicrats like Fuller are more likely to survive than the kind of architects the schools are still producing.

Apropos of something else, McHale once wrote to me, "Allah has the message—and Mohammed is his press agent." On present performance you could certainly put Fuller in the first half of the proposition and, on present promise, you should soon be able to put McHale in the second. This is not the definitive work on Fuller, nor will there be one yet, but when it comes McHale is the most likely man to write it.

NOTE   1. *R. Buckminster Fuller,* by John McHale. ("Makers of Contemporary Architecture" Series.) George Braziller.

17

The Style for the Job

'Toasting,' said James Stirling, 'is a pretty primitive sort of conception. It just doesn't make sense in something rather smooth and elegant like the Braun toaster. I mean, you can burn bread all right in something crude and a bit old-fashioned like your Morphy Richards, but not in the Braun. It's just not right!' There spoke again that hypersensitivity about appropriate character in design that has always needled the Stirling and Gowan partnership. Gowan's manner of expressing it may be less picturesque, but the phrase 'the Style for the Job' is his contribution to a debate that has spread to include the work of Eero Saarinen, and with them, as with Saarinen, this approach has had its pitfalls. But it has paid off in Saarinen's airports, and it has paid off triumphantly for Stirling and Gowan in the new Engineering Building at Leicester University.

It succeeds because job and style are inseparable. In some earlier works, such as the housing at Preston, they seem to have decided the appropriate character subjectively, on the basis of arbitrary sociological decisions. But at Leicester, the first job complex enough to extend their talents to the full, they had neither time, money nor ground-space for disembodied speculation about style: the character emerges with

---

Originally appeared in *New Statesman* 67 (14 February 1964): 261.

stunning force from the bones of the structure and the functions it shelters. It is almost unique in Britain in having no detail, however extraordinary, that is overwrought or underdesigned by the standards set by the structure as a whole. Its character is not only appropriate but consistent in every part.

The building is in many ways as extraordinary as its details. At ground-floor level it confronts the visitor with a blank wall of hard-faced red brick, which is occasionally pierced with a rather private-looking doorway, except at the point where the glazed main-entrance lobby splits this defensive podium into two parts: one a rectangle enclosing the teaching labs, the other a moderately irregular polygon forming the base of two towers housing research and administrative offices. Over the heavy teaching labs there foams, like suds from some cubist detergent, a good head of angular north-light glazing, laid diagonally across the building. Down one side of the block, this pearly translucent glazing rises to four storeys, with the topmost floor of labs strutted well out over a service road that cannot, for the present, be eliminated: the whole complex has had to be crammed onto a site which, by common-sense standards, ought to be about 25 per cent too small for it.

On the opposite flank of the main rectangle rise the towers, but they do not rise in any obvious or tidy-minded manner, since each rests on a lecture-hall that cantilevers out beyond the limits of the podium below. The research tower rises only five storeys above the smaller auditorium, and is relatively conventional in appearance, except that it has one corner snubbed off to clear a legal building line, and its bands of windows are in the form of inverted hoppers, the glass sloping out to shelter flat bands of ventilators underneath. The admin tower, which carries a water-tank on top to give the hydraulics labs at ground level sufficient head of water, has all four corners snubbed off when it finally reaches it typical plan-form, and then rises clear above the research tower.

Between these two main towers rise three subsidiary shafts—a twinned pair for lifts and stairs rising the full height of the admin tower, a smaller one standing only high enough to serve the lower research tower. Where these five clustering towers do not touch—which is usually—the intervening spaces are filled by glazing that in only one case (between the twins) falls sheer and vertical to the ground. In the other gaps it descends in a sort of cascade, twisting to one side or the other, and angling forward to accommodate the ever larger landings that are needed in the lower and more populous parts of the building. This composition of towers and glass is a fantastic invention, the more so because it proceeds rigorously from structural and circulatory considerations without frills or artwork. The solid walls are either of the same brick as the podium, or of the red tiling that covers nearly every square foot of concrete, even floors and ceilings. The glazing (like the tiling) is rock-bottom cheap industrial stuff, just glass and aluminum extrusions. It has no pretty details, just nuts, bolts, bars cut to length on site, and raggedy flashings left 'as found.'

By taking a thoroughly relaxed attitude to technology and letting the glazing system follow its own unpretentious logic, the architects achieved less a kind of anti-detailing (as some critics seem to suggest) than some form of un-detailing that would border on plain dereliction of duty were it not so patently right in this context. But, over and above the rectitude of the detailing, the stair-tower complex offers such bewildering visual effects that words are apt to fail. Both by day and by night (when the stairs are lit by pairs of plain industrial lamps bracketed from the walls) the play of reflections in the variously angled glass surfaces can be as breathtaking as it is baffling. It really looks as if the grand old myths of functionalism have come true for once, and that beauty, of a sort, has been given as a bonus for the honest service of need.

I say beauty 'of a sort' because the visual pleasures of this complex and rewarding building are neither those of classic regularity nor picturesque softness. Its aethestic satisfactions stem from a tough-minded, blunt-spoken expertise that convinces even laymen that everything is right, proper and just so. It is one of those buildings that establishes its own rules, convinces by the coherence of even markedly dissimilar parts, and stands upon no precedents. It rebuffs the attempts of art-historians to identify its sources (unlike some of the other modern buildings on the Leicester campus, which provide a real feast for art-historical nit-pickers), though it has, in some obtuse way of its own, regained a good deal of the bloody-minded élan and sheer zing of the pioneer modernism of the early Twenties. Largely, I think, this is because it really does seem to be a natural machine-age architecture of the sort that must have been in the minds of the *Werkbund*'s founding fathers or Antonio Sant'Elia.

If its attitude to technology is relaxed, its general quality is of a take-it-or-leave-it nonchalance, and this has undoubtedly contributed to the profound and niggling offence it has given in some creepy architectural circles. It is a fair measure of the collapse of self-confidence among students at certain British architectural schools that one of them could write:

> This is a worrying building. Formally it is one of the most exciting modern buildings in the country. Yet its very success . . . calls into doubt the architects' motives and suggests that at times they were only concerned with human function in so far as it provided them with excuses for formal expression.

There follow a couple of paragraphs almost suggesting a hidden hope that it will turn out that the building doesn't work, so that little worries 'about the morality of it' (to quote two more frightened students) might turn out to be justified. The whole proposition here, that a formally exciting building *cannot* be functionally correct, shows the kind of slough into which functionalism deprived of ruthlessness can subside.

Fortunately, Stirling and Gowan applied the kind of radical ruthlessness that conjures convincing form out of service of function, and receives as a bonus, not only the dizzy reflections in the stair-tower, but a nocturnal transformation scene when the building, glowing with its own internal and strictly functional illumination, assumes a mantle of light and mystery that is like no other architectural spectacle the world can offer. *World*—this is a world-class building, one of the very few that Britain has produced since the war, or ever. Its international fame does not rest on its being frightfully British, but on its being resolutely architectural, and in a manner that would justify itself in any company.

The world is now beating a path to its door—where it is greeted by a badly lettered notice announcing that 'this building is not available to the public for visiting or photography.' Not to worry, effrontery or graft will get you in, and any trouble you provoke will help to hasten the day when the University authorities have to face their responsibilities and make proper arrangements for visitors. Architecture of this quality must be public property.

18

How I Learnt to Live with the Norwich Union

Norwich is more nearly surrounded by council houses than any other city in Britain. Even as you sweep in from London, through the monumental avenue of trees that line the Newmarket Road, the Lakenham estate is only just out of view to the right, the sprawling Earlham complex even nearer on the left. Earlham contains some of the most abysmal local authority housing put up in Britain between the wars—hygienic, no doubt, but brutish in its planning, with token acknowledgements of the demands of architecture in the form of fake half-timber on corner houses. Towards 1939, standards began to improve a little, and as a teenager I watched some of the more humane parts of the Earlham complex going up at the bottom of our recently acquired spec-builder-suburban garden. The field where we had dug caves and defence-works, potted larks with an air-gun and horsed around generally was rapidly covered with houses full of slum-cleared families whose younger offspring answered to such calls as 'Come yew haer, gal Gloria, do else I'll lump ya one!'

Gloria's kid brother (or Vera's or Marleen's) passed through my hands some years

Originally appeared in *New Statesman* 67 (6 March 1964): 372–373.

later, during the six memorable months I spent as a master at the remand home at Bramerton across the other side of the city. He was a sharp, narrow kid of the kind the estates seemed to breed in those days, with a welfare state-nurtured IQ that was outside his parent's comprehension, and he stood up in juvenile court to give his mother the farewell she deserved: 'Yew only want me outa the house so yew can goo off with that bleedin' Yank.' He wept, telling me about it months afterwards, and his anguish sums up a painful social revolution from which the city still hasn't recovered. The estates represent a major civic effort in excising blighted housing from the central parts of the city. An urban proletariat has been winkled out of its immemorial stews to be spread thinly in a great suburban ring, and—at what now appears to have been a rather critical moment—this process encountered the U.S. Eighth Army Air Force head on.

Many, if not most, of the preferred American brothels were in council houses, many estate households acquired transatlantic hangers-on who fulfilled the roles of missing men (there was a time when it seemed as if almost all the Norfolk Regiment must be in Japanese prison-camps) not only in the obvious sexual sense but also as handy-men and bread-winners of a sort. PX affluence—cast-off T-shirts, packs of Luckies, comic books, sacks of sugar—fell at random and with maximum psychological and social disturbance on an uprooted working class for whom rationing was just a continuation of undernourishment by other means. We got the obvious victims at Bramerton, but two whole generations felt the impact, and I can still sense it in the city to this day. The base of the social pyramid is unsettled and unstable.

But, if the Yanks hit Norwich in the guts, they hit it in the head too. The first and only time I ever met James Stewart he was with some other uniformed thespians, swapping tall memoirs with Nugent Monck on the stage of the Maddermarket Theatre. The Norwich Players had been at the Madder for almost 20 years by then, and Moncklet had been around the city even longer, and Norwich had almost completely ignored both. Then these college-educated top-sergeants who knew all about the man and his theatre from reading *Theatre Arts Monthly* began to show up, and bring their girlfriends to see the play, and the girls brought their mums and dads, and Norwich discovered that it had a famous theatre and a producer of genius in its midst. Discovered just in time, for he was pushing 70 by then.

What made Monck's career important was not the obvious bit about the repertory stage and his place in the Shakespearian tradition, but the mere fact of his equivocal presence (he was one of my favourite queers) and his refusal to go native. Norwich is a great graveyard of promising careers, where people who might just have made the big time with an effort relax and go small-time instead. It is quite a cushy ecology for a certain kind of intellectual—you can still pick up a piece of gracious property to live in at prices below national averages, and some gracious sticks of antique furniture to go in it; there is a gracious network of art-lovers and music-addicts and some gracious places like the Assembly House for them to congregate in. A man with a modicum of money or talent behind him and an entertaining wife beside him can have a very nice life in Norwich in a sickening sort of way.

But if, like Nugent Monck, he decides not to let the gracious living drag him down, the place can be quite an arena for a determined mind. The indomitable and ever-memorable Gladys Barnard was another one of the same cut. Nobody's fool ('Mr Banham is a young man who thinks he knows everything'), she fought her way up through the local government hierarchy to take charge of the museums service, and leave behind collections of local art, craft and life that would be hard to rival in a comparable city anywhere in Europe—Ulm and Neu-Ulm, for instance, together comprise a very similar cathedral city of about the same size, with one very good museum, but not a museum service of this order. She laid the foundations of what is now an authoritative collection of Norwich School paintings, yet I know that she never kidded herself—Crome and Cotman notwithstanding—that it was more than a provincial by-way in the history of European art.

Survival in this intellectual lotus-land needs a special temperament. I defy anyone to pick out likely survivors in advance, yet they all seem to reveal the same characteristics in their own private ways. And I mean private: the king of the local art scene at present is Davenport, who is so private that his Christian name is never used, even to his face by his closest friends. His achievement in painting, too, is private, for he is a landscape artist of a sort that hardly exists nowadays. But he is no recluse (one of the best general-purpose bar-room vocalists in the business), nor is the meaning of his painting incommunicable—his angry visions of man-made objects in the landscape hit Norfolk people hard, and where they live. But he has only been able to impose this personal and valid vision by relying absolutely on himself and refusing all blandishments to succumb to the flashy and genteel conformism of the school of water colourists who would otherwise have gone on flourishing undisturbed.

Conformism in Norwich would probably be no worse than in other provincial cities, were it not effectively monumentalised in a single dominant industry—insurance. The cultural irresponsibility and stodginess of Big Insurance in Norwich is immediately apparent to anyone who compares the relentlessly quaint image of 'a fine city' projected by Norwich Union advertising with the reality of the urban scene now dominated by the lumping hulk of the Norwich Union's own new office block. But Big Insurance is a law unto itself, and brings into the present century the mental habits of a closed community, an elect, like the Nonconformist pioneers of banking and finance in the city. It is to a Norwich Union executive that legend attributes the dictum: 'Fornication we might tolerate, adultery we might ignore, but marriage outside the company will terminate your employment.' This chosen-brethren approach may have made sense among a tight network of Gurneys and Frys, but it looks pretty antisocial on a giant computerised organisation that seems to have bought up half England. The recent embarrassments over Lord Mancroft show how timid and gutless this conformism can be when seriously challenged.

But imagine what it is like to have to live under the great fat corporate arse of this lot, to pass through an education system which still assumes that a sizeable proportion of its gifted products will automatically go into safe jobs in the N.U., and probably be lost to the cultural life of the city as a consequence: Big Insurance quietly pressures its employees to join the company clubs, associations and amateur dramatics, rather than independent organisations. No wonder the rebels get out, no wonder the independents who survive have to be such tough nuts. This is true of other cities, I know, but Norwich is unique in being a town where it is the middle classes who feel that they are at the mercy of a single industry, a single company.

The new University of East Anglia, though isolated from the city by the Earlham housing estates, may provide the alternative outlets that local grammar-school products need. Denys Lasdun's master-plan for the university is exactly the kind of controversial proposition that the city establishment don't wish to know about, and many local architects, instead of supporting the design, insisted on demonstrating their small-town small-mindedness by complaining that Lasdun's single-building concept didn't give them a chance to share in the spoils. The university project, quite frankly, may still have to be turned into a salvage operation. The proposal to site it on difficult but rewarding land in urgent need of urban renewal, and under the shadow of the Castle, was effectively crushed by the UGC and local fund-raisers, who accused critics of the Earlham site of deliberately rocking the boat and sabotaging the city's chance of ever having a university at all. And having opted for a conventional suburban site, the academic planners have opted for a conventional suburban curriculum as well—the understandable local demand for an engineering degree course was dismissed as 'parochial' instead of being investigated to see what sort of mix it could make with the biological studies that form the other main discipline. Conformism won, and it's dreary old Eng Lit all over again.

Not that the literary culture of Norwich couldn't do with a shot of originality at the moment. The city tends to get the kind of authors the Norwich Union deserves, and to console itself by going on and on about George Borrow, who was all right in his way but that Romany bit is a real drag. Most Norwich citizens quote the wind-on-the-heath tag two or three times a month, but they mean *Mousehold* Heath, that graceless amenity that is one of the city's greatest assets and is deeply bitten into the popular subconscious. Among its gorse and gravel, generations of 11-minus Indians have bitten the dust, generations of teenage maidenheads have perished. To a lad with a bike, a model plane, a catapult or just a piece of wood, it is an inexhaustible resource, within walking distance of the most crowded parts of the city. In spite of the use it gets, the vegetable cover survives pretty well, and when snow covers its scars and half the city comes out with sledges, it is transformed.

Needless to say, a citizens' action group has had to be formed to defend this irreplaceable civic lung. In spite of its value as an open space pure and simple, it is subject to continuous legal nibbling and illegal encroachment. In spite of its unique and hairy character, it is always under threat of being civilised, sterilised or municipalised. Some of the defensive tactics employed by the Mousehold campaigners have upset comfortable square citizens, but this is an area where the city has traditionally worked off its passions and violent tendencies (Kett's rebellion and all that) and the generally stuffy tone of municipal government is liable to provoke desperate reactions even before the situation becomes one for genuine despair. But Mousehold is worth fighting for, because it is a piece of real basic Norwich that every generation rediscovers for itself, just as Magdalen Street is worth fighting for, even if the reasons are more involved. Magdalen Street, indeed, will be the acid test of the ability of citizen action groups to sort out the city's problems to the citizens' satisfaction. It is a textbook example of the multi-purpose street, with interesting people living in medieval courts just behind the most crazy mixed-up set of shops you could ever hope to find, a main commuting artery where you can sometimes stand in the middle of the road for minutes together at mid-morning or mid-afternoon and never see a car. Visually it has survived the ghastly good taste of a Civic Trust face-lift, but how much longer it can survive the increasing traffic pressure is another matter. Unthinking pre-Buchanan solutions, such as bashing holes through it, ought to be impossible after the high valuation which the Buchanan Report gave the Magdalen Street scene. But in Norwich you never know. An administration which believes that 'Norwich City Hall is accepted as one of the finest modern buildings in the world' could believe, and do, absolutely anything.

19

People's Palaces

Instant Xanadus dedicated to the public good have become a drug on the market lately—one people's palace opened, the shell of another shown to the press, the diagram of a kit of parts for the third cautiously released and all in the last month. Each reflects an entirely different approach to the housing of people's pleasures, though each and every one is decidedly 'progressive', and the three-way contrast of the architectural solutions prompts some uncomfortable thoughts about where the cultural Left thinks it is headed.

Completed, the Crystal Palace Sports Centre reveals the social preconceptions behind its commissioning as clearly as ever architecture could. The basic design is from 10 years ago, and couched in the 'Romance-of-Engineering' style then in vogue with the progressive Establishment—Sir Gerald Barry masterminded the overall plan for the complete site, Sir Leslie Martin personally piloted the sports centre through the LCC architect's department. The result has all the vaguely Latin American boldness and hopefully Italian structural acrobatics that you might therefore expect, but is not to be knocked for that reason at all. There is no other stadium in Britain that I would point

---

Originally appeared in *New Statesman* 68 (7 August 1964): 191–192.

out to a foreign visitor without reservations as a work of imaginative architecture, and the enormous sports hall with its pools, courts and practice-pits for practically every form of puntin' a pill about, is probably unique in the world. It is a very exciting structure—and suffers as architecture only when purely 'architectural' considerations have been allowed to take precedence over the business of being a sports-hall.

Just by looking, you can see that they thought of an absolutely splendid roof, a work of art in its own right, carried on a forest of leaning columns. Then, later, they thought of the air-conditioning you need for a sports hall, and how to connect the necessary ductwork in the roof with the machinery in the basement. The solution—a right botch—is four enormous duct boxes, each vastly thicker than any column, and therefore looking as if it is they, not the columns, that support the roof. This duct business has been a perennial problem ever since daring roof structures set in, but it is time to start solving it, by making ductwork look like ductwork, if it is really impossible to get the air-conditioning plant into the roof.

A similar collision between 'architects' architecture' and the earth-people who have to inhabit it occurs in the planning of the hostel block, which has been changed, since Sir Leslie's time, from the horizontal-domestic mode to the vertical-monumental, in line with shifting architectural fashion. The result, whose intellectual elegance and structural cleverness is not in dispute, has a plan-form of six hexagons clustered round a central hexagon containing the staircase—and have you ever tried to get a normal athletic layabout, his tackle, his bed and sundry other furniture into the irregular 76 square feet that are left over after a slightly desperate architect has carved a minimal bathroom and some more goddammed duct-work out of a half-hexagon?

But maybe the athletes will be too impressed to complain, because it is a privilege to be there—the Crystal Palace sports centre will be a kind of shrine for the muscle-bound meritocracy of sport. No matter what old south-of-the-river hands may say about it being a wonderful thing for this kind of facility to be available for 'the people' it will be no use Fred Penge and Arthur Balham trying to book a court or just turning up with their trunks and towels, because this place is not for the people. It is a training centre for specialists who are working their way up through 'the system' towards a lucrative career as amateur sportsmen. The Penges and Balhams of this world will get in from time to time as spectators, but even then they will find themselves segregated from the performers, on a separate circulation system that is never allowed to come down to the level of the sacred turf, blessed cinder-track or perishing pools. The whole planning concept is a paradigm of the new class system of the Welfare State.

This separation of the qualified from the unqualified is deeply bitten into the practical ethos, if not the public pronouncements, of institutionalised socialism as we have it—deriving, I suppose, from the days when socialism was something done on the working class from a great height by Fabians of gentler birth, and the officially encouraged ambition for the faithful plebs was to 'pass for educated.' And coupled with this, a cultural soup-kitchen approach for the under-privileged, hand-outs of free art for those who had been 'unlucky' enough to escape a grammar-school education. I wish that so strong an aura of this approach did not attach to Centre 42's activities—or, rather, I wish they hadn't confirmed everybody's worst suspicions that they are Establishment types doing culture on the poor, by deciding to immure themselves in that made-over, makeshift monument from an OK period in the past.

But there it is—the Camden Town railway roundhouse has the accolade of inclusion in J. M. Richards's *The Functional Tradition* (the industrial revolution decontaminated by Georgian Group sentimentality) and its location on the ground is a perfect topographical symbol of hand-out culture: up the hill are the eggheads of Hampstead, east and south are the deprived ethnic minorities of Camden and Kentish Towns. This one could just about stand if there were striking proof that the building were rewardingly adaptable to its proposed function, but in spite of the rhetoric in the empurpled brochure, the plans drawn up by Architects' Co-Partnership offer a shockingly small return for an estimated outlay of 300,000 nicker. Honestly, any organisation that proposes to spend that kind of money—the brand-new Chichester theatre cost half as much—to lumber itself with a bandaged-up load of Victoriana needs its head examined—or 10 years compulsory exile to Harlow New Town (or Runcorn or Dawley or any of them), a clear site that would give them twice as much usable accommodation for half the money, and a chance to square up to the real problems of the working class without a chorus line of Knights and Dames confusing the issue by viewing it through Ivy-coloured spectacles.

What sticks in my gullet is the second-rate acceptance of a second-hand building as good enough for the job. At least you cannot say this about Joan Littlewood's Fun Palace project. She thinks the 'people' deserve all-new tackle, and if she believes this for reasons as sentimental as Wesker's (ever see her in a pub trying to make the local slag come on gay and spontaneous?) a lot of the people aren't going to argue too hard about her motives. But what is unsentimental—and why the Fun Palace gets my vote—is that she and her architects and tech-men aren't offering any kind of monument, new, second-hand or any-wise. It really is a kit of parts, and for months now Cedric Price, the architect involved, has been driving architectural journalists mad by steadfastly refusing to release any pictures of what the FP will actually *look like*. He may well not know, but that doesn't matter because it is not the point. Seven nights of the week it will probably look like nothing on earth from the outside: the kit of service towers, lifting gantries and building components exists solely to produce the kind of interior environments that are necessary and fitting to whatever is going on.

What matters is that the various activity-spaces inside the FP will not be fossilised in a single architectural *schema* that may become functionally out of date in five years and is out of fashion already, like Centre 42's theatre-in-the-roundhouse. They have been assumed to be functionally out of date the moment they are built, and can therefore be changed—not by sliding screens, parish-hall fashion, but by the complete removal and rearrangement of all enclosing surfaces (floors and ceilings as well as

walls) and since change is regarded as the normal condition, the largest single installation will probably be the means of change, the gantries that make it possible to lift
anything and put it somewhere else. Since there are no exterior walls, the actual enclosed volume of the FP is expected to vary wildly but since it is also to be the first
building in Britain with full (not token) mechanical services and environment controls,
it is quite possible that many activities will need no more enclosure than a roof over
their heads.

Sorry, the word 'building' got in there by mistake (old cultural habits die hard). There
probably isn't going to be any building in the normal scope of the concept at all. What
there will be—if any current concept really covers the FP proposition—is a gigantic version of the three-dimensional chess they play on long interstellar voyages in science
fiction, only any number of unspecified and random players, individuals or groups, can
play, competing for optimum environments for whatever kind of knees-up they have in
mind. So it may turn out more like one of those vast and inscrutable social games in
Van Vogt's *Null-A* novels.

It is all a wild, mod dream, no mistake about it, and this is precisely what gives it its
meaning. It would be possible to produce some sober accounting to show that the Welfare State should start investing in this kind of concentrated leisure plant straight away,
and you could get a committee of interested parties together to draw up a schedule
of accommodation and produce a Crystal Palace Sports Centre situation before it
was off the drawing board. This sort of thing is going to have to be done, institutions
for the institutionalised aspects of leisure. What Joan and her team of 'younger creative nuts' (as she calls them) are trying to create here is an entertainment kit that the
non-institutionalised aspects of leisure can improvise upon, a gigantic junk-playground
for sophisticated grown-up people to whom the handling of mechanical tackle is nowadays as natural as breathing. How far it will work is anybody's guess, but the mere offer
of such a possibility is an unprecedented situation which we cannot afford to pass up.
It is a breakout (not a breakthrough) from a stifling situation in which all the culture and
high ideals have been cornered by the institutions and all the hardware has been cornered by the entertainment industry. Above all, it offers the cultural Left a 'choice, not
an echo' (to coin a phrase): two radically different conceptions of a live popular culture
are on offer, and they are genuinely incompatible. Choose, Bernstein, *now!*

The Great Gizmo

'The purpose of technology is to make the dream a fact. . . . The end is to make the Earth a garden, Paradise; to make the mountain speak.'—Arthur Drexler

The man who changed the face of America had a gizmo, a gadget, a gimmick—in his hand, in his back pocket, across the saddle, on his hip, in the trailer, round his neck, on his head, deep in a hardened silo. From the Franklin Stove, and the Stetson Hat, through the Evinrude outboard to the walkie-talkie, the spray can and the cordless shaver, the most typical American way of improving the human situation has been by means of crafty and usually compact little packages, either papered with patent numbers, or bearing their inventor's name to a grateful posterity. Other nations, such as Japan, may now be setting a crushingly competitive pace in portable gadgetry, but their prime market is still the U.S. and other Americanized cultures, while America herself is so prone to clasp other cultures' key gadgets to her acquisitive bosom that their original inventors and discoverers are forgotten—'Big Kahuna' mysticism aside, even the

Originally appeared in *Industrial Design* 12 (September 1965): 48–59.

Australians seem to have forgotten that they were the first White Anglo-Saxon Protestants to steal the surfboard from the Polynesians, so thoroughly has surfing been Americanized. So ingrained is the belief in a device like a surfboard as the proper way to make sense of an unorganized situation like a wave, that when Homo Americanus finally sets foot on the moon it will be just as well the gravity is only one sixth of earth's for he is likely to be so hung about with packages, kits, black boxes and waldos that he would have a job to stand under any heavier 'g.'

LANDSCAPE WITH FIGURES WITH GADGETS

True sons of Archimedes, the Americans have gone one better than the old grand-daddy of mechanics. To move the earth he required a lever long enough and somewhere to rest it—a gizmo and an infrastructure—but the great American gizmo can get by without any infrastructure. Had it needed one, it would never have won the West or opened up the transcontinental trails. The quintessential gadgetry of the pioneering frontiersman had to be carried across trackless country, set down in a wild place, and left to transform that hostile environment without skilled attention. Its function was to bring instant order or human comfort into a situation which had previously been an undifferentiated mess, and for this reason it is so deeply involved with the American mythology of the wilderness that its philosophy will bear looking into both for its American consequences, and for the consequences of its introduction into other landscapes, other scenes.

Underneath lies that basic confusion about the American landscape—is it a wilderness or a paradise?—that has bedevilled American thought from Walden Pond to the barbecue pit in the backyard, a confusion on which Leo Marx's recent book *The Machine in the Garden* is so illuminating on every aspect except industrial design. Marx observes that the early settlers brought with them from Europe 'the pastoral ideal of a rural nation exhibiting a happy balance of art and nature,' and continues 'In this sentimental guise the pastoral ideal remained of service long after the machine's appearance in the landscape. It enabled the nation to continue defining its purpose as the pursuit of rural happiness while devoting itself to productivity, wealth and power. It remained for our serious writers to discover the meaning inherent in the contradiction.'

Now, from a less bookish standpoint, it might appear that the contradiction between industry and garden is only a local disturbance—local in time as well as space—in a more widespread process of employing machinery to make the pastoral garden-ideal available to the whole nation. Local in time, because one of the surest ways to convert the American wilderness into the American paradise is to let agronomy or industry pass across it and then vanish—as witness the second growth woodlands of Connecticut that have supplanted a vanished agriculture and produced perhaps the most paradisal suburban landscape in the world (or, again, I know areas in the Middle West where the mere mowing and brush-cutting of an abandoned farm will produce a landscape that could have come from the brush of Claude Lorraine). Local in space because the ground permanently occupied or permanently blighted by U.S. industry is still infinitesimal compared with the vast acreage opened up to human settlement by industry's products.

Portable technology closes Leo Marx's contradiction as surely as do the meanings discovered by serious writers: industrial productivity was perhaps the only means of converting the disorderly wilderness into an humane garden. For, if there is rural happiness in America that is in any way comparable with the European pastoral dream—whether noble, as in Palladio's villas, or ridiculous, as in Marie-Antoinette's spoof dairy-maiding—it depends on technology rather than serfdom or chattel-slavery as it did in the Old World. Yes, agreed—the American pastorale probably did start in slave-owning Virginia (through Monticello was full of mechanical ingenuities) but the dream's proliferation beyond the Appalachians, beyond the Mississippi, beyond the Rockies, increasingly depended at every stage upon the products of industry and the local application of mechanisms. For the first time, a civilization with a flourishing industry encountered a landscape that was entirely virgin or, at worst, inhabited by scattered tribes of noble (or preferably, dead) savages.

In Europe and the Orient, industry has had to worm its ways into the interstices of an already crowded pattern of social strata and landownership: over most of the U.S. there was neither society nor landownership until mechanization came puffing in on railroads that were often the first and only geographical fixes the Plains afforded. In Europe, the pastoral ideal is the heir of the medieval *hortus clusus* or walled garden—from the landscape parks of the eighteenth century to the nudist colonies of the twentieth, the pastoral dream has meant withdrawal behind protective barriers to keep out the pressure of the hoi polloi. In America the pastoral ideal is available to the hoi polloi as well, and if he wants wilderness the average man rarely has to drive for more than an hour to find unimproved ground—remember, pockets of undisturbed prairie ecology survive even in Gary, Indiana. The pastoral ideal in the U.S.A. is an extraverted vision, and while Manhattan-based Jeremiahs moan over the disappearance of the wilderness, Europeans (who really *know* about intensive occupation of land) goggle unbelievingly still at the empty acres beyond the filling stations and hamburger stands along the freeway.

THE TECHNOLOGIST ON THE BACK PORCH

Rural happiness in the U.S. was never to be the privilege of the few, but was to be the common property of every member of every family, thanks to domestic mechanization. The good life offered by early visionaries of the railroad-age such as Catherine Beecher, is of enjoyable industry for the entire family, the cultivation of the mind as well as cotton and vegetables; and it already depends, in 1869, on a notable level of mechanical sophistication. As James Marston Fitch pointed out in his key study of the redoubtable Beecher in *Architecture and the Aesthetics of Plenty,* the house she describes in 'The American Woman's Home,' is firmly visualized as a true machine for living in, and already boasts such characteristic gadgetry as a pair of Franklin stoves on the main floor and a hot-air stove in the basement, while the domestic economy practised therein with such devoted industry depends, by implication (as Fitch indicates), on equipment such as the Mason jar.

If Catherine Beecher is indeed one of the Founding Dames of the suburban way of life, then the spread of that way of life from coast to coast depended not only on back-porch technologies (to which I shall return in a moment) such as fruit-preserving, but also on one other major factor which is astonishingly missing from most generalized histories of U.S. culture—mail-order shopping. Whatever Messrs. Colt and Winchester (two more characteristic gizmo-names) may have done to subdue the West, it was Messrs. Sears and Roebuck who made it first habitable and then civilized. Yet their crucial contribution rates no more than the most passing reference, unsupported by discussion or index-reference in Max Lerner's giant coast-to-coast national-economy-sized bromide, *America as a Civilization*. The Sears catalogue is one of the great and basic documents of U.S. civilization, and deserves the closest critical study wherever the state of the Union is discussed.

One thing the student will observe is that the catalogue rarely fails to quote, along with the price and so forth, the shipping-weight of all mechanical kit. This point has its significance in the history of American technology: where distances were great and transport difficult, costs of freightage could overwhelm the economic value of a low-grade product. Whatever was shipped had to have a high selling price, or social value, relative to its bulk and weight, otherwise it was not worth the trouble. Thus, mill-cut timber was only the base material for the balloon-frame house that sheltered the West—what made it possible to give up building log-cabins was, above all else, the incredibly cheap wire nails that began to come in around the mid-century, and were shipped everywhere in bulk by barrel and bag. Here was a product whose social utility rested upon its cheapness and reliability and vastly outweighed its shipping charges. Furthermore, it was a fixing-device that required general native cunning rather than specific craft skill to employ, and so it came readily to the hand of the householder employing back-porch technologies comparable to those his wife was employing in the kitchen. For this is another key characteristic of the gizmos that changed the face of America: they do not require high skill at the point of application, they leave craftsman-ship behind at the factory. Ideally, you peel off the packaging, fix four bolts and press the Go button.

This is what makes Ole Evinrude's invention of the outboard motor so triumphantly American an event. To fit an inboard motor to an existing boat requires craft skills and mathematical aptitudes of a sort normally found only in places with a long tradition of boat-craft, as in the maritime cities of Europe or New England, where boatyards, ship-wrights and the encrusted wisdom of ancient mariners were freely available. But every portage made by the pioneers took them one more river away from any such raft-infra-structure, their boats would normally be the first and only on their particular stretch of water (as are a high proportion of U.S. boats to this day). Their back-porch technologies were unlikely to include either the tackle or the skill to bore a shaft-hole through a keel or transom, fit tube and shaft, make it watertight, calculate (let alone fabricate) the pitch and diameter of propeller, and so forth. But you can order a stock outboard from the catalogue with the right propeller for its own power and your size of boat, fix it with two clamps, add fuel and pull the started. So ideal, and so American is this solution, that other one-shot aids to the back-porch technologist have proliferated—to cite only one, the adapters that make it possible for any hot-rod-crazy to fit any engine to almost any gearbox and transmission. Warshavsky's current catalogue has three pages of them.

ABSTRACT AND CONSEQUENCES OF THE GIZMO At this point we have seen enough of the basic proposition, to formulate some generalized rules for the American gizmo, and examine its consequences in design and other fields. Like this: a characteristic class of U.S. products—perhaps the most characteristic—is a small self-contained unit of high performance in relation to its size and cost, whose function is to transform some undifferentiated set of circumstances to a condition nearer human desires. The minimum of skill is required in its installation and use, and it is independent of any physical or social infrastructure beyond that by which it may be ordered from catalogue and delivered to its prospective user.

As a class of servants to human needs, these clip-on devices, these portable gadgets, have coloured American thought and action far more deeply—I suspect—than is commonly understood. The U.S. tourist hung about with expensive cameras, most of them automated to within an inch of their lives, is a common figure of fun from Jerez to Macao, from Trondheim to Trincomalee, but he is, perhaps, a more tragic figure than a comical one, for it is difficult not to suspect that presented with scenes from cultures that he does not understand he hopes to gizmo them into comprehensible form by pointing the little black box and pressing the trigger. It may not reduce the world to a pastoral, but it will make standardized Kodachrome sense on a screen in the living-room, and it's a lot simpler than learning the language. And if you *must* learn the language, sitting down at a language-lab will give you a gizmo'd knowledge of the tongue far quicker than walking the streets of Amsterdam trying to strike up conversations in Dutch with passers-by (who always turn out to be Chinese-speaking Indonesians, anyhow).

Because practically every new, incomprehensible or hostile situation encountered by the growing American Nation was conquered, in practice, by handy gizmos of one sort or another, the grown Nation has tended to assume that all hostile situations will be solved with gadgets. If a U.S. ally is in trouble, Uncle Sam rolls up the sleeves of his Arsenal-of-Democracy sweatshirt and starts packing arms in crates for shipment long before he thinks of sending soldiers or diplomats—and be it noted that it was a half-breed American, Winston Churchill, who responded in terms that were pure gizmo-culture; 'Give us the tools and we'll finish the job!' Current U.S. foreign policy, Rand Corporation/Strangelove style, revolves disproportionately (it might be argued) around king-sized gadgets whose ballistic complexity and sheer tonnage should not blind us to the fact that they are still kissin'-cousins to Colt and Winchester, and that the abstract concept of weaponry is simply Sears' catalogue re-written in blood and radiation-sickness. And, now that internal subversion has joined the ranks of 'think-able' topics in Vietnam and Santo Domingo (not to mention Harlem and Georgia) don't the departments of State and interior wish there existed some opinion-forming gizmo (guts by IBM and RCA, box-work by Eliot Noyes, graphics by Paul Rand) that could be parachuted down, untouched by human hand, to spread sweetness and light and de-mocracy and free-enterprise for fifty miles around ground-zero. It would beat ugly Ameri-cans any day.

It might work, at that—remember how the transistor radios that have replaced Field-Marshals' batons in every *poilu*'s knapsack helped De Gaulle rally wavering troops in the last agonies of the Algerian crisis. But there are many situations that can't be resolved by gadgetry, however inspired, and the general reliance of the U.S. on gizmo solutions (helicopters in Vietnam, recoil-less rifles in Dominica) appears to Old World observers to have landed America in more messes than it has cleared up. This is not to say that Old World methods such as back-stage arm-twisting or political blackmail would have done any better. It is just that gadgetry is unfamiliar to Old World diplomats and is an easy target for blame.

Unfortunately, gadgetry is also unfamiliar to many of those entrusted with the for-mation of higher opinion and the direction of academic study in the U.S., and loses thereby the kind of intellectual support and scrutiny it deserves if it is to produce its promised benefits in the changed circumstances of today. I have already cited one fail-ure of Max Lerner; let me cite another and then leave him be. In positively the worst chapter of *America as a Civilization,* that on architecture and design, he claims that the U.S. has failed to produce a great domestic architecture, because

> Great architecture is based on belief. Americans have not yet developed a way of domestic life sharply enough differentiated so that a system of belief can be built on it, and in turn give rise to a distinctive architecture. But they do believe in their system of technology. To put it differently, Americans have had greater success with the arts of consumption and comfortable living than with the problem of their life purposes. Wherever they have built structures connected with production . . . there has been a sureness about them absent from the recent fumblings with domestic architecture.

There, if ever, was a man with his finger on the Go button but didn't know it. Even at the time he was writing (1956–57) the under-window air-conditioner and the under-sink waste-disposer had differentiated U.S. domestic architecture from all preceding domestic architectures and introduced new freedoms in design that the pioneer Mod-ern architects never enjoyed, while the consequences have more to say about the life-purposes of most Americans than all the University humanities programmes joined end-to-end. Americans believe in technology and that is where to look for the greatness of their domestic architecture—as every envious housewife of Europe, Asia and South America could tell you. In the process, the structure of the U.S. house becomes little more than an undifferentiated shell within which the gizmos can do their work, and its external form acquires a slightly improvised quality, an indecisive shape. But this is not necessarily to be brushed off as fumbling—it may be necessary experimentation or temporizing until a definitive shape (or some convincing solution of a non-formal kind) emerges to fix the style of the gizmo-residence—experiments like Harry Weese's row-houses in Old Town, Chicago, where the air-conditioners have been built into cupboard-backs that are the least permanent, most easily altered, parts of the structure.

Instances of failures to comprehend the extent and potential of gadget culture are all too easy to multiply, but my concern here is more with the results of this lack of intellectual grip. One outstanding example is the failure to question the present dwindling independence of the gizmo, its increasing reliance upon an infrastructure it could once do without. While the walkie-talkie has cut men free of networks and wiring, the outboard motor persistently grows in sophistication and dependence—it has acquired a dash-mounted control panel and control lines, a steering harness and wheel, external fuel tank and pipe-runs and, occasionally, external electrics as well. As it becomes more integrated with the boat structure at large, it doubtless acquires something of that mystical 'unity' that Old World pundits and New World academics believe to be the essence of 'a good design,' but as it passes out of the capabilities of the back-porch technologist and into the hands of the skilled shipwright, its social usefulness is severely qualified. Again, while Dr. Land's Polaroid camera is finally extricating photography from the Victorian impedimenta that has lumbered it since the time of Daguerre, Detroit is producing increasingly limp-wristed automobiles that find it harder and harder to function away from the smooth concrete of the freeway. I don't wish to sound like William Buckley calling for a return to the hairy virtues of the frontier at a time when increasing affluence and improved social techniques make more expensive and interdependent solutions possible, but there are one or two counts on which these present developments might be held up for closer examination.

WILDERNESS IN SEARCH OF GIZMOS

One such count is foreign aid: many of the development countries, especially in Africa, are in a condition sufficiently analogous to that of the West in the early Sears Roebuck epoch, for American experience to have directly useful relevance. Instead, such countries find themselves being bullied into sinking aid funds in massive infrastructure of a kind the U.S. got along without for several generations, whereas small sophisticated devices that can work without much capital investment under them might produce better immediate results and leave the ground free for even more sophisticated developments in these countries later on. Many Africans are disappointed and suspicious about this U.S. attitude which they regard as the extension of Anglo-French colonialism by other means. In particular they suspect that the aim is to create road surfaces on which the current Detroit product will look less ridiculous than it does on the dirt roads over which Soviet and East German vehicles can bump along regardless, and the other thing they suspect is that the money is being directed into heavy investment in order to keep it out of consumer goods industries that might compete directly with the U.S. One African I know rolled it all up neatly into a big ball of dung by saying 'If the money was ours to spend without Washington's "advice" we would build a factory to manufacture the Japanese Toyota, which retains all the virtues which the Jeep has lost.'

The Jeep makers could doubtless rebut this statement till they were blue in the face, but the fact remains that the Jeep image has lost its ruggedness, has ceased to hold the reputation of a pioneer (and not only in Africa, to judge from the number of Toyotas one seems to see in the mountain states of the U.S.). And there are also some hesitancies, among those who administer or influence aid, that make them un-willing to introduce the independent U.S. gizmo in undeveloped lands; chiefly, a certain squeamishness about introducing familiar brand-names into territories where they might be regarded as dollar imperialism. There is, for instance, a distinct visual and cultural shock in suddenly coming on a Coca Cola dispenser in Latin America or the Arab States: it is apt to look like a visitor from Mars even in the more rural or desert parts of the USA. It has an almost surreal independence of its rough surroundings as it sits snug in its stylists' chrome and enamel, compact, self-contained—an alien. To many sensitive souls it is an offense that they would rather not see perpetrated; and it also implies a criticism of its surroundings.

For whatever unpleasant capitalist habits of mind it may exemplify, it always, in such surroundings, guarantees a higher level of hygiene and technique than the native culture affords. Coke is not a product that can be dispensed through a system of hollow reeds and dried gourds supported in a structure made of adobe blocks, any more than there was ever a wood-burning outboard motor. It imports into surroundings that are—for worse or better—less highly-developed, a standard of technical performance that the existing culture of those surroundings could no more support unaided than could the Arkansas territory when it was first purchased. Unfortunately, much of what has just been said is equally true of Coke machines that stand in some of America's older cities, and this brings up another point about the present crisis of the gizmo that is worth discussing here.

THE CITY AS PRE-GIZMOS ARCHAEOLOGY North America's cities of pre-industrial foundation—Montreal, Boston, New York, Philadelphia through to New Orleans—could be regarded as the archaeological remains of a culture that ought to have died when the gizmos came in. They represent the kind of enormously massive infrastructural deposits that are left behind by handicraft civilizations, for (in the absence of rapid communications and compact artificial power-sources) the only way to get anything even half-way clever done was to pile men up in vast unhygienic heaps (and anyone who has seen the recently published sootfall statistics for East side Manhattan will know that they are still unhygienic today). On such man-warrens were built the only concepts of civilization that we know, but this does not mean that alternative structures of civilization are not possible, and on this basis the culture of the gizmo, with its accompanying catalogue and distribution network, will bear looking into.

And it is being looked into, at this very moment, by every egg-head who claims a 'discriminating attitude toward the mass media.' In, say, Chicago, he consults the catalogue (radio programmes in the *Daily News*) presses the Go button of his gizmo (AM/FM transistor portable) and connects himself to the distribution net (WFMT your fine art program) for the 'Well-Tempered Clavier.' The distributive civilization of gizmo culture is here already—and if that does not sound a very original observation thirty years after Frank Lloyd Wright's injunction to 'Watch the little gas station' let me re-phrase his accompanying deduction that cities are outmoded in a different key. If the nation is to continue defining its purpose as the pursuit of rural happiness, and if its population is to continue expanding at the present rate, then it may soon become necessary to re-suburbanize existing urban sites and to reduce them to quasi-rural population densities. You have only to go up to the Cloisters or Fort Tryon and look around you, to realize that Manhattan Island would be the most paradisal of American Gardens if only they would get New York off it. So I exaggerate? But not very much; there are many semi-urban areas—the centre of Denver, Colorado, for instance—that could still be rearranged to both their immediate and future advantage provided they do not get buried any deeper than at present, in old-fashioned urban infrastructure. The future, at a modest guess, is going to require a much more flexible distribution of American citizens on the ground, and this is going to be much easier to effect if they can pick up their culture and ride than if they are pinned to the ground by vast masses of Lincoln Centre style masonry.

The traditional American wooden house has always sat lightly on its terrain—a smart hurricane or runaway Mack truck will remove it neatly, leaving just 12 posts and 2 pipes sticking out of the lawn. This potentiality seems to trouble architects to the bottoms of their monumental souls, but it has always fascinated U.S. technologues, from Bucky Fuller's Dymaxion houses to the Clark Cortez campers that suddenly seem to be the queens of the American road. Indeed, a self-propelled residential gizmo seems to be a kind of ultimate in the present state of U.S. culture. The Clark's running gear is a hot-rodder compilation of proprietary catalogue components, and once tanked up and its larder stocked it is independent of all infrastructures for considerable periods of time—it need not deposit sewage or waste every time it comes to an overnight halt, so that when it moves off again the next morning, and the grass that was pressed down by its wheels has recovered its normal habit, that piece of the face of America remains as unchanged as if four persons and a package of sophisticated technology had never been there. A piece of the American wilderness had been, briefly, a piece of the American Paradise-garden, and could then return to wild.

NAME IT, THEN WE'LL KNOW WHAT IT IS No doubt this vision of a gas-powered pastorale, a great nation pursuing rural happiness down the highway, is oversimplified, but observe that it has at its heart a discrete and factual object. The Cortez exists already and can be bought ex-catalogue and increasing numbers of Americans will buy them because the most fundamental American response to dreams is to purchase a piece of equipment to make them come true. And dreams aside, the facts about the Cortez are that its residential performance is considerably superior to that of the handsome Jane Jacobs-type brownstone in which I am writing these words, and its mobility is far superior to that of even the most sophisticated trailers because it is just one single compact unit running on only four wheels. For design people at the Aspen Conference this year to respond to the Clark Cortez only with complaints about its colour-scheme or 'It's an ugly brute,' seems a pitifully inadequate response to what may be one of the most portentous events in the history of the North American continent.

Maybe portentous, or maybe not—but in the absence of a general theory of the gizmo by which to evaluate it, we do not know. The number of breaks in the wall of academic ignorance mentioned earlier has been small indeed, even in the twenty years or so since Sigfried Giedion first tickled the topic in *Mechanization Takes Command.* The subject still lacks a radical theorist who will range freely over departmental barriers and disciplinary interfaces and come back with a comprehensive historical account of the rise of portable gadgetry, and deduce from it some informed projections of the good or evil future it affords.

Perhaps his first task might be to think of a better name for his topic than 'Gizmology,' but it may be difficult. The original impetus to write this article came from the impact of a single very precise and concrete image—a man carrying a portable welding plant across the Utah salt-flats with one hand—and the impact of this image was extremely specific. Not 'This man is carrying a portable gadget of typically U.S. format,' but 'This man is carrying a welding plant.' The whole gizmo bit revolves around such unique and discrete objects, named after the specific functions they serve, and this indeed is the prime utility of the whole approach: whatever you want to do, the precise gadget is in the catalogue. But because the whole bit is made up of these genuinely independent parts, each as private and aloof as the Coke dispenser in the Casbah, it remains extremely difficult to generalize about them, even to find them a generic name which will, after they have been a hundred years in the field, acknowledge their nationwide importance on the changed face of America.

Aviary, London Zoological Gardens

Collapsed goal-posts among the trees—this, undoubtedly, is the first impression of the North Aviary from Primrose Hill, and equally undoubtedly it is a very belated contribution to the Arcadian tradition in British architecture. But, within that tradition, it does not belong to the gimcrack wing that gave us so many fake ruins and other collapsed objects among trees; rather, it belongs to the tough-minded stream whose triumphs are the palm stove at Kew Gardens, or Paxton's Victoria Regia house at Chatsworth.

In common with these great temples of acquisitive botany, the aviary is a walk-through exhibition-environment. This is not a total innovation at Regent's Park Zoo, because one is also permitted to share the same physical space as the humming-birds, for instance. But to build on this scale and in the open is a very different problem from the creation of the small, totally artificial environment in which the humming-birds enjoy a manufactured climate secured by double-doored light-trap entrances. In the North Aviary the problem was more that of taming a piece of the existing topography and covering it with an enclosure high enough and broad enough for large birds to fly convincingly—and yet keep the public close enough to avoid the 'Whipsnade effect' of sheer

Originally appeared in *The Architectural Review* 138 (September 1965): 186.

distance and natural surroundings making the exhibits invisible. With very little ingenuity, the form and levels of the present site would probably have made for better-than-
average visibility even with an enclosure that permitted observation only from the outside. The creation of an internal observation route, by means as complex as a dog-leg
bridge without intermediate supports, therefore proposes a significant improvement
over outside viewing—and if the design failed to deliver this, then it would fail as architecture however handsome the covering structure. But quite obviously (though not so
obviously that one does not have to explain it, alas) the bridge offers a bird's-eye-type
view of the cliff-face that no rearrangement of the solid topography could afford, except
by making an equally high cliff directly opposite, and cliff-nesting birds do not nest on
the sides of trenches. The other views, of birds washing and wading in the cascades
for instance, are supernumerary benefits by comparison, though their sum-total is a
substantial additional justification for the bridge.

Some architectural idealists have complained that the bridge is too thick, especially
at its springings from the cliff, and have cited the thin-slab effect of the famous spiral
ramps of the penguin pool in justification. In rebuttal (because this is a very trivial objection) one must point out that both the span and the loading here are of a totally
different order, and that the aesthetic neatness of Lubetkin's ramps had to be bought
at the cost of making their springings almost solid reinforcing-rod with barely enough
concrete to cover. In any case, the user of the bridge does not see its supporting mus-
culature, only a flat ribbon of footpath zig-zagging off into space and protected by handrails and balustrades of no more than domestic strength. It all looks more perilous
than it really is, and has the psychological effect of putting the visitor on what might be
called an even footing with the birds—up in the air, out of contact with the earth's
surface.

Now, from the point of view of critical evaluation, the most striking aspect of the
aviary is that these manipulations of the landscape are not only more crucial to the
proper functioning of the building than is the visible building above ground, but at the
same time they have only the most marginal effect in determining the form of the
'building,' i.e., the covering cage. This is not to say that there were no determining factors at all: the size of the mesh of the netting was effectively settled by the requirement of keeping the right birds in and the wrong birds out with the minimum weight of
metal. There were undoubtedly site-factors that constrained the design, notably the
problem of footings and where to put them. Yet, given all this, a great variety of other
possible structures could have sheltered this rockwork and this bridge; nothing inherent in the programme called for the devising of an experimental *tensistruttura*—
though it is possible that the awkwardness of the site might have constrained a more
conventional design to employ some unpleasantly massive structural members.

Even the present structure is too massive to please the eyes of some people, apparently—which shows, chiefly, how much our common visual approach to tensile
structures still suffers from ignorance and idealism. The stresses in structural mem-

bers loaded at an angle to their axes are of a quite different order to those transmitted vertically along the axes of the columns and piers of conventional rectangular architecture. The ability of astonishingly thin cables to handle these very high loadings in tension tends to give us false hopes of the possible slenderness-ratio of the compressive members that have to absorb, at sundry cock-eyed angles, the accumulated consequences of the cables' tensile magic. Not only this, but stiffness too is a problem in long unbraced struts. In the only previous British structure even remotely comparable to the aviary—Powell and Moya's South Bank Skylon of 1951—the difference between the architects' original idealised concept of feathery lattices in compression, and the brute struts that finally got built, almost unhinged the design visually.

The aviary is one of the few large tensile structures to date in which the original design has not been coarsened in this way. Greater structural sophistication, greater structural realism, and the integration of a crack-hot engineer into the design team from a very early stage, produced a design in which the proportions of the parts are hardly altered from the original model-studies—the diameter of the sheer legs has been slightly increased for the sake of stiffness; that is all.

But, if complaints of overweight structure can be dismissed as idealistic nonsense, some of the objections to under-done detailing are less easily disposed of. While the management of the ends, joints and connections of the main metallic structure seems admirable and convincing, the tailoring of the joints and attachments of the fine-structure of the mesh seems less than housewifely, even when various technical difficulties have been allowed for (it is worth remembering that these problems were not referred to in the early model studies and have, one suspects, been solved *ad hoc*). Again, the failure to introduce optical corrections to the heights of the balustrades produces some careless-looking corner situations where the bridge changes direction—one balustrade up, the other down. And much of the landscaping—notoriously the sculptures for nesting-boxes—lacks the authority of the structure of the bridge and cage.

No doubt this can be altered, and will have to be when more is known about the nesting preferences of the birds; but the failure to detail-out the relationship of mesh to structure in a more convincing manner will be staring us in the face for some time to come, and while it is easy enough to forgive these small failures for the sake of the success of the grand design, they may yet prove to be the difference between a great building of the twentieth century and a major building of the nineteen-sixties.

22

Unlovable at Any Speed

The glow of self-approval was tarnished from the start. Mind you, I still reckon that to acquire so complex a psychosomatic discipline as car driving and pass the test first time at my state of bearded middle-age is not bad at all. But I remain convinced that the examiner had taken leave of his senses: I wouldn't have passed me on the strength of that performance. In fact I was already rehearsing a 'Sorry to have wasted your time, sir' type speech when he said 'Well, that's it. You've passed.'

It's not London traffic that takes the shine off being a driver, either. After five years of cycling I had no illusions left about that. No, it's the damned human race, as usual, and their carryings-on. For a start, being a driver, like wearing a beard, identifies you with a pretty dubious lot of characters. (No, it's not masochism. I did it for a woman both times; beard *and* driving.) Becoming a driver is to join a community (to use a more sympathetic word than it deserves) and a culture (a what?) whose public face has little to commend it.

A bare month after I passed, up came the Motor Show: the Christmas, Easter, Epiphany and Annunciation of the aforementioned community and culture all rolled

---

Originally appeared in *The Architects' Journal* 144 (21 December 1966): 1527–1529.

into one. The Motor Show concentrates the auto-addicts into one big global mass, filters out ordinary human beings, but adds all the professional pushers from Coventry and Birmingham and Dagenham who pander to their addiction. And it adds up to an ugly mob.

To rub in the point, Barry 'Modeste' Humphreys celebrated the occasion by doing (on 'The late show') his impression of that ultimate pusher, the motoring journalist—sheep-skinned, deer-stalkered, piped, handlebar moustached, fuelled by hand-out Scotch and pro lunches and a deep hatred for Barbara Castle.

I hope nobody thought this performance exaggerated—the implication of total corruption ('This is the best car the company has ever made, like all their cars—and I should know, they've given me enough of them') should have given at least two recognisable auto-pundits grounds to sue for libel.

Not that this would worry me too much in itself—we all have a democratic right to go to hell by our own preferred routes. But suppose we want a better route to somewhere other than hell—Hull or Halifax, for instance? Who'd want to build a motorway if it meant pandering to this lot? If the motor trade can't find some new front men, I wouldn't blame B. Castle if she gave up even mending existing roads. That particular relationship got off to a dim start anyhow—remember all that stuff about 'She hasn't even got a driving licence?' She hasn't got a master-mariner's ticket either, nor a commercial pilot's ticket. She's not a paid-up member of ASLEF, nor the TGWU . . . but only the motoring community was bumptious enough to suppose that non-membership of its special interest debarred her from the whole job.

And turn off that smug smile, you architects. You're not much better. The news that Banham is now qualified to perambulate the tarmac in a tin box produces an absolutely standard response from all architects, among them, for instance, a leading light of the swinging, humus-eating Charlotte Street scene, not to mention the most conspicuous non-member of the RIBA, and an equally distinguished research-wallah. It goes thus: 'But you've spoiled everything by learning to drive. People who rave on about technology are supposed to know nothing about it.'

Not only does Ministry of Transport mean Ministry of Motoring, apparently, but technology equals being able to drive a car. I didn't spoil everything by having sweated out a full five-year engineering apprenticeship, adorned with such feats as being, for three days, the only man in England who understood the Stromberg carburettor (then the other handbook arrived, and my plan to hold the war-effort to ransom had to be abandoned). But driving a car makes me a technologist.

Admittedly, for lots of the little people of this world, like classical scholars and hereditary peers, driving a car is their only toehold in technology. But architects, with their far ranging interests and well balanced training, have a practical experience of technology that covers a wide field comprising absolutely nothing beyond driving a car in most cases. That's *another* of the reasons why architecture is too important to be left to architects.

23

Roadscape with Rusting Rails

'But you can't have got sunburned in Los Angeles,' said this girl in London, 'the place is permanently covered with smog!' Yet there I was, tanned and just back from Los Angeles. And there she was, stuck with a cherished misconception. Los Angeles seems to breed misconceptions, and Europeans seem to need them, as models or exemplars of anticipated urban disasters in their own environments. Thus the MP for Hampstead, opposing a proposed London motorway, is reported to have said that 'one of the reasons for the riots in Watts is that it is cut off from the city by a giant highway.' I voted for Ben Whitaker, and will do so again, but this—at least as reported—is a typical misuse of Los Angeles to forecast the future of London.

The cities may be similar, but not in this respect. London cannot have a rational motorway system without knocking down a large part of its massive and densely built structure. Los Angeles can put in ten-lane freeways and only has to knock down a tiny proportion of its dispersed and flimsy buildings. London motorways, like the railways of the last century, would be gashes through millennial history; by comparison, the Los Angeles freeways are laid across almost open country; their relationship to the adjoin-

---

Originally appeared in *The Listener* 80 (29 August 1968): 267–268.

ing land is utterly unlike that of any motorway pushed through South Hampstead and Camden Town. I concede that highways are part of the trouble with Watts—but it's their absence, not their presence, and the absence of vehicles to use them, that cuts off Watts. It's over two miles from, say, the 'Watts Happening' coffee shop to the Harbor Freeway, the access ramps aren't very convenient when you get there, and far too few of the inhabitants have cars to use the Freeway, anyhow. If they had cars, they might be able to drive the distances involved in getting to more lucrative jobs in other parts of the city, but without those jobs, they can't afford the cars. It's a vicious circle of frustrations that tightens round your own white Anglo-Saxon Protestant heart when the daily lady from Watts who cleans the house where you are staying fails to turn up, and you discover that she has been assaulted at a bus stop in the 4 a.m. darkness. And the only reason she was on a bus stop at that un-Christian hour is that if she didn't catch that particular bus she would miss the only connection that would get her to the house in time to do a day's work. Even when you have admitted that there are other ghettos—Mexican ghettos, Japanese ghettos, old people's ghettos, other Negro ghettos and semi-ghettos—and that, even so, only a very small proportion of the city's generally affluent and mobile population actually suffers ghetto conditions, it is still Watts that dramatises the way in which transportation has played a life-and-death role in the history of Los Angeles.

But don't let haters of the motor-car kid you that Los Angeles was created by the automobile. In historical fact, the whole culture of rampant automobilism has been created in an attempt to make sense of a situation left behind by a quite different form of transportation. Ironically, that form of transportation was precisely what is now being naively proposed as the cure for automotive evils: the electric train. In pre-mechanical days, the scattered settlements of Southern California were days apart by ox-drawn *carreta.* When the first railways were built in the Sixties and Seventies of the last century, daily long-distance commuting began almost immediately. In the same decades the separate communities began to provide themselves with internal street-railway systems. And when electric traction became available in the Nineties, it appeared practical and profitable to weld both kinds of transportation into a single urban and interurban system. Several smart operators perceived the glint of gold in electric railways and the land-values they could improve, but the admitted genius was Henry Edwards Huntington. By the time the two decades of rail-laying, company-floating and commercial in-fighting had finished around 1910, and Huntington had emerged as the acknowledged, if not outright, master of the scene, his Pacific Electric Railroad and its associated companies had created the 'City of Southern California' as he had envisioned it, and laced it with 1,500 miles of track.

Not much of it is left to see: Huntington's fancy palace at San Marino and its library and collections; some crumbling romantic stations, rusting rails down the side of wide motorised avenues and boulevards, place-names like Huntington Beach—and the concept of the unified metropolis of Los Angeles, which is his true monument, for a map of the Pacific Electric at the time of its greatest extension is effectively, in size and shape, the map of greater Los Angeles today. As is usually the case after a commercial splurge of this sort, the Pacific Electric was over-extended, uneconomic, and self-obstructing in many ways. As the inter-urban trains opened up new areas for develop-ment, schedules that had been fast and uninterrupted became clogged with supple-mentary stops and innumerable street-crossings. Some routes were never profitable and, in any case, the newly available mass-produced automobile was more convenient than even the myriad services offered by the Pacific Electric's 'Big Red Cars.' Minor services began to be axed as early as 1924.

But the fantastic thing is that the last route was not closed until *1961.* The idea that Los Angeles casually threw away a priceless transportation asset is nonsense—it went on trying for a very long time, longer than some English cities did with their trams. And Watts, perhaps more than any other place, was a creation and a victim of the Pa-cific Electric: while the Big Red Cars continued to operate, it was an important junction and interchange, it was at the centre of things. After 1961 it was in the middle of no-where. Paradoxically, it might still be saved by a Freeway. One of the next to be built should pretty well pass across Watts from east to west, and will involve the construc-tion of a major intersection. Not only should this bring better connections, possibly by special freeway-flyer buses, but the compensation-moneys for compulsorily acquired property could bring capital into the district if everybody played their cards right.

Such things are being plotted now: freeway engineering is a social technique that Angelenos can understand and even trust. Of course they complain about the Free-ways, about the traffic jams and the smog, but these complaints shouldn't be taken too seriously. Whereas, to my standards, a jam is a situation where traffic is frequently halted, for them it is any situation where speeds drop below about 40 miles per hour. For me driving on the Freeways became almost unalloyed pleasure, because Southern California driving is generally so intelligent and considerate and disciplined. But with this circumspect and tolerant attitude to driving goes an entirely intolerant attitude to any imperfections in the system in which the driving takes place. Simply by working better than most other urban road systems in the world, the Los Angeles Freeways have given Angelenos incredibly high standards of expectation.

I think, also, that some fundamental Angeleno psychology is involved. Anything less than perfection they cannot stand, and this absolute temperament shows most sav-agely in their attitude to smog. Fogs and mists are something that the area had long before the motor-car—the Spaniards called it the 'Bay of Smokes,' and some of that smoke probably came from petroleum products even then, because of the open pits of naturally occurring tar, which have caught fire occasionally even in living memory. What is characteristic about Los Angeles smog now is its brown tint, caused by the decom-position of automotive exhaust and other petroleum wastes, under the action of strong sunlight. It also has a characteristic sweetish, oily smell, and stings the corners of the eyes. Officially it occurs on 60 days of the year, on average, but my own counts come out nearer an average of two days a month: this may depend where the count is taken, and what you mean by smog. It can look remarkably like old-world sea mist, or just a rather pretty cold-tea-coloured overcast. In general I remain unimpressed by the air-pollution in Los Angeles; my private test is the survival of white garments, and I find that a shirt that looks grubby in London by 3 p.m. can be worn in Los Angeles for two days, if the exigencies of bachelor laundry make it necessary.

Anyhow, the Angelenos are very impressed by it, and blame the automobile. Personally, I suspect that gardening may have quite a lot to do with it, but you mustn't knock gardening because green things are natural and good. Nevertheless, the maintenance of domestic and commercial horticulture in this desert climate involves pouring prodigious quantities of mist-producing water on the soil of the Los Angeles basin, and this must have done something to the local climate. But the automobile is man-made, and therefore a suitable scapecart. Perhaps the smog is really an emanation of the collective bad conscience of Angelenos, who have mostly escaped quite recently from the Protestant ethic and hard winters of the Bible-punching Middle West, and who may feel that they don't deserve to have so much fun zooming around in cars in the pleasant sunshine.

Most of them, in fact, are completely devoted to the automotive life, and positively proud of the Freeways. Well they might be. Some of the construction work that has gone into them has the unmistakable stamp of great engineering—plus something else. The great multi-level intersection where the Santa Monica and San Diego Freeways cross, for instance, is convincingly monumental when seen from a conventional, static, external viewpoint. The two highest ramps rise, converge and separate in sweeping curves of perfect symmetry, carried on single rows of slim cylindrical concrete columns. But to drive over those ramps in a high sweeping 60-mile-an-hour trajectory and plunge down to ground level again is a spatial experience of a sort one does not normally associate with monuments of engineering—the nearest thing to flight on four wheels I know.

My favourite motorised experience in Los Angeles, I think, was much less advanced, but historically unique. I used to arrange my day, sometimes, to ensure that I finished it by driving down Wilshire Boulevard in the late afternoon towards the Pacific sunset. Nowadays it must be the only shopping street in the world that one would ever want to drive down for pleasure, but Wilshire Boulevard was, half accidentally, designed for just that. Its originator was a wild socialist and friend of Bernard Shaw—Gaylord Wilshire—who gave his name to the first half mile or so of what was to become a great 16-mile avenue. It was not Wilshire who made it what it is, however, but a real-estate developer named A. W. Ross who—according to well-nourished legend—worked out how far the new motorised shoppers of the Twenties would be ready to drive to the stores, identified the areas where the moneyed ones were settling, consulted the map, and discovered that the coming place for shops would be about the middle stretch of Wilshire Boulevard. Partly at the instigation of downtown interests, most of Wilshire had been zoned for purely residential purposes, and Ross had to argue a case, convincingly and in the teeth of determined opposition, for every single site that he and his clients wanted to make over for commercial uses. So it was never the kind of free-for-all type of commercial development of the normal U.S. main street. From the start, the shops on Ross's 'Miracle Mile' had an aura of status, quality and respectability, and it invests much of the rest of Wilshire Boulevard still.

These stores were built for motorised shoppers in an epoch that still conceived of shops in pre-motorised terms. The parking lots were at the back, and you could enter from the back, and there were display windows on that side—still are. But there were windows on the street front as well, and those fronts gave directly onto a conventional wide sidewalk. So it looks exactly like a shopping street in the conventional sense, except that, unlike most such shopping streets, it is not clogged with parked—wrongly parked—cars.

There are still very good shops; it really is a street that can stand comparison with the great shopping streets of the world. It is also beginning to be held up as a model of a 'linear downtown' to planning students in U.S. architecture schools. This I doubt— to imitate Wilshire Boulevard strikes me as putting the clock back. It seems to be a unique monument to a transitional phase in the rise of planning for the motor-car. Better to leave it so, as the true heart of a city which, in its size, shape and physical equipment, is all one vast transitional monument to the rise of mechanical transport. Los Angeles is a city founded neither on rock nor water, but on wheels, and in Watts, on the Freeway, or Wilshire Boulevard, you know it.

24

History Faculty, Cambridge

It was James Gowan, not Jim Stirling, who explicitly voiced the axiom 'the style for the job' (with its corollary implied: 'a different style for every different job'). So Stirling-baiters who have been poised to savage him for re-using the Stirling *and Gowan* style of the Leicester Engineering Laboratories on the new building for the History Faculty in Cambridge are out of luck. In any case, the History Faculty is a pretty daunting demonstration of how little the details have to do with fixing a style. Conspicuously, the brick and tile surfaces with all those neat gutters and corners and balustrades reappear at Cambridge, so does a large acreage of standardized industrial glazing, and so even do chamfer-corner stair-towers, but the result is an entirely different style of building.

Much of the rhetorical effect ('expressionism' according to Professor Pevsner) of the Engineering Laboratories was due to a very demonstrative separation of the different functional volumes—towers, auditoria, workshops, etc.—and their further

Originally appeared in *The Architectural Review* 144 (November 1968): 329–332.

differentiation by a repertoire of widely contrasting surface treatments—blank brick, smooth glazing, angled glazing, north-light glazing, free-form glazing—each of which tended to be used on only one type of functional volume. The whole complex seemed to be springing apart, with each volume asserting its independence. The History Faculty building, by contrast, is folded back on itself, into a snug and relatively unassertive format, without any very strong projections or major breaks of its silhouette (the stairtowers have a completely different effect from those at Leicester). Also there are, effectively, only two visible surface treatments: the hard red brick or tile, which is largely restricted to the plinth in which the upper part sits, and the standard industrial glazing which surfaces almost 75 per cent of the upper structure above the plinth.

There is, as at Leicester, an alternative kind of glazed surface; where Leicester has the specially designed diagonal north-lighting, Cambridge has a specially-designed giant skylight over the reading room of the Seeley library. But whereas Leicester's north-lights erupt spectacularly all round the perimeter of the workshop area and are a compelling part of the total visual image, Cambridge's skylight is quite difficult to see from outside the building and contributes nothing to its silhouette. It is a crucial part— perhaps the most crucial—of the whole design, it registers strongly in Stirling's widely published isometric drawing of the scheme, yet to see it properly in real life the visitor must retreat almost among the pilotis of the adjoining building by Casson and Conder on Sidgwick Avenue. Only from there can you appreciate its stepped-pyramid form, uncommonly like a slice out of the greenhouse of some monumental Victorian botanic garden.

This glazed pyramid has been the other great hope of the Stirling-baiters, and again they appear to be out of luck. For months now, stories of the monstrous solar heat gain through all that glass have been assiduously circulated by that persistent group who, still smarting from their defeat when Leicester was shown to be as functional as it was spectacular, were assured that this time they really had Big Jim hooked on a charge of indictable formalism. This time it would stick, because the stories of sweltering temperatures in the reading room that were going round the lunch-tables of the Architectural Association were all perfectly true and based on personal observation . . . except that the observers had apparently failed to note (or to mention) that the heating throughout the building was being run full blast at the time to help dry out the structure.

Admittedly, the view of the thermal environment put forward by the architect and the servicing consultants in documents circulated to the press is not very inviting—peak temperatures reaching 90 deg F under the most extreme conditions, and the ventilating system only able to trim 10 deg F off that figure in the main reading space. But it is difficult to know when or how often such extreme conditions will ever be reached in the climate of Cambridge. My own personal observation is as follows: on an unannounced visit in mid-August, on a day of continuous sunshine and very little breeze, at 2.15 p.m. and with outside shade temperatures of 74 deg–77 deg F and no mechanical ventilators working. . . . I found the interior warm, but not so much so that it was necessary to remove my jacket. If it had been any hotter I would not be writing this article.

Since shade temperatures in Cambridge hardly ever hit even the seventies in term time, and the ventilating plant is there for use when they do, the glass pyramid must be accounted a reasonable, responsible environmental device, not a formalist extravagance. It is, of course, far from being the simple green-house lean-to that many people seem to imagine; instead, it is a properly sophisticated glazed roof, fulfilling—mechanically and visually—a set of simple rules laid down in 1914 and studiously ignored by the architectural profession ever since.

Firstly, it is a widely separated double skin; the inner skin being of obscured glass (in fact, a built-up sandwich, as was the obscured glass at Leicester) to prevent glare and to give an even, shadowless general light throughout the reading area. The small part of the lower skin, which has been glazed clear to show the ventilating plant in the top of the pyramid, does admit a triangle of unrestrained sunlight, but only on a few days around midsummer, and this does not fall into the main reading area.

Secondly, the air-space between the two skins is environmentally active because it is, in general terms, controllable; in winter with all the louvres in the vertical steps of the pyramid closed, the trapped air can be held fairly still as an insulating blanket to reduce heat-loss. In summer, with all the louvres open, external wind-pressure can combine with internal stack-effects to sweep out heated air from under the upper layer of glass. It should be noted here that, although the three ventilating fans are housed in the truss-space between the upper and lower skins of glass, they do not serve to move air through that space. Rather, they serve to augment stack-effects in the upper part of the main library space itself, extracting foul air from the apex of the pyramid and exhausting it direct to atmosphere through the louvres in the penultimate step of the pyramid.

Thirdly, general artificial lighting comes from twinned strips of fluorescent tubes flanking the main truss members within the roof-space, but no attempt has been made to introduce radiant heating from between the two skins of glass; instead, artificial heating is supplied by convectors all around the base of the pyramid, providing a blanket of warm air to travel up under the obscured glass, and thus prevent currents of chilled air descending on the necks of readers below.

Given the strip lighting, the main outlines of the structure within the glazed roof-space will always be visible, come sun or come darkness, to any reader in the space below who cares to look up at it. Whether or not this has any assessable psychological value is difficult to assess (my own ideas seem to be at variance with those of the architect, as will appear later), but it makes this the least boring luminous ceiling in the whole of recent architecture. It is both explicit, and inherently interesting, and has needed no additions to style it up or compensate for visual deficiencies. Even a complete layman with little knowledge of either mechanics or architecture (a professor of Modern History, say) would be able to see (and sometimes hear) the roof going about its business of mediating between inner and outer environments, and understand what was going on.

With the pattern of shadows from the structure above marching across the obscured glass as the day proceeds (an astute reader with Boy Scout training would be able to tell the time by them presumably) and fading into the night pattern of parallel lines of fluorescent light, it will present a continuously interesting overhead spectacle . . . only *interesting* is an inadequate word for this spectacular roof. It is absorbing, not only for its inherent visual qualities, but also because those qualities derive from Stirling having followed the precepts laid down by Paul Scheerbart in *Glasarchitektur* over half a century ago.

I am quite certain that Stirling did not follow them knowingly, because I know he has never read them. Scheerbart derived them from common-sense, observation and imagination; so did Stirling. Nevertheless, it is fascinating for an historian like myself to see that when Scheerbart's precepts about the use of a diffusing inner layer, the use of an insulating blanket of air between the two skins, the placing of light sources between the skins (but not heaters) and all the rest of it, the result is quite as marvellous as he prophesied it would be in 1914. I have not yet seen the History Faculty from outside after dark so I don't know if it fulfils the Scheerbartian role of *ein ganz selbstandig Illuminationskörper* (Leicester fulfils it magnificently, of course, so one has hopes) but in one way the interior goes right against Scheerbart's ideas, and the approved orthodoxies of illuminating practice as well. Wherever light is required under opaque, not glazed, ceilings, it comes from naked fluorescent tubes, without shades or diffusers, mounted on surfaces painted hard gloss white. As described, it sounds awful; as experienced it is never troublesome (light for reading will be supplied locally by fittings on the desks) and lends a certain sparkle to distant views through the bookstacks, etc.

At least, that is how it appears in the main reading room. In the smaller seminar rooms and offices the situation may prove different. There are bound to be complaints about the lighting because that is a fashionable thing to complain about, but even when allowance for human cussedness and academic conservatism has been made, it seems possible that detail modifications will have to be made in some of the rooms because of localized patches of glare or shadow. Already, in some of the smaller rooms on the west face of the building and in corridor spaces on the top floor, there have had to be remedial alterations to cope with thermal problems (extra ventilation, venetian blinds, etc.).

However, there are some persistent minor doubts about the environmental conditions in the smaller spaces which stem less from the basic design of the building (it should be remembered that its orientation had to be turned through ninety degrees after design was completed, through no fault of the architect) than from the detail provisions made for controlling heat and light, and the level of performance demanded of the occupants. The environmental controls provided are hot-water convectors in the upstand beam on the edge of the floor-slab, ventilating louvres in the patent glazing, and venetian blinds hung in the space between the glazing and the upstand. Now, with the laudable intention of preventing direct draughts, the louvres are placed so that they are masked by the upstand, and their control handles are therefore a little difficult to reach. But they are also masked by the venetian blinds when these are in the down position (which they normally will be on days hot enough to require adjustments to the louvres) and it is quite easy to get the control handles fouled up in the slats of the blind.

Situations like this are governed by Murphy's Law (also known as Finagle's Law) which predicts the probability of mechanical disaster by the formula: If anything *can* happen, it will. Such probabilities are high anyhow, but in this case they are likely to be raised by the fact that most of the occupants of the building will be humanities-oriented, and therefore likely to fall below the national average in mechanical literacy and competence. Controls that get fouled up through mismanagement by the occupants will tend to be left in that condition while the occupants take verbal revenge on the architects. If revenge is to be taken anywhere, it should be on the University Grants Committee as the agents of a policy of allocating building budgets too skimpy to permit decent environmental installations, which in this case would be either full automation of the environment, or controls sophisticated enough to provide idiot-proof local manipulation. As it turns out, the excellent basic environment provided by Stirling and his consultants will require some skill and intelligence for its proper employment throughout the building. Not only in the smaller rooms, but in the large volume of the reading-room as well, the environment requires conscious manipulation by a responsible human being. The control-console for heating, lighting and ventilating is incorporated in the island desk which is also the command post from which an assistant librarian supervises the library and its contents, so that the whole life and human situation of the library falls under the hand of a single person—let us hope that the library gets the kind of captaincy (or stage direction?) it deserves.

It may seem eccentric to have begun thus, with the environmental mechanics, in discussing a building in a context where problems of style and cultural values are usually taken to be pre-eminent; but the peculiar relationship of the History Faculty building to the Cambridge scene can only be tackled in this way, to my opinion. Let me explain at once that my opinion is that of a persistent user of both libraries and seminar rooms, with fairly well-developed professional reflexes, especially where libraries are concerned.

What makes a library a good place to work in, and thus an effective contributor to the cultural values of the university of which it is a member, is complex, and ultimately engages almost every known aspect of architecture. That engagement begins with the creation of a satisfactory life-support system of heat, light and ventilation, such as has been discussed above (this is obvious, yet there are too many libraries that fail even at this physiological level, and every scholar has his private black-list). But even in terms of physical comfort the matter is a good deal more subtle, and extends well beyond what mechanical services can provide.

Thus, the business of working with books is a primarily optical affair, but the provision of adequate light of the right colour and quality does not in itself give adequate service of this function. It is physically impossible to keep one's eyes on the print for more than a certain period of time (varying with one's own psychosomatic make-up and the nature of what is being read) and what is seen when the eyes are lifted is crucial. Not only must the length of focus change, but what is seen in long focus must possess certain qualities too. As far as I can make out from my own experience, what is seen must be totally different from what is on the desk in front of the reader. It might be the view out of a window into the campus or city beyond, or it might be an architectural interior striking enough to hold the interest of the viewer—not an endless perspective of bookstacks and eight-foot high suspended ceiling, but something like the hand-crafted space-frames of Mackintosh's library at the Glasgow art-school, or the laughable domes of the Bibliothèque Nationale.

The History Faculty does not provide external views from its reading room that can be actively enjoyed—and this is not intended as a value judgment on other buildings in the Sidgwick Avenue development; simply that it is not possible to see much, even from the reading desk in the long window beyond the bookstacks. The interior views, on the other hand, are long enough to provide a real change of focus, have architectural interest in their own right, and also offer a change of subject matter, since anyone looking up from his books at the galleried cliff of acoustically slotted white wall will catch glimpses of non-readers proceeding to and from class-rooms and studies at the various levels.

Such reminders of alternative patterns of activity seem to be a more than visual relief, but in providing them, the building appears to be running counter to the architect's uttered intentions. In conversation, Stirling speaks of the business of reading as if it were an intensive process from which the reader ought not to be distracted, and therefore explains the tall upstand parapets of the access galleries as being high enough to prevent the heads of persons in the corridor being seen from the reading room below, and those parts of the parapet that have been raked back to a narrow cill at the top as providing psychologically valuable views down into the reading room (thus giving a sense of unity between library and class-room activities). But it seems to me that an even greater psychological value resides in the views *out* of the reading room into the life of the galleries, especially where the parapet is cut down to knee-height, as it is at two points at each of the lower levels. It is difficult not to feel that in matters like this Stirling is proceeding on sound human instincts that undermine the functionalist rationalizations he likes to produce as *post facto* justifications of his designs. As usual, the disparity between architect's rationalizations and user's observations does nothing to invalidate the quality of Stirling's design—as any reader will agree as he straightens up from his books, stretches his shoulders and raises his eyes either to the spectacle of donnish heads bobbing along above the parapets, or to the three ventilating fans, painted in strong farm-tractor primary colours, nestling like newly landed agricultural space-satellites in the peak of the roof.

The exterior offers nothing so spectacular to the view. The projecting stair-towers and the end walls are explicit about vertical circulation and sectional organization, but can hardly be said to dramatize these. This ineloquence becomes extreme in the patent glazing that covers most of the exterior and remains, in light or shade, curiously and craftily obtuse. It presents a glass surface that avoids doing any of the things that glass is supposed to do in Modern Movement mythology—it is not glamorous or fabulous, reflects nothing of interest and reveals remarkably little of the interior functioning of the building. It presents itself to the view simply as an inexpensive way of keeping the weather out; one that might—but for the fact that there are advantages to be gained from admitting daylight to the interior—equally well have been corrugated asbestos.

To get away with this architecture of dumb insolence in Cambridge requires more than just derring-do; it requires the self-confidence that comes from knowing what you are about, and it implies an attitude. Self-confidence first: that patent glazing is not neutral or neat. The temptation to make it so (as proof that you are a gentleman as well as an architect) would have overwhelmed some architects confronted with Cambridge, but Stirling has permitted roughnesses, irregularities, misalignments. This is in no way to disparage him or the glazing system, which is meant to be assembled thus, and has the necessary degrees of tolerance to even out local inaccuracies. To have assembled it more neatly and with greater nicety of alignment would have been, and would have looked, merely affected—like most other modern architecture in Cambridge.

The attitude which seems to be implied in this self-confidence is that Cambridge is a university, rather than the shrine of a cult. All the other modern buildings in Cambridge—even the very good ones, like Harvey Court—seem somewhat pre-occupied with trying to prove themselves scholarly adepts at the rituals of the cult, like collegiate planning, historical erudition, urbanity, and so forth. They come on like provincials earnestly trying to pass as long-established dons, and betray themselves by accents and mannerisms that don't ring true. By proceeding as if the cult did not exist, and therefore not having to prove anything about it, the History Faculty building leaves itself with no problems of accent or manner. Style and detailing derive intrinsically from the building itself, not extrinsically from some more or less accurate apprehension of contingent cultural factors.

The building is indifferent to the architecture that surrounds it and therefore appears to mock it, but is not indifferent to Cambridge, nor does it mock it, as a university. The commission did not arise from some self-advertising endowment nor an attempt to capitalize the name of an ageing statesman, but from the manifest needs of history teaching. The design was chosen from a very limited competition whose entries were closely scrutinized by men deeply involved in running the university and teaching in it—the Sidgwick Avenue Committee and the two appointed members from the History Board, Geoffrey Elton and M. I. Finley.

These last two stood by the design, and the architect, through thick and thin and the barbed onslaughts of Hugh Plommer. They stood by it on functional grounds; more strikingly, they stood by it on aesthetic grounds as well (Finley: 'I do not want to debate the aesthetics of the building either; I like it.') Anybody who wishes to maintain that this is the wrong kind of building for Cambridge must face the fact that this is the kind of building the History Faculty wanted badly enough to defend it in the Senate, and that they clearly were not in the market for either a pseudo-jewel-casket like the Beinecke Library at Yale, nor a joke fortification like the new library at Trinity College, Dublin. Unlike those two august institutions they are not lumbered with illuminated missals and humanistic manuscripts. The History Faculty just has a lot of undergraduates and a lot of current literature and a fairly numerous teaching staff, and commissioned a building which could bring all these neatly and effectively together.

Clients and architects knew what they were about, and therefore had the confidence to do what they had to do without bravado or false humility (both of which are endemic in buildings actually under construction in Cambridge at present). The result, respectful to Cambridge at the more fundamental level of what Cambridge actually does, presents a startling critique of buildings that have tried to be respectful to Cambridge at the superficial level of what it looks like—the more startling in that no critique appears to be intended. The mystique of 'the Cambridge tradition' is neither sent up nor put down. It is not even treated with the contempt it probably deserves; it is almost as if architect and clients had failed to observe its existence because they were too involved with the living body of Cambridge to notice the coffins into which other architects have tried to cram it. The sad thing is that Cambridge opinion will eventually accept it as part of 'the Cambridge tradition' and then no one will have the guts to pull it down when the useful life for which it was designed has come to an end.

The Wilderness Years
of Frank Lloyd Wright

'Let us now praise famous men in chronological order.' Really, the keeping of cen-
tenaries is among the dottier rituals of Western culture. The purely numerical magic of
10×10 drives us to comb the works of famous artists, politicians, architects, plain-
tively inquiring: 'What survives of his achievement 100 years later?' Since this is a
purely rhetorical question, deserving the answer 'Who cares?', the centenary orator
hurries to ward off this vulgar riposte by inventing achievements that had not been noticed before—for Frank Lloyd Wright, to cite the case in point, the alleged invention
of 'indeterminacy,' 'cluster' and 'territoriality.'[1]

So why am I bothering to play the centenary game? Because I think there are some
things that did, factually, happen in Wright's career but which have eluded historical
understanding and critical attention; and they have centennial connections that justify
their re-examination 100 years after his birth. For me, there is no question of what survives of Wright's achievement. Nearly all of it does, looking better than ever. But there
was an awkward passage in the chronological middle of his career that we know very
little about. In that architecturally waste place, two major themes of American history

Originally appeared in *RIBA Journal* 76 (December 1969): 512–518.

intersected with Wright's career and changed it, I believe, in ways we may have failed to comprehend. And both these themes were the same age as Wright himself.

One was the completion of the transcontinental railway. The driving of the golden spike into the ceremonial tie of laurel wood at Promontory, Utah, on 10 May 1869, a month before Wright was born, had an obvious symbolic quality that is not to be mocked. With the barrier of mountain and desert breached, the United States were now physically, as well as legally, united. The world's most expansive single-language, single-landmass culture had taken the most crucial step toward becoming a communicative unity, in which all parts were in effective contact. And over nearly two thirds of that landmass, from the Mississippi westward, this culture was a wilderness that had virtually no local history before the railroad. (We ramble on nowadays about America's post-industrial culture, but most of the U.S. had no pre-industrial culture of consequence at all.)

It was an unprecedented development in the history of the human race, and Wright was born into it as his native environment. He grew up in a continent in which even the wildest and most remote areas were becoming accessible within two or three days from his native middle west, accessible in ways they could not have been to the Founding Fathers less than a century before, nor even to Walt Whitman a generation before. That 'wilderness of unopened life'[2] discerned by Whitman in his own mind, and in a semi-legendary west that he had not seen, was physically accessible to Wright.

The fact that it hasn't turned out as Whitman (or Wright) hoped—'Where is the Mississippi panorama/And the girl who played the piano?/Where are you, Walt?/The Open Road goes to the used car lot'[3]—all that much-publicised failure of the American Dream cannot reduce the historical magnitude of the fact that the accessible physical wilderness gave the dream of the mythical wilderness a power that few national myths have possessed before or since. The man who has never felt the power of that dream, who has not experienced days when he is forced to believe it even against his better judgment, will never understand much of the America that lies west of Bowling Green, Ohio.

That dream, solidly underpinned by universal mobility, is an essential part of the America we know, one of the most crucial factors separating North American culture from that of the old world. Elements of the dream, which is an extension of the arcadian or pastoral vision, came from Europe in the first place, of course, but were soon undergoing powerful local modifications in their transatlantic context. For example, whatever private versions of a pastoral arcadia may have existed in the individual minds that drafted the Declaration of Independence, they possessed one collective version of it so true that they never needed to hold it to be self-evident: that it was possible to maintain a lively and creative culture without cities. European pastoral had existed as an ideal antidote to the real evils of the cities; but in the infant U.S., cities were still of so little consequence compared with the palladian life of the great estates and plantations that pastoral had already begun to change its role as arcadia came physically closer. Thomas Jefferson was prepared to encourage the trend by combating the rise of native manufacturing industries that would reinforce the growth and power of cities.[4] The objective of the young republic would be 'to define its purpose as the pursuit of rural happiness,' as Leo Marx has put it.[5]

The pursuit of that rural happiness was to lead to the postulation of a tamed arcadia, the ideal suburbia that never quite exists anywhere but is always just round the corner. The physical realisation of this 'middle landscape' (Leo Marx again)[6] was to involve two major 19th century phenomena powerful enough to smash a less potent vision—industrialisation and democratisation. In spite of Jefferson's suspicion of 'the mobs of the great cities,' the dream that had been conceived as aristocratic and agrarian touched ground in most of the U.S. as an egalitarian vision based on advanced manufacturing techniques.

PIONEER HOUSEHOLD For architecture, these transformations seem to have been more disturbing than we have commonly acknowledged. In the new states opened up by the transcontinental railroad, dream and technology, plus an aversion to the fixed patterns of social interdependency that immigrants had left behind in Europe, combined to produce a culture based on isolated, atomic, self-sustained family units—the so-called 'pioneer household'—increasingly armed with mechanical aids and less supported by outside social relationships than in any previous communities above the subsistence line.

In the year that saw the birth of Frank Lloyd Wright, the full architectural implications of this situation were weighed up, and the proper conclusion drawn—not by an architect, but by that redoubtable educator and feminist, Catherine Beecher. For years she had been addressing herself to the problems of domestic economy in the new territories and publishing the results in a series of books, each of which pushed her concept of the house itself further into unknown territory. In *The American Woman's Home*[7] of 1869 she produced her final and most radical proposal: a lightweight balloon-frame structure enclosing a core of services.

Such a solution reverses the traditional priorities of farmhouse architecture, concentrating the investment in a sophisticated mechanical core instead of in a massive exterior shell, calling at long range on an advanced industrial technology with which it is connected only by railway, rather than exploiting the available material resources of the ground on which it stands. As envisaged by its inventor, the house was never built; like the ideal wilderness of Walt Whitman, it was part of a neopastoral dream of the good life in the middle landscape. But the circumstances of the real wilderness soon drove other house builders in the same general direction. The American woman's home is the idealised ancestor of every U.S. suburban tract house, lightly built and heavily serviced, a dream that money can buy. And before we sneer, let's acknowledge that it is the ideal ancestor also of Wright's Usonian houses, the Eames house, Philip Johnson's glass house and most of the other U.S. domestic architecture we have been brought up to admire: skinny weatherbreaks full of expensive services.

As I have just suggested, these two dream realities of the middle landscape—the accessible wilderness and the American home—meet in Wright's Usonian houses and in the Usonian town planning of Broadacre City. Yet they meet there in a slightly garbled form. Their true meeting in the purest forms of the American Dream came just before Wright's Usonian period of the early 1930s, in the wilderness years of the previous decade. I believe that somewhere in those years he passed through some crucial experience, if not an actual crisis, that effectively separates his early career from his later work.

I take it we are no longer so historically naive as to accept the implicit proposition of some of Wright's more idolatrous admirers—that he was the resolute exponent of a single philosophy and style of architecture throughout his career. Patently, the first Mr Wright, and the last, were different kinds of architects to an even greater degree than is customary in long careers at the drawing board. The first Mr Wright, from the time he left Sullivan's office to the time he left Chicago in 1909, was the architect in residence to a shrewd and godfearing White Anglo Saxon Protestant suburban community, for which he designed the prairie houses and Unity Temple, and for whose business connections elsewhere he designed the Larkin building in Buffalo. Had he built nothing else, had he quit when he ran off with Mamah Cheney, his achievement would still have made him America's greatest architect to date and the world's best domestic architect since Andrea Palladio.

AMERICAN WORLD FIGURE The last Mr Wright—the cloaked and be-bereted pseudo-bard, instant grand old man, architecture's gift to the mass media, one-man Victorian revival and creator of plaster monuments to American provincial self-esteem—that Mr Wright can be seen emerging already by the middle 1930s, just before Falling Water and the first phase of the Johnson Wax office complex. The difference between the first and last Mr Wright is summed up by something very unpleasant that Leonard Eaton said to me recently about Wright's clients: 'Before 1910 it took intelligence to employ Wright, but after 1935 it only took money.' The architecture seems to reflect a reciprocal change in the architect.

This still leaves a gap of 25 years in the middle of his career, and a man can change a lot in a quarter of a century. In Wright's case, the changes seem to come in fairly perceptible steps. Thus his elevation to the rank of a world figure in his own eyes comes at the very end of that quarter century, when he began to meet people who actually called him to his face 'the world's greatest architect' or—more subtly—could show him with scholarly expertise, like Edgar Kaufmann, how he rated in the world historical picture. But his elevation in his own eyes to the rank of a specifically and consciously

American world figure belongs to the 1920s; and the pretence of Americanism is more interesting than the pretence to world rank. Indeed, I suspect that the quasi-messianic claim to a worldwide mission is what garbled the purity of Wright's American Dream. Or, to put it another way, the vision of an American architecture that he developed in those wilderness years was almost too pure, too ineffable, to be uttered abroad without dilution by a rhetoric more conventional and more corny than it deserved.

A TRIPLE WILDERNESS The growth of that American vision can be traced through the biography of those years of triple wilderness: triple because there are three different kinds of wilderness wrapped one in another. There was, first of all, the professional wilderness, the exile from the work and clientele to which he was accustomed. In adulterous flight with the wife of a client, Wright had cut himself off, in 1910, from his whole Chicago practice; the works he did later in that city were rare, unrelated to one another, often backward looking. Thus uprooted, he had, almost for the first time, to face up to the reality of a world outside his midwestern cabbage patch. He had been outside it before, but only as a tourist. The impact that Japan made on him while he was working on the Imperial Hotel in these early wilderness years was very different from that of his holiday trip in 1906—so much so that in the *Autobiography* he mentions the earlier trip only as a parenthesis in his account of the long building campaign at the Imperial Hotel.

But these experiences were received with a sensibility that was sharpened by more than professional distress, for these were the years also of his spiritual wilderness. Beginning in August 1914 with the appalling massacre of Mamah Cheney and her children, and sundry other persons, at Taliesin by the butler, Wright suffered a psychological battering that would surely have unhinged lesser men. The whole incredible story—a cross between *King Lear* and *Peyton Place* with additional dialogue by August Strindberg—was to last for all of 15 years until he was 60 and finally married to Olga Lazovitch, the last and most durable Mrs Wright. Throughout that decade and a half, psychological uprootings alternated with physical displacements, each exacerbating the effects of the others.

Where did these displacements take him? Earlier to Germany and Italy, now to Japan, but more often than not to the southwestern states of the U.S., especially in the years when Taliesin and his home state of Wisconsin were forbidden him by threats of legal action or bank foreclosures. In these years Wright was not the midwestern Chicago based architect we automatically think of when discussing his work. Instead of living and working in the suburbs of a great and established 19th century metropolis, Wright was now living in, say, La Jolla on the California coast, or working in Phoenix or Los Angeles, a temporary resident of the putative suburbs of great cities whose form was yet to be revealed.

Los Angeles, for instance, was initially little more than a staging post on Wright's visits to Tokyo for the Imperial Hotel, and though it retained something of that status throughout the wilderness years, he did also build up the outlines of a Los Angeles practice. He appears to have found the scenery and the potentialities of the place promising at first, though later he acquired the common habit of sneering at the city as 'a desert of shallow effects' and at its 'Boulevard Wilshire.' Nevertheless, he began with high hopes and good intent, setting out to build for Aline Barnsdall 'a California Romanza,' a 'natural house . . . and naturally built, native to the region of California.'[8]

Completed, the Hollyhock house 'on this beautiful site, Olive Hill . . . under the serene canopy of California Blue' was certainly unlike the houses Wright had designed to be naturally native to the region of the middle west; it is most significantly natural to the region of California in being pure Hollywood, down to and including the geometrical banalities of its conspicuously *beaux arts* plan. Most writing about the house has little to say about the plan, however, and a great deal to say about its supposedly Mayan shapes; and a great deal of art-historical energy has been wasted—in my opinion— in pursuing the exact sources of those shapes in pre-Columbian architecture.

It is a waste of time because, confronted with the physical presence of the Hollyhock house, one is much more impressed by the sheer wedding cake prettiness of its detailing and the fact that, like the shallow effects all around that Wright affected to despise, it's all built of stucco over wooden studding. In this way, at least, it is entirely native to that region, which is almost entirely stucco built. And the backsloping walls of its upper parts have sources much nearer home than Mayan architecture. They look to me like the first visible influence on Wright's work of what was to be his third and truest wilderness: the high desert states and their Indian *pueblos*.

CONCRETE CONSTRUCTION If Wright himself had not yet seen those *pueblos* in 1920, and the adobe construction that give them their characteristic form, his admirer, assistant, follower and Los Angeles office manager, Rudolph Schindler, certainly had, and had recorded them in drawings.[9] Now this touches on a sore topic. Wright came to loathe Schindler, to damn him on one occasion as an 'amateur'[10] and on another as a 'draft dodger'[11] (not that Wright took any very active part in the war he claimed Schindler had been avoiding). Yet there is abundant evidence, even in Wright's *Autobiography,* that without Schindler the Hollyhock house would not have been completed, and the lodge gate at the entrance to the estate is an admitted work of this Viennese 'amateur.' Schindler, indeed, may have played a larger part in this phase of Wright's career than is generally credited, for he was far less the submissive pupil than Wright's other assistants and apprentices. Never a mere shadow of the master, he alone survived with a creative personality of his own.

Schindler being so fashionable at the moment, there is a grave temptation to see his hand in everything new in Wright's work of the period. Nevertheless, there are at least two topics where his presence is extremely suggestive. One is concrete construction: Wright did not use it for the Hollyhock house, but did employ his celebrated

*Chrysler New Yorker,
late 1950s, fin
detail.*

*Cadillac, 1953,
badge and chrome
detail. Used in PRB
film for the Arts
Council of Great
Britain;* Fathers of
Pop, *1977.*

*Adolf Loos, Steiner
House, 1910.
Vienna, Austria.*

*Adolf Loos, Ameri-
can Bar, 1908.
Vienna, Austria.*

Alfred Koerner,
Grosses Pflanzen
Haus, 1905.
Dahlem, Berlin,
Germany.

The Palladian Bridge, c. 1740. Stowe, England.

Buckminster Fuller, Home Dome, 1964. Carbondale, Illinois.

James Stirling and James Gowan, Engineering Building, Leicester University, 1963. Leicester, England.

James Stirling and James Gowan, Engineering Building, Leicester University, 1963. Leicester, England.

Cedric Price,
Fun Palace Model,
c. 1960.

*Cedric Price, bridge,
North Aviary, London
Zoological Gardens,
1965.*

*Cedric Price, North
Aviary, London
Zoological Gardens,
1965.*

Charles and Henry Greene, Gamble House, 1908. Pasadena, California.

Rudolph Schindler, Lovell Beach House, 1925. Newport Beach, California.

Ice cream wagon,
Cummins of Crewe,
1974. Crewe,
England.

Tennessee Valley Authority, Norris Dam, completed 1936.

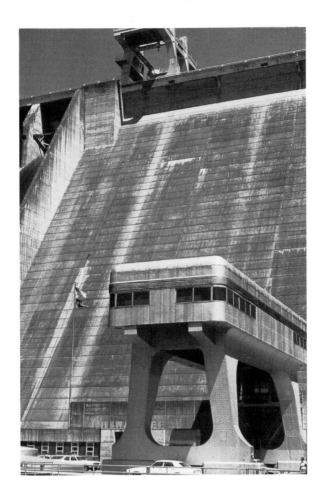

Tennessee Valley Authority, Hiwassee Dam, completed 1940.

Norman Foster,
Willis, Faber,
Dumas headquarters,
1977. Ipswich,
England.

Norman Foster,
Willis, Faber,
Dumas headquarters,
1977. Ipswich,
England.

Norman Foster,
Willis, Faber,
Dumas headquarters,
1977. Ipswich,
England.

Airstream camper, c. 1940. Door, window, and structural details.

Mission church and belltower, originally built in the seventeenth century. The tower has been re-built several times after earthquakes. San Juan Bautista, California.

Mission church, arcade, seventeenth century. San Juan Bautista, California.

*James Stirling,
Michael Wilford and
Associates, Staats-
galerie, 1984. Stutt-
gart, Germany.*

*Giacomo Matte
Trucco, Fiat factory,
1916–26. Lingotto,
Turin, Italy.*

*Giacomo Matte
Trucco, Fiat factory,
1916–26. Lingotto,
Turin, Italy.*

*Pierre Chareau and
Bernard Bijvoet,
Maison de Verre,
1932. Garden
facade. Paris,
France.*

*Pierre Chareau and
Barnard Bijvoet,
Maison de Verre,
1932. Entrance
facade. Paris,
France.*

Renzo Piano, Menil
Gallery, 1986.
Houston, Texas.

Renzo Piano, Menil
Gallery, 1986. Gal-
lery interior before
installation.
Houston, Texas.

Airship hangar, 1932. Clam-shell doors. Moffett Field, California.

Airship hangar, 1932. Interior, shown on Armed Forced Day, 1980. Moffett Field, California.

'textile blocks' in one form or another in all the other Los Angeles houses. The local precedent for the use of concrete in domestic construction would be the architecture of Irving Gill, whom Wright had known long before, through Sullivan's office. But just across the street from Gill's famous Dodge house, Schindler was using concrete construction in his own house in 1921, a couple of years before Wright did so. Furthermore, the man-high tilt-slab wall units of Schindler are a neatly intermediate size between Gill's monolithic walls and the foot-cube textile blocks of, say, the Millard house.

But there is another topic in which Schindler must figure, though it is a rather cloudy one in which it is hard to discern his exact role. On the ground among the Hollywood hills one is very struck by the way these California houses of Wright's not only occupy their hillside sites in a manner different from that of the midwestern houses—which is understandable, given his regional intentions—but also in a manner which seems to deliberately flout all those well-known dicta about 'of the hill, not on it.' The Ennis house, for example, is well and truly on its hill; far from respecting the land form, it simply exploits it as a viewpoint from which to glower down over the city below. Or again, the enormous project for the Doheny ranch spreads Cecil B. de Mille type architecture right across the face of an innocent sandhill in Sierra Madre, completely obliterating it, using it as no more than a prop to support the terraces and steps.

Now we know that, a little later, Schindler effectively selected the site of Neutra's Lovell house;[12] did he also select the site for Wright's houses? The Millard house, for example, was moved from an already purchased flat site to a new one on the side of a ravine. And if Schindler had a hand in these matters, what sensibility did he bring to the task? The question is worth asking because the Vienna exhibition earlier this year of work done by Wagner's students in Vienna around the turn of the century revealed some exercises in hillside siting that Schindler may well have known;[13] they look startlingly Californian, and are some years earlier than anything similar designed by Wright.

The matter can be left open. The point to be emphasised is that in California, Schindler or no, Wright was in collision with cultures and traditions he had not previously had to work with. That they shook him, as well as disappointed him, there can be little doubt. Above all, they were the introduction to this first working encounters with the true wilderness, which never did disappoint him; he was ultimately to make his second home in the desert, at Taliesin West.

And the desert also shook him, as it must shake anybody. Not only is it ravishingly and inhumanly beautiful, but it marks the situation where the accessibility of the wilderness becomes frankly disturbing; driving out of the great cities of the southwest you come upon it too soon, before you can adjust yourself to its psychological impact. In three or four blocks of suburbia you can go from well-kept and watered gardens to untamed desert; you can walk 50 yards from the kerb of a well-metalled and properly policed freeway and stand where no human foot has stood before.

Conditions must have been wilder still in Wright's first desert years, and the impact that much greater. But on his raw-rubbed psyche the impact must have been greater still because of the extraordinary manner and company in which he first saw the desert. In 1922, in one of his blackest moments, there suddenly appeared a kind of fairy godfather, in the form of Albert M. Johnson, the president of the National Life Insurance Company of Chicago, brandishing $20,000 for studies of a new skyscraper HQ that he had in mind. Johnson was also a religious enthusiast, and had it in mind to create a place of retreat to be presided over by his wife. One day he bundled Wright into his Dodge tourer and drove him out to see the site of this proposed fundamentalist Eden—a cool 1800 miles away in Grapevine Canyon at the top of Death Valley! The site was already occupied by the eccentric and enigmatic Death Valley Scotty, proprietor of a mysterious and possibly mythical gold mine. Wright was unimpressed by Scotty, suspecting that his gold mine was Albert M. Johnson, but very impressed by the scenery: 'Nature staged a show for us all along the way!'[14]

Wright appears to have made at least one extensive project for the Grapevine Canyon site, of which drawings survive. In detail, this design seems to lie pretty close to the Hollyhock house, but only in detail; the larger elements of the design are strewn about the Death Valley topography with far greater freedom than in any previous projects of comparable scale, like the unbuilt McCormick house, or even contemporary large projects like the Doheny ranch. However, the projected retreat remained no more than a project, and Johnson's attention wandered. All that finally got built was Scotty's incredible castle.[15]

Yet it was in the desert, the true wilderness, that Wright was ultimately to achieve freedom in planning: freedom from axial symmetry, from right angles, from centralised spaces, which had persisted in the geometry of all his earlier work, even when the functional relations and human use of the spaces were at variance with the formal plans. These desert designs of the late 1920s, with their irregular planning, look to me like the true link between the first Mr Wright and the last.

What brought Wright back once more to the desert was an appeal for help from an old pupil, Albert Chase McArthur, who was designing the Arizona Biltmore Hotel outside Phoenix and wanted to use concrete block construction. The final result was technically less advanced than either had hoped, and visually an eclectic collection of Wrightian motifs from various periods. But while working on it, Wright met Alexander Chandler, chief citizen of a small town near Phoenix to which he had given his surname. Between them, Chandler and Wright cooked up a hotel project to out-Biltmore the McArthurs: San Marcos in the Desert. The project was remarkable, but not so stunning as the temporary camp that Wright and his assistants built as living quarters for the duration of the design process.

Ocatillo Camp, named after the desert flame-flower, deserves to be recognised as one of the classic personal statements of 20th century architecture, ranking with the Glasgow Art School, the Barcelona Pavilion, or Notre Dame du Haut at Ronchamp. But it also has about it the air of freshness and new invention usually associated with the beginning of an architect's career; and as far as Wright is concerned, I think it was, in fact, the second beginning—even though the Depression nearly made it a false start.

In the *Autobiography,* Ocatillo and its associated activities occupy only 10 pages, but they stick out from the rest of the book because of their almost unalloyed cheerfulness, as if something happened to Wright then that later events could never corrupt. The desert seems, again, to have caught him in a receptive mood and inspired him to enthusiasm. It also inspired in him the first full-blown organic analogies drawn from Nature, the sort of thing that became his commonplaces later but are hard to find in his earlier writing. Not only were the structures 'to grow up out of the desert by way of desert materials,'[16] but he also proposes the forms of the mountains behind San Marcos as the source for the asymmetrical pitch of the gables, and the growth habit and surface ridges of the *sahuaro* cactus as the model for a whole new architecture. And it was the desert that in some way made it impossible for the new architecture to be symmetrical: 'Out here in the great spaces obvious symmetry claims too much, I find, wearies the eye too soon and stultifies the imagination. Obvious symmetry usually closes the episode before it begins. So for me I felt there could be no obvious symmetry in any building in this great desert, none especially in this new camp.'[17]

Wright meant it: Ocatillo's snake fences loosely enclose a compound which is also framed by small buildings dispersed apparently at random, their local symmetries of plan almost impossible to read from any ground-level viewpoint. The randomness is only seeming, however, because a geometrical platt does underlie the plan, an accumulation of 30°/60°/90° triangles similar to those of the gables. Related systems of triangular composition immediately appear in other projects of these desert months: in the Owen Young house, in the Cudney house, which was named after the *sahuaro* cactus, in the great project for San Marcos itself—and in that other San Marcos, the towers of St Marks in the Bowery which eventually got built as the Price Tower at Bartlesville, a true *sahuaro* structure as Wright understood it.

STRUCTURAL LIGHTNESS Wright came to understand other things, too, at Ocatillo. The buildings round the perimeter were little more than stiff tents of boards and canvas, very flimsy by district surveyor standards, but adequate to the environmental needs of a desert community—more than adequate, indeed, for their management of diffused light went far beyond the simple service of environmental need. Wright, however, was most impressed by their structural lightness: 'I believe that we pay too slight attention to making slight buildings beautiful or beautiful buildings slight. Lightness and strength may now be synonymous. Usually we spend so much too much to make buildings "last" as we say. Unqualified to build, we are still making caves for cavedweller survivals.'[18]

Wright had designed lightweight constructions before, as late as the Hollyhock house, but they had been put together by professional builders. The practical experience of getting Ocatillo built with his own hands and those of his assistants made him see its advantages and architectural potential afresh; in the accessible wilderness he was rediscovering what Catherine Beecher had learned in Wright's native region in the years just before his birth, reassembling the dream of rural happiness in an unsullied middle landscape.

Just as analogies drawn from the *sahuaro,* its internal structure and external ribs, underpin the whole design for St Marks in the Bowery, so the practical assembly of Ocatillo Camp underpins many of the structural peculiarities of the Usonian houses of the 1930s. What was not of stone in those houses was of skinny wooden panel construction, the panels meeting at frequent right angles as they framed useful closets and alcoves, bracing one against the next like the lengths of the snake fence at Ocatillo. Parts of the plan of the Herbert Jacobs house, for example, are simply the Ocatillo fence reduced to rectangular format.

That was almost 10 years later. The Ocatillo adventure ended with the Wall Street crash of 1929. Chandler abandoned the San Marcos project, Wright's expected fee became another giant bulge in his overdraft, and in the following winter the desert Indians looted the camp for their own structural purposes. Wright's first wilderness period was over, though he would be back in less than a decade to begin his permanent encampment at Taliesin West. But he had seen his true wilderness and was changed by it; new themes emerge in his writings and designs, and pervade his work for the rest of his life.

Thus, in the *Autobiography,* the first attacks on the city follow immediately after the account of Ocatillo: for example, the 'angry prophecy' against urban concentration.[19] Wright sees now that cities may have been necessary to support the civilisations of the past, but that the same great civilisations had been killed off by excessive urban concentration and overbuilding. He produces his own version of Jefferson's dream of a culture without cities—the project for Broadacre City, a city of Usonian houses and *sahuaro* towers distributed at suburban densities through a regulated middle landscape, elaborately serviced by mechanical power and private transportation.

Yet even as the great model of Broadacre City was being built, the desert dream was being obscured, the vision was going wrong. In saying that it went wrong, I am not supporting the criticisms of Broadacre City that are commonly made. The low densities don't frighten me; the proposals for family self-sufficiency, of a sort, on an acre of land, were not just romanticism—U.S. government agencies in the Depression were pushing official programmes advocating the same idea as the answer to crying social needs. Furthermore, family living at these densities was a pretty accurate vision of the standard package into which the middle landscape would be subdivided in ideal postdepression suburbia.

Where I do see Broadacre City going wrong is in losing touch with the physical and psychological realities underlying the American Dream, and trying too hard to be architecture in the academic sense of imposing permanent form on transient process, trying to legislate not only human life but the laws of Nature as well. As Wright worked and reworked the scheme, making it more and more architectural in the orthodox sense of the word, so it becomes more and more ludicrous from a practical and mechanical point of view. Its sky fills with nonflyable helicopters, its roads with unmanageable automotive grotesques that are required to negotiate inherently dangerous traffic intersections.

If Wright had been vouchsafed a true vision of America in the wilderness, and was already losing it in luxuriating architectural self-indulgence, the clue to this loss is found in that observation of Leonard Eaton's about Wright's clients. By the middle 1930s, Wright was being rescued from the professional wilderness, not by the astute client class who had driven him out of Chicago in 1909, but by the cultured offspring of well-established east coast money. The pioneer of this new type of client was Edgar Kaufmann Jr, who neatly avoids Eaton's strictures about needing only money to employ Wright after 1935, because he, in fact, appeared on the Taliesin scene in 1932, and it needed intelligence and vision to actually start the process of recovery.

Edgar Kaufmann paid for the great model of Broadacre City, again a gesture one must applaud, but it shifts the emphasis in Wright's work away from the construction of useful buildings for real people to inhabit, and toward the creation of purely aesthetic monuments to Wright's formal genius and the bank balances of his patrons. Though Wright was allegedly annoyed at being treated more as an historical influence by the Museum of Modern Art exhibition of 1932 than as a living presence,[20] he was flattered by the role of elder statesman and oracle, and soon fell into attitudes that suited the role. Undoubtedly, this only brought to the surface personality traits that had always been there, but he was now prepared to capitalise on them, particularly in his new sub-profession of strolling lecturer, beginning with the Princeton discourses of 1930. In his lecturing persona, Wright visibly—I suppose I should now say legibly, but some performances do survive on film—relies on his personal charm and charisma much more than on logic or information. The correspondence columns of the RIBAJ in 1939 and 1940 show that the charisma that worked in the U.S. did not necessarily work for him in Britain.

For Wright was, however tarnished the vision, still intensely American. In the decade when the previously European trained ascendancy in U.S. architecture was being replaced by a new ascendancy who actually were Europeans, refugees from Germany and elsewhere, Wright's double dyed Americanism had a peculiar value, and not only as a witness to his fellow Americans. We can now see that the vision gained in the wilderness could have had a value for the rest of the world, if the world had been in a position to listen and look. Whereas, for most of Europe's major architects, the events of 1929 were the beginnings of their wilderness and uprootings, for Wright they presaged the end of his worst troubles. While the rest were pulling back into themselves, retrenching spiritually and entering a decade where their ideas had to stand still, Wright was opening out confidently into the new career that began at Ocatillo Camp.

While the rest were reduced to academic reworkings of their 1920s visions of close-packed tower cities—the old futurist aesthetic petrified in cultural embalming fluid—Wright's Usonian vision of Broadacre City started the forward movement toward the real future again. If I have criticised that project for its architectural overelaboration, it is nothing to the sheer architectural arrogance, fixity and abstraction of Le Corbusier's Radiant City, or the hidebound functionalist categories of the Athens Charter. For all its faults, Broadacre City bore witness, in a necessary time, to an alternative vision of civilisation, a vision gained in a wilderness of unopened life that no European could ever truly know.

NOTES

1. See Edgar Kaufmann Jr, 'Frank Lloyd Wright: The 11th decade,' *Architectural Forum,* June 1969, p. 38 ff.

2. The phrase is D. H. Lawrence's.

3. Louis Simpson, *Walt Whitman at Bear Mountain.*

4. *Notes on Virginia,* 1785, response to Query XIX.

5. *The Machine in the Garden,* New York, 1964, p. 226. The whole of my argument is deeply affected by Marx's brilliant but one-eyed study of the impact of technology on the American pastoral tradition, and also by Morton and Lucia White, *The Intellectual versus the City,* Cambridge, Mass, 1962, though I have reservations about their conclusions.

6. Marx, *Machine in the Garden,* p. 23 *et passim.*

7. New York, 1869, and see also James Marston Fitch's invaluable study, 'Our domesticated utopians,' in *Architecture and the Esthetics of Plenty,* New York, 1961.

8. Frank Lloyd Wright, *Autobiography,* New York, 1943, p. 226.

9. See plate on p. 52 in the catalogue of the Schindler exhibition, Santa Barbara, Cal (and elsewhere) 1967 etc.

10. Wright, *Autobiography,* p. 228.

11. Finnis Farr, *Frank Lloyd Wright,* London, 1962, p. 194.

12. This is not yet documented scholarly knowledge but well substantiated gossip.

13. See plate 34 in the catalogue of 'Die vergessene Wagnerschule,' Vienna, 1969.

14. Wright, *Autobiography,* p. 255.

15. The detailed building history of this remarkable complex seems very little studied, though Finnis Farr gives a sketchy version (without apparently knowing that Wright made any designs): *Frank Lloyd Wright,* p. 142.

16. Wright, *Autobiography,* p. 307.

17. *Ibid.,* p. 309.

18. *Ibid.,* p. 311.

19. *Ibid.,* p. 317.

20. Farr, *Frank Lloyd Wright,* p. 194; and for a slightly different version, see Peter Blake, *The Master Builders,* London, 1960, p. 270.

» The 1970s

FROM BOYHOOD REYNER BANHAM'S interests had been very wide indeed, his curiosity particularly aroused by the unexpected and the incongruous and most particularly by anything with wheels and/or an engine, so that when he was given the opportunity to write for the weekly magazine of social comment, *New Society,* on almost any subject that intrigued him, he took the chance and ran with it to the end of his life. Most of the articles chosen for this book from the '70s and '80s are from *New Society.*

It has been asked why so many articles in the years when he was living in the United States should still have been written for British and European magazines. This can be answered by saying that he was asked to write for American architectural magazines, but not on any regular basis for the weeklies. His long-established relationship with *New Society* and its editor was unique (and he thought, privileged), and after his arrival in the United States in 1976 he saw himself, as already suggested, as an American correspondent for U.K. readers.

The move to the State University of New York at Buffalo in 1976 from University College, London, had its difficult aspects, especially as he left a city where he had a thriving career in writing, speaking, teaching, broadcasting, and television. But Buffalo had something about which he became more and more enthusiastic in his three and a half years there—its great industrial history and the spectacular remaining structures from the city's prosperous heyday in the late nineteenth and early twentieth centuries.

U.S. industrial buildings of that time were known to be the inspiration for the modern movement in architecture in Europe, and the sight of these magnificent pioneering buildings, especially the grain elevators (recognised on the spot from photographs in European architectural books of the 1920s—Mendelsohn, Corbusier et al.), still standing in isolated splendour though long abandoned, inspired Banham's summer courses at SUNYAB and culminated in his last major book, *A Concrete Atlantis.*—M.B.

26

Power of Trent and Aire

A litany for that late moment when you turn out the bedside light: "Let not Drax falter nor Cottam pause, for without their like all will be dim in England." You may not know these names, their location may well be remote from yours, but they affect your life more intimately than you care to believe. They are among the more accessible of Hinton's Heavies: generating stations of 2,000 megawatt capacity along the Trent—Cottam, West Burton and Ratcliffe—and the Aire—Drax, Eggborough and Ferrybridge C. And if they go on the blink, TV pictures will shrink and heaters go cool over much of England, for they are all part of the computer-controlled supergrid that supplies the basic power for most of the country.

But if they are so big and important, why do we hear so little about them? For a start they are not glamorous, sabotaged or atomic; they burn old-fashioned coal—though they burn it with a sophistication that makes atomic power look primitive, and with an efficiency that substantiates the too-often-mythical "economies of scale."

Secondly, they are not visible from Hampstead and Highgate and therefore they all escape the notice of opinion-makers and public mouths—though they are well-known

Originally appeared in *New Society* 15, no. 398 (28 May 1970): 926–927.

to various in-groups such as birdwatchers (because of some accidental amenities they have created for our feathered friends).

But chiefly, I think, because the Central Electricity Generating Board secretly hoped no one would notice them, and tried to make them self-effacing. The 2,000mw pro-gramme was launched at a time when the whole electricity business was under heavy pressure from amenitarians, and it seems almost as if Sir Christopher Hinton and his advisers, aghast at the literal enormity of what they were about to commit, tried to find ways of making the supposed offence less noticeable. Honestly, there was no offence, but the leap in size from the previous generating plant could make anyone nervous.

The statistics don't really tell the layman much—even when you have translated all those megawatts into domestic light-bulbs, the answer is still a number with seven or eight noughts after it. But if you start comparing the physical plant with other large objects you have to realise what league they are playing in, and it's a very Big League indeed. The average sort of chimney for one of these stations is at least the size of the Post Office Tower; the cooling towers are about the height of the spire of Salisbury ca-thedral or of St. Paul's; and Battersea power station would almost go inside one.

To anyone brought up on the standard pious myths about the small-scale delicacy of the English countryside, this must sound like Total Destructo Corp at work. But what does a 700-foot chimney look like at Drax? Answer: not even half that size, because there is nothing at Drax with which to compare it, except other equally over-scale ob-jects, such as the cooling towers. Like the other five, Drax sits in the water meadows of a broad valley-bottom, rising from a flat low horizon without a human habitation or other conventional structure in the same view.

There is, in fact, a little Victorian railway building in the foreground at West Burton, but it hardly registers as part of the picture. The only one where scale comparisons are really revealing is also the only one that is at all well-known—namely, Ferrybridge, on the A1 north of Doncaster. From the main road, it is just another scale-less Heavy in a rural setting, but if you leave the A1 and go round to the high ground at the back of the station, the landscape suddenly becomes basic drift-from-the-north stuff, with pigeon lofts and broken pavements and cleared house-sites and shuttered shops—and even the cooling towers of the earlier, smaller Ferrybridge B stand up like mountains behind that lot.

With the others—such as Ratcliffe, just beyond the A6 intersection on the M1—it is a quite different optical effect that gives the only clue to scale. Going north on the motorway, for instance, Ratcliffe's 600-foot chimney and eight monster cooling towers come into view over a hill on the right, long before you reach the intersection. But even after you turn off, and are driving straight towards them, they still don't seem to get any closer. It is this apparent recession alone that tells you that they must be very big—big enough to cause serious misjudgment of distance—because there is simply nothing else against which to measure them.

Ratcliffe, the most accessible of the Trent group, exhibits all the standard features of the 2,000mw type—chimney, cooling towers, a boiler house some 800 feet long by 200 high, switchgear buildings the size of aircraft hangars, office block, dust precipitators, a megaton coalyard, a private railway loop to bring the coal in and haul the dust away: all gathered together in a composition of parts that looks natural and convincing and right, and at home in its riverside landscape, even if its size remains inscrutably vast.

But as you actually drive into the station, and get close to the buildings, you become aware that all this natural and industrial grandeur has been fiddled about and meddled with and busied over by some other race of beings whose scale, by comparison, is that of ants. The broad self-confidence of the designing sensibilities that created the hugely elegant forms of the cooling towers and chimneys has been niggled away in the smaller structures and the ground-level parts of the larger ones—and all this is, ultimately, the result of the CEGB over-reacting to the pressures of the amenitarian/conservationist lobbies.

I'm not saying that the board shouldn't react at all—as the body responsible for effluents, for instance, that have raised the temperature of the Trent to a level that threatens unpredictable ecological changes, the CEGB has a manifest duty to take all the relevant advice it can get, and act on it. In fact, the board takes a lot of advice and acts on as much of it as can reasonably be expected. As it happens, the kind of riverside site that gives good communications and handy cooling water, is also the best from the point of view of visual amenity, because of the advantages of these ambiguities of scale. In the valleys of the Trent and Aire, the board could hardly get it wrong, and most of its choices of site are very good.

Choice of site, indeed, solves as much of the amenity problem as it is within the power of human ingenuity to solve, but in the mental climate of the late fifties it was mandatory to do more. The board had to perform in public certain approved prophylactic rituals of Establishment magic: it had to make a big show of calling in architects. Given the peculiarities of building in remote sites rarely seen by the public, plus the conspicuous irrelevance of the architectural contribution—reputedly responsible for less than 2 per cent of the total investment—the whole operation became a licence to architects to do their nuts in rural privacy.

It was the sight of the extraordinary architectural goings-on at Drax last summer that alerted me to the extent that this new dispensation had turned the clock back to the bad old days of the brick cathedrals. Admittedly, Drax is the most extreme example; but all six of the Trent and Aire Heavies I have now seen exhibit some symptoms of irrelevant architectural overkill.

Brick cathedrals? Ah, there was an heroic episode in the history of technology and taste: the day they killed off the brick cathedrals!

It all happened in the early fifties, lads, when great and good men looked upon this green and pleasant land of ours and noticed that it was being disfigured by architects who were making technology an excuse to do *old-fashioned* architecture, and were dressing up power stations in a monumental style, when they ought to have been coming on crisp, clean and modern. What it really amounted to was that the style that had made Battersea a popular landmark before the war had become unfashionable among the architectural pundits, and too expensive for the nationalised industry to bear. Sensing the changed atmosphere just in time, Farmer and Dark architected Marchwood in a skinny, modern, machine-aesthetic style and even offered to leave some of the equipment out in the open air without benefit of architecture at all. They became the heroes of the hour, and Robert Furneaux Jordan, surveying the battlefield from the safety of the *Architectural Review* in April 1953, exulted: "The dross, the stylistic cage has gone: the only major building left is the turbine hall!"

Heigh-ho—with the onset of all Hinton's 2,000mw Heavies that "major building" was to become so major that men of goodwill would tremble right down to their cold feet and call back the dross, rebuild the stylistic cage. The Hinton regime at CEGB began by calling in Lord Holford (thus ensuring a good hot-line to the Royal Fine Art Commission), setting up the board's own in-house Architectural Division (which has subsequently shown signs of becoming the only really useful part of the whole exercise) and wading into some major PR operations.

Now, to be fair, the role of the external architects (many of them new blood, doing their first power stations), under this new dispensation, was originally envisaged as far more radical and comprehensive than it had been in the brick-cathedrals period. As consultants, they were intended to have some say in the design of all structures great and small, their location on the site, the surrounding landscaping and even the exact line of the sites boundaries. The intention was ambitious, and much was made of it. The catalogue of the 1963 "Architecture of Power" exhibition in fact singled out for special emphasis Gordon Graham's model studies for the bulk forms and grouping of West Burton.

But between ambition and performance there has been a persistent and widening gap. In the end, there has been very little that architects could do about the shapes of the main forms or their grouping, and precious little that landscaping could do either, when the structures it was supposed to hide were between twice and 150 times the height of the tallest, deciduous greenery available. Even decisions about colour are pretty irrelevant at this huge scale and in average British weather—though the amber cladding of Cottam's boiler house has become the house colour for the whole station, and West Burton's differently coloured cooling towers were not quite such a ridiculous idea as they are sometimes made out to be. (Unfortunately, all of these have faded badly except the yellow one.)

However, there was still plenty that the architects might have done for the environment of these stations' large workforces. Yet all I heard were the familiar old complaints: unworkable laboratories, impractical colour schemes, the uncontrollable sunglare in offices, buildings raised on podia from which one could fall because of the absence of handrails. I report these various complaints regretfully, because nearly all the architects involved are more or less close friends of mine, and more regretfully still because they contain truth as well as interprofessional jealousy.

Even if it is not true that "there is nothing they can do about the machinery, so they take it out on the human race," there is manifest truth in: "They are determined to make a personal statement somewhere, so the office block gets over-designed, a bloody jewel!" The architected parts of Hinton's Heavies are getting very precious and arty indeed.

Take Cottam, for which the architects were Yorke, Rosenberg and Mardall. Under the huge amber flank of the boiler house, the ancillary buildings for workshops and the like are detailed in a neat and sensible combination of metal, glass and concrete block that is both sharp and cool; but, for the office block, the same idiom has been over-wrought and made gratuitously rhetorical, and the whole thing is raised on a sort of truncated brick pyramid to emphasise its status as the kind of artwork the rest of the buildings are not.

At Drax (architects: Clifford, Tee and Gale) things have gone even further. Less a brick cathedral than a concrete bunker, it exhibits that obsession with ribbed surfaces and forceful projections that have their origins in Brutalism and their confirmation in that craze for the work of the Nazi's Todt Organisation that fluttered architecture's fashiony fringes in the mid-sixties. Not restricted to the office-block scale of buildings, it has also erupted on the control-room side of the boiler house with an uninhibited gaucheness rare in recent British design.

Further criticism must be withheld here because the spaces inside—not yet completed or visitable—may prove to be workable and habitable, but the pretentiousness of the exterior is bound to arouse grave suspicions. Whatever Michael Shepheard, the CEGB's chief architect, may have hoped that consultant designers could do to "bring down these vast envelopes to human terms" has clearly been frustrated at Drax by the consultants' inability to resist what he calls "the temptation to be grandiose."

But if the prognosis for power-station architecture looks less reassuring now than at any time for the last ten years, the blame must lie not only with the architects, but also with the board. During one of the PR exercises of the late fifties, Lord Holford said: "Genius cannot be hired; but standards can be set." But the evidence of the eyes is that the board tried to do something like hiring genius, and failed because it did not try hard enough to set standards.

The board has been quite astonishingly indulgent to the foibles and fantasies of its external architects, as if by hiring a big-name Fellow of the RIBA it could excuse itself from further architectural responsibility. Fortunately for us, if uncomfortably for the board, its apparent complacency has been sabotaged from within; the in-house Architectural Division, disenchanted with its unprofitable role as a kind of internal pseudo Fine Arts Commission, trying to vet external architects' work, has been transforming itself into a highly competent design-and-development team.

Along the way it has designed some neat, serious and economical buildings. Not power stations yet, but district offices, training centres and the like. One of them picked up a *Financial Times* industrial architecture award this year, thus pleasing and surprising the board and giving heart to some of its more concerned architectural employees. But surely this award also carries with it a clear duty for the CEGB as a public body. It can no longer pretend that it does not have the talent to design a model 2,000mw station itself. Quite clearly it now *has* the capacity to "set standards," in Lord Holford's phrase, not only by exhortation but by tangible example as well. We could all use a station that stands up to the closest architectural and financial scrutiny—as well as looking like a successor to Stonehenge when you stand too far away to be distracted by detailing.

The Crisp at the Crossroads

Among the triumphs of progressive technology that Luddites and Leavisites alike have lately been spared is the toad-in-the-hole-flavoured crisp with a hole in it! Scores of other equally nutty (literally so, in some cases) flavours for the familiar old potato crisp have been mooted lately. Don't imagine that cheese-and-onion or barbecue-bacon exhausts the ingenuity of the industry, now that flavours are sprinkled on as a dry powder before the crisp is cooked.

Not all the possibilities have got beyond idle brainstorming (blackberry-and-apple? smoked salmon? how about *crème de menthe*?), but the story about the party that was stoned right out the window at Redondo Beach by LSD crisps is true, apparently, and one memorable week in Montreal I breakfasted (for reasons beyond human belief) on Boursin, instant coffee, and rainbow crisps. Rainbow? You bet; red, blue, green, white, natural, and all tasting like cardboard.

The potato crisp is at the crossroads, and to judge by the sundry aromas arising from the secret kitchens of R-and-D departments, the industry can't guess which way it will go. Whoever guesses right could make a real killing. The value of Britain's annual

---

Originally appeared in *New Society* 16, no. 406 (9 July 1970): 77.

crop has doubled since 1964 and now stands around 62 million quid—crunch that! In the process, Smiths, with only 30-odd per cent of the market left, has had to concede victory to Golden Wonder, with over 45; and the old basic salted crisp has lost almost half the market to new fancy flavours.

It's been a real stir-up, and it has consequences for the arts of design, because the old basic crisp they still eat down at the Rovers' Return, even if it is doomed elsewhere, was unique among the works of man in being as neatly related to its pack as was the egg to its shell. Different kind of neat, but almost as instructive to look at.

For a start, it is an inherently unconformable shape. The cooking process that makes it crisp also crumples it into rigid but irregular corrugations. There is no way to make it pack closely with its neighbours, so that any quantity of crisps must also contain an even larger quantity of air. Bulk for bulk, as packed, crisps contain even less weight of food than cornflakes, and thus give conviction to the myth that they just *can't* be fattening.

This sense that there is no diet-busting substance in crisps is reinforced by their performance in the mouth. Apply tooth-pressure and you get deafening action; bite again and there's nothing left. It's a food that vanishes in the mouth, so, I mean, it can't be fattening, can it? It certainly isn't satisfying in any normal food sense; the satisfactions of crisps, over and above the sting of flavour, are audio-masticatory— lots of response for little substance.

The pack is analogous in its performance. Keeping the crisp crisp means keeping water-vapour away from it; and until recently the only cheap, paper-type flexible materials that formed effective vapour-barriers were comparatively brittle and *in*flexible, and thus produced a lot of crinkling sound effects whenever they were handled. What with the crisps rattling about inside, and the pack crackling and rustling outside, you got an audio signal distinctive enough to be picked up by childish ears at 200 or 300 yards.

But, more than this, the traditional method of sealing off the top of the pack produced a closure that could only be opened destructively and couldn't be resealed. So eating crisps was an invitation to product-sadism. You tear the pack open to get at the contents, rip it further to get at the corner-lurkers in the bottom, and then crush it crackling-flat in the fist before throwing it away. It's the first and most familiar of Total-Destructo products and probably sublimates more aggression per annum than any quantity of dramaturgical catharsis.

However you look at it, or listen to it, the total relationship of crisp to package is a deafening symbiosis that comes near to perfection. And it's the kind of perfection that not even a towering genius could have invented from scratch. The neatness of the relationship has almost a vernacular quality about it, like some survivor from a lost golden age of peasant technologies that have matured long in the wood and hand: the oar, the axe, the rolling pin. But in the crisp's case, the golden age was recent, a threshold between two ages of industrial technology—the transitional period between the grinding poverty that 19th century social moralists found so repugnant and the new afflu-ence that 20th century social moralists find so repugnant.

In the history of rising genteelism, the potato crisp is a key piece of the technology that enabled a woman to go into a pub and still emerge a lady. By asking for "A bag of crisps, instead," a lady could avoid having another drink without dropping out of a round; could participate in the social rituals of receiving goodies from the bar, or passing them on to others, without finding herself confronted with yet another jar of ultimate senselessness—and, above all, without incurring the accusations of airs, graces, and "going all la-di-dah" that would follow if she ordered Babycham.

Now that categories like "woman" and "lady" are no longer distinguishable, or worth distinguishing, when any bird can share a joint or a bottle of plonk with any bloke without being mistaken for what she wishes she wasn't, the ancient function of the crisp is crumbling almost as fast as the crisp itself. For, in its new functions, the crisp just does not possess the mechanical strength it needs.

Next time you go to one of these functions, and find yourself thinking that a splodge of onion dip would go nicely with the glass of foaming Silesian sherry the dean has just pressed on you, have a good look at the contents of the bowl of dip. The chances are that you will see a surface so pocked over by the shards of wrecked crisps that it looks like the Goodwin Sands during the Battle of Britain. For every Smith or Golden Wonder that actually comes up with a scoop of dip, four or five will die the death between the fingers of the would-be dipper.

Right now, the British crisp certainly isn't keeping up with technological adventures abroad—those big, white symmetrical ones from Holland, for instance. They may look and taste, like foamed polystyrene, but they have the structural strength to lift a lot of dip. Even so they are a poor shape for the job, compared with current models of the American "taco chip."

I don't know how long the taco chip has been around. I didn't really become con-scious of it until I was doing my own housekeeping in Pasadena last winter. But its mastery of the problems of a savoury-dipping culture was immediately apparent. A cheerfully synthetic product, not notably derived from sliced spud, its flavour patently sprinkled on, not bred in, the taco chip comes on in equilateral-triangle format, about two inches on the side, handsomely tanned and only slightly wrinkled.

Not only is it better-looking than the pallid old spud-based product, but it also has the mechanical strength (without being inedibly tough) to take advantage of the excel-lent dipping performance it derives from its sharp, 60 degree corners. All in all the taco chip is a classic U.S. "engineering solution," a worthy manifestation of the spirit that puts men on the moon and Mace in the campuses.

The surest indication of the crisp's escape from the pub-and-chara context of prole-cult is the fact that something like 40 per cent of the product is now bought as part of the weekly groceries in suitable family-economy packs, while licensed premises now handle only 10 per cent of the trade. Scotland, apparently, is still where the bulk of Britain's crisps are eaten—a surprising statistic since it is difficult to relate the crisp's low ratio of substance to side-effects with the Scots alleged sensitivity to value for money.

For, if food value were the criterion for purchase, the crisp would be unsaleable. It isn't even an economical way of buying calories, compared with, say, porridge. Crisps—taco chips and their likes must be seen as ritual substitutes for solid food, the kind of token victuals that ancient peoples buried with their dead, the nutriment of angels rather than mortal flesh. In fact, the more I think about the comparison with porridge, the more worried I get. Could it be that the world's greatest anthropologue has got his polarities wrong, and should have written, say, *The Boiled and the Crisp*?

28

The Historian on the Pier

The Municipal Pier at Santa Monica, California, is a building that a historian might study for any number of external and fashionable reasons—as one of the sacred places of pop art, perhaps, or as a multi-level "megastructure" in the ocean, 1,600 feet of motorised environment poised over the Pacific breakers. But the prime reason for studying it is that its history is interesting in its own right, and raises some fundamental questions about the nature and methods of architectural history.

Almost all the readily available historical statements about the pier are misleading. Authorities are agreed that the pier was built by the municipality in 1921 with the proceeds of a loan bond issued the previous year, but this statement is not true of the whole structure. Legally, it consists of two piers, built more or less simultaneously and in continuous contiguity. One, the longer, with the harbour master's office in the end, is the Muni proper. The other, the shorter, is an amusement pier built by Arthur Looff— sold to the Santa Monica Amusement Company in 1924, and now most commonly called the Newcombe Pier, after the family that has run it for years.

At beach level, the two piers are easily distinguished by their structures. The

Originally appeared in *New Society* 17, no. 433 (14 January 1971): 66–67.

Municipal, with its massive timbers and properly disposed angle bracers to resist lateral loads, bespeaks civic caution and responsibility—a strong pier, built to last. The Looff, on the other hand, seems to stand on as little timber as will bear the traffic, probably depends on the adjoining Muni for lateral bracing, and generally answers to the norms for commercial structures on the southern California shore.

But this structural separateness is pretty irrelevant to the way the double assembly functions. The amusements on the Looff would be almost inaccessible without the roadway provided by the Muni. The Muni itself would have only limited reasons for existing nowadays without the bars, restaurants and other concessions on the Looff. Yet this symbiosis of function can hardly be said to have been designed. Almost perfect it may be, but it is a perfection of mutual growth and adaptation. When the Looff was young, it was a traditional amusement pier, with rides and a rollercoaster and, above all, a famous ballroom—La Monica—which survived for many years in different guises.

La Monica was finally demolished in 1960, leaving only a tattered fragment of stuccoed balustrading behind. That fragment was practically all that survived of the whole pleasure environment created by the amusement company. The site of the rollercoaster is now largely occupied by a go-kart track and a standard, prefabricated, matslide. But what now occupies the site of La Monica, the departed ballroom? In the words of Joni Mitchell's song, "They paved Paradise and put up a parking lot." Where there was once, doubtless, a sprung floor, there is now blacktop tar spread on the basic plank structure of the Looff's decking, and further back toward the shore there is a paybox for a normal commercial parking operation. This change of use symbolises the process that has united the two piers. Under the influence of "normal" automobile pressures, the Looff has now become a piece of normally used roadside land, a parking lot behind a roadside strip of shops. And the Muni, these days, carries only a normal road, complete with standard parking-meters along the kerb. A piece of Road-America has got stuck out over the Pacific, complete with the world's oldest offshore parking lot.

Now, all this may well be a moderately interesting sidenote to the recent history of Internal Combustion City, Los Angeles, but does it really deserve such attention? Californians with local knowledge would say: "That's the wrong pier. You ought to be talking about Pacific Ocean Park."

POP, within sight of Santa Monica pier, is a natural subject for a conventional architectural historian. First, it has just been destroyed, so he can rail at the uncultured insensitivity of a depraved age; second, it was used for the exteriors in *They Shoot Horses, Don't They?,* so it is in fashion; third, it was remarkably good of its kind, perhaps the most concentrated amusement pier ever built; but, fourth and chiefly, its landward face was a running sequence of pure Hollywood versions of all the architectural styles of the world, done in lath and plaster. It was immediately accessible to the architectural historians' normal procedures of making stylistic comparisons within the standard format of identically dimensioned colour-transparencies, and that would be a compelling reason for *not* discussing Pacific Ocean Park.

I find this kind of instant stylistic juxtaposition increasingly suspect when applied to architecture. In painting, it does not bother me. Leonardo's *Gioconda* and Raphael's *Fornarina,* being portable art-works, could be hung side by side for comparison. So there is no falsity in exhibiting slides or photographs of them side by side and making academic capital out of it. But for *La Fornarina* substitute the Farnesina palace by Raphael's pupil, Baldassare Peruzzi, and for *La Gioconda* substitute, say—because it is also in France and connected with Leonardo da Vinci—the Chateau de Chambord, and you have a juxtaposition which is a historical nonsense because it is a physical nonsense.

The mere fact that Chambord, and the Farnesina were begun within a decade of one another matters little, compared to the fact that they are, and must remain, some 1,000 kilometres apart. Putting them side by side falsifies them both by giving them a fictitious common context. It matters, fundamentally, that their contexts are as different as Trastevere and the Forêt de Sologne. If they had been built elsewhere, their whole meaning would have been different.

Duccio Turin, Professor of Building at London University, recently put "fixity" at the very top of his list of eight distinguishing characteristics of buildings. "The final product of the building industry is fixed to the ground on which it is erected," he added. "One could almost say that it becomes part of it."

Now, if this is the first feature of a building, then architectural history should acknowledge it. The point about a mobile home, even, is less that it moves, than that it *can* be moved. The percentage of its useful life that it spends in motion is infinitesimal, and during that time it is not normally inhabited, and is not therefore architecture. Its possibility of motion underlines the fact that it is only architecture when it stands still on a particular piece of ground.

The history of any piece of architecture is bound up with the history of the parcel of ground on which it stands. We all know what happened to the house built upon sand, to cite the most obvious example, and the one most relevant to Santa Monica pier.

The present structure has not yet suffered the great fall of the biblical house, in spite of its arenaceous foundations; but the history of the parcel of sand it stands upon is totally entangled with that of the pier itself, beginning with a mystification about the year in which it was built. Though the authorities are agreed that this was 1921, there is a bronze plaque alongside the entrance to the harbour-master's office, stating that the pier was built in 1909. More confusing still, there is abundant photographic evidence of the pier being built at that time, and in reinforced concrete, not wood.

In fact, the experimental concrete pier of 1909 was destroyed by the rusting out of its steel reinforcement. The wooden pier that replaced it in 1921 inherited, among its multiple functions, the prime function of the concrete Muni—to carry the town drain out to sea, and for that reason was the same structure in the eyes of the municipality. This salubrious civic function was apparently abandoned before the twenties were out, when Santa Monica's sewage system was connected to that of the City of Los Angeles. The point at issue, historically, is that Santa Monica pier stands where it does because the municipality was already on this parcel of ground even before this pier was built.

However, it would be naive to suppose that municipality and pier stand in any simple cause-and-effect relationship, with the pier passively reflecting changed intentions ashore. A pier on this same site is, indeed, the reason why the city was founded. Work on a first pier began in March of 1875, as the seaward terminal of the Los Angeles and Santa Monica Railroad. Pier and railroad alike were part of a project to give Los Angeles a second harbour, by arranging to connect the city with the deep water of Santa Monica Bay.

The standard route from the pueblo of Los Angeles (downtown, as now is) to Santa Monica had, in fact, been established only in the previous decade or so. It followed the ancient Spanish Camino Real, out of the pueblo as far as the tar pits at La Brea, and then skirting the edge of the higher ground to the north until it hit the shore between the edge of the high ground and the swamps and sand dunes to the south. At the point where the road hit the shore, boats could be beached and the tar from the pits at La Brea could be loaded into them. That point was called Shoo-Fly Landing, because of the defensive action that had to be taken as a consequence of the stench. It is the only logical point for any form of surface transport to come to the ocean on this coast. The Santa Monica Railroad followed the same route and emerged at the same point; and so did the Santa Monica Freeway.

But if the land-form dictated that the first Santa Monica pier should stand at Shoo-Fly Landing, it was *only* the land-form, and not the city of Santa Monica itself. The settlement comes after the railroad and the railroad comes, in a sense, after the pier, whose one possible location at Shoo-Fly Landing fixed the details of the project.

One can see the pier as the seed or trigger which has precipitated the whole development of Santa Monica—from being southern California's first resort city up to its present eminence as the home, both of the most famous think-tank, the Rand Corporation, which stands just inland of the pier, and of that most dramatic of all the institutions for curing the ultimate private evils of southern Californian society, Synanon House, which has always occupied one or another of the ancient resort hotels within sight of the pier.

In a discussion, hitherto unrecorded, Lord Llewelyn-Davies, in search of a rock-bottom or last-ditch definition of architecture, uttered the phrase: "In the last resort, architecture is that which changes land-use." This is not a complete definition of architecture, any more than Professor Turin's concept of fixity is a complete characterisation of a building. But it is an essential definition of architecture, because the prime reason why any building is designed is to alter the use of some particular parcel of land, in order to render it a better environment for some human activity.

The classical art-historical methods, used by most architectural historians, do not handle buildings that are seminal in this sense, but only in a narrow and restricted cultural sense. Buildings are adjudged seminal if they introduce a new style or a new typology—something like Brunelleschi's Pazzi chapel or Le Corbusier's Pavillion Suisse, both of which are highly seminal in the stylistic and typological sense, much less so in the sense of what they did to the land use of a particular district.

Ironically enough, close studies of the relation of building and land are often conducted by the "narrower" type of architectural historian in order to discover the precise date of a building and thus to place it in a stylistic or typological sequence. But all this fascinating and humanly relevant information is then relegated to an appendix or footnote, because it has no place in the context-free categories in which these cultural sequences are constructed. Santa Monica pier reminds us that the strength of architectural history is that it is founded on physical objects, and can always rejuvenate itself by going back to these objects in order to ask new questions about them.

29

The Master Builders

The pictures over the bedhead have gone, but the hooks for them are still there, and so is practically everything else that was there in Aunt Julia's time. Looking at the picture of the room in her day, framed on the writing desk beside the portrait of Aunt Julia herself, you realise that the only difference in the scene is your own 1970s presence. The room was built around her expressed needs, but it is as habitable now as when she moved in during the spring of 1909—the Gamble family, to whom Julia Huggins was maiden-aunt-in-residence, were astute clients and the brothers Charles and Henry Greene architects of practicality.

If that had been all there was to it, living in the Gamble House today as a guest of the University of Southern California would have been no more than a convenient and comfortable experience, for which one might feel decently grateful. But not as honoured and privileged as one, in fact, does—nor as intrigued, involved and envied. As clients the Gambles were as inspired as they were astute, and the practicality of the

---

Originally appeared in *The Sunday Times Colour Supplement*, 8 August 1971, pp. 19–27.

Greenes was subsumed within an architectural vision of romantic genius, equalled in their generation by Frank Lloyd Wright and, perhaps, Charles Rennie Mackintosh, and by no-one else at all.

Even so, the comparisons that one inevitably makes with the Greenes' mighty contemporaries can be misleading; their work in Pasadena is profoundly *sui generis,* unique and unmistakable. It has affinities with the Shingle Style of the Eastern U.S.— so called because of its predilection for wooden shingles as an external cladding material, but notable for the complex, picturesque silhouettes it gave to even modest houses. However, historians force the Greenes' work into that category at their peril— like trying to dismiss Shakespeare as a Jacobean dramatist. The Greenes evolved a blend of traditional architectural skill (in planning and the like), informed taste in the fine arts (connoisseurship, you could say) and craftsmanly detailing (robust, subtle, sometimes both) that would not have made sense in either Wright's Chicago, or Mackintosh's Glasgow, or the New England resort towns where the Shingle Style evolved.

The added architectural dimension that separates their work from their contemporaries' is still impossible to define verbally, but has something to do with the reason they, and the Gambles, were in Pasadena: the climate (psychological as much as meteorological) of Southern California. It was an environment for life and work that was to liberate, transform, the views and performance not only of the architects of the Greenes' generation, but equally spectacularly those of the next—the Germans and Viennese, especially Rudolph Schindler and Richard Neutra, who arrived after the First World War.

For the Gambles, this house on select Westmoreland Place, which was a short service road separated only by a ten-foot strip of landscaping and trees from Orange Grove Avenue, the residential main street of Pasadena through all its transformations from orchards through health resort and snob suburb to its present condition as the Hampstead (near enough) of Los Angeles . . . for the Gambles this was a winter cottage— all 8000 square feet of it. David Gamble was a director of Procter and Gamble, whose home base was in Cincinnati—where the winter climate is a very good reason for going to California; and the house is craftily adjusted to take full advantage of Pasadena's gently nuanced winter weather. Charles Greene had, indeed, given "Climate" as the first of the four conditions affecting the style of a house, with "Environment" second, "Materials" third, and "Habits and Tastes—the life of the owner" only fourth.

From Climate to Life, the Greenes knew why people were in California in the winter. They had come West in 1893 to see their parents who were living in Pasadena because of Mrs. Greene's health. They decided to stay and get their teeth into the problems and potentialities of California, abandoning what might well have been careers of conventional success and prestige as erudite Classical Revivalists in Boston. Or might not have been . . . their father, Dr. Thomas Sumner Greene, had apparently developed some radical views on the human environment while the family were living in cramped quarters in St. Louis; at that same time, Charles and Henry were going through the experimental Manual Training School at Washington University (yet another hopeful 19th-century probe in the general direction of where the Bauhaus was later to be discovered).

Whatever potential lay in these peculiarities of their background was released by California, and there expressed in an architecture whose strength lies in concealed contradictions that reflect their dual background: it looks casual, but is fundamentally formal; honestly handicrafted, but only where it shows and in a style consummately integrated from more diverse sources than were normal even in that most eclectic period of American architecture.

It is the handicraft style of the Gamble House that reaches you first—the house is obsessively made of wood. So are most of the houses of North America, except that in the Greenes' work the obsession is manifest in every visible square inch of the material. Wood that is merely structural necessity is left pretty rough, and quite roughly assembled, if it is in places not normally seen by genteel eyes—roof-spaces, cellar, and so on. But all the wood which is, so to speak, in the public domain has been lovingly wrought, almost to the point of fetishism. Every surface has been rubbed down by hand, every corner rounded away, every joint and fixing made elaborately explicit. The same visible technology of wood invades all the furniture as well, and in some rooms it becomes difficult to tell where furniture ends and house begins—the sideboard of the dining room is a projecting bay of the house-structure, with its own roof and windows, and the whole room is more like the inside of cabinet-makers' work than any normal sort of interior decoration.

The Greenes were lucky with their craftsmen—they needed to be—but they were also prepared to devote endless supervision to their work, and more than just supervision. Peter Hall, contractor for the structure and most of the furniture, was someone they had virtually set up in business themselves. Not unnaturally their work is therefore seen as a crowning triumph of the Craftsman Movement, the American wing of William Morris's Arts and Crafts in Europe. But having said so much, one must then tread warily; there is craftsmanship and craftsmanship.

The style being promoted by Gustav Stickley in the *Craftsman* magazine, and in his so-called Mission furniture, was square, direct, only marginally relieved by visual artifice—a dark and more massive version of Voysey's furnishings in England, more or less.

There are a few Craftsman pieces in the Gamble House; they emphasise the extent to which Hall and the Greenes were after something else. Their work is much more subtle, refined and—for want of a less compromised word—*artistic* than the true Craftsman style with its plain, honest, Teddy Roosevelt virtues. What Charles and Henry Greene seem to have arrived at is almost craftsmanship as a style of decoration and a way of ordering the visible elements of the structure, a repertoire of usages for shaping ends, fixing brackets, notching corners, strapping joints, pinning mortises—if it was anything you could do to wood, they found a way of making decoration of it; and the technique spread over to other materials, too, so that one finds equally obsessive detailing on, say, the leather-work of the straps that support the lighting fixtures. It is beautiful, no doubt about it, but an environment where every square inch of surface was a major sensuous experience could easily prove cloying—as is so often the case with European Art Nouveau.

What saves the Gamble House is complex, and derives from the family as well as from the architects. The Greens framed all this elaborate woodwork in an architectural context that is ample and orderly. The rooms are large, so that there is room to stand back from the detailing; sheer space lends an air of ease and relaxation on every floor, from the broad entrance-hall flooded with light through a 12-foot spread of decorative Tiffany glass, to the so-called billiard room in the roof, low-ceilinged but wide, panelled and windowed like the saloon of an old steamer.

And orderly; the spread of terraces and sleeping porches at the northern end of the house gives it an informal, spreading air that is deceptive. In spite of its size, the house is compactly planned, the rooms ingeniously fitted together in groupings controlled by a strict, if hidden, symmetry. Occasionally the symmetries are explicit—the dining room balances about an axis which runs from the sideboard to the french windows that give on the terrace, while the big living room has virtually true bi-axial symmetry, fireplace and window-bay fixing one axis and balancing about the other.

What the family contributed to the equable impression given by the house is not only their own life style, in which a love of beautiful objects and fine workmanship is embraced within a love of space, nature and the open air . . . not only all that, but also a feeling of continuity into the present day. Although the house has been in the joint care of the City of Pasadena and the University of Southern California since 1966, it is still pervaded by the Gambles, their presence, their tastes and habits. Partly this is due to the persistence of people—Aunt Julia, bless her, lived till 1942 and left her mark long after the original builders had died (David Gamble in 1923, his widow six years later), stray cousins stay overnight even now and James Gamble (grandson of David) presides over the meetings of the advisory board. But more than this, the present curator of the house, Randell Makinson, is not only the world's leading Greene and Greene scholar (inevitably) but has known the house (and the Gamble family) since he was a student, and was the first person to whom the Gambles broached the idea of handing the house over to a public organisation. Through Makinson, continuity of something like family sentiment pervades the running of the house even now. That unmistakable "museum chill, that no amount of flower arranging can warm," has at no time possessed it. The Gamble House lives.

It lives *as a house*, and the life it possesses involves the visitor. But whether it lives as part of the developing history of modern architecture, I don't know. For me it will always be something of a beautiful dead-end, a sudden halt when the wood-building traditions that the Europeans had brought with them across the Atlantic and the North

American Continent confronted Japanese architecture from across the Pacific in exquisite deadlock. In the next architectural generation this confrontation between the
American heartlands and the culture of Japan was to take a curious and baffling turn,
when Frank Lloyd Wright used Los Angeles as a staging post on his trips to Japan to
work on the now-demolished Imperial Hotel. Some commissions in Los Angeles and
Pasadena appeared in the process, and he brought out his young follower Rudolph
Schindler to supervise them. Schindler was to stay and flourish as an independent architectural talent; but Wright, having adorned the sandy hillsides and canyons with half
a dozen romantic houses, became disenchanted and left them behind as a puzzlingly
unrelated interlude in a career whose main action was always elsewhere.

But that's Los Angeles: interludes, baffling; ends, dead or honourable; middle
periods, missing or mysterious; beginnings, promising or blighted; starts, false or
sudden—these seem to have been California's contributions to modern architecture,
rather than sustained and mature achievements, and make it one of the most fascinating territories in the world for the student of modern buildings. But part of the fascination lies in that word 'seem,' because we are still very ignorant of what happens there.

The common attitude of writers on modern architecture is still to regard California as an interesting backwater, in spite of the fact that, on any reasonable accounting
of quality and quantity, Los Angeles ranks alongside Paris and Chicago as a world
centre of modern domestic, with some three-quarters of a century of inspired house-
building to its credit. But it all got missed out and passed over, because the history of
modern architecture was written by German-speaking historians largely about German
refugee architects, and mostly read by 'cultured' Anglo-Saxons who could imagine
nothing much coming out of Southern California except Sunkist oranges and Chaplin
comedies.

Even Richard Neutra, who took care to maintain contact with centres of academic
power and journalistic influence back East, got far skimpier treatment than his mani
fest qualities deserved. Still, by the time he died last April, the world did know of Neutra as the designer of the Health House of 1930 with its advanced technologies of construction and its sensational hillside site, and it knew, too, his fabulous desert houses
done immediately after the Second World War, and it had read his books (though not
as diligently as he would have wished). But those who had no strong contacts, or
couldn't be bothered with that kind of thing, like Rudolph Schindler—but for whom
Neutra would never have been in Los Angeles in the first place—simply fell out of the
historical record. Only in the Fifties did they begin to get their due. The breakthrough
was the chapter in which Henry-Russell Hitchcock put together "Frank Lloyd Wright and
his California Contemporaries" in his compendious *Architecture: Nineteenth and Twentieth Centuries.* This at least gives credit to the Greenes and their contemporary Irving
Gill, though it manages to dismiss Neutra in one reference and a footnote ostensibly
about something else, and has nothing at all to say about Rudolph Schindler.

Little more than a decade later, this omission of Schindler is already totally incredible, yet none of us who reviewed the book for learned journals uttered a word of complaint that I can remember. I must have known of Schindler's existence at that time, but had no idea of either his potential importance or his quality as a designer. His importance is this: that in isolation from his Viennese training and origins, and inspired by his work with Frank Lloyd Wright, he invented "the white architecture of the Twenties" at the same time as his European contemporaries, and quite independently of them. This achievement punches such a hole in the accepted, Europe-centred view of the rise of modern architecture, that it actually threatens the livelihoods of some professional academic architectural historians, and there is quite a busy little sub-industry at work desperately trying to find ways of disproving Schindler's precocious originality. Lay readers may find this difficult to credit, but the U.S. architectural history industry in a bad mood can resemble a Madison Avenue novel in its bitchiness, neurosis and insecurity.

The situation is exacerbated by the fact that Schindler was also an uncommonly good architect, to whom flashes of genius occurred at a rate above the world average; there is no hope of brushing him off as a stylistic freak. If he is to be considered at all, then he must be considered seriously, because his Pueblo Rivera apartments and Lovell house are the equal of anything Le Corbusier had done up till the same time (1926), while the house he built for himself and Clyde Chase in 1921 transcends, in my estimation, anything done by anybody (including himself) before Le Corbusier's Villa Savoye of 1930.

It is difficult at first sight to see what is so marvelous about the Schindler/Chase house. Difficult to believe, for a start, that you can be in the right neighbourhood: Kings Road, just south of the Sunset Strip, is in a convulsion of redevelopment, single-family houses going down before the bulldozers (Irving Gill's splendid Dodge House went early in 1970 amid howls of public outrage) to make a shambles of churned debris on which heroically undistinguished stucco apartment blocks are duly constructed. And when you have convinced yourself that you are at the right address, it is difficult to see any architecture at all amid the bamboos, banana palms, lemon trees and god wot that has grown up since the house was built. Yet all that greenery is part of what the architecture is all about.

If one sets up the Schindler house in contrast to the Gamble House, then the first and most fundamental contrast lies in their response to the same immensely habitable California climate. The Gamble House, in spite of all those terraces and sleeping porches, is still a pretty compact, block-like concept, in which indoors and out are still identifiably different. Not so the Schindler house, which seems to take blocks of that climate and fold itself loosely around them. This, in itself, represents a major gesture of liberation for one trained in the solidly monumental tradition of Otto Wagner's teaching in Vienna, and who was still designing compact, clear-cut buildings in Chicago in 1914, and later yet was Frank Lloyd Wright's site-architect in Los Angeles. But here, in 1920–21 it seems as if the sun has burned away all his past—or nearly so.

There are plenty of learned pundits around who will point out that there can never be a genuinely fresh start in architecture, that it is improper to suppose that anyone could design a house as if there had never been houses before. Yet the Schindler house comes disturbingly near to being a totally new beginning. At the start of the decade when the European modernists were to make a big deal out of the attempt to achieve "interpenetration of indoor and outdoor space" Rudolph Schindler in his California isolation had it made already, with his alternations of open-sided rooms and open-roofed courts.

The arrangement of rooms and courts is, in fact, quite orderly, even with touches of disguised symmetry, but it isn't easy to grasp at first, because what emerges from the occluding boscage seems to be a random collection of inexplicable blank concrete walls, wooden eaves, Japanese sliding screens, outdoor fireplaces and the like, capped by glazed sleeping porches. Yet the basic plot is as simple as it is neat. Most of the double house (Mrs Schindler and Mrs Chase, old college friends, ran it as a single household at times) is assembled by joining, end-to-end, variants on a single standard room type, which has a massive concrete wall at its back (towards the street), a flat wooden roof, and sliding glass on the side towards the court or garden. Construction pictures, taken before the sleeping porches were added on top, show an almost fortified-looking structure squatting low in bare scrubby desert earth, and it is not improper to see in this image the influence of Schindler's visit to the Indian Pueblos of the Western deserts.

This contrast of the former desert and the present jungle is typical of the apparent contradictions that run all through the design and its history. For instance, the residential polarity of the house has reversed, and Mrs Schindler now lives in the former Chase rooms, and lets off the former Schindler parts as studios for architects and the like. Or the construction, which looks appallingly flimsy, but has stood half a century—and that is a long time in Los Angeles, so that one mocks the workmanship at one's peril.

Certainly it is a cheaply built house, and a simply built one—but never stupidly built. There is something very crafty, though not craftsmanly, about the way it has been *thought* together, rather than assembled, and a deceptive air of casualness in the way concrete meets wood and wood meets glass, as if Schindler were saying "Architecture? It's easy. Construction? No sweat." And comparing his attitudes to the intellectual agonies that were screwing up the work of his stay-at-home contemporaries, his good luck in being out of Europe and into California is clear.

But he had not really left Europe behind. I sat in the room where Frank Lloyd Wright had waited to apologise to Schindler after their inevitable quarrel, and looked at the ceiling and marvelled how much sheer old-fashioned European professionalism could survive such a sun-change as Los Angeles had wrought on Schindler. Everything is, in fact, symmetrically disposed; clerestory window answering clerestory window; beam answerable to beam, in doubled pairs that recalled Mackintosh's Art School in Glasgow; the joists of the roof deck (visible because there is, in fact, no ceiling at all) disposed in three panels, the joists in the outer panels at right angles to those in the centre, and so forth. His right hand did not lose its cunning, but his creative mind lost its inhibitions.

It is in the use of concrete that this emerges most strikingly. No, sorry, it is the light switches that are most striking—usually a plain chain pull emerging from an equally plain hole drilled in the woodwork, so that years of use have worn the wood into a freeform keyhole shape. The concrete, I should have said, is *instructive.* Its use at all is an oddity—most of Schindler's work, like almost everything else in Los Angeles, is made of wood and stucco. Concrete, the symbolic proof of modernity in Europe, was an oddball or underground material in Southern California, and typically appears in the work of individualists like Irving Gill, or work done on behalf of genuine eccentrics like Death Valley Scotty.

In the Schindler/Chase house, it is used as something between an adobe wall and a plank fence. It was cast on the ground in slabs a metre wide and a shade over two metres high, and then tilted up into the vertical, where it stands, tapering from some 20 centimetres at the bottom to 10 at the top. It would have been almost impossible to tilt these slabs up into position edge to edge, because they would have caught on one another and fouled, so a relief has been formed for most of the length of each vertical edge, and if left unfilled would have made a sort of mediaeval archery slit between each slab and the next. For security and weatherproofing the slits are filled with strips of fluted glass, which admit unexpected shafts of light into the backs of the rooms.

The wooden structure of roof, glazed walls and sleeping porches rests on these massive concrete abutments in a pretty nonchalant-looking manner, but the nonchalance conceals a good deal of sound practical sense, particularly in the avoidance of expensive carpentry details. As an amateur constructor myself, I was constantly recognising usages I had worked out on my own for avoiding, e.g., having to notch a beam or upright where they meet—in other words, avoiding the kind of details that Charles and Henry Greene and their craftsmen had gloried in, so that the contrast between the two houses runs right through from the largest considerations to the smallest, from attitudes to climate to attitudes to saw-cuts.

Yet both were shaped in essence around the same California climate; neither could have happened in any local culture in the world. Both are *thoroughly* Southern Californian, though neither is *typically* Southern Californian—the sort of situation that drives tidy-minded historians and critics out of their heads. There is no single style of architecture that characterises the area, because the only quality that typifies the style of life there is the ability—real or illusory—to invent or adopt any style you like. Charles Greene's four determinants of architecture—Climate, Environment, Materials, and Habits and Tastes—contain only one moderately fixed term, and that is the climate.

Los Angeles's range of environment, from the beaches to the foothills and the deserts, is without comparison in the other metropolises of the world; no local building material is good enough to establish a hegemony over the range of importables; the habits and tastes are anything you like to name. The result is a kaleidoscope (other cliches like 'spectrum' or 'mosaic' are too orderly in their implications) of styles that can produce not only the Greenes' beloved woodwork, Irving Gill's restrained Mission style and Schindler's free-association ad-hockery, but also the fantasies of Hollywood Baroque, the keen sobrieties of Charles Eames's steel house or the total originality of Simon Rodia's ceramic-crusted towers in troubled Watts.

The mixture defies categorisation, but creates an open, flexible situation in which a determined client and an imaginative architect can do their thing without too much fear of what the neighbours may think. A home in Pasadena or Hollywood, or Malibu or Huntington Beach, can be (as Frank Lloyd Wright said of a different situation) "a more organic expression . . . the delightful thing that imagination would have it"—which is rough on us historians, but very good for architecture.

30

Rank Values

It was the closing meeting at Cross-in-Hand Stadium—closing, being dismantled even, on a town-planning objection, which looks odd at first sight because it's quite a pretty place: a 300 yard concrete oval hidden from the Eastbourne road by two meadows and a belt of trees, and only the pen of a great nature poet could have done justice to the men's bogs, wattled enclosures nestling in a grove of birches. The racing there isn't pretty though; it's *rank.* Not in the J-Arthur-Gong sense, but in the Tom Wolfe sense.

I always knew what Wolfe meant by the term. But even he, in *Kandy Kolored Tangerine Flake Streamline Baby,* could only define it obliquely ("made of 100 per cent guaranteed lowest-grade Japanese plastic"), but at Cross-in-Hand enlightenment struck like a bad egg. "Rank" is anything that has got detached from the bottom of an accepted value system. What races at Cross-in-Hand—bangers, stock cars, superstox, hot rods—is not the bottom end of British motoring sport, it doesn't even connect with the official hierarchy. Certainly the Royal toffee-nosed Automobile Club has recently "recognised" the rulebook of Spedeworth Limited, who operate such circuits, but this feat of condescension does not necessarily admit stock-car drivers to regular RAC-

Originally appeared in *New Society* 21, no. 516 (14 September 1972): 510–511.

sanctioned events. The Spedeworth rulebook does not insist on your having a valid driver's licence—an RAC requirement that has kept many a boy racer out of the big time after a visit to the magistrates' courts.

Other manifestations of rank culture, for purposes of comparison, would be the Cloggies cartoon strip (but obviously nothing else in *Private Eye*), Steptoe Senior (but not Alf Garnett), Jaywick Sands, jokes like "What's black and bumps into pianos?" (answer: Ray Charles), Waitrose and other own-brand supermarket lagers . . . which brings up an important point. Having fallen off the bottom of an established value system doesn't mean you have no values; Waitrose lager is not bad, and at Cross-in-Hand Stadium they were a really sharp rank crowd; their applause was not casually bestowed, but with discrimination. For standing a car on its roof, a yelp of approval; for rolling it right over, a roar of applause and *pro rata* for the number of rolls, plus actual clapping if it could then be driven back into the race. For winning a race, only polite murmurs because that wasn't the object of the exercise—except for the last race of the day which was a proper demolition derby, where the money went to the last car capable of moving under its own power.

"Car" is strong language here. In real motor racing, the Graham Hill stuff, there is still some metaphorical substance in the myth that the racing car of today is the family car of tomorrow. Down in rank Spedeworth country, where there are no myths, the banger racer of today is the family car of yesterday after it has failed its MOT. Thirty seven of them lurched to the line for that last race, unsplendent in matt-finish colour schemes of multitone rust and Woolworth spray paint, stripped of all glass and any peripheral components such as lamps that might have resale value, some with their back ends blow-torched right off behind the wheel arches.

The winner was an Austin station wagon (in fact, big Austins won all the banger races). In the apparent absence of any other gears, it backed the full length of the top straight between the accumulated wreckage, kapow! into the front of the only other survivor and smashed his front wings down over the wheels so that he couldn't move. It rebounded about 18 inches, and in its moment of triumph the motor stalled. There was a microsecond of utter silence, and then a howl of congratulation went up.

The scene was really something. Around the 300 yards of track, 37 wrecks were now distributed, two upsidedown, one on its side, one burned out, two still smoking, several hissing quietly as their split radiators emptied, three hooked on the cables of the safety fence, five locked together by tangled metal at one turn, two seemingly friction-welded in eternal deadlock at the other, most immobilised because they had run over parts of their own internals and were reduced to fuming frustration.

It was a right elephants' graveyard of butchered machinery, and it was what the rank crowd had come to see, of course . . . "Of course?" This is one of those "everyone knows" situations. Everyone knows that car-racing fans go to watch the crashes and the bloodshed. The media certainly "know" this, emphasising deaths by fire and mutilation, serialising Jackie Stewart's so-called diary with its chronicle of dead friends and the bravery of rich little widows. Only we're not talking about serious Jackie-Stewart-type car racing here. Cries of "Thank God!" in Jackie-Stewart-type circles, who feel that the ghoul squads who used to sprint up to half a mile to be at a crash scene before the dust had settled and the blood stopped dripping, did the sport's image no good, and are relieved that the ghouls now go to stock-car racing.

Except that, *if* that is where they have gone, then everyone "knows" it wrong. If you want to see bloodshed, don't go to a Spedeworth circuit. In a whole day of miscellaneous motorised mayhem, there was only one (gore-free) stretcher case, which was the first I have ever seen at one of their meetings. No Sir, if your bag is seeing handsome young men mangled and burned, follow the Grand Prix circus and the big-time sports car events like Le Mans. Fair enough actually; one of the things that gives Grand Prix racing its peculiar moral standing among sports, and its strong claim on front-page headlines, is that it is an ultimate risk sport. You get killed.

Thanks to padding, safety harness, low real speeds and plenty of crumpling tin between man and landscape, stock-car drivers live to crash and crash again. So what the hell have the rank crowd come to see if it isn't blood? Answer, something much more threatening; they've come specifically to see metal bent. They've come to see motor cars, top goodies of the consumer society, and the glowing symbols of Sunday-supplement success, reduced to a coughing, leaking, geriatric impotence; scarred, wounded, dragging unhinged doors like broken wings; limping on shredded tyres, their front wheels bent pigeon-toed under the toothless maws where the proud chrome of the radiators once gleamed.

It's marvellous, and completely shameless, the ultimate sadoporn of a product-obsessed culture. It is the terminal subversion of the power of material things, far more subversive of the established value system than most political or philosophical railings against materialism because it is seen to *work*. Sermons and fine words halt no automobiles, but the average Spedeworth driver could stop a dozen in an afternoon.

Obviously, it is too subversive to be allowed to continue. A society that can tolerate the brutal death of foxes and stags, the maiming of racehorses, and noble spectacles like that, can't be expected to stand idly by and allow motor cars to be degraded in public. I said it was the closing meeting at Cross-in-Hand. There was a tombstone on the cover of the programme; but more than that, something happened during the lunch break like nothing I have ever seen at a sporting event anywhere. Most of the crowd formed up on the circuit in a close-packed column of four, with banners, to go on a last defiant protest march past the houses of "the Commander and his cronies," as they called the five determined objectors who gave evidence against Spedeworth at the planning inquiry that had finally closed the track.

By my count, two and a half thousand, out of a crowd of 3,000, went on the march, being joined outside the circuit by another thousand-odd locals who were not stock-car fans but felt sufficiently pissed off at what they saw as the thwarting of the democratic will by a few powerful representatives of entrenched privilege. That's about four times as many as turned out for political demos in Ulster the same afternoon; but you can guess which got the national TV coverage.

In some ways I think the Cross-in-Hand demo was quite as important as the Ulster ones. Admittedly it was too "dirty" for your committed general-purpose protester because commercial interests, as well as democratic principles, were at stake. Nevertheless, all else being equal, it was an important gesture by the Sussex underdoggery; and the things that aren't equal have to do, precisely, with the nature of rank culture, thus:

A very similar ruckus has blown up over the racing circuit not far away at Lydden in Kent. There are many and deeply felt local differences between the two cases; but the basic issues (and a number of other car, cycle and motorboat circuits in the Home Counties) are much the same. All motorised sport causes "noise, parking problems (disputed here), inconvenience and disturbance of the amenities," and that can be very tough if you have moved to this kind of area to get away from specifically that kind of thing. There is no way of bucking these issues; all forms of motorised sport are costly enough to need the support of paying crowds, and all forms of motorised sport have noise as part of their attraction. Quiet motor sport is about as much fun as low-proof whisky or coitus interruptus.

Anyway, it can't be made to fit into the established value system's stereotype of the "countryside" as an area of solitude and silence; and planning authorities will therefore usually find against it. As far as Lydden is concerned, they finally haven't. Could it be because there is one, critical, difference in the social standing of the two cases? There is banger racing at Lydden from time to time, but the main fare offered is conducted under the full panoply of RAC regulations. It's only Minis and other tiddlers and saloons, because the track doesn't meet the safety standards demanded by the Jackie Stewart big-time connection; but, however humble, it's still proper motor racing. The actual sport may be slow, grotty and (during the winter Rallycross season) mud-caked, but properly licensed members of the Establishment race there and—like John Gott, chief constable of Northamptonshire—even get killed doing so.

They belong, they're all right, they're inside the value system. After argument they can proceed to make as much noise as Cross-in-Hand and attract comparable crowds. But the rank enthusiasts of Spedeworth fell off the bottom of the value system (if they were ever on it) and a society that is prepared to subsidise the destruction of public property (namely, British Rail rolling stock) by Everton or Celtic supporters on a more or less weekly basis isn't able to let Sussex's submerged tenth smash up their own property on private land.

Cries of "Here, hold on a minute!" from everyone, including Everton supporters. I'm quite prepared to hear that the commander and his friends are perfectly happy to let Spedeworth bend metal for fun and profit as long as they do it somewhere else, but the effects of the 1947 Planning Act haven't left much-where-else at all. Everton supporters can think themselves lucky that the powers-that-be accept football rowdyism as an inalienable right of the labouring poor.

Since rank motor sport involves the use of automobiles—something that the powers-that-be have always begrudged the labouring poor—the chances of banger-racing and the like ever being legitimised are a bit scant. But maybe it's better that way.

31

Paleface Trash

Yeuk! James Burke was wearing one; so—incredibly—was the standard-issue short-back-and-sides astronaut sitting next to him. The camera began to pan right; could it be that . . . yes . . . (groan) . . . as Patrick Moore hove twitching into view, live by satellite from Cape Kennedy, he, too, was wearing a bolo tie. It was enough to make me give up wearing them altogether.

Of all the many forms of "airport trash," of all the art forms peculiar to the tourist industry, the bolo tie is the most peculiar. It belongs, almost exclusively, to the western states of America, but it is no part of the standard export image of The West. Hardly any of the so-called Western shops in England ever had them, and those that did never knew what to call them: "Lanyards? . . . er, lariat ties . . . er?" said the girl in the old Oxford Street Western store.

I finally learned their real name in a tourist trashmonger's on Fremont Street, Las Vegas . . . which reminds me that Tom Wolfe didn't know what they were called, either,

---

Originally appeared in *New Society* 23, no. 542 (22 February 1973): 426.

when he wrote his famous Las Vegas piece. In the description of Tom Blaney, the creator of the giant illuminated signs, the best he can manage is: "a Texas string tie, the kind that has strings sticking through some kind of silver dollar or something situated at the throat."

The strings are often real leather thongs, or simulated leather plaits, or knitted like bootlaces and don't actually stick through the silver dollar or whatnot. They pass through some kind of clip or buckle on the back of it, so that the dollar can be slipped up and down them and will stay where it's put. Not only does this make it possible to take a bolo tie off and on, it also leads to their alleged functional justification, which is an almost perfect capsule of Middle-Americana. You can slide the dollar down, and wear your shirt a couple of buttons open for comfort; and you can button up and slide the dollar up again, when you enter a restaurant or some other joint you might be thrown out of for not wearing a tie.

My first bolo came from the airport at Seattle—Tacoma, which isn't strictly the West. Its clasp was in the form of the Thunderbird off a totem pole, which makes sense locally. The bulk of bolos on airport stalls aren't local in their references, however. They are straight plastic dude-ranch stuff; crossed Remington rifles in plastichrome, on a free-form permastone plaque, boots, saddles, horseshoes. And they're standardised from St. Louis to the Pacific Coast. But you never see anybody wearing them. They must be bought for the giggle, or out of boredom between planes; taken back east; and forgotten.

Of course, some—like Tom Blaney of Federal Sign and Signal Corporation—have their own personal bolo symbols—like his silver dollar—which they have invested with something of themselves. How many such bolos are custom-made I don't know; but I doubt if they need to be. If you work the racks (in the old rag-trade phrase) at the airports and tourists traps with diligence and imagination, you can usually find some real oddities among all the plastic dudeware. And they might as well be customised, because you'll never see another like them outside the shop.

They range from New Mexico roadrunner birds in pseudo-bronze, through coins and skulls in genuine metals, to objects having real value, craftsmanship, and stuff like that. For instance, stone arrowheads, made of real stone by real Indians living on actual reservations. As physical artefacts their shapes may be only a shade more regular than some of the thinner free-form gem-stones; but their claim to be human products emanating from a particular culture gives them an altogether different status. And they are part of what is currently the most interesting and ambiguous part of the bolo situation.

The better bolos all seem to come from the desert states, from Utah, Colorado, Nevada, Arizona, California. They illustrate Indian themes and are made (in varying degrees) by Indians and not, like the "Indian beads" that hippies used to affect, in Hong Kong. They may yet become a significant art-form, a reservation industry like rug weaving that could stand on its own feet economically; an item of apparel that would enable

Americans of conscience to identify a little with the Indian community without dressing up stupid.

They depict Hopi or Katchina dancers, sand-painting symbols, Zuni snakes and eagles and other totemic animals, sun discs. They are made, as often as not, in what are now the canonical materials of Indian export art, low-carat silver and chips of turquoise, or in tolerable enamel imitations.

Usually, the turquoise is thinly sprinkled on the silver. But if you are prepared to sport more than ten bucks for a bolo, you can often find, somewhere, sun symbols or feathered heads, mosaiced from wafer-thin slivers of coloured stone, set in a matrix of silver wire, and then polished down so that they look almost like Limoges. I have been told that this particular technique came in, like the horse, with the Conquistadores.

It may be true. What clearly did come in with the Conquistadores is the range of simplified Spanish baroque motifs that turn up in the Indian connection. If you saw on television the *Horizon* programme about the Navaho a year or so back, you will have seen practically every single member of the witch-doctor/psychologist seminar, wearing really splendid Hispano-Baroque bolos of heroic size. Gave me a shock, too, because I have never, ever, to the best of my memory, seen a south western Indian wearing one off-camera.

Bolos really don't seem to be normal Indian gear, anyway. They seem to belong somewhere along the uneasy join between the present condition of the American Indian, and the palefaces' cherished mythology of the Old West. For me, this is the bolos' ultimate fascination. Their ambiguity, their dubious authenticity, is their main recommendation, for reasons that I will endeavour to explain sensibly.

My own relationship to "the Indian thing" is a blank. I have read and heard all the arguments—political, legal, economic or macrobiotic—about their present plight. I have duly seethed with liberal rage at their exploitation. My stomach has heaved at the piles of beer bottles and puke left at the entrances to their (alcohol-free) reservations. I have talked to some Indians who cared to talk. But between me and Indians ancient and modern, present (as at Taos) or absent (as at Mesa Verde), there seems to be a glass wall that I do not feel separating me from any other culture I have encountered on its own ground.

I must go back and make my peace with this situation sometime. But, for the present, the way of the Indian remains for me inscrutable and private. At Taos—*even at Taos!*—which is fairly open and touristy, I found that there were scenes and persons, such as a woman swathed all in white who stood still on a roof-terrace for practically an hour, at which I could not point a camera because it would have seemed a gross invasion of privacy.

I could not bring myself to intrude. In the same way, I do not covet genuine Indian art-works and ritual objects. To possess one would be a kind of anthropological pillage as far as I am concerned. It's their religion, their magic, and I don't feel I have any right to mess with it. But I remain totally fascinated, like everyone else who has seen the pueblos. And if I feel a glass wall between myself and them, my nose is pressed hard against it. And the bolo tie, Indian in format and possibly in workmanship, is still paleface trash; safely this side of the glass; something I can wear with a clear conscience.

32

Power Plank

Tread softly if you carry a big stick; but tread how you like if you carry a clipboard, because no one dare question your authority. Few portable artefacts pack such symbolic power as this piece of plank with a bulldog clip at its top. Sceptre, sword and crozier may lose their sway, but the man with the clipboard commands instant respect. And the reasons why are probably traceable to our old friend, the Military-Industrial Complex.

Within the established hierarchies of that complex, there are fine gradations of personal power that cannot be indicated by brass badges, or the colour of a pay-slip—crucial slender margins, quite different from the gross differences of power enforced by, say, the police or footy referees. Those have important uniforms, and carry notebooks, but when they have taken a name or issued a caution, they *put the notebook away again.* Not so the clipboard, which must be permanently in hand and visible, and thus distinguishes the NCO in charge of stores from the equal-ranking NCO who, from

Originally appeared in *New Society* 24, no. 560 (28 June 1973): 762.

a position of weakness, is trying to get something *out* of stores. Alternatively, it distinguishes "staff" who happen to be visiting the shop floor in dirty clothes, from honest members of AUEW whose clothes are dirty because they are never *off* the shop floor.

Anyhow, when I was a member of the military-industrial complex myself, I had a marvellous ringside view of the clipboard being used to indicate crucial microgradations of power, even among upper staff. Test-pilots and test-observers alike wore flying overalls, leather helmets and intercom headsets, but the pilots had their notepads strapped to their thighs, so that they could jot down Observations Essential to the War Effort ("Skein of geese over Quantoxhead") without removing more than one hand from the business of flying. Observers, however, who were sitting down the back among their gauges, had nothing better to do with their hands than make notes, and so carried clipboards.

This may sound like a mere functional discrimination, but it was also an essential means of enforcing the strict social structure ordained by our chief test pilot, who had decreed that observers, like pilots, were entitled to cups of steaming black coffee when they came back frozen from the empyrean, "as long as they don't drink it in the pilots' mess, but in a standing position in the corridor outside the kitchen." Any observer with ideas above his station who tried to sneak into the mess would be betrayed by his clipboard, and immediately ostracised by all decent people. Nor dare he abandon his clipboard, because he might then be mistaken for mere AUEW members, like myself, who were occasionally issued with flying gear in order to perform suitably menial tasks aloft.

So, if you're insecure about your precise rung in the hierarchy, the old power plank can be very reassuring, and there's no lack of functional excuses for carrying one. There are always lists to be checked, boxforms to be filled out, agenda to be worked through, scores to be ranked. Sociologists know all this stuff, of course, but keep quiet about it for obvious reasons—the clipboard is their margin of middle class ascendancy over their subject matter. But don't think that the subjects resent this; the sight of the clipboard tells them it's Role-Playing Time, and they can get to work battering babies, vandalising playgrounds, resenting immigrants, being influenced by violence on the box, and making up stupid rhymes for the Opies.

However, there is also an important role-ambiguity in the, as it were, bi-polar nature of the clipboard itself. The board serves to support the questionnaire that is being filled out, and the clip serves to stop it blowing away. But the clip also symbolises the power of the board-wielder to take, and clip down, pieces of paper from those over whom dominion is given. Thus a ticket inspector will secure under the clip dubious tickets, receipts (and carbons of receipts) and other documents by which he accumulates control over his clients. Ditto the waterguards in customs sheds. And in both cases it's made worse by the fact that the rotten bleeders are in uniform and we are not, so they don't *need* to gain power over us by this modern equivalent of securing nail-parings and locks of hair.

So there's a pretty rich vein of social and psychological pay-dirt in clipboards; but where's the expertise about them? Who designs them? When did they mutate from a piece of plank with a loose clip over the top, to a snub-cornered board with a purpose-made clip riveted to it? What's the morphology? What's the bi-polar Levistrology?

I checked out our family holdings in clipboards. We have four for some reason, and the most basic is one of those nasty pieces of hardboard from Ryman's that everyone seems to own these days, with a heavily styled (horizontal ribs) clip and no means of identification, except the words "Made in England" on the back of the clip. But we also possess the same device bound in Royal Blue PVC with a slightly different clip (but possibly from the same stylist) bearing the unmistakable symbol of W. H. Smith since they went "Good Design," but—and mark this—made in Holland. In other words, the power-symbols of Euroburocracy are here before we're properly into the common market.

The other two are more instructive. One appears to be a vintage classic, equivalent in its field to a Red Label Bentley or 30/98 Vauxhall. For a start, the board is genuine plywood and *varnished.* The clip is modest in form, with a simple round head to the lever. The blade, however, has the words *East-Light* in a neat rectangular border super-imposed on that great period image, a sunrise, while the top right-hand corner of the board has a transfer about the size of a large postage stamp with the lapidary wording: "EAST-LIGHT: when re-ordering specify East-Light board-clip No. 51 (mounted on polished hardwood) also give size 4to or F'cap."

Board-clip!? Sounds a bit Purcell Room, doesn't it, like *forte-piano*? The whole thing looks as if it comes from the late twenties, but did they have clipboards then? Is it a collector's piece? Is there an East-Light Owners' Club, or an East-Light Register for locating discontinued spare parts? Perhaps other East-Light owners would care to contact me, especially the long-wheelbase F'cap model, and we could have a rally at Woburn or something as dreary.

From classic to plastic: the fourth board looks like an attempt at a radical innovation, Alex Moulton style. It came from a back-to-college display at the Ralph's Super-market on Sunset Boulevard. It is bound in black PVC, has a very modest clip—but *two* boards. The plastic binding not only forms an envelope pocket on the face of each board, but also forms a simple hinge between the boards, which close over like the covers of a book. It's a real break from the classic format all right, only it's particularly useless. You can't handle it as a clipboard without folding the spare board right round behind the main one, which splits the plastic hinge a bit further and allows papers tucked in what is now the outer pocket to fall out unobserved.

Its only real advantages are in the area of symbolism. It obviously outranks plain clipboards, not only because it's more complex but also because its contents are concealed when it's closed. It thus gives me a slight edge when, say, working on a television programme where practically everybody on the crew—director, director's personal assistant, studio manager, camera assistants, make-up girl even—brandishes a power plank. At tea-breaks, when all the boards are on the table, so to speak, it's possible for me to get some idea how far the others have got with their To-Be-Dones, shooting schedules, footage counts and so forth, but they can't see where I have got to with proposals to mess the script about.

It looks as if the next stage in clipboard development has got to be in this direction. Special-equipment clipboards with stop-watch holders already exist in motor sporting circles, and some sociologists who are still into quantification have had hand counters mounted on theirs. But where are the clipboards with built-in lights for night observations, with perspex canopies to keep the rain off, with slide-rules down the edge, with navigational protractors, with bullet-proof backs for Queen's University, Belfast, sociologists? Yes, I expect they are all on file in the Patent Office, but until they are in Ryman's and Smith's they are not doing what they could to enrich the hierarchical symbolism of a visually egalitarian society.

33

Iron Bridge Embalmed

A close, steamy day—real Shropshire weather—in the gorge, and the place choked
with coachloads of tourists. The Iron Bridge still heaved its experimental arches in
shaky temerity across the Severn to the Benthall bank, but instead of its perfect semi-
circle of cast iron being reflected in the river to make the perfect circle you see in the
old prints, the water was penned, interrupted and diverted by caissons of sheet steel
in which men were at work stabilising the footings of the arch.

So, within sight of its bicentenary (1977), the Iron Bridge in Coalbrookdale, most
sacred relic of British industrial archaeology, was visibly well on its way to its final fate
as a fully charabanced and properly mummified piece of Our National Heritage—like
the Tower of London or the lions of Longleat. As part of the official British Travel Association's vision of Britain, protected by the Ironbridge Gorge Museum Trust *and* the
Friends of the Ironbridge Gorge Museum, it begins to look like a good nitty-gritty
idea being relentlessly smothered by Portmeirion-style gutless genteelism.

The trust's own bookshop—next to the cleared and sterilised area by the bridge-
head, tastefully re-Georgianised and filled with Coalport pottery—seemed to sum up

---

Originally appeared in *New Society* 25, no. 570 (6 September 1973): 587–588.

what was happening well enough. But what really tolled the bell for me was the notice in the window announcing that Barrie Trinder would autograph copies of *The Industrial Revolution in Shropshire* (Phillimore) there at noon the next day.

We had come up to the Dale specifically to read Trinder on location, and before we set out, that old book trade autograph-copy promotional dodge would have seemed the last thing that the rusted and sooted relics of our manufacturing forebears needed. But right there on the territory it began to look all too apt. It has been a lowering experience for over 20 years (almost to the day, since I first saw it) to watch the Iron Bridge going from simple neglect in the early fifties when it passed into the un-safekeeping of the county council, and began to be vandalised to its present condition of embalmed municipalisation. It's good to have it preserved, and good that its footings are being made secure, but the gardenesque devastation of everything around it is relentlessly eroding its visible and tangible meaning.

This is not, I hope, sentimental niggling that the Gorge has ceased to be a scene of picturesque decay. What's at stake is the whole problem of the relationship of buildings to landscape, which in the Ironbridge/Coalbrookdale area is a matter of acute historical importance. Thanks to the activities of the Museum Trust, the landscape problem has expanded to practically territorial scale. The area covered by the trust's activities runs something like four miles, from the dam of the Upper Furnace pool at Coalbrookdale to the entrance of the Tar Tunnel at the foot of Hay Incline. At this point the length of the Blists Hill Open-air Museum runs back through its woods and glades some three quarters of a mile from the Severn's bank. That's a lot of landscape, and it's all relevant, but the relevance is vanishing under a load of erudition and good intentions of which Trinder's book is unfortunately typical.

It looks, and feels in the hand, as if it is going to be just what the inquiring visitor needs at this point: the local equivalent of Georgina Masson's *Companion Guide to Rome* or Hugh Honour's likewise to Venice. These are big-league comparisons, which *The Industrial Revolution in Shropshire* invites by its encyclopaedic and learned text, and the world-wide historical importance of its subject. But it cannot be made to function as a guidebook, and that's what is so desperately needed. The trust's standard-format pamphlets on individual monuments don't fill the want, either; they are too limited in content, too destructible in use and too easy to lose in the field.

Trinder's book doesn't set out to be a guide. It is a straight-up-and-down social and economic history of his selected piece of the Industrial Revolution—all the usual stuff about turnpikes, Methodists, gin, Chartists, poor-law commissioners, Friendly Societies, strikes (you got a lot to answer for, Asa Briggs!), parish registers, smallpox . . . to be fair, there are only *two* references to smallpox, as against 65 to steam engines and something over 500 to aspects of ironworking. So no one can complain that this thorough and painstaking book is off-balance except me, and I think it is off-balance in exactly the way in which the whole Ironbridge Gorge Museum Archaeology Industry is running off-balance at present.

The trouble is that the scholarly view of the industrial revolution of the 18th century is obsessed with the concepts of capital and workforce. In the atmosphere of diffused marxism (more properly, I suspect, engelism) that pervades British academe, it is the anonymous and amorphous movements of cash and labour that are felt to be most powerfully real. But that's a bum feeling in the Gorge, where it is hardware and brick-work, water and iron, that matter. Grand general statistical overviews mean nothing here; everything is specific, unique, local and peculiar—because of the landscape.

The south Shropshire coalfield consists of a rather ramshackle plateau handily stuffed with useful minerals, into which the upper waters of the Severn have carved a gorge some 300 feet deep, thus creating a set of techno-topographical challenges and opportunities without equal in the world at that time. It was that mating of machinery and mineralogy that made Coalbrookdale "the wonder of the age."

If you don't believe me, go and stand on the pioneering cast-iron bridge and look up and down that most dramatic part of the Gorge with its mixture of tree-clad crags and cliff-hung edifices of commerce and industry. Or stand down the hole by Darby's re-stored 1777 furnace at Coalbrookdale, with generations of brick and stone retaining walls supporting the upper pool above you, and the arches of the railway viaduct stilt-ing above that. Or halfway up the grassed slope of the Hay Incline and marvel, not only that the technology of 1793 could move boats up and down its 1,100 foot length, but that the darn thing (thanks to Shropshire topography) has water at the bottom *and* the top!

And when you've done that, follow the signs for the Tar Tunnel, which I reckon to be the most manic and fantastic of all these early confrontations between technology and geology. Conceived originally as an underground canal running back directly from river level to mine-workings deep under the plateau, it finished up as a railway reaching 1,000 yards under Blists Hill and a drainage culvert from the mine-workings there— and the source of the tar that gave it its name. The tunnel intercepted a number of natural seepages of bitumen, yielding a total of up to 1,000 gallons a week, which William Reynolds, the proprietor, processed and sold with proper entrepreneurial zeal.

You enter the tunnel now through an unpromising door in the back cellar of an aban-doned shop—exactly the kind of unforgettable scene-setting that is being eliminated through misplaced tidymindedness elsewhere. Its brick-lined, horseshoe section, not always tall enough to stand up in, electrically lit at intervals, and you can go about 100 yards in increasing chill and damp before you're stopped at an iron grille. Tar still seeps through the brickwork at a number of points, but about 70 yards in, a hole on the right of the tunnel affords a low view into one of the tar pools, dark, glassy, enigmatic under a single spotlight.

That's the place; the chill centre of the whole "great human exploit." Somewhere to pause and reflect in tranquillity on the sublime and picturesque impressions with which the senses have been battered throughout the visit. Impressions of a landscape where every prospect seems to command prime sites for "a gravity-feed operation"—raw materials in at the top of the hill, finished products out at the bottom, and a millstream down the side to keep the wheels turning, and great stone foundations, cinder banks, tall glassless windows, broken walls of engineering brick to prove it all happened.

Do you wonder that 18th century visitors went out of their tiny Enlightened skulls on viewing it in the original flaring colours preserved for us in de Loutherberg's pictures? And don't you regret that no one around the industrial archaeology business today seems capable of going out of theirs, or of transmitting any of that excitement if they feel it. The whole presentation of the museum complex is listless where it doesn't seem faintly grudging—none of the exhibits in the open air anywhere is labelled, for instance.

That's why I feel it's all going down the drain of established academic culture. Barrie Trinder's book is packed with well-researched information, much of it twice—occasionally twice on the same page, almost word-for-word! Somewhere under this mountain of academic overkill lies buried the physical presence of the Shropshire industrial revolution. There is, in fact, only one publication in or about the Gorge that rises to the occasion historically or in any other way, and that's the car-windscreen sticker proclaiming "It all started here" [insert picture of bridge] "and we've been there!"

That's more like it, but still doesn't deal with the real problem, which is the failure to respond to the physical presence of the scene and its buildings and artefacts. Trinder's defenders (and they'll be numerous in the present creepy state of the trade) will argue that it's unfair to abuse him for this—that he set out to write a scholarly study, not a pop guide. But that really reinforces my point, by implying that it's not quaite naice to go out of your skull over this collision between industry and topography. In complaining that he failed to write a guidebook, I am really expressing my bewilderment that anyone with eyes in his head and aching muscles in the back of his legs (oh, those inclined planes!) could want to write anything else.

Sundae Painters

Ice cream waggons must be about the biggest invisible objects in residential Britain. If they are "seen" by adults it is metaphorically—as problems, as threats to the road safety of children, their chimes an invasion of environmental privacy. But next time a waggon enters your field of concerned liberal attention, try looking at it with your eyes instead, because the chances are much better than evens that you are looking at a genuine, good-as-autographed David Cummins.

Cummins? Cummins of Crewe (Crewe!?) produce about 500 ice cream vans a year, and totally dominate the British market. David Cummins, of the founding family, is the man who must be credited with designing (for want of a more accurate word) this highly saleable product. And you won't find him sitting down to a drawing board to do it. More likely he will fumble out a fag packet and a ballpoint and "We'll do a curve something like this, then a sort of thing here, and try to bend it round underneath . . . huh?" The rather shaky drawing, smaller than the thumbnail alongside it, will be for most of the

Originally appeared in *New Society* 28, no. 601 (11 April 1974): 82–83.

back end of a van, or at least for the whole of the complex bit at the point where the tail fin meets the roof and the back window. "But sometimes," Cummins says happily, "we just draw in the dust on the side of the body!"

He's what intellectual circles would call an autodidact. Left school a couple of weeks before his A levels; came into the firm to work on the refrigeration side; learned the trade by sitting next to Nelly, as the saying goes; and took over from Nelly as soon as he realised that that worthy was doing it all wrong ("Technical college? Useless—full of retired railwaymen converting fractions to decimals and back"). His drawing would get an "I for incompetent" in any design school. He knows what an isometric is but can't draw in perspective. Yet his drawings sell more vans, he claims, than photographs would. They give all the information that's relevant; isn't that enough?

Within the works it certainly is. He's working in a kind of vernacular situation which—in spite of the novelty of its materials (fibreglass) and technology (soft-serve ice cream, and stuff)—is the way the master masons of the Middle Ages are supposed to have worked. Whether they did or no is arguable; but, for generations of design theorists now, right back through Gropius to William Morris and beyond, it has been an article of faith that in the Middle Ages there were no drawing-board designers, and the master mason clambered about the scaffolding making design decisions on the spot and explaining them to his workforce by scratching thumbnail sketches on a corner of tile and saying, "Let us make an ogee somewhat after this manner, then a quodlibet here, and curve it (God willing) upon the buttock side . . . Prithee?"

Not that Gropius himself ever worked like that. In spite of his expressionist rhetoric about "abolishing the snobbish distinction between artists and craftsmen," it is not recorded that he clambered about the scaffold of the Bauhaus building in Dessau, saying, "*Machen Sie eine bogen, und Etwas hier damit . . . u.s.w.*" They don't do that kind of thing in the places where they worry about design, only in the places where they worry about getting the product on the road and working for its living. . . .

The particular non-medieval vernacular in which Cummins works isn't as old as he is. He might *just* have been in long trousers when "somewhere about 15 or 17 years ago, say 1955," the family garage built its first ice cream van, after a period of building trailers and station waggons ("because they didn't have to pay purchase tax") for friends. Those 1955 prototypes have a distinctly Noddy-car air; the front ends were pure cartoon-faces. But the idiom clearly comes, in fact, from the bus-body traditions of the time, complete with the double-drooping styling line down the side.

Those were metal bodies over a wood frame, and the waggons stayed basically metal panelled for years. The fibreglass revolution struck remarkably late, when the big fat Bedford CF van-chassis became available at the end of the sixties. The greatest triumphs of the Rocket-Baroque phase of the Cummins vernacular had been a couple or four years earlier than that, when the space race and Batman had provided a linked set of images that looked entirely appropriate servicing the queues outside the Science Museum in the school holidays.

Although tail fins and Batman imagery persist, the whole style has calmed down, matured. Paint is taking over the prime visual role. It's always been important, of course; and from the very beginning Cummins colour schemes have always divided in the same way, with very few exceptions: cream or white above the droopy styling line: pink, sludge blue or sharp green below ("Just done a brown one. . . . D'you think brown's all right for an ice cream van?"). Now, however, these two fields of colour are being colonised by a new tutti-frutti of detached motifs and flourishes. Batman, Robin survive, joined by Disney characters; but the merchandise itself, a whole repertoire of different types of ice cream is taking over, garnished with swirling ribbons and stars. And a slight touch of history here and there, where imitation awning stripes, like on the original hokey-pokey carts, adorn the visible side-panels of the roofs.

Occasionally an ambitious van buyer will ask to have a scene painted on his machine. There were two in the shed last month; one with knights jousting and a castle in the background, the other a Mediterranean village (sic) with a palm tree. The knights were frankly awful, the palm tree spread was OK (even if its iconography leaves the package tour industry with a lot to answer for). But neither seems to me to have much to do with the real ice cream vernacular. It's all those dancing ice lollies, overloaded cones, stupefying sundaes, zooming wafers, and saucy Ninety-nines, that are what it's all about, framed in brackets and dotted lines, looped with ribbons and punctuated with stars. And these are legendary—in the sense that there's a legend about them.

Almost the first I ever heard about Cummins of Crewe was from an ice cream vendor one dozy hot July afternoon off the Balls Pond Road (honest!). Trade was quiet, though he had the bonnet of the Bedford up to keep the engine cool. We passed the time of day, and I admired the paintwork, and he told me it was all done with such obvious loving care because the painters were "little old men who'd been doing the numbers and stuff on railway carriages at Crewe before they closed the works."

Not a word of it's true. The basic paintwork is done by regular automotive paint-job specialists like you might find at your neighbourhood body-shop, and the fancy stuff is done by a couple of signwriters named Wilf Cross and Terry Colvin. Though I did feel that a touch of the legendaries was creeping in when Cummins explained that they *used* to have a signwriter named Pasquale Ferrugia, and that what I was assuming (privately) to be a bit of motel art from Venice, on the office wall, was the view from Ferrugia's room on the Grand Canal. Cummins's face was perfectly straight as he told me this, and the painting *was* signed Ferrugia. . . .

However, not all is paint that seems so . . . some of the figures and ice creams are standard transfers. But the ribbon work has to be painted. So, for some reason, do the sundaes. Next time you come upon a Cummins van, have a look at those cherries, each executed with a couple of twists of the brush. They're as delectable a *morceau de peinture* as you'll come upon in a month of.

The Sundaes (and the ribbon work) are also indicative of a certain easy-going self-confidence that pervades the style these days. There's nothing tentative or provincial about it, and that's just as well since Cummins are now on a "Today, Crewe; tomorrow, the World" trajectory. Already selling their ice cream waggons to Europe and even Italy (real coals-to-Newcastle stuff), not to mention Hong Kong, they now have a body shell that goes across the Atlantic, fully trimmed and equipped, and drops on to a standard Chevrolet chassis when it gets there.

Regrettably, only the prototype "American machine" had a genuine Cummins paint job. The production models will go in underpaint, and will receive local artwork. Admittedly, there are good commercial reasons for this, and the style of Cross and Colvin is more than an ocean different from that of the heavy American coach-painters and Kustomisers. But it might still marry up to some of the more exotic American work. I'd really like to see one of those sundaes and its ribbons floating over the desert scenes that Art Himsl currently paints on Californian supervans.

Meanwhile, I'll settle for the Cummins product as it stands, residual tail fins and all. More than that, I'll salute it as one of the better things to be seen on our roads today. And watch out for Cummins on water too, because he builds and hires out special narrow houseboats for use on the local canals. *In steel.* And when I asked why steel, when everybody else was building rental boats in fibreglass and he had a factory full of fibreglass wizards, he simply said, "You should see them after they come back after a couple of days' hiring . . . all those narrow stone bridges."

And there was this pile of chairs in the yard: "We're doing a night club in an old cornmill." In a fit of extreme thickness I asked who had designed it, expecting the name of an architect. "Well, we did. I mean we're sort of making it up on the spot, you know." By then I *should* have known.

35

Bricologues a la Lanterne

Among the dottier myths that haunt the "world of discourse" in which I operate is that of the *bricoleur*. It comes—appropriately enough—from *La Pensée Sauvage,* but—equally appropriately—has already taken on mythographic aspects that Lévi-Strauss himself never intended:

"The *bricoleur* is still someone who works with his hands and uses devious means compared to those of the craftsman. . . . The *bricoleur* [dictionary definition: odd job man or handyman] is adept at performing a large number of diverse tasks; but, unlike the engineer, he does not subordinate each of them to the availability of raw materials and tools conceived and procured for the purpose of the project. His universe of instruments is closed and the rules of his game are always to make do with 'whatever is at hand' . . . the engineer is always trying to make his way out of and go beyond the constraints imposed by a particular state of civilisation, while the *bricoleur* by inclination or necessity always remains within them."

Those are the actual Lévi-Strauss words as quoted in the most consequential bricological text to date, *Adhocism* by Charles Jencks and Nathan Silver (1972), where the

Originally appeared in *New Society* 37, no. 717 (1 July 1976): 25–26.

bricoleur is set up as the archetypical make-do-and-mend patcher and improviser and thus the patron saint for their "new" gospel of improvisatory design. However, the bricoleur has also come in patron-handy to ecomaniacs and alternative technologists, to architectural dissidents reacting against the sophisticated rigor mortis of "system building," to Popperian proponents of piecemeal planning as against comprehensive redevelopment . . . and *haute-bricolage* has been detected by some critics in the work of Marcel Duchamp and Robert Rauschenberg.

This, however, is not the role for which Lévi-Strauss intended him. The passage from Jencks, quoted above, is a brilliant piece of selective editing from which the original meaning has been totally mislaid. If you go back to the text (around page 16 in most translations) you will find that the bricoleur is not part of any anthropological statement or argument, but more like an extended metaphor or parabolic gloss on one.

Much as the parable of the Good Samaritan appears in the gospel less to claim virtue for Samaritans than to make a point about the nature of good neighbourliness, so the bricoleur is there less to claim virtue for do-it-yourself than to illuminate a point about the nature of mythologies—that they are cobbled up ad hoc out of folk tales and fables that are to hand, rather than purpose-designed to explain the Cosmos.

Time, I think, has had one of its little revenges hereabouts. When *La Pensée Sauvage* was written, the polar opposition between Bricoleur and Engineer could have been understood as it was intended—as a cute expository device of almost mathematical elegance. But by the time the book was translated into English, it had reached the status of being almost the Third Testament, so every word in it had to be read as gospel. To judge from conversations around design schools (and much of *Adhocism,* too) the bricoleur is now established as a kind of third-world alternative to science and engineering, pottering around in his *bidon* in the *barriada,* improvising, as like as not, a wheelchair out of Coke cans and dismembered rollerskates—so that his neighbour, legless and blinded after the attentions of the local junta, can get to his begging pitch outside the Hilton Hotel.

In the same mythography, the engineer (who confusingly includes the scientist according to Lévi-Strauss) is of course the black-tie-and-white-shirt figure in the air-conditioned and fluorescently lit laboratory, feeding his computer with data that will require the rape of several thousand *tonnes* of rare earths from the ancestral lands of the last tribe of matrileneal, head-hunting, three-toed-sloth-worshipping, etcetera, etcetera.

You know the picture. . . . But the point is that even if you subtract all that current eco-loving, Volvo-driving, culture worry, and get back to the bare bones of the original polar opposition, it still isn't true. Lévi-Strauss's engineer is an even more mythological figure than his bricoleur. Even if, as Jencks sagely observes, the difference between Bricoleur and Engineer is one of degree, then on any evenly graded scale from the one to the other, practically everybody, *including* the engineers, is going to be up the brico end, with hardly a soul at the other. The Lévi-Strauss engineer, conceiving and procuring everything specially for the project, may possibly exist in exam papers at the Ecole Polytechnique, but nowhere else in engineering as generally understood.

The reason for this should be obvious enough. Engineering, as generally understood, is a true child of bourgeois capitalism. Its *ultima ratio* is still profit. There is normally far less profit in using specials and one-offs than in using whatever is at hand, on the shelf, in the stores, ex-catalogue. As Bruce Archer used to say to his industrial-design students at the Central School: "Stop designing nuts and bolts. They're all in the book!" And this applies right up to the commanding heights of engineering technology, where money is supposed to be no object.

Thus is it not true even that "you can't bricolate your way to the Moon." The Apollo excursions were engineered down to the last accountable fart and belch *because* they used that irreducible off-the-peg component, man himself, accepting the "constraints of a particular state of civilisation," instead of going beyond them and insisting on fully automated observation devices (as the Russians tried to do with Lunokhod). And as anyone who reads the ads in the colour supps will know, all sorts of standard kit like cameras and wristwatches went on the Apollo jaunts "as found," or nearly so.

Again, until the 98 per cent purpose-designed Ferraris began to dominate Grand Prix racing last year, we had seen nearly a decade in which the commanding heights of automotive technology were occupied by Formula One racers that were bricolated together out of Ford motors, Hewland gearboxes, Girling brakes, and so forth. Even now Ferrari doesn't make his own spark plugs or brake pads, for goodness sake.

Where you are most likely to encounter the purpose-conceived and purpose-procured product is at levels so modest they aren't normally thought of as engineering. The plastic comb in your pocket was the product of just the kind of monomaniac "universe of instruments" that Lévi-Strauss attributes to engineering: made in a machine specific to comb-moulding out of specially blended comb-plastic. Or take the current basis of the whole culture and technology of third-world economies (if what you see on the box is to be trusted), to wit: the yellow plastic bucket! That is the end-product of a process in which every component, procedure and material is specific to the production of plastic buckets.

But just because the Lévi-Strauss engineer is a kind of one-dimensional polemical caricature (or can serve as one) and is a purely academic construct, unsullied by the kind of observation of real life that anthropologists used to be expected to be careful about, he is very handy for academics bricolating theories out of other people's books. He appeals fatally to the kind of mind that likes to work with cultural monads.

That's why he literally suits the book of Jencks and Silver. Products of a period of architectural education that tended to reduce all its students to cultural monads by insisting that they re-design everything from scratch in one-to-one correspondence to its specific function, they discovered bricolage not for what it was—the way the world has always worked—but as a gospel of salvation. And since a gospel needs a Satan, the engineer had an immediate role in this new bricosmology.

What's worrying, ultimately, is that an elegantly contrived but trifling metaphor should come to be regarded as a revelation about the nature of design. Worrying in that it is only a symptom of the general ignorance about engineering among those who profess to tell us what's wrong and what's right with western culture, and—above all— what's wrong with engineering as a part of that culture. I know one shouldn't tell tales out of school, but I remember that during the period that *Adhocism* was being written, one of the authors, challenged on a point of engineering ignorance, actually rang me up to ask if "there's a good book on technology I could read?"

People who can believe that mass bricolage is a sovereign remedy for "forces and ideas that hinder the fulfilment of human purposes . . . large corporations . . . philosophies of behaviourism . . . modern architecture" because it is the opposite of the faceless "technostructure" of engineering, should think again, carefully. Modern bricolage, on the evidence of the illustrations in *Adhocism* (and the pix, at least, do observe the real world) works *only* with the offcuts and discards of engineering. Not a single unmanufactured piece of natural material, not an ass's jawbone nor a twig of willow appears in this conspectus. The bricoleur's universe of instruments proves—in this version—to be just another colonial dependency of the dreaded technostructure.

Touchez pas au brico! It could be injurious to your health if you don't know what it's about. After all, and at the end of the day, the bricolage to end all bricologues is the use of a lamp post as a gallows!

36

Lair of the Looter

For a seemingly harmless building, the Getty Museum at Malibu, California, has had to withstand an awful lot of flak. Most of it, of course, has been directed at the man behind the building—the last of the big looters, balancing his collection on top of a cliff that might have been better left as nature intended it. And that's not "another story" either, because much of the popular success of the museum has nothing to do with the architecture, but a lot to do with its being the lair of the last looter. Getty-gawping is not so very different from Bedford-gawping, or Devonshire-gawping.

Except that the museum is vastly better designed for gawping than Woburn or Chatsworth—beginning with the vast parking garage underneath. Not that the building was ever inhabited by JPG himself—growing popular legend to the contrary. It was conceived as a pure museum, yet that is not the source of the pronounced "museum chill" that pervades it. That comes from the excessive zeal of the designers, who sought to lift the design above controversy—and have had nothing else since it opened.

Originally appeared in *New Society* 40, no. 761 (5 May 1977): 238.

The basic premise of the design, as announced by the founding tycoon, was to make an accurate reconstruction of the Villa of the Papyri at Herculaneum (probably the biggest loot-strike ever in the history of predatory archaeology). The plan of the villa has been known since the site was tunnelled through in the process of rifling it in the 1750s, and this is straightforwardly reproduced at Malibu. It is a plain square Roman country house with an atrium and an internal court, and a long water-garden in front with a peristyle all round it.

Delicious! You look from the vestibule down the long colonnaded water through a cleft in the wooded cliffs to the Pacific Ocean beyond, and it's as adorable and sybaritic as the sites where the Romans built the real thing around the Bay of Naples. Only this particular real thing was not built in one of those crotchy clefts where Clodia and the Poet did their well-known numbers, but on flatter agricultural land with no such view of the water. The Getty site works well, though, since the ravine makes for easier access to the parking below—but shouldn't they have found a more comparable Roman model?

Benefit of the doubt, I think. It does work, and it looked *so* gorgeous in the deepening, purpling evening, with the ocean shimmering under the romantically hovering lights of the police helicopters. What one can't forgive is the grindingly remorseless accuracy of the detailing. Actually, no one has any real idea what the finishes, surfaces, applied ornament of the original were like, apart from occasional tunnelers' *aperçus* through the lava that buried Herculaneum. Norman Neuerburg and the other historical consultants have therefore been forced to invent—no, *bricolate*—a repertoire of details from other, more accessible, Roman remains of comparable age, scale and function.

They have done it with such bureaucratic precision and lack of wit that it is, I think, pointless for Getty-bashers to try and question its accuracy. Neuerburg, I am sure, can quote chapter and verse for every triglyph, bucrane, niche and astragal, because I have heard him doing it, in tones of mortal offence at being queried. The erudition and workmanship are as impeccable, and absolutely deathly, as this kind of pluperfect reconstruction must always be.

But they are also *relatively* deathly, as well as *absolutely* so. There happen to be good cases for comparison all around, as anyone who tries to cry "Pure Hollywood!" with a gesture of dismissive contempt, will soon find. The gesture sticks in mid-contumely, the cry will not pass the larynx. For Hollywood was never like this, in spite of the millions spent boasting about the thousands that were spent on accuracy. Bad taste will out, every busby gets berkeleyed over some telling detail. Getting classical architecture, in particular, enjoyably screwed up was (and is) one of the great national sports of southern California.

You don't even have to go the ten or twelve miles to Hollywood to see it, either. A ravine and a canyon west of the Getty lair is a housing subdivision called Sunset Mesa, which offers some half-dozen variants on the same basic tacky house-type. One of these has a cheerfully loony cut-price Ionic portico. Confronted with all this *klassisistischkitsch,* the Getty is just an exquisite corpse, and—equally obviously—is not pop architecture, as maintained by defenders like David Gebhard from fake Spanish-colonial Santa Barbara up the coast. Whatever the erudite likes of Gebhard may say, this is, very definitely, high art. What makes it despicable, despite its virtues, is that it is *failed* high art, but not failed in the way that would make it camp, in Susan Sontag's terminology. (Remember Susan Sontag?).

The failure lies in a crunching lack of sympathy for the key exhibits to which it was specifically intended to be sympathetic—the Roman sculptures and reliefs. Far from looking at home, they look lost. The setting deprives them of their residual life and makes them look like junk, in contrast with the mummified completeness and high finish all around them. The missing noses, toes, fingers which were their warrant of antiquity and authority now make them look worn out and discarded. You wonder what they're doing in a smart new motel like this.

Motel? The comparison seems to me unavoidable. If you are going to make a high-art/low-art scene about the relationship of "Roman" statuary to modern "Roman" buildings, then the appropriate benchmark in this case seems not to be any glyptotek, museion or gallery, but Caesar's Palace in Las Vegas. That is far from being my favourite along the Strip (though it has many fans among high-art pop-fanciers) and its detailing is nearly always pretentiously wrong-headed and Mickey-Mousical. But it does have a sumptuous air of nouveau riche dissipation and fat-city pleasures, of stern middle class morality coming apart at the seams, that hits you again and again as you peer into the capacious and elaborately decorated interiors that the Romans built in those now-buried pleasure cities under the shadow of Vesuvius.

That air is coldly absent at the Getty. It doesn't even have the distant echoes of imperial sadism that lend nasty life to some of the other villa sites around Naples. No blood was spilled here, nor sperm, nor wine, nor other vital juice. No one even puked in the pool nor pissed in the fountains. Nor will they—the custodians hover, like thought-police, between the ancient marble and the ever-new stucco ornamentation. Two or three different and equally sinister time-travel novels seem to have got telescoped into a single van Vogt nightmare. *Let me out!*

You go into the water-garden again; it is darker now but the architecture is only seen in mercifully detail-less silhouette. The sky glows still with the last aftermath of sunset and the ocean still gleams. The air suddenly smells as delicious as the scene looks. What a marvellous idea the Getty Museum must have been. If only someone else had thought of it!

Valley of the Dams

Arrived in the heart of Redneck Macholand, with our thirties-radical sensibilities ready tuned for instant disappointment at the almost certain discovery that not a single Good Ole Boy was even remotely interested any more in the renowned social experiment of 40 years ago whose remains we had come to visit . . . only to discover that it was the story of the hour on local TV, the newsreader milking every last drop of irony from: "Run-off from the past two days' heavy rain now covers an estimated 3,000 acres of the valley bottom above Tellico dam. Authorities emphasise that sluices in the newly completed dam have not been closed; the causes of the inundation are purely natural."

The joke is that the sluices of Tellico dam may *not* be closed for a while yet, because of litigation to lift an Endangered Species Order, issued on behalf of a rather dim-sounding minnow called the snail darter. This is a variety whose only known home is the river above Tellico, and it may perish if the water deepens. Mother Nature's 3,000-acre *jeu d'esprit* could only be seen, here in Knoxville in the shadow of the

Originally appeared in *New Society* 41, no. 772 (21 July 1977): 138–139.

Smoky Mountains, as a slap in the face for "them ecologisers up in D.C.," who had stayed the closing of the sluices in defiance of united local opinion.

For this is territory where every smallest child has heard from his grampaw how dams have saved the ecology, the economy and even the culture of the local folk. Tellico almost joins onto the end of Fort Loudon dam. They span the Little Tennessee and the Tennessee proper, respectively, just above their confluence. They are one of the first (Fort Loudon, 1943), and probably the last, of the works of the Tennessee Valley Authority.

Sic transit. . . . In 1943 when Fort Loudon was completed, TVA was ten years old, having been instituted with extraordinary despatch in the first *month* of Roosevelt's first term (though after years of lobbying, wheeling and dealing by Senator Norris of Nebraska): a piece of social and physical engineering of a scale (it affected seven bordering states as well as Tennessee) and profundity (the re-shaping of a ruined society) difficult to match even in the Russian five-year plans. In that decade, its performance as well as promise made it the paragon of enlightened regional planning, advanced conservation, social renewal and modern design. Praised by Lewis Mumford, Julian Huxley and other top Herbivores; illustrated in all the best architectural magazines; an image of a future that millions went to war to make the world safe for.

Now, however, the activists who have set the Endangered Species legislation to work see themselves as Davids of the good battling against Goliaths of established power, who care naught for ecology, conservation or the future.

What went wrong? Nothing much. Fashions in radicalism change, but some have more durable effects than others. Current eco-radicalism ultimately aims to leave nothing new behind, simply to hold the balance of Nature where it is. That particular variety of snail darter may have been headed for extinction anyhow, in which case its preservation might prove to be a monstrous act of human arrogance. But it will never *look* anywhere near as arrogant as the act of pouring tens of thousands of tons of concrete in a massive wall across a river valley and impounding a sizable lake behind it.

Yet that particular kind of arrogance may have, for instance, saved the city of Chattanooga from almost annual flood disasters, and thousands of human lives with it. I don't know how you make a moral balance between the saving of the snail darter, and the restoration of the human, animal and arboreal ecology of an area the size of Britain, after earlier generations had ripped and stripped the valley into a bleak wilderness. What I do know is that the surviving monuments of the early days of TVA, especially the upstream dams like Norris, Hiwassee and Fontana, have an overwhelming physical grandeur that extends consistently down to their smallest details, and seems unavoidably to reflect a grand vision and a high purpose in the men who built them.

Even if I had not met any of these men, I think the vision and purpose would still have come through. Of course, it's difficult for anyone of my generation to be impartial about the works of TVA. They are part of the body of socialist legend on which I grew up, they were as integral a part of the iconography of the left as the Odessa Steps or the double portrait of Sacco and Vanzetti. I could never look at them with totally neutral eyes, but I have now seen them with changed eyes. For decades I knew them only in the original heroic black and white photographs—white concrete and black sky because of the period's almost mandatory yellow filter. But now I have seen them in the Ektachrome of real life. And they're *better!* Even the ones I visited out of a sense of duty, expecting them to be boring in a distinguished sort of way, like Watts Bar, are better in real life than they were in the sacred icons.

Watts Bar, on reflection, is a site that focuses quite a lot of the history of TVA, its putative regress from all right to all wrong. It's a multi-purpose downstream dam, built across a broad stretch of the Tennessee in a fairly flat, rolling landscape that can look like the lusher parts of Dorset. Its 19 sluices help to control flow and flooding. Dams like this, combined with massive re-afforestation upstream in the mountains, help keep the Big T within bounds. But the lakes they impound have created a tourist industry as well.

The lakes are also navigable by commercial traffic, and by the left bank there is a massive lock that lets big ships and barges up and down: one link in a navigation system that nowhere has less than eight feet draught of water throughout the year. (Thus resolving a problem that has officially bugged Tennessee since the 1820s.)

Over the lock and across the river, on stilts along the top of the dam runs a state highway (a multi-purpose dam really works for its living!), rising over a hydroelectric powerhouse by the right bank and up to the control room on top of the bluff, the switchyard behind it and the public viewing room cantilevered off the front of the bluff. All TVA dams have public viewing rooms, and wall-to-wall/floor-to-ceiling glass on one side of the control room, so that the People of the United States can see what's going on.

That's a lot of socially useful business to concentrate on one relatively simple piece of civil engineering. But that's what TVA was originally all about. Just downstream below the bluff, however, is the much illustrated Watts Bar coal-burning plant, built to satisfy wartime energy needs (it went on line in 1942). Beyond that again rise the cooling towers of the still-unfinished Watts Bar nuclear power station.

Now there's a certain historical justice about this, since so much of the infant TVA's power-output was gulped down by the Oak Ridge atom bomb plant over the other side of Knoxville. But the three stations together—hydro, coal and nuke—all too clearly mark the steps in TVA's seemingly irresistible transformation from a great social experiment into yet another North American energy conglomerate.

That transformation is far from total. Much of the original multi-purpose social programme remains. But it has become an even smaller percentage of the authority's business. And speaking of business, it has now moved its headquarters into two conventional, leased-from-a-developer office blocks in downtown Knoxville, as if to emphasise its assimilation now into the world of Big Energy. In the process, its image has been skewed—permanently, I suspect—so that extremists of both left and right agree in seeing it as just another monster public utility. Hell-bent on ecological destruction, if viewed from the left; or creeping stalinism, when viewed from the right.

Both views are somewhat true; as is the uncomfortable feeling that TVA has, somehow, been going steadily downhill. People in the authority itself betray their sense of it. The security guard who showed us (and a few other visitors) over Hiwassee, resplendent in his grey-green Smoky Bear uniform glittering with silver badgework, spoke with evident contempt of fossil-fuel power. He harked back to the days of pure hydroelectric generation almost as a prelapsarian paradise (a phrase he could never have managed in his Good Ole accent full of disintegrating diphthonged vowels, but that's about what he meant).

At Hiwassee, it was a sentiment worth meaning. It's not the highest of the upstream dams (Fontana is, at 480 feet), nor is it the most obviously prestige-laden (that's Norris, named after George Norris, creator of TVA). But as early as John Kyle's book of 1958 (*The Building of TVA*), Hiwassee was "considered by many people to be the most beautiful dam built by TVA. However . . . it is not frequently visited."

Twenty years later, that's more true than ever. It's still not much visited because it's so remote. But it is spectacularly well worth the two or three hours of elbow-wrenching mountain driving it takes to get there. A tall dam in a deep, steep valley full of trees, down into which you zigzag, seeing the dam at each turn of the road, tree-vignetted in its preferred role of a noble work of man at home in the bosom of Mother Nature. On the final approach, you come at it straight and level along the valley bottom, river on left, the switchyard's humming, glittering space-frame on right.

Square ahead of you rises the cliff of concrete—weathered after its 36 years but not cruddy. Under your feet is the powerhouse, with two gigantic circular hatch covers for servicing the generator sets, let into the platform on which you're standing. Against the foot of the dam itself squats the carefully architected and conscientiously modern entrance/control-room building, faced in shutter-patterned concrete to match the dam, with the word *Hiwassee* in giant, three-dimensional metal letters of plain, blunt sanserif form.

But what holds the eye is one of the happiest inventions of TVA's first phase, the mobile gantry crane that fishes generator components up from the hatchways when they need servicing, and puts them back when they're done. Travelling on rails right across the platform, it stands on four massive straddling legs. Its machinery is contained neatly in an elegant Streamline-Moderne housing, the shape and size of a futuristic railcar, appropriately snub-cornered and finned right round with continuous ventilator grille. That gantry occurs at other dams too, like a giant aluminised watch-beast from an old science fiction epic, keeping guard over the good works below. But at Hiwassee it's seen at its best and most convincing at the best and most convincing of all TVA sites.

It's the epitome of a vision of gentle technology, tamed power, in the service of, you know, all the *little* people out there; the farming cooperatives, the fertiliser plants, the tourists, the Good Ole Boys, the People of the United States, to whom every one of these dams is formally dedicated in that same plain blunt lettering above the maps and explanatory murals in every visitors' viewing room.

It ought to be as flaccid as any other political rhetoric or governmental pretensions to style of the period. But it isn't. The style is so consistent, so carefully thought through, that the vision holds. Nothing that has happened to TVA since can really tarnish it. There are still gentle giants in the land.

38

Grass Above, Glass Around

The Willis, Faber and Dumas headquarters in Ipswich has taken just over two years to go from nine days' wonder to architectural respectability (RIBA Eastern Region award). But it remains almost as inscrutable as ever. It ought not to be. Most of us by now can "read" a glass-walled office tower without difficulty. Many of us, indeed, are demonstratively bored by *having* to read them as often as we do. But then, what Foster Associates have designed in Ipswich is not a conventional rectangular tower, but a seemingly free-form four-storey plan, waving about as it pursues the outlines of its site, slickly clad in dark, unmodulated glass from eaves to pavement.

The decision to build in this way in the historic heart of downtown Ipswich can be defended—and has been—on purely functional and economic grounds, as architects are wont to do. But when you have said that, you have said nothing about why it is a controversial, important and (possibly) extremely good building to have on that particular site. All that part of the argument must turn about purely visual, formal and

Originally appeared in *New Society* 42, no. 783 (6 October 1977): 22–23.

symbolic aspects of the design, because what Norman Foster has done is to mix, without apology, two completely different (some would insist, utterly opposed) sets of architectural approaches, expectations and customary usages.

In the traditions of the Modern Movement in Architecture, glass is of the party of order and hygiene. It stands for the replacement of the slums of the huddled poor by clean crystal towers. It stands for the illumination of the dark places of vernacular superstition by the pure light of rationality. World-wide, it has become the symbolic material of clarity, literal and phenomenal. As such it is—or was—universally delivered in crisp rectangular formats, pure and absolute, impervious to local accidents and customs. It was therefore appropriate to all the aspirations of the founders of the United Nations, who gave it canonical form in their headquarters tower in New York. Less felicitously it proved equally apt to the ambitions of great multinational corporations. Worse yet, to the avarice of downtown developers the world over.

In Ipswich, this last manifestation is represented, just across the street from Willis Faber and Dumas, by the Franciscan Centre development. But the glass vision is there bowdlerised by the sixties' most favoured substitute for architectural thought, *beton brut*—off-the-form concrete, here so poorly detailed, so neglected and unloved, that it is already growing moss! The architecture of rationality runs down into the architecture of profit and loss; and being without profit, is accounted the deadest of losses.

Against this kind of design is normally set a different Modern tradition which has had many names at different times, but is most fully represented by the doctrine of "Townscape," advanced by the *Architectural Review* in 1950, and elaborately developed over the years by the *Review*'s two brilliant draughtsmen, Gordon Cullen and Kenneth Browne. It has had its triumphs—notably the Festival of Britain—and, in spite of attempts by writers in the *Review*'s arch-rival, *Architectural Design,* to prove the contrary, continues in the "Contextualism" of sundry German, Dutch and Belgian gurus that AD is pushing at the present time. Essentially, it is an amalgam of picturesque contrast and surprise, with circumspect (and usually sentimental) respect for what the Italian phase of the movement would have called the *ambiente pre-esistente,* plus recycling, rehabilitation and so forth. Above all, *not* putting up standardised glass boxes all over the world.

That is the latter tradition that Foster's acquiescent pursuit of the boundaries of his given site appears to support. It's not what he usually does: his nearly complete Arts Hangar at the University of East Anglia pays no visible respect to anything at all in its surroundings. So he seems to have made even his faithful fan club uncomfortable, as well as making the opposition feel they are being got at. Yet he has, indeed, made his glazed perimeter follow the soggy curve of a postwar traffic improvement on one side, the irregular joggles of existing mediaeval streets on two others; and only on the fourth has he imposed a rationalised straight line on an irregular sequence of property boundaries—and that is the least seen of all the elevations.

But then to hang (literally) an uninterrupted and unaccented sinuous curtain of glass all round this "historic" perimeter. . . . For many good souls it's too much to take, even at the purely conceptual level. No, *especially* at the conceptual level, since, given the tendency of good-guy ideas to cluster, even when they have no logical connection, the Contextual, "herbivore" approach has lately taken on board the moral load of energy conservation as well.

Now "everybody knows" that glass is an energy-wasteful material. Yet Foster Associates have the gall and (tough luck, herbivores) the figures to show that this is a reasonably energy-efficient structure—partly because its very deep-plan four-storey format gives a low ratio of glass to internal volume (and the glass is deeply bronzed as well), and partly because much of its roof is clad in one of the oldest and most reliable insulating materials known to vernacular wisdom—growing turf!

But: turf on top of a high-technology building full of air conditioning, escalators, computers and stuff? Once again, separated expectations, different architectural languages, have been shotgun-married without apology or regard for the niceties of academic discourse, where turf is perfectly acceptable as long as it is on small-windowed, irregular technologically low-profile buildings. Academic polemicists might do well to remember that the man who reminded the present century of the roofing virtues of growing turf was none other than the true and onlie begetter of the universal, damn-local-traditions, glass-skinned, pure rectangular office block, Le Corbusier himself.

And so on. The pity of it is that so much of this academic debate is about matters which are marginal and trivial to the important business of seeing the world better housed, better serviced, better symbolised—but are matters suitable for academic debate. And Willis Faber and Dumas makes fools of them all. For what really hurts is that the building delivers precisely those anecdotal and serendipitous pleasures to the trained eye that the *Architectural Review* campaigned for 30 years ago and that the Contextualists have now rediscovered via linguistics and a kind of populist neo-marxism . . . delivers all that by doing exactly the kind of architecture they would unobservantly claim couldn't do it.

As I recall, it is since Theo Crosby's rather Radical Chic *Environment Game* show at the Hayward four years ago, that the cry has been for more craftsmanship, more detail, more decoration, more incident. All those qualities that the standard, off-the-peg, minimalist glass wall could never give, and was therefore deemed uncultured and dehumanising. Foster's wavy wall, with its storey-high sheets of glass butted edge to edge without framing, is even more detail-free than glass walls usually are. Yet when you look at the building you see almost nothing but craftsmanship, detailing, incidents, decoration, historical values—all reflected from the buildings on the other side of the street.

Look upon its featureless facades, and you shall see every period of East Anglian urban architecture from Low Gothic to High Brutalist, and almost every catalogued historical detail from *abacus* to *zygus*. Spire and dome are there, chimney and gable, column and pilaster, arches round, ogival and pointed. Better still, by choosing your viewpoints with creative care, you can manoeuvre an artisan-mannerist gable (reflected) on top of a modern matt-black metal ventilating grille (real), and make them fit together exactly. Indeed, you need to keep your eyes peeled and your wits about you, because the facade can deliver sequences of this sort of effect quicker than you can keep up with at normal walking pace.

The reason for this quick-change display of visual puns, oxymorons, metaphors and other tropes, is that the facades are curved but the glass is flat. So no two adjoining facets are in the same plane and thus reflect non-adjoining subject matter. Everything is reflected in tall vertical slices, with violent visual discontinuities between the content of one slice and the next. You may, for instance, on the incurved side toward Friars Street, observe the same facing building reflected (in part) twice, several panes apart. The intervening facets are taken up with a quotation from a totally different building opposite, a short length of Willis Faber reflected at right angles to itself, and a tree apparently in a different part of Ipswich altogether.

These are exactly the kind of visual effects—surprise, truncation, concealment, confrontation—for which Townscape always campaigned. Looking back now on the discomfiture the *Architectural Review* clearly experienced when confronted with this building (that did so many things the *AR* held dear by architectural means the magazine's editors affected to abominate), it would be difficult not to smile, but for the contemptible intellectual contortions the editors went through to find something definitively bad with which to damn it. After two pages of praising with faint damns, they finally produced their polemical master-stroke (sic): the possibility of *two* such buildings:

"One Willis Faber and Dumas building may be a revelation, but two facing one another make a prison."

Come off it! Two such facades facing one another would not (just) reflect a lack of craftsmanly detail on both sides of the street, but also—as in all facing-mirror situations—the viewer repeated to infinity in both directions. Not only does that flatter the viewer, but it is a form of ego massage which the editors of the *Architectural Review* enjoy all over their editorial offices every day of the working week, for their premises are notoriously the most bemirrored in the business. Perhaps they're just jealous. Perhaps it is not flattering to see a bankrupt ideological position reflected to infinity. Perhaps they should put turf on their heads and see if that looks any better.

39

Summa Galactica

Picture, if you will, a heroine dressed all in virginal white, who never gets raped or even kissed, in an exploitation movie that has already grossed so much at the box office that *Jaws* looks like a minnow and the *Exorcist* like a Wayside Pulpit. The mind boggles. But then *Star Wars* (which doesn't hit the UK till December but whose pre-publicity is already all around us) is a boggling movie—especially if you fail to pick up the clues to its deceptive simplicities early enough.

The last possible moment at which you can hope to get on, and hang on, is probably where the bar tender points through the throng of variously fur-covered, balloon-headed, pig-nosed, cyclopean, and even more extraordinary creatures yet . . . points, that is, through the normal crush at his murky, extra-galactic *cantina* at the fastidiously detailed (made in Britain!) gilt robot in the doorway and barks, "*We don't serve their kind in here!*"

It's an old joke, as comfortingly familiar in science fiction as a mother-in-law joke would be in vaudeville. But it has a new twist now, because—obviously—Android Lib would see to it nowadays that the Equal Rights Amendment applied to automata, as

---

Originally appeared in *New Society* 42, no. 786 (27 October 1977): 190–191.

well as to men, women, gays, goys, Jews, blacks, yellows, Hispanos, Amazing Hulks and things with five tentacles coming out from under each ear. The Biological Chauvinist Piggery of the whole episode pushes the frame of reference back before 1968 or so. *Star Wars* may well be the first historical costume drama of SF, and as thoroughly researched as *Roots.* Which makes it about the most complicated simple-minded movie ever made.

This simplemindedness is the true reason for its stunning success, however. It's a straightforward interstellar western. It is a rattling good yarn with an entirely surprise-free scenario, unencumbered by characterisation or acting (apart from some Rommel impersonations by Peter Cushing), but driven at breakneck speed by real pacey-pacey cutting, and a soundtrack that rarely leaves you time to think.

Not that there is much, at that level, to think about—except that, since Kubrick's *2001,* the pundits have come to expect that any expensive SF movie has got to be a vehicle for pretentious cracker-mottoes about Man, God, Destiny and all that. So Alec Guinness's *Star Wars* valedictions, "The Force be with you," have been scrutinised up, down and sideways for evidence of a New Deism, or even worse, when all they are, in truth, are SF conventions.

For, outside its rattling good yarn, *Star Wars* is about science fiction conventions— all of them, a kind of *summa galatica* of downright Thomist encyclopaedism and inclusiveness, subject only to the *terminus ante quem* implied by the datedness of the barroom sequence. This is SF before J. G. Ballard and his quality reduced it to the level of literature: SF of the period of John W. Campbell Jr's most authoritative editorial years at *Astounding* (later, *Analog*) magazine; the period, roughly, from Asimov's first robot stories to Frank Herbert's *Dune.*

George Lucas (of *American Graffiti*), who wrote and directed, knows all that stuff. Too few of those who have wasted good newsprint trying to explain "the phenomenon of *Star Wars,*" seem to know any of it at all. Most were thrown completely off-track by the statement (by whom?) that Lucas had originally intended to make a Flash Gordon movie. The more one looks at *Star Wars,* the less likely that appears. Literally "appears," because the movie's visual sources are nowhere in that area. Its imagery comes from the non-comic-strip pulps like *Astounding* and *Galaxy* in the fifties and sixties, from their great illustrators and cover artists like Chesley Bonestell and Kelly Freas, and *above all* from the written words themselves.

This is an intensely, attentively, literary film. Which is what has made so depressing the failure of the literary critics, even in the *Times Literary* (you should pardon the expression) *Supplement,* to realise what it is all about. Regular cinema audiences don't seem to have this problem, and Lucas pays them the compliment of never supposing for a moment that they will. The narrative pauses neither to explain its references nor to underline its allusions. There's no time, and should be no need.

Most of the first quarter of the story takes place on the arid planet of Tatooine, where the two robots have been deliberately marooned with their crucial strategic information, in the hope that someone who knows what it is all about will pick them up and send the info on to the rebels. In the event, they are picked up by the Jawas, diminutive figures in quasi-Capuchin hooded habits with curious loops and lengths of plastic tubing protruding here and there from their garb.

Now, this was not just a fancy of the costume department. Practically all the audience within our earshot flashed on the fact that this was a reference to Frank Herbert's *Dune* ecology, where the desert folk, the Fremen, wear special gear that conserves and re-cycles all their body water.

To my knowledge, none of the regular critics have picked up this reference, or the fact that it apparently extends and resolves the problem left behind at the end of the *Dune* trilogy. That problem was: can the Fremen preserve their ancient and noble warrior culture without a reversal of the ecological process that is turning their desert into irrigated farm land? The implication of *Star Wars* is, so to speak, "Neither!" The desert has returned, but the mighty Fremen have been reduced to tinker bands of midget secondhand-robot dealers, travelling in armoured vehicles whose silhouette against the sky looks deliberately reminiscent of old-fashioned gypsy caravans.

An interesting and cynical concept, but surely a bit much to be riding on the back of a rattling good simpleminded yarn? No, this is the level at which *Star Wars* is complex, and sustainedly erudite. For instance, I knew I had come across the Jedi knights somewhere before, and was only momentarily deflected by Alec Guinness's first appearance in pre-faded Zen strip. The Jedi Order's mixture of chivalric dedication and mod technology has got to come, not from Tolkien, as *TLS* correspondents aver, but from Ernst Juenger's *On the Marble Cliffs.* I don't suppose anybody much around the team that made the movie, or around us in the cinema, had ever read it, either in the original German or in translation, yet it's been soaking into SF since the early fifties.

That concept has some uncomfortable overtones. It got Juenger into trouble in some quarters because it smacked of Nazi revanchism, postulating as it did an oathbound secret *corps d'élite* defending the inner secrets of western culture. That's a theme that runs through more than just SF of course. It's already there in most readings of the Arthurian legend. (Was it Clive James who pointed out what a creepy band of fascists the knights of the Round Table would appear today?) Anyhow, what seemed to reinforce the Juengarian connection was that the decor of the final sequence—and this is something every pundit *and* most of the audience picked up—unmistakably recalls Leni Riefenstahl's *Triumph of the Will,* banners and all!

Shocking or not, this sits well with the chivalric theme that informs most of the movie, and nowhere gets in the way of the cowboy aspects of the yarn. But chivalry does do something funny to the ending, generally. Thus, after the final crucial action sequence which—for all it takes place in spacefighters over the topography of an artificial Death Star—is a classic Western gulch ride, with the hired gun, who was thought to have taken his bounty and split, coming back to ride shotgun on the hero and keep the baddies off his tail . . . after all that does boy get girl, or girl get boy? Neither and both. The princess Leia goes off with both Luke Skywalker, the hero, and Han Solo, the hired gun, arm-linked between them, just good buddies and as pure as the Coke commercial the tableau suspiciously resembles.

And that's the nearest thing to sex in the whole movie, and a great tribute to Lucas as a science-fiction scholar. The princess, played by Carrie Fisher with all the emotional depth of an underdeveloped Polaroid, remains throughout an unsullied figure in her virginal white Roman nightie, and shatter-proof hair-do which seems to be something to do with early pictures of Eleanor Roosevelt. But when the action gets rough, she mucks in with gun and boot.

A tomboy? No, the exact phrase is: "You're a real brick, Leia!" To put it any higher would make her sound too much a Joan of Arcturus, and she's not spooky enough for that. But she is certainly as remote and unreachable as any mistress of a medieval troubadour, even when she is slopping around in peril in the waste disposal system of the Death Star (in a glorious send-up of Wajda's *Kanal:* is *nothing* sacred?).

In a movie which has been lavishly overpraised for its special effects, and grimly over-scrutinised for philosophical mystifications (and will occasionally rejoice British viewers by its resemblances to *Dr Who*), the pure white princess is the touchstone, not only of devotion to a chivalric ideal, (ie dumb but noble) but more than that, of true scholarship. She is not a nostalgically idealised girl-figure like those in George Lucas's previous, and equally excellent, *American Graffiti.* She is an accurate reading of the way heroines really were in the brave science-fiction days of old. *Star Wars* is not nostalgia; it is history.

40

Pevsner's Progress

David Watkin, *Morality and Architecture: The Development of a Theme in Architectural History and Theory from the Gothic Revival to the Modern Movement* (Clarendon Press: Oxford University Press)

Apparently graven in stern Roman capitals on weathered masonry on the dust-jacket, the title of David Watkins's reworked lecture promises something more lapidary and more portentous than proves to be the case. The relationship between morality and architecture could be of considerable—even life and death—interest to the world at large, but what the book contains is a series of scholastic complaints about moralizing in architectural writing, from Pugin to Pevsner.

The lecture, when originally delivered in Cambridge in 1968, was—quite properly— valued as a mind-cleansing squib. Reissued almost a decade later, ballasted with a full apparatus of footnotes, and weighed down with the assumed mantles of Popper, Butterfield and the supposed Peterhouse tradition of anti-Whiggery in historical writing,

---

Originally appeared in *The Times Literary Supplement*, 17 February 1978, pp. 191–192.

it now looks more like an attempted academic takeover of the current fashion for knocking Modern Architecture and all its works, and all its apologists—but especially Pevsner, whom Watkin attacks for the last third of the book with an animus that seems to go well beyond normal Cambridge passions for self-righteous rectification.

Watkins clearly recognizes his own extremism: indeed, he exaggerates its extremity by going out of his way to ward off criticism (or invite admiration) for his temerity in attacking Sir Nikolaus. The effect is not convincing; it will not do for him to say that in criticizing one aspect of Pevsner (or Pugin, J. M. Richards, Viollet-le-Duc, and others who get the treatment) "it is with no wish to question the value of the whole", because all Pevsner's major works, most of his minor ones, and every different kind of Pevsnerian writing, get worked over—even obiter dicta about individual monuments in *The Buildings of England.*

These last are accompanied by some further apologetics about not being "intended as an assessment of the general importance . . . of an amazing triumph of energy, productiveness and erudition unequalled . . ." and this is no more convincing than what went before, because what Watkin is offering is a totally different view of history, and the historian's work, from that pursued by Pevsner. Had Watkin the same powers, productivity, and erudition as Sir Nikolaus, he would have done it all differently. Or not at all, for the fundamental weakness of the book seems to be that he cannot see Pevsner whole, does not understand that what Sir Nikolaus hath wrought is not divisible into "energy, productiveness and erudition unequalled" on the one hand, and damnable Whig heresy on the other. In criticizing one aspect he does, in fact, attack the whole, because he has—with possibly mistaken accuracy—identified the core of Pevsner, his belief in something very like the currently discounted concept of Progress, or even the Christian idea of salvation as understood by Pugin.

Now there is nothing inherently improper or repellent about Watkin's intention to censure Pevsner for Whiggish historicism in imputing direction and purpose to History, and importing morality into architectural judgment. Moralizing in architectural judgment was famously deprecated by that delicate aesthete Geoffrey Scott, in *The Architecture of Humanism,* before Pevsner was in his teens, and of recent years Pevsner-bashing has been an accepted academic field-sport, especially among those like Watkin and myself who have been his pupils. We have all had our difficulties in not tittering at his insistence that artists like Gauguin and the Douanier have a place in the progress of modern design "from William Morris to Walter Gropius", have found his emphasis on a coherent *Zeitgeist* in every significant period misleading, constricting and often glibly rhetorical, and been dismayed by his persistent blindness to the importance of some kinds of architecture and design.

Yet that Zeitgeistical approach had, perhaps still has, and may have again, a special usefulness whose value Watkin appears incapable of comprehending, and whose point he misses, through a weird mixture of intellectual muddle, ignorance of his material, and rigidity—rather than rigour—of method. "Muddle", in accepting Pevsnerian valuations when he does not have to: for instance, he finds it ironic that William Morris "attacked the machine in his writings while using machines in his business", yet Morris the Luddite is almost entirely an invention of Pevsner's—younger left-revisionists (like Ian Tod in his Durham MA dissertation) have shown that, by quotation no more selective than Pevsner's, Morris can be made to appear pro-Machine. "Ignorance," in (for a glaring example) his elaborate attempt to destroy Pevsner's view of the "worldliness" of Renaissance architecture (where the "religious meaning of a church is replaced by a human one") on methodological grounds, not to say forensic ones, as if he did not know that Rudolf Wittkower had devoted two telling pages and some heroic footnotes in *Architectural Principles in the Age of Humanism* to demonstrating Pevsner *factually* wrong—Renaissance church plans demonstrably did display religious symbolism.

Such muddles may be due to no more than inattention, or failure to read what he has just written, but they can be classics of self-cancelling argumentation, as on page 28 of *Morality and Architecture,* where Watkin tackles one of the key topics in all historical assessments of modern architecture—the use of glass:

> Thus a persistent tradition in modern architecture, from the glazed staircases of Gropius's Werkbund building of 1914 to Stirling's glazed History Faculty buildings at Cambridge of 1964, has been the belief that glass has some special and unchallengeable role as the expression of the spirit of modernity. In fact its use is generally an aesthetic urge disguised as a technological necessity and in the History Faculty, for example, certainly cannot be justified by "convenience, construction or propriety".

The use of "in fact" presumably registers a belief that these two sentences are somehow in opposition, but neither in logic nor in fact (a distinction not often enough made in Cambridge) are they mutually exclusive. Glass has satisfied that particular aesthetic urge precisely because it has that special role as an expression of modernity, at least since the publication of Paul Scheerbart's *Glasarchitektur* in the year of the Werkbund building. And while we are talking about muddle, is it not better practice to compare comparable data when comparing buildings, in which case the dates in the passage above should be "1912 . . . 1964" (commencements) or "1914 . . . 1968" (completions)? Furthermore, I have no recollection that the use of glass in either building was justified or excused by either architect except in terms of external necessity—in Gropius's case it was claimed to be an offer he couldn't refuse from a manufacturer, while in Stirling's it was claimed to be the only cladding material that was feasible within the penny-pinching budget imposed by the University Grants Committee. While you are getting your breath back after those two claims, you might like to work out how a "use" can be an "urge" disguised as a "necessity."

"These, however, are minor blemishes", says a standard *TLS* reviewer's bromide, indicating that the nit-picking has come to an end, and grudging praise is about to begin, but in this case it cannot be so. The next stage is major blemishes; to wit, rigidity and what can only be described as chronic historical insensitivity. The rigidity is the saddest aspect of the book, because it purports to derive from Karl Popper, of whom I believe it to be travesty. Yet there can be no doubt that Popper has had as curious effects on art-historians as on the CIA; in both cases *The Open Society* seems to be held a pretext for the closed mind. I have heard an art-historian of great distinction rebut an objection with the phrase "That is a Hegelian idea, and Popper has disproved Hegel!" (Members of the audience sitting nearer the front claim that what he actually said was "and Popper disapproves of Hegel!" but there are limits to my credulity.) For Watkin, it seems, anything deemed by him to be historicism must be false because Popper (and to a lesser extent, Herbert Butterfield) would disapprove. Like an inquisitor of the House Un-American Affairs Committee, Watkin seems to demand "Are you, or have you been at any time . . ." and finds the case proven simply on the answer to that one question.

Dragging in the CIA may seem like cheating, but Watkin (in the seclusion of a footnote) is prepared to compare Pevsner to Goebbels—which is not the worst example of his insensitivity to the historical situations in which his subject-matter found themselves, but not far off. Indeed, it seems that the rigid imposition of this one-valued view of historical writing can only be pursued in the absence of any real feeling for the periods under discussion, and fortified by other rigidities outside the argument—Watkin advances under the banner *DOM* (which has page v all to itself), and from time to time comes close to that kind of vindictiveness of which only Christians seem capable.

This insensitivity spans a spectrum from the ridiculous to the tragic. At the ridiculous end must stand Watkin's half-page twitting Pevsner for trying to bring "even so slight a thing as a chocolate box" within his historical system, apparently not knowing that the design of chocolate boxes was a matter of wide (albeit joking) concern in the 1930s (cartoon of an aesthete pointing the finger of scorn at a sunset and shouting "Chocolate box-y, chocolate box-y!") and that Pevsner, as a living human being, could hardly fail to comment. At least part of that comment is valid still—"Neither a circus scene nor a still life of fruit has a natural and easily understandable relation to chocolate".

The tragic extreme of his insensitivity is revealed in a phrase that has already given widespread offence: "as a Jew, Pevsner found it prudent to leave Germany". Now, this statement is true by the standards of Josef Goebbels, but Watkin, who is very scrupulous about the religious affiliations of certain composers he believes misrepresented by Pevsner, is quite unscrupulous about Pevsner's profession of Lutheranism (which might have given him pause at a number of points in his argument) and, as for the word "prudent" . . . well, it is prudent to run for the door when the house is on fire and collapsing about your ears. The man's life was in danger, for pity's sake, and he feared for his family.

Watkin seems able to handle the realities of the 1930s only by comparing text with text, which of course gives him one of his better coups: Pevsner's use of the word "totalitarian" as a term of apparent approval in the concluding paragraphs of *Pioneers of the Modern Movement*. It is a usage that has been much commented on since, and not only among Pevsner-bashers like Charles Jencks, but most have been prepared to allow that in 1936 it might not have meant exactly what Allied wartime propaganda and Joe McCarthy had made it mean twenty years later. In Watkin's single-valued world, however, it seems that words can only have one meaning ever, and for this reason Pevsner's next worst crime after that "totalitarian" has to be his use of the word "historicism" in a sense different to that intended by Karl Popper. It has always been perfectly clear what Pevsner means by the word, and it is difficult to find a more convenient label to describe what he is discussing when he uses it, and it nowhere impinges on its other meanings, including those used in discussing historiographical techniques, but Watkin responds with the kind of epistemological seizure exhibited by Lévi-Straussians when someone uses the word "structural" to describe the way a building, not a mythology, is put together. For Watkin, it is quite simply "misuse".

Furthermore, it seems neither true, nor very observant, to propose that this "misuse" leads to a "failure to recognize that he is himself a historicist in the sense defined by Popper." The matter, I suspect, is one of indifference to Pevsner; he might even be pleased to be a historicist in that sense. He has never, that I can remember, denied his intention to push certain views of history; conversationally at least he has acknowledged himself a propagandist for that kind of architecture which was pioneered from William Morris to Walter Gropius. The whole proposition is a bit like accusing him of allowing his mania for all things English to blind him to the fact of his forty-odd years' residence in Hampstead!

Nevertheless, Pevsner's kind of historicism in its English context is part of everybody's Pevsner-problem, not just Watkin's. Butterfield's anti-Whig particularity is not the only aspect of English intellectual establishmentarianism that Pevsner has offended. There was a certain inevitability in Watkin's exhumation of Sir Edwin Lutyens as his ultimate weapon against Sir Nikolaus—indeed it is rather surprising that he holds back the architect of New Delhi until the last six pages of the book. Pevsner's not over-respectful attitude to the Classical tradition in British architecture has been resented ever since the Reith Lectures of 1955, and Lutyens is simply another slighted classicist to add to the long litany (Thorpe, Webb, Inigo Jones, Gibbs, Holland, Chambers, Adam . . .) of those whom—it is alleged—Pevsner hath despised and rejected. That was for being "Un-English" but the case is worse with Lutyens, whom Pevsner in a long, considered and appreciative review of Christopher Hussey's *Life,* treated as less than serious—"Building with Wit" was the title of the review. Watkin has either missed that article, or has set it on one side so as not to distract from his professed concern at the way Lutyens has been deliberately suppressed, and rendered an un-person, in the *Outline of European Architecture.*

It might be that the reason for this is that Pevsner (like me) would find preposterous Watkin's claim that Lutyens was one of the "two or three most brilliant and successful architects England has ever produced", but it is equally likely that the real reason for Lutyers's non-appearance in Pevsner's *European Architecture* is that his style does not fit Pevsner's periods, that like Sir Walter Raleigh in *1066 and All That,* he was eliminated for being "left over from a previous reign". There can be little doubt that Pevsner has been responsible for some major omissions, suppressions and diminutions of movements, men and reputations in order to keep his generalized pictures of styles and periods in manageable shape. There have also, equally certainly, been some over-valuations, notably of Walter Gropius and the Bauhaus.

But, as Tom Wolfe said of Marshall McLuhan, what if he is right? Pevsner nailed his colours to the Bauhaus even earlier than Sigfried Giedion did. Some of their intellectual manoeuvres, both Pevsner's and Giedion's in the cause of demonstrating that the Bauhaus/International style must triumph, seem as doubtful to me as they do to Watkin. But it is evident that he picked a winner. Never mind whether that particular style is "legitimate" or "totalitarian": it remains an observable fact that increasingly, throughout the whole of the two middle quarters of the present century, it has become the visibly dominant style of "our times" and will continue so for some while, since there is no sign of an effective replacement for it yet.

Watkin, like the present editors of the *Architectural Review,* Charles Jencks and the "Post-Modernists", Simon Jenkins of the *Evening Standard,* and a host of others, may not like this dominance, and few of us can care for what debased versions of the style have done for the downtowns of so many cities, but it must seem historically irresponsible to pretend that it has not encapsulated the architectural ambitions of our powers-that-be as surely as High Gothic, or Anglo-Palladian, or any other dominant style carried the equivalent ambitions of the bishops, earls, kings or princes of their times.

Now, Pevsner's success as a stylistic talent-spotter could be due to a number of things: luck, undue influence on later events, or a true perception of how things happen in history. All three are indeed there; he was clearly fortunate to be set on course by Gropius almost before he knew that such a thing as a "Modern Movement" might exist; he certainly was influential in shaping the ideas of two if not three generations of architects, historians, and critics, so that all were inclined to make his prophecies come true. And at least one of the reasons he was so influential was that his historical generalizations looked true at the time, and in many cases still look good.

Anyone who believes he can find direction and purpose in history must be capable of producing comprehensible pictures of the historical process and they will be comprehensible only in so far as they can cut through the glitter and confusions of "the Brownian movement of random events" to reveal patterns (true or false) that lie within. The discovery and delivery of such generalizing patterns is one of the services that historians render to the lay members of society. Indeed, the ability to generalize convincingly and usefully is one of the tests of a great historian, and is also one of the reasons historians' reputations are so perishable, since changing circumstances will undermine the conviction and utility of any generalization. But it also explains Pevsner's impact in the 1930s, 1940s and even 1950s, when architects and lay-folk alike needed help in understanding what was going on.

Given such generalizations it is, admittedly, very easy to endow them with personalities, parts and passions, and it is—alas—not a very long step from such glib observations as "The Roman Baroque prefers elliptical floor-plans", to more sinister historicist rhetoric about "the architectonic mission of the German *volk*". Yet their utility persists, and Watkin avails himself of them as much as any historian: "the historicist and *Zeitgeist*-inspired historian will tend to regard modern collectivist ideas as right; he will be ever anxious to deal wholesale with humanity, to label individuals as types, to identify them in classes. . . ."—a sentence in which he himself labels individuals as types and identifies them in classes.

The relative blackness of pots and kettles is not the point at issue here: Pevsner's performance is. He got it right. He got it more right than Giedion or Henry-Russell Hitchcock. It behooves any of us who disapprove of his methodology, or dislike his particular favourites and are concerned at his omission of *our* particular favourites, to recognize that he produced a picture of the architecture of his own time which was useful, applicable, and has had demonstrable predictive power. If it was Whiggish historicism, or the kind of moralizing that comes naturally to a self-made Lutheran, that made it possible to do that, then so much the worse for Butterfield and Popper.

Indeed, a good Popperian, I feel, should salute rather than abuse Pevsner for having offered a falsifiable hypothesis about the main style of twentieth-century architecture in the Western industrialized world, and having seen that hypothesis resist falsification for forty years. It is, of course, only one of the many historical services he has rendered us, but its success should command respect, and give pause to those who would deprecate any of his methods.

41

Taking It With You

"It's not that caravans are bad housing . . . but that most housing isn't as good as caravans," or so said Alison Smithson (architect, novelist, spouse of architect and Edinbrugian *philosophe* of a prime Brodieish vintage). The remark was given the automated brush-off then, much as it would be today. "Everybody knows . . ." that caravans are portable slums and that caravan-sites are "ghettoes of poverty." Indeed it remains a fact that even the best-built caravan, if mounted on a brick foundation, not wheels, could be condemned by the district surveyor as a legally "dangerous structure" (so could a London bus!), but it is also still a fact that if you are buying basic habitability, a caravan gives you more for your money than anything on foundations the district surveyor could approve.

Footloose intellectual freebooters like Buckminster Fuller may have no difficulty with this concept of mobile homes as high-value housing . . . but most of the rest of us, and especially architects, are not at home with the idea, particularly when we contemplate the seemingly permanent environmental mess that usually surrounds them. The learned Smithson herself has been pretty acid about most of the mobile homes that

Originally appeared in *New Society* 45, no. 826 (3 August 1978): 252–253.

actually cross her field of vision. So what was she on about? Just being flip and ala-mode in the modish sixties, or is there some shining Platonic ideal of a mobile home that once blessed her eyes?

You bet your re-cycled Mary Quant wellies there is! It shines forth upon the roads of America, but gleams quite frequently upon the highways of Europe, Africa and Asia as well. Three or four generations of modern architects have worshipped it, after their fashion and usually from afar, though ex-Bauhausler Marcel Breuer built one into his own house in the forties.

It's called the Airstream; it's been around since the early thirties, when it was dreamed up by one Wally Byam, and its smoothly streamlined polished-metal form is accounted one of the classics of modern American design. Like all classics (or Platonic ideals) it is supposed to be "for ever," changeless. Like that other Platonic ideal on wheels, the VW Beetle, it has in fact undergone continual detailed changes while being praised by bat-eyed liberals for its avoidance of "annual face-lifts à la Detroit."

The outline (if not the details) of the dream has changed little since it was first in-vented—not by Byam but by pioneer aviator Glenn Curtis. Like many another elegant snob in the late twenties, Curtis was appalled by the motley roadside hostelries he had to stay in while motorin' to Miami, and decided to take his own stateroom with him, in a streamlined capsule articulated to the back of his touring car. The Byam ver-sion was a regular towed trailer, not an artic, but was essentially the same proposition: a clean, efficient, highly-serviced, totally independent living-unit "wherever and when-ever you choose to go or stay."

Air travel (as much as yachting) and aircraft technology were the inspiration of these streamlined sleepers, which were near enough contemporary with the first transconti-nental sleeper airliner, the Douglas DST, later to become that workhorse of the air, the Dakota or DC3.

What's odd about the Byam-waggon, however, is that it has only lately come to actually *look* like its distinguished contemporaries such as the DC3 or Bucky Fuller's (equally aircraft-inspired) Dymaxion cars. Unlike the Volkswagen, which has gone on looking like the same made-in-Germany tin jelly-mould from its beginnings to its recent end, the Airstream has contrived to finish up looking like a Classic of Early-Thirties American Functional Styling, but only after 45 years of detail refinement.

From its beginning until the middle sixties, the Airstream's metal panels did not join in smooth three-dimensional curves, but were faceted, like the planking of a boat, al-most, and its windows were not round cornered and flush with its sides, but had bent metal guttering over the top. Even after the plank effect had been smoothed away, the windows still had awkward corners, and it is only in the seventies that the Airstream has really been stylistically fit to stand alongside, say, the gantry-cranes of the TVA dams as proud witness to the spirit of the New Deal!

Not surprisingly, therefore, it bathes in the glow of nostalgia playing around "The streamlined decade," and its design-styles—the current Broadway smash, *On the*

Twentieth Century, celebrates that great thirties train in sorry lyrics and tepid tunes, but the sets are a *knockout;* it's the first musical about industrial design! The Airstream fits that scene obviously, but what about ten years ago, or 20, or even 30 years ago when Breuer discovered it?

The fascination, for architects and designers, lay in its nearness to a full realisation of Le Corbusier's dream (the whole profession's dream, therefore) of *une machine à habiter fabriquée en série;* a house engineered like an aircraft and manufactured like a car, Bucky Fuller's "Standard of Living Package." It was thus that the tragically late and lamented Ray Wilson celebrated the Airstream at Cambridge in the sixties; a snug weatherproof shell stuffed with capital-intensive technology, delivered to your address and replaced when it obsolesced. In spite of the vastly greater prestige of Apollo, Salyut, Soyuz and Skylab, and fighting off the earthbound challenges from the self-propelled Clark *Cortez* camper in the sixties, and General Motors Motorhome in the seventies, the Airstream has visibly remained the *beau ideal* of capsule-fanciers like Archigram, who frequently collaged it directly into their Plug-in, clip-on cities—where you could "live in the same house at several different addresses or several different houses at the same address."

The appeal of the Airstream, however, was always more visual than intellectual. It may be a very neat concept, but even in its facetted primitive forms it was an immensely appealing image. And it still is. Its polished aluminum exterior skin has the craftsmanly elegance of a Douglas aircraft; its miscellaneous doors and flaps and plug-points and ventilators have that aptness and tidy detailing which is supposed to derive from unaffected engineering practice, but which actually requires enormous self-effacing sophistication on the part of the designer. Overall, it sustains those neo-classical traditions that were built into the soul of western engineering around the time of James Watt, memorialised in aphorisms like: "Style is a word that has no plural."

That's the outside; what about the interior? Go on, guess! Wrong, wrong, all of you! Except for the cynic in the corner who has been reading Martin Pawley's *Private Future.* At least one of the fascinations of the capsule-dream was always the supposed private fantasies that could be contained within those sealed shells. Imagine convoys of gleaming streamliners zipping along the interstates, passing boring farms and tedious state capitals and dull townships while those within conduct Japanese tea ceremonies, perform exquisite tortures with obscure Transylvanian leather objects or declaim Pindaric odes while dusky maidens anoint their heads with rare unguents. Imagine away . . . the facts of the case are that the interiors of Airstreams are of a studied, deep-carpeted, wood-grained, value-free neutrality hard to match outside a Holiday Inn, and leave (physically) no room for fantasy.

This concentrated ordinariness has always been part of the deal, I suspect. Wally Byam's creed (oh, yes—it's a movement, practically a religion, being an Airstreamer) speaks of "bringing the world to your doorstep" but what he must have meant was "taking your doorstep to the world." Whether the view through the aircraft-style windows is Miami, Monument Valley or Mount Ararat, you are snug and secure in a piece of regular American suburbia.

In some ways this is an even more sensational situation than if an Airstream should prove to contain a cinema-organ or a seraglio, and it is a cultural fact that Americans have been warily shaping up to of late. A recent cartoon showed a man unloading tables, chairs, a standard-lamp and a television from a trailer home in the middle of some wild forest glade, what time his wife says: "I thought we came here to get away from it all, but you've brought it all with you!" Within the Airstream's perfect techno-logical shell lies the promise that, after all, you *can* take it with you.

42

Hotel Deja-quoi?

We need a new dead cliche to replace *déjà-vu* in certain media-related usages. Partly because the phrase has become so narrow in its meanings—when a TV critic says *déjà-vu* she means its re-run time again; when a theatre critic says *déjà-vu* it means he still can't tell Barbra Streisand from Millicent Martin; and when *New Musical Express* uses the phrase it's because *that's* what they probably think "Devo" is short for. But more than that we need a familiar phrase to label the ever-increasing frequency with which fact imitates illusion.

What's *not* at stake here is any element of design or purpose: an architect's perspective or couturier's scribble is a thin illusion that is deliberately intended to fatten out into three-dimensional fact. And of *course* the moon landing looked exactly like the simulations; in that surprise-free scenario they could have done the whole thing in the studio, were it not for this Boston Irish maniac who had written the contract in such a way that they actually had to put Neil Armstrong's foot up there in physical fact.

Originally appeared in *New Society* 48, no. 861 (5 April 1979): 26–27.

But both simulation and fact were boob-tube events as far as you and I were concerned, as well as being connected by a chain of planned causalities. It's a very different matter when three-dimensional concrete fact and two-dimensional media anticipation are separated by 40 years of non-causal disconnection. Yet here I was in this hotel lobby in Detroit thinking, "Vincent Korda Strikes Again!"

Vincent Korda? That's right—one of the Hungarian Connection who did so much to make British films of the thirties barely distinguishable from American ones. He was the man who got the design credits for all those sets in the movie version of H. G. Wells's *Things to Come,* which the art-history books insist on crediting to the former *Bauhausler* Moholy-Nagy. Actually, if you watch *Things to Come* very closely you can pick out the two tiny sequences which are by Moholy, and that leaves Korda 99.8 per cent of the film. That doesn't necessarily mean that Korda actually *designed* it, of course; I used to know this man who was at the old Ealing Studios and he said. . . .

Sorry, and yes—agreed—*Things to Come* was intended to be a seriously prophetic film, a work of extrapolation about what could really happen, rather than pure unbridled fantasy. On the short haul its prophet-and-loss account was pretty good; the anticipations of wartime chaos, and guerrilla aftermaths still hold up—especially the supermacho sheepskin liberty-bodice gear affected by the warlords in the movie, and by commandos in real life, during world war two.

But Raymond Massey and his parachute *übermensch* never came to restore order and decency after the chaos was over—though I do sometimes wonder about the *intentions* of General Westmoreland and middle-period strategy in Vietnam. From somewhere about the fictive 1950 onwards, illusion and reality drift relentlessly apart. Until you get to the Hyatt superhotels, and especially those designed by John Portman, for they recreate in all-too-concrete fact the kind of gigantic interior space that most of us recall as *the* image of the latter sequences of *Things to Come.*

The giant space in question is the central piazza of Wells's (Korda's?) city of the future, rising umpteen storeys high to a glazed roof—ditto John Portman's hotels. The huge space is ringed by pedestrian galleries and traversed by flying walkways—ditto (within limits) Portman's hotels. Vertical transportation in the Korda Piazza is by visible elevators in transparent ducts—and that kind of transportation has been the very trademark of Portman ever since the Peachtree Center in Atlanta over a decade ago.

The clincher, however—and a very unsettling one for me—is the trees. High up in the entirely artificial man-made environment of Korda City, rows of ornamental trees grow—looking not unlike the rows of trees that have graced visionary (but not factual) architecture ever since romantic neo-classicists began to hypothesize reconstructions of the tomb of the Emperor Augustus, around 1780.

Portman's trees don't come in rows, but in large oval or circular concrete planters, bracketing off the visible structure high up above your head when you enter at foyer level. The fact that they are different from Korda's in detail, but so alike in intention, is what makes them so convincing. Portman clearly is not imitating Wells's City of the Future; in America it would be inappropriate for him to take over the detailed symbolic forms of a projected society which is obviously both *planned* and European.

In the world of commercial fun he must, obviously (since he believes in it), add fairground details to his elevators, for instance, and have them splash down—almost literally—in floodlit lily pools at reception level. Yet the overall effect is so like, that you are really brought up short and forced to ask what are the connections, however tenuous, between Portman and Wells.

In a generalised sort of way, there is of course a connection between *all* modern architecture and Wells, *via* the Italian futurists before world war one. Their interest in Wells is known, their influence as the architecture of the twenties, and the sixties, is demonstrable and will probably prove to be infinitely revivable. Like the "great tunes that will not go away" (*Mack the Knife, Maple Leaf Rag, Yesterday,* and so on) the futurist vision/version of the Wellsian city is one of the things the 20th century is made of.

Where Portman most disturbingly connects back to Wells, however, is in the closure of his great spaces; the futurist's cities were open to the blue skies of Italy. Wells's cities were usually roofed over, as was the Korda version, as are Portman's gigantic lobbies. That wouldn't be all that odd if they were just lobbies in hotels, like the Ritz or the Waldorf or old mother Claridge. But Portman's lobbies aspire to be something vaster, and the vaster they get the nearer they draw to the Korda vision of a roofed multi-story piazza.

Now, that Korda version is true to Wells; his cities tend to be enclosed systems (remember the squalid rooftop scenes in *The Sleeper Wakes*?) looking inward in a rather paranoid manner that is perpetuated in later science-fiction futures, such as Asimov's sealed cities that ordinary citizens dare not go outside. And a great Portman hotel is just that—Renaissance Center in Detroit is almost a complete city in itself, inward-turned and virtually sealed against the legendary squalor and violence of downtown Detroit. Indeed, it has what look like defensive outworks between its entrance areas and the city beyond.

It's all uncomfortably like one of those self-contained cities planted on the face of an alien planet that were so common in SF, but it also summons up that persistent Wellsian dichotomy between the beautiful people in their beautifully controlled environment and the lesser breeds—violent or stupid—outside (or below) who toil to support them. And, hold it! Before your unquestioned liberal reflexes deprive you of understanding, let me report that all the really beautiful people inside the Renaissance Center that night were *black,* and that practically a third of the folks who were still strolling the terraces and bridges at 2 am, or sipping drinks among the ornamental plantings by the sparkling fountains, were also black. That's something that nearly all the regular intellectual future-fictionists (Huxley, quite as much as Wells) got wrong—supposing that privilege and racial stereotype will always be related to one another.

But Wells—or possibly Portman—got the rest of it right. This is the city of beautiful paranoia to the life. To step into Renaissance Center is to step into the World of Wells. Perhaps the new cliche we are looking for needs the homophone pun on *Puis/Puits,* which works in French (whereas *Then/Wells* doesn't in English) and would give us *Déjà Puis*—Already then, or Wells Already.

Valentino

Simply Filed Away

Real Los Angeles experts pride themselves on being able to walk you straight to the tomb of Rudolph Valentino without hesitation or false turns. (My own rating as an expert is given by the fact that I still make one wrong turn, the last one.) No doubt, non-experts readily fantasise an image of the tomb, complete with an elderly veiled woman bending to place one red rose on the marble slab, amid all the rhetoric of Forest Lawn's funerary fantasmagoria. . . .

Except that Valentino's tomb is not at Forest Lawn; in fact few of the Los Angeles tombs that matter are at Forest Lawn. No real, dyed in the wool (or died-in-the-swimming-pool) Angeleno would be seen *dead* there, it's too touristy and too common-place. After all there have been other Forest Lawns right across the states since the middle of the last century, and the accident of authorship that made this far-flung one the setting for Evelyn Waugh's *Loved One,* also made it an allegory of America, *all* America, as viewed through the shit-coloured spectacles of ingrained European prejudice.

Originally appeared in *New Society* 49, no. 875 (12 July 1979): 86–87.

Forest Lawn is not L.A.—or rather it is no more L.A. than any typical bog-standard franchise outlet is, like McDonald's or Howard Johnson's. Quintessential L.A. lies buried elsewhere in Tinsel-town, and Valentino is—how shall I put it?—filed away in *Hollywood* cemetery, along with such other substantial relics from real life as the Chandlers and the Otises of the *Los Angeles Times,* and the 20 composing room workers who died when the anarchists bombed the paper in 1910. And Douglas Fairbanks—the Mary Pickford half of the tomb was still unoccupied, the last time I looked, but that lack of symmetry has presumably been remedied now. And General William Andrews Clark, who gave his library to the University of California, and other solid worthies.

Now, General Clark's tomb is an exact replica of a small Roman temple, done in blinding white marble, reached by a bridge over a reflecting pool. It is a work of studied rectitude, of almost bourgeois conformity, and that really is the natural style of the Hollywood cemetery. The kind of cheapo whimsy you might so easily expect is hard to find there—almost the only example of note (noteworthy enough to appear in the publications of the semiotic fringe of architectural history) is the Bigsby monument, capped by its true-to-life model of an Apollo rocket, symbolising the vertical hopes of the defunct, and its two flanking inscriptions "Retired, by God" and "It was fun." That kind of yucko looks weirdly out of place in the Hollywood, where inscriptions tend to be as tersely proper as the architectural detailing of the monuments is correct. It is a field of regular urns and obelisks, temples and sarcophagi, under the palms and olive trees and—at our last visit—jacarandas at their fluorescently floribund crescendo.

What, if anything, seems decadent about the Hollywood cemetery is a sense of a great style in incipient decay, and if you want to see that style at its full strength, untroubled by doubt or hesitations, then you must leave the Hollywood, go down Western Avenue to Washington Boulevard and turn up Mariposa, which delivers you straight into Rosedale Cemetery.

And that is a stunner! Older than the Hollywood, it occupies a gently rising rectangle of land, and up through the middle of it winds a mighty avenue of palm trees. Never have I seen palms like these; the trunks as thick and close as the columns of a Doric temple, but a solemn matt black-brown in colour, crowned by heads of greenery that you hardly notice, so solid is the funeral pomp of the double rows of the trunks.

They match the style of the tombs, which are tough-minded, uncompromising and proper. The names on the marble and granite are in raised letters that follow the styles of the great Victorian wood-letter type-books—Gothicks and Grotesques, Ionics and Egyptians—their polished forms standing proud of the pick-tooled surface of the stone behind, and the imagination that shaped the tombs themselves gives form to the same defunct virtues of nobility, simplicity and primitivism.

E. H. Jones, for instance, lies in a tidy little temple, but unlike General Clark's suavely precise *Maison Carré,* this one makes a point of appearing primitive. Its walls are of coarse, rock-faced rusticated stone, instead of smooth white-marble ashlaring, and its columns look curiously naked in their absence of details. But this is not ignorance or incompetence; every line and surface speaks of knowledge of that learned longing for a true, aboriginal architecture that runs back through the classical tradition through Sir John Soane and the Abbé Laugier to Serlio, Alberti and other theorists of the Renaissance.

Just to emphasise the solid base of this memorial tradition, the Jones tomb is confronted, obliquely, by two monuments that would be gravely sensational anywhere. One is about 20 paces away, the other maybe five times that distance, and both are pyramids! The nearer, Shatto, is a properly primitive pyramid, again in rock-faced rusticated blocks of grey granite, sober, stable, self-contained.

The other is black and highly polished with an "Egyptian" entrance and gilded papyrus capitals to its columns. The effect is almost shocking: here—O Isis and Osiris!— among the dry sandy fields of southern California is what strikes the eye as an almost exact quotation from Karl Friederich Schinkel's famous Berlin Opera sets for *The Magic Flute.*

I doubt it was accidental. Whether the iconography is meant to be Masonic, Mozartean or merely memorable, this cuts too close to the heart of one of the most profound and persistent burial traditions of the European intelligentsia. Never mind "everybody knows the pyramids"—including the one on every dollar bill—but not everybody knows about that ingrained preference for elementary geometrical solids (like the square pyramid or the cube) that grows out of German neoclassicism, and surfaces in strange places like the theories of Cézanne and the paintings of Paul Nash, and current nut-cults about pyramids.

Why we forget that tradition, I suppose, is that it is over-familiar; the pyramid and its skinny cousin, the obelisk, adorn so many European monuments that we can hardly see them anymore. We need to stumble on them in strange places; not necessarily in Rosedale Cemetery—Adolf Loos, the great, bent, Viennese architectural theorist of the turn of the century laid it down thus: when we find a mound in the forest, six feet by three, formed into a pyramid with the spade, we become serious and something inside us says, "Here lies. . . ."

And that, said Loos, "ist architektur," and we had been sent to Rosedale to see an example of that dictum made real. But its impact—knowing, assured, impressive— was more than an illustration to a familiar quotation. It sat there, a thing in its own right, rich in allusion but self-sufficient in form, Whoever did it, did a classic. . . .

Valentino? Well, he's actually in the Cathedral Mausoleum in Hollywood Cemetery; a decent, stiff but inoffensive classical building with an entrance in the middle of its long side. You go in the entrance, past about ten of the twelve stone Apostles, and turn down the second aisle on the left. The last transept but one on the right contains his mortal remains—box 1205. It's at about face level, right at the end next to the window. The bronze scutcheon bears only his name, Rodolfo Guglielmi Valentino, and his dates. The two standardised glass vases in the brackets on either side are pretty well crammed with roses, of which one is red, as legend requires.

But the whole thing has that traditional European reticence (Peter Finch, gentleman, is at about knee-height on the other side of the transept) that has nothing to do with the "up front ersatz" fancies of Forest Lawn, but a whole lot to do with those two pensive pyramids at Rosedale.

» The 1980s

IN JANUARY 1980, Banham transferred to California from the East—not to his old love, Los Angeles, but to a post in art and architectural history at the University of California at Santa Cruz. Up to then his teaching had been, almost exclusively, in architecture schools. He now relished the opportunity to look more closely at contemporary art as well as architecture. And he was nearer to his new love, the American deserts, first discovered when he was researching the Los Angeles book. Now he could visit a different desert every weekend for his book *Scenes in American Deserta,* this time not curiously examining phenomena out in the great big world, but looking at the unexplained reasons for his own reactions to those hauntingly vast spaces.

The extraordinary scenic beauty of Monterey Bay and the position of his house by the ocean were a constant nourishment, but he had been a big city person for many years, and when the invitation came to take up a professorship at the Institute of Fine Art at New York University he was surprised, delighted, and highly honoured. His tenure was tragically brief because of his swift terminal illness. His inaugural lecture was written in hospital and published posthumously in New York and London. It is included in this volume.—M.B.

In 1988, the Design History Association founded the 'Annual Reyner Banham Memorial Lecture' at the Victoria and Albert Museum in London. The lecture series is organized in cooperation with the Royal College of Art and the Victoria and Albert Museum. Banham was a founder member of the Design History Association, and one of the first to promote design history as an area of academic study.

The Haunted Highway

At Remsen Corners, Ohio, the electrical problem changed from chronic to acute (possibly terminal) and left us stranded with a flat battery and an almost dry tank outside a filling station that was neat, shiny, highly coloured, fully equipped—and *shut*! Public holidays in the States are often observed with a fanaticism that overrides even commercial zeal, and not only was the gas station locked up, but the classic white wooden American farmhouse next door was curtained and empty—they'd even taken the dog with them. Nothing but silence and a light dusting of hoar-frost over the spreading flat fields and a grey-white mist.

In fact, help was but ten minutes' walk away, and we were repaired and awheel again by ten the next morning. But before we got into our stiff-upper-lip routine and set about salvaging our situation, we stood by the back bumper of the car and had a short psychological slump; and in that blank pause, the freezing silent desolation seemed to bite into our awareness of the whole continent. Far and fast as we drove, the mood stayed with us almost to the Pacific coast. America in a trance—or just unplugged at the mains.

Originally appeared in *New Society* 52, no. 918 (19 June 1980): 297–299.

After Tulsa the mood acquired elegiac overtones, and sustained them for almost 1,500 miles to Barstow in California. For the whole of that distance, Interstate 40 is haunted, dogged, mocked almost, by the mouldering remains of one of the great highways of modern legend. Just what this was all about didn't fully strike me until our first meal-stop out of Tulsa. We ate at a laconic, plastic, biker-movie sort of lunchroom next to the frozen pool of one of the two fairly grotty motels in the middle of the place, which otherwise seemed to consist of two or three filling stations and a thin line of houses and behind them, the inevitable mist-bounded circle of flat, frosted fields.

But just as we were pulling out of town, I saw this sign, "El Reno Correctional Center," and something went click. *El Reno on Route 66!* Yes, El Reno on that "legendary highway thru' the sick psyche of the hitch-hikin' nation." That legendary highway that will officially cease to exist next year, but has already died by obsolescence and replacement along most of its hallowed length.

Legal extinction will never equal the traumas and emaciations of partial abandonment, however. Where Sixty-Six physically survives it is usually—as at El Reno—in short loops and parallels to Forty, like the oxbows of an old river, furnishing services to the new Interstate. When you see the "Gas, Food, Lodging" sign you pull off Forty, and there they all are on a bumpy stretch of historic Sixty-Six. The whole classic desert section from Seligman to Kingman in Arizona, taking in Valentine and Peach Springs, has now become a 90 mile oxbow of this kind.

Even more affecting (if you have any Soul of the Road in you) are the short sharp stretches, mostly in the Texas Panhandle, where they haven't yet built the last links of Forty, and traffic is suddenly forced back onto the physical remains of Sixty-Six whether it needs food, fuel, or not. And there you are, unexpectedly tooling down the main drag of somewhere like Groom, Texas. The only enduring physical structures in Groom are the tall grain-elevators by the rail-tracks that parallel Forty/Sixty-Six for ever and ever. All other structures in Groom are low, crumbling, accidental, ephemeral—cement-block motels, streamline filling stations, Moderne cafes, all with large, but battered illuminated signs, their plastic as crazed and broken as the stucco on the buildings. Groom clearly wasn't built in a day—more likely, in the two hours before dawn on the day the legend of Sixty-Six was born.

And it will die with that legend; not because the mystic number Sixty-Six has been taken away from it, but because fewer and fewer Americans in the future will be able to cram all their worldly goods in the back of the waggon, scratch "L.A. or bust!" in the dust in the back window, and drive, drive, drive into the golden sunset. Groom's doom prefigures in the gasoline-short USA that is to come, and its warning was repeated wherever old Sixty-Six got close to Forty, like a skull by the trail, or a tomb by the Appian Way. The last such *memento mori* was at Ludlow, in the Mojave Desert. That is the absolute end, the last grim stub of Sixty-Six before Forty itself is extinguished by Interstate 15 at Barstow. There was one coffee-shop in working order, but everything else along that bitter end seemed to be abandoned gas-stations with wheelless cars in the forecourt, or vandalised cafes with not a sheet of glass in their windows, but the black-leatherette bar stools still in place along the counter, and even the napkin-dispensers still gleaming nickelled through the dust and debris.

So the glory is departed—no more hitch-hiking GIs with their bed-rolls, no more grizzled philosophers with a big dog in the truck behind them, no more golden girls in MGs, no more migrating families with "their all in the U-Haul" hitched behind the Plymouth, no more Easy-riders with their tall "Ape-hanger" handlebars, no more Volkswagens with New Jersey licence plates and surfboards racked on the roof. . . .

They are still around, in fact. We saw samples of practically every legendary denizen of the Interstates, but the sense that they may soon be gone was ever-present; that the whole Road-America culture was crumbling—as at Groom—or cocooned—as at Remsen Corners—waiting to be rediscovered by historians or archaeologists of a distant, or even near future.

Very near future. They're at it already, as anyone will know who has come across a copy of David Macaulay's *Motel of the Mysteries* (Hutchinson). A Brit, now teaching at Providence, Rhode Island, and an architect by training, Macaulay has a useful list of semi-humorous books of busy, well-informed drawings behind him (*Cathedral, Pyramid, City,* and so on) that have become the staples of school architectural history courses. About three years ago, however, he came up with a book/exhibit called *Great Moments in Architecture* that revealed a fully developed satirical wit, a tendency to draw mock-Piranesis and a preoccupation with Pompeii-as-Las-Vegas.

THE MACAULAY *Motel of the Mysteries* is the first full-scale display of this new Macaulay. Telescoping
OF AMERICA Pompeii, the Tutankhamen show and European contempt for motel culture (remember *Lolita*?), it does the standard fourth-form lavatorial jokes about archaeologists mis-constructing ancient sites and artefacts. Some of it is very funny, much of the anti-archaeologist stuff is almost in the same league as *Anglo-Saxon Attitudes* (even the erudition is almost up to Angus Wilson standards), and the whole thing is uncomfor-tably like—if not Groom—then, say, Amarillo, Texas. It is just possible that the next, and last, motel to be built on Sixty-Six off Forty in Amarillo might be called the *Toot'n' C'mon.* (I told you the humour was fourth-form, didn't I?)

However, *Motel of the etc,* represents the motel in its mature, developed form. What's weird about places like Groom is that much more primitive motels can be dis-cerned there, abandoned or still in use. And not just Groom; on another trip and an-other highway, I have stayed in motels that were not so different from the one in the great first-ever motel movie, *It Happened One Night.* And at times like that, being a historian to the marrow, I have wished that some Pevsner of the Interstates had written a multi-volume *The Motels of America,* giving dates and attributions and off-the-cuff critiques: "Overwrought plastic window-trim on street front. Splendid sculptured shag rug in tones of orange in front office. Textured blue ceilings. Original 1956 ice-machine in back courtyard."

In the meantime, *Americans on the Road* by Warren James Belasco (MIT Press) is another implicitly valedictory work, a first stab at that "decent book on the history of motels," that people keep asking after, though its subtitle, "From autocamp to motel, 1910–1945," reveals that it is really a *pre*-history of the building type, and stops just at the point where true motel-culture, and the legend of Sixty-Six, begins to emerge.

The strength of the book, which has a guaranteed place in all American Studies libraries, is that it is a thorough-paced social history of Americans awheel and the civic and commercial installations created for their comfort and accommodation. It has a real treasure chest of a bibliography, and will be welcomed by academics.

And that's what's wrong with it, too. It smells of the study and the lamp, not of those boring, sweaty, interminable miles of dust and sun glare between Denver and Topeka in high August, or that feeling that there is no escape from Nebraska, on which so many travellers comment. I get no sense that Belasco ever smelled the lure of sheer distance in some clammy pre-dawn parking lot in Terre Haute, Indiana, or felt that characteristic slumping of the muscles as you steer the car into its appointed parking space under the tall Days Inn, or Motel 6, sign after 700 miles of dark-to-dark driving.

Instead there is a slightly toffee-nosed air of superior wisdom after the events: "Maybe motorists took the wrong path. Instead of escaping to the road, perhaps they should have looked for answers closer to home." And maybe Christopher Columbus should never have set sail; perhaps James Watt should have made tea with that boiling kettle, instead of inventing the steam engine. . . .

Where this sense of ivoried unreality is most disturbing, however, is in Belasco's over-tidy expository diagram of his historical process, which goes: random camping, 1910–20, municipal camps, 1920–24, pay-camps, 1923–26, early motels, 1925–45. These time slots are, *of course,* based on scrupulous documentation, but if you take especially the middle two out of the library and into the field where people are clearing sites, laying concrete, building brick toilets, adding cabin units, and stuff like that, then those three or four year intervals are too short to be credible. If there were recognisable motels by 1925, then there were probably primitive motel prototypes as early as 1920. Belasco himself records cabin-building as early as 1922, and it would take a finer-tuned legal mind than his to determine just where to draw the line between a "camp" with a few cabins, and a small "motel" with tent-sites. Motel *practice* clearly anticipated the motel *concept,* let alone the coining of the word, as early-twenties rural entrepreneurs grappled with the problems of ripping off the passing motorists for fun and profit.

Belasco's historical apparatus is too pat, too neat an academic mechanism to look convincing outside the cloistered groves (actually the Library of Congress) where it was assembled. Somewhere on one of those service-loops of Sixty-Six, in the corner of the lunchroom of a crumbling stuccoed motel, there must be an old-timer in faded fatigues and a three-day stubble who can recall, in the B-movie phraseology that old-timers really do speak in the west, where and how it all began: "Just by the grade crossing outside of Williams (or Ash Fork, or Essex, or Winslow), mister, round about Twenny or Twenny-one, just a few Maw-and-Paw cabins, run by a couple name of Johnson, or Jackson . . . Jimson? Don't rightly remember, but anyways. . . ."

They're real, I've met them, given them lifts. They're all like Walter Brennan, and they do the essential *Boyhood of Raleigh* numbers for travellers on the haunted highways, except that they describe a past that is here, not a future out there. Someone (I hope) is already taping their memoirs; certainly the recording of roadside artefacts and buildings has been going on ever since Ed Ruscha first published *Twenty-Six Filling Stations,* and that was 15 years ago. There is, too, a Society for Commercial Archaeology which seems to specialise in documenting stainless steel diners. So it's all happening, and perhaps this is what the U.S. will have instead of industrial archaeology, Coalbrookdale and the Iron Bridge.

However, I don't intend to be around when they begin the Big Digs at Ludlow or Groom. Macaulay can record the patient sifting through smashed formica and rumpled chrome strip in search of sundae glasses and syrup dispensers, and Belasco can write it all up in a historical scenario that no one now living in those places could recognise. For myself, I would much rather be around when the archaeologists stumble on that perfect, sealed time-capsule at Remsen Corners, every nut, bolt, wrench, tyre, spark plug, oil can, shining in its appointed place, even the rescue truck, a-gleam with chromium, neatly slotted into the only piece of clear floor-space large enough to accommodate it, the locked pumps outside with their hoses coiled just so, like soldiers at ease on parade, rapt out of time in a pool of frosty white silence broken only by the very, very faint hum of the fluorescent security-lights inside.

I *know* where the music died.

45

Dead on the Fault

To the memory of Maria Antonia Castro, says the small square slab at my feet, *Wife of F. A. MacDougall, died 30 May 1855, aged twenty-five years.* She was a niece of General José Castro, sometime Governor of the state, and commander of rebel cavalry who had defeated John Fremont and the legendary Kit Carson. . . . Put foot to ground in San Juan Bautista, and you tread on the early history of the State of California!

Tough history even for a well-connected woman like Maria Castro. She was already widowed, and ailing, when she married MacDougall. He cared for the declining twelve-month of her life, and inherited the task of raising her sons. He also inherited huge areas of real estate, which he promptly sold off at a smart profit in California's first land boom. The history you tread out here is, above all else, the history of the anglification of a traditional *ranchero* economy, and a declining mission culture.

For Maria's memorial is in the floor of the north aisle of the last and greatest of the California missions, the only one that is still self-supporting, not an embalmed ward of the state, and now the focus of deep, fierce and inscrutable Hispanic sentiment that even the most crass of outsiders cannot but sense. We began to hear about San Juan

---

Originally appeared in *New Society* 63, no. 1055 (3 February 1983): 187–188.

as soon as we came to this part of the world—a shrine; a truly magic place; a real centre of people-energy, man; exquisite; the essential mission.

Not all of that may be apparent at first approach, through the usual agribusiness mess and dusty sidestreets of your average small town in "Steinbeck country" (the TV version of *East of Eden* was largely filmed in San Juan Bautista) but as you penetrate deeper the style begins to change—false-front stores, galleried adobes, fancy-carpentered Anglo houses, all suggest that this must be a town where the second half of the last century failed to happen. And that's about true; like Stamford in Lincolnshire, San Juan was a coaching town (a team-change on the Butterfield Stage) that the railways ignored.

Time did not stand quite still, however. The ranching economy survived, and the flat valley-bottom was put down to intensive market gardening, and the town, pocketed in a ring of pretty hills, evolved very slowly, keeping its extraordinary live links to the past. The silver mines up the canyon may have failed, but the last mission Indian did not die until 1973, and the long tradition of the church has delivered the mission into the 1980s looking, sounding, even smelling unlike any other.

It is large, and its three-aisled plan is almost unknown elsewhere among the Spanish missions. Like all big adobe constructions, however, it is solid, lumpy and nowhere quite upright. Yet it is rendered graceful by delicate country-rococo painted garlands on the massive square columns between the aisles . . . decorations that apparently still follow the designs and colours of the original work, done by an Irish carpenter who jumped ship in San Francisco, and finished up married to yet another Castro and Hispanicised as Felipe Santiago (not bad for Tom Doak!).

The three ponderous adobe vaults also give the mission church acoustics so stunning that local choirs and orchestras compete decorously to perform here, but the music I am hearing right now, as I stand with my left foot by Maria Castro's modest memorial, comes from the fiddles, trumpets and deep-backed guitars of the Mariachi Caltecas, for this is the midday Mass of the Day of the Dead, one of the two great annual festivals of San Juan Bautista.

The other is the Fiesta Rodeo, the celebration of the *ranchero* culture—equestrian parades and clattering harness all hung about with silver ornaments, the *caballero* gear that has snobs and yobs alike filling the plaza outside the mission with western hats, the rodeo itself, and then the streets running with beer and piss at night and the stores boarded up against the ritual violence.

El Dia de los Muertos is different—but that doesn't mean that it's anything like Eisenstein's *Que Viva Mexico* either! It is relaxed and a bit arty and more bucolic and very friendly (gentle even) though quite loud when the music gets going, and "historical" in the demotic California sense that people dig heirloom suits and uniforms and velvet gowns out of the mothballs and, cheerfully heedless of whether or not they are matched for period, stroll around in couples like the extras on Main Street in a routine western.

Quite half of them will have their faces made up (masks are rare) as Death's Heads and will have forgotten about it before midday, so that one has weirdly normal conversations with street vendors, uniformed officers of the peace, local dignitaries, parking attendants and strangers, all looking like death and perfectly cheerful about it.

Ordinary folks, with their kids, will be mostly picnicking or listening to the music in the Plaza, a regular rectangle of grass about the size and smell of a smaller English village green: One side of the Plaza is entirely occupied by the external arcade of the mission; the lower end is closed by the Plaza Hotel and the ancient home of the Castros (from whom there is no escape hereabouts, it seems!). Across from the mission stands an enormous false-fronted livery stable, then the Zanetta house with its outside galleries, its palatial pretensions and its large upstairs ballroom, and the only other building on that side, at the upper end, opposite the entrance to the mission church, is the so-called Dressmaker's Cottage.

The fourth side of the plaza, between the cottage and the church, is without buildings. Instead, a double row of trees stands along the top of a short, steep drop to the flat valley bottom. The rodeo grounds are down there, and the tiered seating for rodeo-fanciers is simply built down the slope, a natural grandstand.

But this is no commonplace declivity; it is the local manifestation of the most portentous geological feature in all California—the dreaded San Andreas Fault! Whatever else is marvellous, magical and unique about San Juan is given heightened impact, profounder emotional charge, by the visible and unavoidable presence of this slumbering threat of that ultimate doomquake that occupies the thoughts of every Californian for some part of every waking day. On this cheerful day of the living dead the symbolism is so obvious that you can't be bothered, but the threat is always there under the trees and sunshine.

Meanwhile, the mass is over and the crowd is drifting down to the low end of the Plaza, where a platform for speeches has been set up in front of the gap between the hotel and the Castro adobe, for this is no ordinary Day of the Dead. After years of work, the state parks service has finished (at last!) the restoration of all the secular buildings that front the Plaza. Last night there was a great fandango danced on the newly-repaired maple floor upstairs in the Zanetta house; today there are ceremonial discourses from the mayor, the priest, the man from the parks—and from someone who has been visible and omnipresent all day, a stocky Hispanic figure conventionally dressed in jacket and slacks, shirt and tie, but with a splendid flat-brimmed hat worn rakishly low on the brow: Luis Valdez!

Valdez? The name should mean something to members of the *bien-pensant* left, even outside North America. While it would be bizarre to describe him as an Hispanic Joan Littlewood, there are similarities and he admires her work. His *Teatro Campesino* is an historical consequence of the road-and-field politics of the grape-picker strikes in the sixties that made César Chavez a world figure, and its style is song-and-dance agit-prop. It is also loud, energetic and funny. If you have seen his regular musical *Zoot*

Suit, then that is not *Teatro Campesino* (being more of an adult *West Side Story*) but might be described as an urban equivalent that replaces the folk, mythic and rural strains of the *Teatro* with street-smarts and big-band pizazz.

The real *Teatro Campesino,* country-bound in spite of its sophistication and deep literary sources, has found in San Juan a near perfect operational base, within striking distance of both big city resources and campus creativity but close to the surviving roots of whatever makes Californian Hispanic culture something distinctive, and in the visible presence of the agricultural labour that made it politically necessary.

And it was clear, as the day progressed, that the *Teatro,* as embodied by Valdez and his busy aides, is now a kind of third force in the town, making it a community energised by powers spiritual, temporal and theatrical. The physical presence of the *Teatro* is not normally conspicuous, their permanent stage is half a block off the main drag, at the back of the *Jardines de San Juan* restaurant, but on this Day of the Dead one was aware of their animating activity behind practically every public act—the place has more style than is halfway decent for so small a community!

Just how the three powers feel about one another is not altogether clear—this, after all, was a day of goodwill and welcome to all—but one had the feeling that Valdez might just take over completely one day, and make the place a permanent festival that would put Spoleto and Salzburg right in the shade—or that what would crumble when the Fault terminally stirred itself, would just be an elaborate stage set, the quake itself an ultimate production number or comic act of audience participation, leaving the church with the authorised Apocalyptic script, but no one left to play it!

For the present, however, as the afternoon grows late, the triumvirate of church, state and theatre holds its productive equilibrium, to the clear advantage of the town, for such is the international clout of *El Teatro Campesino* (who at one point persuaded Peter Brook that he should act, not just direct) that they have been able to bring to this almost unknown country place the last goody of the day, the prestigious *Folcloricos* group from Mexico City.

A few hundred souls are still sitting on the grass, listening and eating; the "historical" costumes are still strolling around the perimeter of the Plaza, and from the upper gallery of the Zanetta house, we can see the other little miracle that makes San Juan magical. Beyond the trees on the fault line; beyond the rich, flat valley-lands, the modest dry-grass hills that enfold every view from the town are beginning to take their sunset aspect, the low golden light modelling their humped outlines and sharp valley like draped green velvet.

You can see that almost anywhere in Steinbeck country, but around San Juan they seem particularly artful, irresistibly fetching. Could this too be Valdez's fault. . . .

46

O, Bright Star . . .

. . . of constabular authority, resplendent on the uniformed bosom of the female deputy sheriff who had just meticulously hand-checked my carry-on luggage. *Hand*-checked— no x-rays or metal detectors; they keep up the ancient skills and value-systems in that high inter-mountain country where Marlboro Men roam in their pick-up trucks and elegantly-worn blue denim. Indeed, it's all so macho and hairy-chested that you have to wonder how they ever managed to deputise a *woman*. . . .

Musing on these matters while waiting for Sagebrush Airways flight 665 to whisk us away to less arid climes, I watched her go back into her office and close the brown plywood door behind her. On the door was a very much enlarged version of the same star of authority, about 18 inches across, presumably a plastic decal to go on the side of a patrol car.

This badge of authority bore looking at: like all good sheriff stars it had points, six of them. The points had round knobs on their extremities, and the triangular spaces

---

Originally appeared in *New Society* 64, no. 1068 (5 May 1983): 188–189.

within them were filled in with distinctly Victorian foliate decoration. And there were words, like *Sheriff* and *Robson County,* on scrolls, surrounding the Great Seal of the State in the centre.

It is not often that one has a chance to study such an object in magnified detail like this—to get an equally good look at the one the deputy was wearing I would have had to lean close enough to get myself arrested.

Neat, I thought; fascinating. But the pleasure of seeing a sheriff star under a microscope, as it were, was suddenly terminated by a dread thought which persistently afflicts all those who profess the trade of design-historian: *Who designed it?* Sheriff stars can't just happen; some person or group had made decisions, based on taste or tradition, standing orders or divine revelation, and had thus determined its form and iconography.

And I had no idea who. Similar horrors of ignorance have doubtless afflicted persons of my calling confronted with the bright-work on British bobbies' bonce-cosies, or the heraldry on the reverse of Maria Theresa dollars, or all that squiggly stuff around Her Britannic Majesty's Principal Secretary of State inside the front cover of your passport, but I was stuck, there and then, with the problem of who designs sheriff stars.

It's taken a long time to find out, because a certain reticence surrounds the whole topic. There is no literature that I or our indefatigable campus library staff have been able to turn up, and bare-faced inquiries directed at law enforcement personnel tend to get very dusty answers—*don't* ask a policeman, because he will immediately suspect the worst; there are far too many unlicensed stars and badges in circulation already.

In the end, it was the sheriff of Salinas, caught with his guard down when my credentials were up, who broke the silence and told me where his department went to buy their insignia, and this lead (the appropriate cliche, you'll agree) led me to Acme Star and Badge Co, and that's not their real name either, but the company's reticence is catching.

Actually it led me in the first place to a telephone conversation with the company secretary, who sent me their catalogue, which confirmed that I had indeed got on to the right kind of operation, and then to an extended conversation with the proprietor, which confirmed that I had also got on to an enthusiast—to put it very mildly indeed.

I probably should have guessed this last from the rhetoric in the trade-literature I had already received:

"All of our badges are hand-made and use silver solder for ribbons, attachments etc, and these consume enormous amounts of silver. Since our solders are 45 per cent and 66 per cent silver these costs reflect ultimately in the price.

"We could change our methods of construction and utilise lead solder but that would just make an inferior product, and in this plastic world quality will not be eliminated at Acme Star and Badge Co. The only companies that remain in business are firms that are serious about their craftsmanship."

In this plastic world, it turns out, about a dozen companies in the whole of North

America are serious enough about their craftsmanship to have survived, four of them here in California, and mostly firms about the same size as Acme, with an output of less than 10,000 pieces a year. Not quite a cottage industry, then; more like the little maisters in Sheffield, only in this case spread across a continent.

Not that the premises were anything like Sheffield, when I got to them: three 1920ish single-storey shop units on an island of older development amid all the urban renewal in downtown Oakland. The firm was founded before the turn of the century, but has only been on this site since 1971, when it was urban-renewed out of its old building, and the present proprietor has only been in charge since 1968. The entirely convincing air of unshakable traditionalism that pervades the operation may thus be no more than an optical illusion by now (the old shops must have been comfortably well-worn before they moved in) or it may be generated by the process of manufacture, as we shall see.

The first impression on entering the front office is that you have walked into a badge freak's paradise. In the glass display case on the wall are some 100 badges and stars, some labelled as being from the early 1900s, while under the glazed top of the counter opposite are another 120 or more, loose on jewellers' trays. Pay-dirt for the badge design-historian, but how to mine and refine it?

A TIMELESS WORLD The more you look at this board the less sense of orderly stylistic or technical development you can discern. Some of the most ornately Victorian are clearly recent, some of the most obviously modern-movement, in plain undecorated silver with stern sanserif lettering, are among the oldest on display. Perhaps we are looking at a world of design that has become timeless, frozen out of the tides of fashion. But if that is so, then whence the very large variety of different designs, not at all the narrow range that would normally come from a static vernacular?

The answer, again, lies in the production process, which is in itself something of an historical monument. The raw stock is bronze strip, plated with the appropriate gold, silver or alloy on one face, and the blank star is punched out on it on a Roussell punch—which, like most of the machinery employed, comes from Providence, Rhode Island, another bit of American traditionalism. The blank is then taken to a Standard Machines die-press, and the foliated decoration in the points is bashed into relief on it. Three or four thumps are needed to make the embossing deep enough, and since the metal work hardens, it has to be taken away and annealed between thumps, acquiring a coating of oxide that dulls it to anything but a bright star.

Then another thumping press raises its centre into a dome, if that is what's required. The lettering is drawn on by hand, meticulously with a sharp-pointed scriber, to ensure its just spacing and proper arrangement before it is punched into the metal with hand-held letter-punches, a small hammer and finicky precision. This done, the recessed letter-forms are filled—in a positively mediaeval way—with a slurry of coloured ground glass and water, and popped into a minute and non-mediaeval electric oven in order to fire the slurry into enamel.

The now more-or-less complete badge or star comes out of the oven looking like an archaeological relic, all blackened and blotchy. But some smart fettling by hand, before it goes into a tumbler to be sloshed around with a quart or two of steel balls to take out every minutest scratch or blemish, and out comes as supernaturally gleaming a star of authority as you could ever hope to see.

Now, this technology permits someone to do quite a lot of designing without ever having to put pencil to paper. Where dies, ribbons, etc, are compatible, a good deal of mix and match is possible—decorative devices can be selected, rejected, omitted, for instance, or the same infill patterns can be applied to stars with or without knobs on their points, the whole thing could be domed or flat, and so on. The possible variations are, theoretically, a mathematical product of the numbers of compatible dies, and there are supposed to be at least 300 assorted dies on the shelves along the work-shop wall (it looked a lot more to me) and there are thought to be about the same number in the "archive" or "mausoleum" of abandoned patterns.

Currently, Acme are recovering old designs from the archive and finding them sale-able, which is one reason for the historical confusions. Another is the fact that rather few absolutely new designs are being created from scratch because they have lost their old die-cutter, and failed to find anyone trained to work at his bench, in spite of advertising as far afield as Germany. They can farm out their die-cutting, but I got a distinct impression that they don't really care to do that; it would be a concession to the plastic world, somehow.

Whether the cutting of totally innovative designs was ever common I now take leave to doubt, and at the moment it is patently unnecessary. For the foreseeable future, Acme should be able to cruise along on its large visible stock of existing designs and variations, and the hidden assets of the mausoleum—especially in the present con-servative (not to say nostalgic) climate of opinion out in Law'n'Order-land. That still leaves the design-historian with his ultimate problem, however: accepting that day-to-day designing is done by choosing motifs from catalogue and archive, where did those motifs come from in the first place?

Are they all variations from some unique original sheriff badge, some kind of *Ur-stern* or Platonic Idea shining untarnished in the dawn's early light of American law-enforcement? It would be tempting to think of it as something profoundly simple and unadorned, but that temptation should be resisted because—as far as I can ascer-tain—such a badge would have been made in the early 1850s (when New York police are first described as wearing stars) and would therefore be likely to be crusted with early Victorian ornament, acanthus leaves flourishing in every point, plaited borders on every edge, droopy scrolls for the lettering—something like Acme's present No. 646 as worn by the Oregon Highway Patrol, perhaps.

I doubt we will ever know; the origins of this prized emblem are probably lost behind a jungle of foliation, borders, state seals, scrolls, ribbons, heraldic beasts, sunbursts, republican eagles . . . and bitter arguments about whether to have five, six or seven points. Those arguments are still proceeding, or something very like them—while I was perusing Acme's stock of stars and badges, the company secretary was on the phone, burning the ears off someone at a local YMCA about the arrangement of the lettering on their official seal: "No way; the 'Founded 1897' should go around the *bottom* of the circle, right? Then the 'YMCA' goes across the middle, and 'Commerceville' goes around the top, OK? Oh, you're welcome, but you shoulda asked me first 'cause I could have told you all that stuff."

I think I heard an official seal being designed. If I'd hung around a bit longer, perhaps I might have heard a sheriff star being designed? Within a settled idiom, design does not necessarily require drawings, but that's something they *dare* not tell you at the Royal College of Art or its American equivalents. It's only *originality* that needs drawings!

47

Stirling Escapes the Hobbits

Moriturus Caesar . . . and all that. About to die, I salute the editor of *New Society* for allowing me to do it all over his columns. My death will be at the hands of the Paranoiat (or Taste Police) and its instance will be my praise of the new addition to the Staatsgalerie in Stuttgart. That addition is the work of James Stirling, Michael Wilford and Associates—and as anyone will know who keeps up with the English highbrow weeklies (professional, intellectual or satirical), the only approvable attitude to James Stirling is one of sustained execration and open or veiled allegations of incompetence.

At first sight that is odd. His disaster rate is about average for super-star architectural practices in Britain in the last two decades, and he has done nothing remotely as obscene as the Hunslet Grange housing estate in Leeds. But that counts for nothing in this argument. He has put up buildings in Oxbridge, where the Hobbits of the intellect can see them (they can't see Leeds—"North of Banbury, isn't it?"), and for being thus visible he will never be forgiven.

So my doom was probably sealed as soon as anybody knew I was off to Stuttgart. Disinformation was readily volunteered about Stirling's art gallery. The roof leaked and

---

Originally appeared in *New Society* 70, no. 1137 (4 October 1984): 15–16.

the walls were so damp that plants were already growing out of them. The external cladding was having to be replaced two months after the opening, and was covered in protest graffiti anyhow. The only graffito I could find on arrival looked like a spoof by the management, and the rest had apparently been removed by magic. The cladding story had to be grudgingly disavowed by the editors of the *Architects' Journal,* the story about the roof could not be checked on the spot, and the veritable plants growing out of the walls had been put there on purpose as part of a classicising joke about Piranesi's engravings of Roman ruins.

The doubts expressed about the actual gallery spaces I can share to some extent. But the design of all gallery spaces these days is very moot, and Stirling was unlikely to please everybody. For me it was less that the means and mechanisms of the lighting were too visible above the glazed ceilings, but that in combining ancient forms— rectangular plan, coved cornices and central lanterns to admit light—with the wide spans made possible by modern structural techniques, he had created spaces that were almost disorientingly expansive. I felt an awfully long way from the artworks at times.

But galleries as such are a very small part of what museums need nowadays. What they usually need most desperately, when they expand out of their earlier accommodations, are all kinds of auxiliary spaces that lead up to the point where art and public finally confront one another: everything from cloakrooms to conservation laboratories, by way of lifts for the disabled and small auditoria. About all this kind of stuff I have no complaints of substance within, and really nothing but praise without.

Indeed I have to say that I was almost knocked out by a level of sustained inventiveness and poised wit that I haven't seen in a new building for a long time. The site demands inventiveness anyhow, not just because the new work has to make visual and functional sense in relation to the older museum alongside, but because the ground slopes up fairly steeply from the Konrad Adenauer Weg in front to the Urbanstrasse behind. The solution, basically, has been to put the galleries round three sides of a square courtyard at the top, with the open side of the square looking down over a series of terraces which contain all those necessary etceteras that support the exhibition of the art—in this case, *literally* support.

So far this is only a bit more than functional and sensible. Where the design takes off into the realm of inspiration is in the management of a circulation problem peculiar to the site. The pedestrian way up from the *Weg* below to the *Strasse* above begins by ramping across the faces of the terraces, then plunges into a deep rotunda in the centre of the gallery courtyard, climbs around half its perimeter, and finally passes through a narrow slot in the highest parts of the building to emerge at upper street level next to a couple of enormous high-tech air intakes.

The rotunda is the real key to the design as the visitor experiences it. Serving as a sculpture court for the whole museum, it also brings light down into the back of the entrance hall below. Glassless windows in its upper parts enable museum visitors to look down on both their fellow art-fanciers and those who are merely crossing the site; and to admire the ingenuity with which the two circulation patterns never actually interfere with one another, nor does the public foot-way constitute any threat to the security of the museum itself.

All this big sweeping geometrical terracing and its monumental intruding cylinder would be handsome and clever even if it were finished only in standard, value-free modern white. Stirling being Stirling, however, it isn't finished in anything of the sort. The walls are mostly covered in what appears to be multi-hued sandstone masonry, rising at gallery level to huge, plain, coved cornices—an Egypto-*Zauberflote* touch that is echoed in the pair of dumpy-Doric columns between which one enters the rotunda from below. The ramps have enormously fat Kandy-coloured handrails in pink and blue, the entrances are sheltered by greenhouse-roofed canopies suspended on constructivist-looking steel bracketing, and the entrance proper, once you have gone inside, proves to be floored in a yelping garden-green compound that has been the talk of Germany for months.

Such free-form bravura may sound like the usual post-modernist omnium-gatherum of eclectic historical details, but isn't. Stirling is not only one of the most visually erudite architects of his generation but—like Le Corbusier, his first hero—is also extremely observant of things which are not particularly architectural, and can turn practically any of them to architectural effect. If the visitor to the Staatsgalerie will look around him at the city beyond with only moderate attention, he will see that with barely a couple of major exceptions—the pit-head gear re-deployed as a lift shaft, the aforementioned Piranesi plantings on the top of the rotunda—the details seem to come from the museum's immediate urban surroundings.

Stuttgart is—in its civic and governmental moods—a stone-faced city, given to large, serious cornices and the like. The segmental-arched window openings that Stirling employs so freely, are equally freely employed throughout historical Stuttgart. But the greenhouse-roofed canopies at the entrances are the local downtown bus shelters. Where the museum's less grandiose minor accommodations break out above the stone-faced terraces, or up at the back of the site, they display the regular yellow stucco (and even the dotty round windows) that were the commonplaces of Stuttgart's rebuilding after the air raids at the end of the second world war, the vernacular townscape of Fassbinder's *Maria Braun*.

In modern architecture, this sort of thing used to be called "cribbing," especially by Stirling and his mates who made no bones about it ("Okay, then, historian Banham; name my influences!"). But when the post-modernists and other wets of academe moved into the act, it was elevated to the status of *typology* or *contextualism*. What Stirling and Wilford have done at Stuttgart could just about be called typological in the sense that it looks something like yer typical art gallery, and contextual in that it looks something like its context—ie, the neighbourhood.

Contextualism, however, has been increasingly taken to mean looking so nearly exactly like the neighbourhood that no one will notice that you have done a new building at all, and that is what recommends it to Young Fogey pundits of the David Watkin/Roger Scruton neo-conservative tendency. Stirling can do that number, too, as his extensions to the Architecture Building at Rice University in Houston testify, all looking so like the blandly third-rate architecture to which they are attached that you don't immediately twig what a first-rate piece of work he has done.

The relationship to the Stuttgart context isn't like that at all. This is a big bold building, commanding on its site, respectful of the older museum next door as one professional to another, and—above all—a sort of celebration of the city of Stuttgart itself, and its architectural traditions—including the proud place it occupies in the mythology of modern architecture because of the manifesto houses by practically every accredited Hero of Modernism that survive from the exhibition of 1927 on the hill of Weissenhof overlooking the city.

The ultimate strength of Stirling's design, as William Curtis pointed out recently in the *Architectural Review*, lies not in its classical references, but in its underlying discipline of modernist compositional methods. Stirling himself is prone to compare the plan with that of Berlin's Altes Museum, because of the central rotunda. But the way everything else is put together goes back to the more formalist aspects of Modernism, such as he was taught at Liverpool in the forties. It is on the basis of this inward strength that he can compliment the city of Stuttgart by making what are very high-level architectural jokes about it, and *for* it.

The best of these jokes is that the necessary ventilation for the car parking under the lowest terrace has been made by way of a couple of "accidents" to the front wall. Gaping holes have been made where blocks of stone have apparently fallen out, and there they are, lying half-buried in the grass by the sidewalk—and everybody in that well-informed city knows that the exact location of each "fallen" block, and the exact degree of its burial in the grass, were meticulously designed by Stirling and Wilford, and equally meticulously executed by the German builders.

They like that kind of wit in Stuttgart, where the well-known proverb, "A German joke is no laughing matter," has a special meaning, it seems, which Stirling is able to tap—as no German can. This is a building that could only be built in Germany, but no German could have done it; only someone with Stirling's special relationship to that culture.

At which the Oxbridge Paranoiat will doubtless exclaim, "Then, why doesn't he go and stay in Germany for good?" (Like "Why don't all you bloody socialists go and live in Russia?") That is actually the wrong question on the right topic. It should be: How can so quintessentially English a Liverpudlian Scot as Stirling only find architectural happiness outside his native isles?

The immediate answer would have to be: "Budget." As Michael Wilford said recently of the demise of their scheme for Columbia University in New York, "We are expensive." But good budgets are a product of will as well as affluence, and tend to come from clients who want *architecture,* not just square footage of floor area. German culture, since about 1800, has seemed to want architecture, and to attribute to it almost magical powers, both in civic and cultural life, and in the *Bildung* of the individual human being. No wonder those who saw Stirling at work on Stuttgart, and in meetings or the site, report that he has never seemed so cheerful, so relaxed.

He needs the break. Who knows what the Oxbridge hobbits will try to do to him when his Tate Gallery extensions are opened?

Fiat

The Phantom of Order

Last year's grand international consultation (don't *ever* call it a competition) on the future and re-use of the old Fiat car factory at Lingotto in the inner suburbs of Turin, was demonstrably a gilt-edged occasion, since the exhibition of the proposals, mounted in the abandoned building itself, the sumptuous accompanying literature and all the associated manifestations clearly cost a pretty *lira* or two, and the architects consulted included our own James Stirling and Sir Denys Lasdun, as well as other heavy-duty talents from both sides of the Atlantic.

Like the equally grand consultations to find an architect for the second Getty Museum in Los Angeles, it may prove to be one of the major architectural events—or possibly non-events—of the past year or so. But why all the bother? Locally, the issue seems to be simply that Fiat is Turin, and Turin is Fiat. The company embodies and symbolises the industrial power of the city, and the factory commemorates all that labour history and union politics that have marked the long years of the love-hate

Originally appeared in *New Society* 72, no. 1173 (18 April 1985): 86–88.

relationship between Fiat and its workforce. Indeed, one reading of local history would insist that the plant was built in its very straightforward concrete-and-glass form in "deliberate and concrete response to the factory occupations, the demand for syndicalist control, the workers' councils."

More than that, however, the Lingotto plant is just the biggest thing in town. A single building four storeys high and half a kilometre long, with a press shop and other ancillaries at either end that bring it up to almost the full kilometre, it outbulks even the most grandiose of Turin's baroque monuments. Its disappearance would not only remove a big piece of local history, a memorial, a symbol, it would also leave a huge hole in the skyline along the via Nizza.

It would also remove a building whose unique position in the history of modern architecture cannot be equalled anywhere in the world. Hence the international interest of which Fiat is so acutely aware. Yet it was the work of no great or famous architect, and the name of its designer—Giacomo Matte Trucco—seems to attach to no other building that is known at all. Nevertheless, its status has been that of a masterpiece ever since it began to be known in 1920–21. It got into all the forward-striving books by people like Le Corbusier immediately, and into English language texts by the likes of Lewis Mumford within a decade. For this rapid acceptance there are two reasons, I think: one is that it fulfilled a modernist myth; the other is that it had a terrific gimmick.

The gimmick is the most obvious attribute of the building. How else could it be a gimmick if not obvious, even if it is a travesty of the designer's intentions to call it one? The building has a high-speed test-track *on its roof*! Two 500 yard straights are linked by high, embanked curves at either end. The track is reached by spiral ramps of extraordinary ingenuity—and beauty—that thread their way up through floor after floor. The undersides of the ramps are reinforced by concrete beams that radiate from the columns around the central well like the ribs on the underside of water-lily leaves. They were in all those Anglo-Saxon books in the thirties, but in the twenties all the *real* modernists had already been up the ramps and had then had themselves photographed standing on the roof. The photographs of D'Annunzio, Marinetti, Le Corbusier I have seen recently; those of Gropius and Owen Williams (the engineer who gave you the Empire Pool at Wembley, the *Daily Express* building, and those appalling bridges on the first section of the M1 motorway) I have not seen for some time, but I bet they are all in Fiat's comprehensive archives, together with those of everybody else who ever was anybody in modernism.

Including, recently, myself. It was a weird experience—like finally arriving in the Sistine Chapel, Niagara Falls, or somewhere else that you've heard about since ever. But it was radically different in that this is the one you *must* arrive at by car, and experience from a car. To do it any other way would be almost a blasphemy, like arriving at a pilgrimage church in the Middle Ages with anything but bare feet. The Fiat company car came up the ramp, slowly enough for me to enjoy the structural ingenuity going on all around, and finally emerged through a narrow slot round the back of one of the bankings and there was that famous view of 500 yards of rooftop straight, stretching ahead to where the banking curved up to the left at the other end.

It was exactly like all those commemorative photographs, and I almost expected to see the ghost of Corbu standing there with his white pants, black jacket, glasses and briar pipe (though I now know it is quite a different ghost who has the best claim to walk the circuit of that roof).

Round that famous circuit we went—and after one single lap you knew why Fiat gave up using it for serious testing. A *high-speed* track it emphatically is not. Even a modern Fiat, with all that clever suspension geometry underneath and good Pirelli rubber wrapped round its wheels, is in tyre-squealing, body lurching trouble on those banked curves even at a modest 60kph. The curves are desperately tight, and have to be or the track wouldn't fit on top of the building. But something seems to be un-settlingly askew with their geometry, too, as you come on and off the banking. What all this must have been like in the early twenties, when Fiats stood tall on their high-pressure "knife-edge" tyres and artillery-style springing but could, every one of them, do better than 70k . . . well, *exciting,* that's for sure!

Which is what the whole design is about anyhow—the excitements of the automotive age. Giovanni Agnelli, the boss of Fiat when Lingotto was conceived in 1914, wanted an American-style factory like Ford's famous (and even longer) plant at High-land Park in Detroit. But what separates Lingotto from American plants of the same period that I have been studying recently, is sheer rhetoric. The American plants are useful and fairly cheap facilities for manufacturing things in. Fiat, which is uncannily like an American concrete-framed building in all its details, is also a public statement about modern manufacture, about modernity itself. Marinetti hailed it (of course) as "the first invention of Futurist construction."

He got it wrong. Had he known what he was talking about, he would have had to damn it with the foulest epithet in his inflamed vocabulary: *passeiste.* By the time Lingotto and its ramps were finished in 1926, it was already becoming *passé* by American standards, for Henry Ford was getting out of multi-storey Highland Park, and moving more and more of his operation into huge single-storey tin sheds at the River Rouge. Lingotto was really a monument—a memorial to a myth of modernity, and of America as the home of modernity. The racetrack on the roof was the final and necessary symbolic flourish, like the stone laurel wreath on the head of a statue.

That last simile I have borrowed more or less directly from Edouardo Persico, the most intelligent, eloquent and tormented of the younger Italian architects who perished under the Mussolini regime. Disappointment was probably the core of his torment. As the youngest member of Musso's pioneering embassy to the Soviet Union in 1923, he must have hoped that the fascists would keep open the links between their radicalism and that of the left, but he was barely back from Russia before he had the first of his political troubles and found himself in jail. From then until his death in 1936, he had the sort of existence that can be immensely productive in both design-work and writing, yet remains somehow marginal to real life. For part of that time, he actually worked at Lingotto. Out of that experience he produced, in 1927, his first architectural writing.

It is an extraordinary piece of work, dominated by the sheer bulk of the building, and its intimations of a secret order beyond the human:

> Atop the building, the test track is like a king's crown, and just as a crown symbolises some essential and dominating Idea, so here the car and its speed are celebrated in a form that presides over the work of the factory below, not only in terms of the rationality of utility, but also according to some secret standard that regulates the ends of things. A mysterious logic of harmony—which the architect has followed intuitively as a sign of authority—has elevated the track to the summit of a work of man; much as the authority of a crown on the head of a king transcends the merely human face below, and weighs upon it with the force of a dominant rule.

I don't think this has anything to do with the Divine Right of Kings—however well such a concept might have suited Agnelli, *Il Re dell'Industria*—but it has a lot to do with the desire for a comprehensible sense of order in a disorderly world, where the old rules of God had been banished and replaced by . . . well, *nothing,* except the dictates of a rationality bent to the service of madmen like Mussolini.

An order beyond human lunacy had its desperate attractions. Persico describes the workers waiting to enter the plant for the morning shift:

> They do not speak, they do not move as they would in other human assemblies; they wait. All things are already in order, nothing can be changed; everything obeys an order which is not the expression of human will, but of a wisdom submissive to the Laws. They await the Laws; they are a people still confused, without order, an image of humanity without rules . . . they have more need of order than of bread.

As one who, long ago, used to stand amorphously in a waiting crowd, silent in front of the gates of quite a different factory, I can vouch for the observational truth of that. I don't, however, buy that apparent appeal for order at any cost, even though I know that it is not an appeal for the corporate order of the new fascist state but more likely an amalgam of Persico's disciplined Catholic upbringing, and the *Ordine Nuovo,* "a just society, an orderly society, made up of equals," imagined from prison by Antonio Gramsci, the only other Italian thinker of the period whom I find as sympathetic as Persico and organiser of the syndicalist occupation at Fiat after the first world war. But in the abandoned hulk of Lingotto, that thirst for order is an ever-present factor.

Those vast empty floors, almost purged of signs of human use or occupation, and inhabited only by endless rows of square concrete columns that stretch to apparent infinity, obeying no visible law save those of perspective . . . See, it's catching! The phantom of order conjured up by Persico will not go away now for me. On the roof, even if I can't take the test track too seriously, it seems okay to be yer regular cheerful modernist, but in the body of the works, a different order . . . damn, there it is again . . .

seems to prevail, and here Lingotto is superficially very like its American predecessors.

I have seen the inside of a lot of abandoned American industrial real estate over the last few years in the course of my researches, and I kept catching that quality, long before I re-discovered that Persico text. Cleaned and abandoned, with vast windows and endless rows of regular repetitive columns, these clean well-lighted spaces have an uncanny and deeply reassuring calm. The noise and bustle of production, the bulging accumulations of racked products, have long departed. All that remain are rational frameworks for human activities—awaiting their orders. But even in what remains of Ford's "Old Shop" at Highland Park, the only American site that has anything like the historical importance and cultural consequences of Lingotto, they are just neutral containers for which alternative uses, if any, will be found by the normal mechanisms of the market economy.

Lingotto is not just a neutral container. Too much cultural weight, too much self-conscious pursuit of modernism, too many quests for the order of the Laws, still haunt its 70 year old concrete. Whatever their real motives, Fiat are perfectly right to propose that its future be taken out of the hands of the market. But I see in none of the competition entries—sorry! *consultative proposals*—much real sense of that phantom of order which Persico left to stalk its echoing floors and which ascends by the two spiral ramps to the track that crowns the whole enterprise with a "a concrete image of speed . . . where nothing may deny the car."

Modern Monuments

In many an attempt to make learned (as opposed to common) sense of the new Lloyds Building, and other examples of High Tech architecture, one will read references to some mysterious *Maison de Verre.* But what "House of Glass" is meant? Everybody knows that Modern Architecture is "just a bunch of glass boxes," so it could be anything or nothing. Or is it perhaps a Platonic ideal; some pure conception of the ultimate glass box that has been trying to get itself built ever since Modernism came in?

Retrospectively it almost is just that—if you look for a comprehensive prototype for all the mechanistic romanticism and engineer-styling that comes with recent British High Tech buildings, you are liable to find yourself falling backwards through time until you soft-land in the late twenties, touching down in the *Septième Arondissement* of Paris, outside an uninformative gate in an equally anonymous standard Rive Gauche facade, where you have to address an electronic squawk box to be admitted.

Inside, you confront a wall of glass bricks set in concrete in a black steel frame at the back of a standard Paris-type courtyard, with two steel ladders flying up on either side, and some massive floodlamps carried on clever steel brackets. Even if you know

---

Originally appeared in *New Society* 78, no. 1246 (14 November 1986): 12–14.

it from photographs, the physical presence is still a shock in that traditional-type context. This is not modern architecture as it is generally understood; not the modern architecture of Gropius, or Le Corbusier, yet it is unmistakably "modern" in its materials, its aesthetics, the kind of earnest life-style it implies.

It's as if its architects, the French Art-Deco superstar Pierre Chareau, and the Dutch modernist, Bernard Bijvoet, had invented an alternative Modernism to the one that is in all the books, and that is why the *Maison* isn't in those books; not in Giedion, not in Pevsner (which is probably why it isn't in Banham, either; I caught up with it later), not in Hitchcock, nor all those lay-person's "introductions" to modern architecture. It appears briefly in Tafuri's revisionist *Modern Architecture,* and in William Curtis's equally revisionist text under the same title. But—sensationally—it's not in Frampton's *Modern Architecture; a Critical History,* even though he has made himself the world expert on the house. Known and admired it is still "un-assimilated to the canon."

In a way, it almost threatens the canon, which is probably why it is so much in vogue at present. The interior, in particular, is not only a knockout, but it suggests even more forcibly than the façade how Modern might have been quite different. On the ground floor are doctor's consulting rooms but they are not in the standard chrome-and-glass iconography of Modernist hygiene; there's wood, and the metal is black. Everything is rational but different; sliding doors rotate on hidden pivots, screens concertina away on curved tracks.

From the consulting level you go upstairs—at a low angle on a light-metal open-riser staircase that is mounted on a hinge at the top and sliders at the bottom, with low hand-rails spread so wide that they seem intended only to catch you if you fall off!—and at the top you come into what must be one of the greatest rooms of the 20th century, irrespective of style or period. It is two storeys high behind that wall of glass bricks, which becomes a wall of light when seen from inside. Photographs make the room look too tall and too dark; whereas the reality is marvellously luminous and spacious in all directions.

The furniture is stolidly well-made Art Deco wood, but everything else is strictly "Machine Age." The originator rubber floor is still in place and intact, though it looks its age; exposed steel columns rise through the space, jointed with dozens of hefty nuts and bolts—but partly clad in expensive marble! Electrical conduitry and switchgear are all in view but the main light-fittings are partly concealed and heating comes out of metal grilles in the floor and every cubic inch of wooden cabinet work is carried in skinny black metal framing that is a continuation of the handrails around balconies and stairs. And it is all lovingly handcrafted, as if even the metal was cabinetmakers' work. It shows how good modern architecture might have been if it had been properly made!

And, looking at all that neat black metal, some of it perforated even, you can see only too clearly where so much current black and perforated High Tech furniture (the stuff you see in Astrohome in Covent Garden) had its origins. The wheel of fashion has creaked around, and the house that didn't fit the canon a decade ago is now the house that everyone wants to see. Which is very tough on doctors trying to practise on the ground floor and the descendants of Dr Dalsace (who built it), trying to live on the upper floors.

This happens to all inhabitants of great modern architecture, of course—some owners of houses by Frank Lloyd Wright in Chicago suburbs really do keep a sawn-off shotgun handy, because their openlawned front yards don't give any protection against marauding architecture buffs.

This whole issue of public access to private dwellings that are monuments in the history of culture is something you don't have to be called Bedford or Bath to know about, but there is a twist in the case of the *Maison de Verre:* can a work of such determined Modernism be *historic,* a *monument*? It is surely a contradiction of the intentions and nature of Modernism for its products to stand around long enough to become monuments anyhow, even if some of the exhibits in the Museum of Modern Art in New York are *over a hundred years old*! I still get a funny feeling whenever I write a phrase like "the modern tradition" even though I know it stands for something real, and I think that at least one of the reasons why we have been having the "crisis of modernism" that gets academics so excited at conferences is that we are faced with the problem of forcing a lot of anti-historical material into historical categories that it was deliberately designed not to fit.

The problem is worse when the monument in question is as private unto itself, as independent of the institutionalised movement of Modernism, as the *Maison de Verre.* You can see this clearly enough if you contrast its case with that of Weissenhof Siedlung, in the suburbs of Stuttgart. Built in 1927 as a public demonstration of modern housing, master-planned by Mies van de Rohe, it is not so much "assimilated to the canon," it *is* the canon. Its white-walled, flat-roofed buildings by Le Corbusier, Mies himself, Gropius, J. J. P. Oud, Peter Behrens and others, including mystery men like Mart Stam and rank expressionists like Hans Scharoun, represented the first major rally of modernist architects, the first all-modern community whose townscape one could walk about in.

This past summer, at my third visit, there was nothing casual, dis-regardful or bashed up about the Weissenhof scene as there had been when I first visited it after the war. The great German *Kulturschutzmaschine* has taken over; all is now neat and tidy, the buildings put back like 1927. All that saved it from being completely mummified and spooky was that the restoration work was not absolutely completed; the famous apartment block by Mies van de Rohe was only half done, and one could sneak into the unfinished parts where the crews were still at work, and see original structural steel exposed, original brass handrails, even original bath-room tiling, and those horizontal strip windows that still give such spectacular panoramic views over the ring of mountains that frames the city below.

What else saved it from being a total mausoleum was that people actually live in it, hang ludicrous chandeliers in their living rooms, put cheerfully wrong curtains in the windows, hang surprisingly provocative underwear out to dry, and generally behave like living *Volk.* The effect, for me, was very strange; it is good to see quality buildings being given the upkeep they deserve but is the embalmed result *modern* any more?

I think not—unless you treat Modern as just another historical style, like Rococo or Flamboyant, which is very definitely not how any self-respecting modern architect, dead or alive, has ever regarded it. The problem seems worse in architecture than in the non-constructive arts—*Finnegans Wake,* for instance, has been procrusted into the canon of great literature it set out to mock rotten—but the persistence of the classic (oh?) monuments of architectural modernism is of a different order, and they defy "interpretation" in ways that other arts do not.

Great works of architecture—and ancient ones tend to be as resistant as modern ones—seem to populate the history of western culture in a nonconforming mode and on a different time-scale that together make nonsense of the seamless web of "Zeitgeist." Impressionist painting, impressionist literature, impressionist music, even impressionist sculpture—but impressionist building? Only at the expense of voiding the word of usable meaning. Could it be the same with Modern, and that the "permanent masterpieces" of modern architecture operate under a different rule book in which the canon is almost irrelevant, so that the houses on the hill of Weissenhof can sit around being public, canonical and *kulturgeschichtlich,* and the *Maison de Verre* can go on being private, uncanonised and category-proof, without being any the less significant for being so unconformable?

Or will the *Maison de Verre* turn out to be the basis of an alternative canon? More and more architecture pundits have lately been running this up the proverbial flagpole to see if anyone else is paying attention. The usual format of the argument, made explicit in the catalogue of the massive exhibition *Vision der Moderne, das Prinzip Konstruktion,* at the Deutsches Architektur Museum in Frankfurt this year, is that historian-propagandists of modern architecture got the *Zeitgeist* twisted, and propagandised a style (that was to become canonical) of closed volumes, simple geometrical forms and smooth surfaces, while offering to trace its ancestry from objects like the Crystal Palace and the Eiffel Tower, that were open-work, complicated and less smooth than rugged.

If High Tech is that ancestry reasserting itself (and Lloyds looks very much like it) over the established canon, then the *Maison de Verre* has its uneasy place as the first example of a modern architecture true to its claimed parentage. But does even that make it a permanent monument, like, say, Stonehenge?

Building Inside Out

The house of Wonko the Sane—as readers of the fourth volume of Douglas Adams' *Hitch-hiker* trilogy will recall—was up the California coast and apparently inside out, with bookshelves and carpet on the outside and "rough brickwork, nicely-done pointing and guttering in good repair" within. The reason for this state of affairs, *Hitch-hiker* fans will also recall, is that Wonko has been forced to conclude that the rest of the human race were stark staring bonkers, and has therefore deemed the rest of the world an insane asylum with him alone living "outside" it.

Hitch-hiker fans probably thought that their brilliant author made all that stuff up out of his undoubtedly fertile imagination. It is just possible, however, that the basic idea, if not the details, came from observation, not imagination, for Adams is very good at observation, especially about California. If we may transpose "up the coast" to Santa Monica (something which often seems to happen at about three in the morning) then we have, not a half-dozen blocks from Wilshire Boulevard, a house which indeed seems suspiciously Wonky.

Its roof may not quite be the M. C. Escher-after-a-night-on-the-town extravaganza

---

Originally appeared in *New Society* 81, no. 1282 (24 July 1987): 11–13.

that Adams proposes (though it has been compared to *Caligari*) but, under a particularly berserk piece of that roof, resembling a rough-carpentered cube of glass which has pitched over on one corner and thereby become the "kitchen window," one may stand at a regular kitchen sink, looking out over a normal bourgeois tiled wall and a shelf of better-than-Habitat glass . . . and Wonkily insecure in the knowledge that directly behind you is the *outside* of the window of the living-room! A very decent, vernacular, well-made Craftsman style bay-window ten feet wide, with the gable of the master bedroom above it.

The situation is actually Wonkier than that. Most of the *original* house on the site is now inside the *present* house on the site, but the totality adds up to a single house, not one inside the other, largely because the bare frame (remember we are in wood-building country, not brick) of the older house has been stripped of its exterior cladding and interior lining, so that one can constantly see through former walls, and occasionally floors, from one room to the next. However, these aspects of the house, though highly subversive of normal real-estate values, do not disturb the neighbourhood as much as the fact that most of the exterior of the total house now consists of materials like chain-link fencing and corrugated iron.

This last consideration also establishes that we are *not* looking at the work of a do-it-yourself eccentric; such precisely judged flouting of the norms of suburban culture has got to be deliberate and knowing. The house is the work of a professional architect; his name is Frank Gehry and he would be the hottest property in North American architecture right now if anyone could work out what to make of him. More garbage has been written about him than any other architect of his generation, but all attempts to push him into any known taxonomy—even postmodernist—tends to leave him uncategorised and cheerfully insisting that he is just an old Jewish poppa who builds things as best he can.

At one level, that is a perfect description of him. He is quite Jewish, as well as late-fifty-ish, and the legends about his Jewish momma are thick on the ground—from how she came to Hollywood to break into the movies (pure legend) to how she once insisted on continuing to scrub the floor of his office on her hands and knees as important clients were arriving (just possibly true).

As to building things, he certainly knows all that stuff. Even if the stories about him having started out as the developer-builder of cut-price condominiums are also legendary, he had plenty of hands-on experience before he got into architecture as such. And, of course, there are legends about him being an autodidact, but in fact he had an art training (if all the top-class Los Angeles artists he knows would send one work apiece, it would be the most spectacular art show in the city's history) before doing regular architecture school at the University of Southern California, and that is a fairly normal education for a California architect of his generation.

His earliest independent work was fairly tidy-minded mainstream modern—tidy-minded enough for the professionalism and natural design talent to be immediately comprehensible and an award-winning studio for the graphic designer Lou Danziger of 1964 established him as a coming man. I visited the studio in 1969 to borrow a camera to take some pictures of Santa Monica pier (one of which appeared in *New Society* in 1971) and was immediately struck by two things: the studio-space seemed to be entirely occupied by a full-size pool table, and the whole building showed suspicious affinities with classic modern studios of the twenties in Paris.

Later, in conversation, I found out that he had lived for some time in Meudon-Val-Fleury, which is notable territory for studios of that period. That conversation took place in London and—appropriately enough, I now think—in the joke-Hindoo setting of the Mumtaz Indian restaurant by Regent's Park. The next extended conversation was in a stolidly Italian "Family"-style nosher back in Santa Monica. I said, "Why is everyone looking at me; haven't the Mob seen a bearded man before?—It's not that, but you are sitting where Spiro Agnew always sits when he comes in here with Frank Sinatra," and it was clear that we were now in Gehry the Celebrity country.

So he got jobs like the refurbishing of the Hollywood Bowl band-shell, and went on to design for the Rouse Corporation, urban-renewers extraordinaire, for whom he did the Santa Monica Mall shopping center, and other prestige jobs. But at the same time he did more and more private houses, and they got Wonkier and Wonkier, because he let the basic stud-and-crud construction show through in more and more eccentric ways, developing a style which in Santa Monica itself looks just like normal local cheapo construction.

This enables pundits who are stuck on how to explain him to do the "Everybody's crazy in Los Angeles" ploy, and leads to occasional critical embarrassments. Particularly with a house he did for an ex-lifeguard right on the beach, which looks so much at home there that many of those who know it only in photographs suppose that the house next door, adorned with oars and life-belts, is part of his design, whereas that one really *is* local do-it-yourself vernacular.

The real piece of Gehry-ism in the Norton House ("My pride and joy"), however, is that the ex-lifeguard's study (he became a script writer) is in the form of a lifeguard's elevated look-out box, the sort of memory manipulating that has become almost a Gehry signature. But the places where he was able to strut his stuff as an artist-constructor were in the exhibition-installations he designed for the Los Angeles County Museum of Art, and the temporary accommodations of the Los Angeles Museum of Contemporary Art. The more-recently completed permanent home of the museum is by the Japanese architect Arata Isozaki (a sore point, I suspect), but Gehry's rehabilitation of two former garages as the "Temp Contemp" is so preferred by many art-folk that the museum has taken out a permanent-type lease on it.

By the time it was completed, he stood revealed as a real nutter, who is also 100 per cent certifiably architect, the kind of creative talent who alters "the topography of architecture in America," as they say in pompous circles. He may also alter the topography of world ditto, since there is no one like him (except possibly James Stirling, to stretch a point) and the rest of the world is taking notice even faster than the rest of America.

The work that the rest of the world seems to think is purest Gehry, and shows what he can really do when he has full steam up, is the mini-campus for the Law School of Loyola Marymount University on Olympic Boulevard hard by downtown L.A. There is, obviously, a certain piquancy in an old Jewish poppa designing for a hard-core Catholic operation that flies the name of a founding Jesuit in its title, but maybe it needs a Wonko street-smart sense of humour (and Gehry grew up along this very stretch of street) to make this kind of designing deliver its allusive and illusive (and even elusive) potential. The given site is a sloping rectangle of nothing, between some routine Los Angeles modern-style academic buildings and the boulevard itself, looking across at a townscape which is irredeemably Angeleno ho-hum-drum.

There are a number of obvious ways of dealing with such a site—so Gehry did something completely different. The earliest sketches show a long general-purpose building down the side of the site and in front of it—can it be? Yes they are!—a row of small classical temples. The final version that got built is even better, because the classical temples have become reused ruins, roofed brick boxes fronted by rows of detached columns made of totally inappropriate materials like sheet steel, have been joined by a Wonko version of a chapel and belfry done in plywood and clear plastic sheet, and have been regrouped not in a row but to frame a loose sequence of semi-enclosed spaces, into the middle of which the long general-purpose building precipitates a flying staircase in trick perspective.

For reasons known only to his usually better-informed self, local architecture critic John Pastier has called the result "a Smurf Acropolis," which is exactly what it isn't. What it clearly recalls (and Gehry himself has confirmed this more than once) is the Forum Romanum, with its mixture of classical temples, green spaces and baroque churches. And what could be a more apt hatchery for Catholic lawyers, given canon law's double heritage from Rome and Christianity? But there is a double whammy here as well—in the city of Los Angeles, which has notably failed to generate a convincing or conventional urban centre, the Loyola Law campus is a wonky reminder of the very oldest kind of civic/religious downtown known to the western tradition.

Yet the whole conception is free of the pushy, pasted-on, pastiche classicism that makes routine postmodernism so tedious. There is not a single classical detail to be seen anywhere, but Merrifield Hall, which is the centre of the scheme, is a plain brick box, just like the original Curia in the Forum where the ancient Romans did their legislating, and that is the pitch at which the whole design operates. If you know your architectural history it is a subtly erudite pleasure to be there. If you don't know architectural history it is still a pleasure to be there if you know the heavy-handed boredoms of the other campuses around the Los Angeles basin.

Yet, even at this elevated critical level, this is still where-else-but-L.A. country, as at the Norton house or his own wonky home. For they are all in some way, commentaries on the "eternal laws of architecture" in terms of local building techniques. Commentaries, that is, on the academic disciplines of architecture (history, draughtsmanship and all that) in terms of the brute facts of how things actually get built (wood, concrete, finance and all those) in the world outside the ivory-painted crudboard towers of academe.

I was holding forth on the virtues of Loyola at a meeting of my fellow architectural historians, pointing out that, contrary to what routine postmodernists might have done, the columns in front of the temples of instruction were base-less and capital-less, when a voice from the floor said "but not pointless!" And that's it; among all the base-less posturing of routine postmodernism, Gehry looks wonkily sane and to the point.

51

In the Neighborhood of Art

As current art museums go, the Menil doesn't. Strikingly at variance with prevalent trends like the postmodernism of Stirling's *Staatsgalerie* in Stuttgart, the gentlemanly Contextualism of Harry Cobb's Portland Museum or even the Academic Modernist-Revivalism of Richard Meier's High Museum in Atlanta, it is headed in some totally other direction, for which we will ultimately learn to be grateful, but the immediate effect, for both public and pundits, is liable to be bewilderment and (alas!) hostility.

The collection it houses will present no such problems; it is of such pervasive quality that everyone will agree that the only decent human response to it is honest envy . . . all those Magrittes, those Ernsts, those Mattas and Victor Brauners, the filing cabinets full of Joseph Cornell boxes—and the twice-hallowed tribal objects, whose original numinousness has been doubled by their historic provenance in our own culture ("This one came from Captain Cook's first voyage").

Originally appeared in *Art in America* 75 (June 1987): 124–129.

Envy also for the staff, curatorial, scientific, craftsmanly and administrative who have been provided for as in no other museum to date. Not for nothing is the Menil known as "the revenge of the professionals," for professional work-space accounts for almost 60 percent of the total space, and on prime floor levels at that—no more workshops in dripping basements, photo-archives on makeshift mezzanines, offices crammed under roof-timbers, or loading docks like abandoned mineshafts. Not everyone is going to be grateful—high-flying museum staff are men and women of pronounced and idiosyncratic opinion—but the whole conception of the building appears to hold the proper housing of expert staff to be at least as important as the proper housing of the works of art. Not even Isozaki's MOCA in Los Angeles, with its staff in the air and its art underground, makes such an issue of housing the *Werkleute* as if they were as precious as the *Kunstwerken*.

But all this happens within a structure that doesn't even try to look like a museum. "Like an upmarket UPS depot" was—I think—intended as a kindly characterization of the design, but it is a fair sample of the bewilderment the exterior has stirred, even before its completion. The project had barely been published as drawings when Stephen Fox in the 1983 issue of the Houston architectural magazine *Cite* supposed that "the Menil Museum could easily turn out to be overwhelmingly non-Monumental." Such critical self-contradiction is not surprising; recent well-regarded museum designs, and even redesigns like the Isozaki/Polshek project for the rear of the Brooklyn, tend to make—and to be valued for making—major monumental gestures of civic and cultural intention. Standing in conspicuous and history-loaded city-center locations, they tend to come forward with important messages for the citizenry as a whole. Renzo Piano's Menil (strictly, Piano and Fitzgerald's Menil), on the other hand, relates visually to its own neighborhood and very little else. This may be a properly "user-friendly" gesture in Houston, which tends to pride itself on being a "city of great neighborhoods," but there are clearly those who feel that this is an inadequate mode of address for the home of such a world-class collection.

It is, however, a uniquely interesting neighborhood, this long strip—much of it Menil property—running west from Montrose Avenue between Richmond to the south and Alabama to the north. It is interesting not only because it contains the University of St. Thomas campus by Philip Johnson (1957) and Howard Barnstone's Rothko Chapel, but because, as it continues westward, it reveals its earlier incarnation as an unassuming residential neighborhood which would be pleasant in any North American city. In the present state of Houston, however, it is like an oasis of humanity, or a time-warp return to the suburban innocence of some Andy Hardy Golden Age. The decision to sustain this almost idyllic character—people walk dogs and hold conversations on street corners, and I still haven't seen a single jogger there—seems to come from the de Menils themselves, though it clearly has the informed support of everyone else around the organization.

But how does one fit a major art gallery—we are talking here about a proposition almost comparable in size to the Frick in New York or the Yale Center for British Art in New Haven—into a suburbia which is on the average only one-and-a-half stories high, without crushing the neighborhood flat? Partly, the gallery itself has slipped into its surroundings at their own scale—auxiliary activities like the auditorium, bookstore and restaurant are to be housed in single-story, garage-scaled structures across the street between Sul Ross and Alabama.

The main building, however, is a whole block long and 165 feet deep, and three-and-a-half stories high; to make that look at home requires resolute bloody-mindedness as well as surreptitious tact, and that difficult synthesis is written all over the face of the building. Tact proposed a boarded exterior painted the same gray as the neighborhood houses, following the color scheme already decreed for properties along Branard and Sul Ross streets by Howard Barnstone, the Menils' long-term architectural adviser. Bloody-mindedness decreed a skinny but highly visible and purposeful steel frame with emphatic verticals picked out conspicuously in white paint.

SUBTLETY IN STEEL It all looks very simple, and indeed that is what it is, but simpleminded it is not. Behind its neat boxy forms and almost diagrammatic structure, this is a very subtle and complex building indeed. Even the detailing of the steelwork is rich in allusion and modern-movement history, local and remote. Locally the echoes are of Mies van der Rohe, which may sound strange, but one should remember that, next to Chicago itself, Houston must be the most Miesian city in North America. Quite apart from Johnson's works for the de Menil/St. Thomas connection, and Mies's own extensions to the Museum of Fine Art, there is also the work of the "Rice connection": Howard Barnstone himself, Anderson Todd and a small host of their pupils, partners and followers. Almost anywhere, it seems, in the rambling, unzoned dystopia that makes Houston an urbanist's nightmare, one may stumble with relief on neat steel-framed structures with "made-at-IIT" written all over them, and as often as not the exposed I beams of their exteriors are painted white against their gray walls.

But the design also pays tribute to an unlikely and exotic source of inspiration—the steel-framed "Case-Study" houses done in Los Angeles in the '50s and early '60s by Craig Ellwood, which were admired quite separately and for different reasons by both Renzo Piano and Walter Hopps, the Menil's director, even before they met. After they had been introduced by Dominique de Menil (at the suggestion of Pontus Hulten), architect and director decided to admire Ellwood together, and update his nifty steelwork details. So the Menil looks doubly at home—Miesian and suburban—and faintly Angeleno-exotic at the same time; and anyone who still thinks that architectural steel is reductionist or value-free should speak carefully when on Branard Street.

Most of what has been spoken so far about the building has been on quite another matter, however: the sunshade "platform" that runs right through the building from end to end and front to back. Insofar as the Menil may be called a High-Tech design, the sunshades are the reason for doing so, but although they constitute a separate architectural element that could stand on its own—almost literally so, if I read the structure correctly—without the rest of the building, they are the very heart of the whole conception, and the basic section of the museum is largely generated by them.

That section is a sort of double-decker sandwich. The first layer, at grade level, consists of galleries on the north side, the grand corridor that runs the full 500-foot length of the block, and some equally high-ceilinged workspaces on the side toward Branard Street. The second layer, which forms the lighted ceilings of the galleries and the shaded "piazzas" (an appropriate Old-South term) around the perimeter, is the sunshade platform. Above that comes a shallow, and mostly open, floor of mechanical and other services (virtually invisible from ground level), and above that again the range of rooms that runs the full length of the Branard side and includes the secure-storage "treasure chambers" where the bulk of the works will reside when not sent downstairs for public display in the galleries. (It will still be possible to view the works in these fastnesses by special arrangement.)

THE
ENVIRONMENT
OF ART

The sunshade platform, and the mechanical floor above, thus provide the most crucial environmental controls for the whole operation—though there is also a minimal service space below grade, and a quite separate "energy building" half a block away to the south, which is the main source of environmental power, but keeps insurance-intensive elements like natural gas fuel out of the gallery building proper.

Conditioned air is distributed to the galleries under the floors, but it also circulates through the walls themselves, so that no moisture-sensitive art work finds itself hung on a damp wall (always an important consideration in a climate like Houston's). The floors are stained almost black, so that the strips of bronze ventilation-grille are hardly visible; the walls are painted white, and over them spreads a light of—frankly—ethereal beauty. That is not the kind of language that I use very frequently, but the quality of the light that enters the Menil through the sunshades is breathtaking. The only gallery light that I can compare it with is that in Louis Kahn's Kimbell in Fort Worth, but whereas the light under the vaults there is mysterious and largely a matter of optical illusion—it looks natural but is heavily supplemented with artificial—the daylight in the Menil is honest, pellucid and without additives.

Such quality was not easily got. The original inspiration was a small art gallery in the Israeli kibbutz of Ein Harod, lit by sunlight bounced off its flat roof onto the underside of curved reflectors, and thus into the gallery space below. Though striking, this solution was not adequate to the Menil's requirements (among other things, it allowed direct sunlight into the gallery at certain times of day), and the development of the double-curved reflectors that were finally devised required an intensive and prolonged collaborative effort by Piano, his engineering partner Peter Rice, the systems engineer Tom Barker, and the computational and experimental resources of Ove Arup and Partners in London (the normal operating base of Rice and Barker). The reflectors are made of ferro-cement, which is very heavy, and are carried on a system of trusses built up from ductile cast-iron elements that are almost Victorian in their elaboration—though reckoned by Rice to be the skinniest reasonably possible, to carry the weight and yet minimize light loss and shadowing.

Compared to other gallery-roofing systems currently in use, it looks almost unbelievably complex—Peter Rice is not exactly famous for simple or obvious engineering solutions—but on performance it has manifestly been well worth the complication. The quality of the light is like nothing else, anywhere—certainly not in any regular vanilla "universal space" type of gallery—and may well set standards to make other architects lie awake at night. And like one or two other triumphs of unaffected functionalism, it is blessed with an unsought bonus.

A LITTLE
LIGHT-MAGIC You can't see what it is at first, though you can see that there is something strange about the light on the underside of the reflectors, something other than the inevitable change of color and intensity as the sun crosses the sky. What has happened is this: a late revision in the design of the almost flat glass roof above the reflectors means that alternate runs of glazing are sloped in opposite pitches (originally all the runs of glazing were to be sloped in the same direction), and this in turn means that alternate reflectors receive light that is slightly differently diffracted as it angles through the glass. And that in its turn means that alternate reflectors are slightly cooler or slightly warmer in color. The effect is very, very slight (it barely shows on my color slides), but it is *just* sufficient to transform perfect illumination into living lighting.

The actual light levels are quite low, to protect the works of art on show. Although the illumination can get as high as 800 lux near a window under strong sunlight when the general illumination peaks at about 500, for most of the days of the average year it stays down near the 150-lux mark which was the figure they designed for. Now that is really quite dim compared with everyday outdoor light levels, yet the human iris adjusts for the subdued illumination, and the eyes remember these marvelous galleries as being radiantly pearly-bright. Since it is for these galleries, as a setting for the matchless collection they display, that the Menil will be valued, critical opinion about the architecture will in due course skew round to find ways of acclaiming this as a great building. Its "reductionist" steel frame will probably be discovered to have the virtue the architect himself attributes to it—"frugality"; and its "overwhelming non-Monumentality" will turn out to be "contextually sensitive," or something.

For Dominique de Menil herself, however, it will simply be "a functional building," though designed by an architect "who combines imagination with classicism in spite of the modern technology," housing what she insists "has always been a Houston collection." The rest of us will observe that if this is a Houston neighborhood collection, the world could use a few more such neighborhoods, and that Renzo Piano, whatever qualities he may or may not combine as an architect, has here achieved a building that has put the magic back into Functionalism.

52

On the Wings of Wonder

The thing I will miss most about rural California will not be self-consciously country-style events like the Pumpkin Festival at Half Moon Bay, or Santa Cruz County Fair or the Gilroy Garlic Festival, but, more likely, the air shows. This has to be partly Banham atavism—I acquired the taste in my Biggling infancy from being taken to see Sir Alan Cobham's Flying Circus. But there is a special technocultural resonance to Californian versions like the Watsonville Fly-in and the Salinas Air Show, which is partly historical/ environmental, and partly the recent sociology of aviation.

Historically and environmentally, it is a matter of the extraordinarily benign climate of most of California—even the most decrepit antique string-bag or loony home-built can expect 360 days or so of flyable weather in the year, and the bland blue of the local empyrean never seems to look anything but user-friendly. No wonder that the first scheduled air-mail was in this state, and that making planes has been one of the dominant industries since the twenties. What the recent history of aviation has contributed

Originally appeared in *New Society* 82, no. 1294 (16 October 1987): 18–20.

to the mild blue yonder is an awful lot of secondhand aeroplanes of every shape and size, and a lot of people who know how to fly them, or enjoy messing about with them or can observe them with an educated eye.

What we are talking about here is an informed public for aviation, not just a mass audience for noisy spectacles—as well as the Chicano extended families, the keen Asian strivers and the beery red-necks who tend to make up the bulk of the paying customers, there is also a hard core of frighteningly knowledgeable retired air-line pilots, active owner-builders of radical plastic-bodied "experimentals," Korean and second world war veterans.

But where one sees the hard core most clearly is at the Watsonville show, the least pretentious and most amiable of the local fixtures. Strictly speaking, it is just the Watsonville Antique and Experimental Fly-in. It has no highly paid or heavily hyped star performers; it is a "fly-what-you-brung" meet. Anyone with the right kind of licences for self and plane can show off doing aerobatics if they feel the urge and there is time in the schedule, but what is really going on is a mass rally of the recreational aviation community. Some will come in their trailers and campers just to be there and greet old buddies from way back when. But most will be on their own wings, and for a couple of days before and after the show the air over Monterey Bay is full of improbable machinery, puttering slowly to or from Watsonville.

You might see a flight of four or five Ryan trainers from the thirties, polished shiny as jewels, or a back-to-front Rutan Varieze (direct ancestor of the back-to-front Voyager that flew round the world nonstop earlier this year). You might see a home-built Poggenpohl powered by a Ford Model-T engine, or a legendary Beech "stagger-wing" biplane, or a Curtis JN4 Jenny, the aeroplane that taught America to fly in the very early twenties. And you realise that there is a whole demotic subculture up there in the canopy of California blue that really has no equivalent anywhere else in the world.

It all comes to rest on the unassuming Watsonville tarmac; there are dinners and dances; those who can afford it spend the night in a motel, but some will sleep in old buddies' trailers, and others, out of principle or poverty, will pitch a tent beside the plane or just drape a groundsheet over a wing and sleep on camp beds under its shelter.

In the afternoons, the paying public is let in to wander (and wonder) among the rows of parked aircraft ancient, modern and plain unlikely (there was this thing looking like a park bench with an airscrew on the back and a pilot seat on the front and casters underneath; unbelievably, it flew). To show willing and entertain the punters, a thin succession of elderly and underpowered biplanes will take off and perform a few gentlemanly loops and rolls, accompanied by friendly applause from the groundlings.

The serious air shows are very different occasions; nobody jumps the ropes at Salinas in September—indeed, to get anywhere near the front of the public viewing area you have to rent a private "box" at vast expense, and even then you are nowhere near where the performing aircraft park. There are plenty of nonperforming aircraft parked behind the stands to go and gawp at; some will be the same planes from Watsonville in June, but more of them will be military, including current service machines. It is all very heavy metal and professional, and public performance is what it is all about.

And ceremonial. The flying day begins with a formation of aerobatic planes drawing a vast smoke circle in the sky, through which U.S. Army parachutists descend to the strains of the national anthem, one of them with Old Glory fluttering from a weighted line hung from his crutch, others with trails of variously coloured smoke coming out of their boots as they swoop and swerve and occasionally "execute a canopy-relative work."

"Canopy-relative work" simply means sitting on top of the chute of the next guy below you in the drop-pattern, but the phrase brings us up against the least lovable aspect of the heavy-metal shows; the corrosion of language. The running commentary on the parachute drop is always given by Captain somebody, and in a mixture of Ollie-North Jingo-speak and technical jargon. In fact, the National Security Council prose-style may just be para-babble with the canopy-relative words left out.

It used not to be so bad, but ever since the Grenada caper, an increasingly super-heated miasma of Rambo-Reaganism has permeated more than just air-shows— British TV viewers may think themselves lucky that all they got for commentary on the last Olympics was the usual load of Colemanballs; what we got in the States was the assumption that the Olympics were a rerun of Grenada, and that sport was just the continuation of gun-boat diplomacy by other means, with rhetoric to match.

The main impact on the airshows, however, has been a constant hammering of the American-ness of what you see before you, which can lead to ludicrous results at times, as when the announcer at this year's Moffett Field show had to admit that the "Team America" aerobatic squad were actually flying *Italian* planes—"But the motors are American, the wheels are American, the electronics are American and [on a note of rising hysteria] practically every nut and bolt is American."

The other most conspicuous effect is that where music is required to accompany the performance (which it never is, really), it now tends to be conventionally patriotic, so that aerobatic sailplanes, which once used to perform in blessed silence, and then later to nothing more offensive than (how did you guess?) Albinoni, now tend to do it to the strains of *America the Beautiful,* or worse.

Fortunately, however, the bulk of what we all come for is so deafening that music, or even commentary, is pointless. What the groundlings have mostly come to see is, for instance, wing-walking, which to some extent is just nostalgia for the good old days of barnstorming, but I have to admit that it is pretty riveting to see an old Waco biplane doing outside loops with a girl braced against the wing struts on each side. And they have also come to see the heavily hyped military aerobatic teams, which always turn out to be boring because these monster jet-fighters are so fast and unwieldy that they are out of sight most of the time, trying to turn round and get back into the same county as the airfield.

The exception to this rule is the Canadian Snowbird squad; for a start there are nine of them in the formation, which means that they can do really complicated choreographies and, since the planes are modestly powered trainers, they can keep the action over the airfield and in view of the audience all the time. But, chiefly, they have so much pizzazz, precision and show-biz style that they make the U.S. military squads look klutzy. Just starting up the jets before take off is now such a production-number—three with red smoke, three with white smoke and three with blue, with each plane's mechanic kneeling in front of it *at the salute* before waving the pilot away—that on one occasion they got a standing ovation before they had left the ground!

MANIA AND PERFECTIONISM They are a hard act to follow; there is only one act that can, and that is civilian—the Christen Eagles. In many ways, the Eagles are quintessential central California country aviation, built in the local boonies by Dick Christensen who became almost offensively rich in the early days of Silicon Valley by making very clever tools for doing incredibly small things, and then gave it all up at the age of 30, and decided to pursue his hobbies, like ranching and flying. Only he pursued them with proper Silicon Valley mania and perfectionism, and not only are the planes (developed from the Pitts biplanes you can see aerobatically advertising cigarettes at British meets) marvels of technical proficiency and visual presentation, but all three are flown by former world-class aerobats, and they do things to make sensitive souls do catharsis in their pants.

For a start (literally), they will do flick rolls straight off the ground as they take off three abreast—which requires not only nerves of high tensile Krytonite but also absolute faith in the reliability of the engine, and the attentiveness of the other two pilots. Airborne, they tend to spend as much time upside down as the right way up, and a good deal of time flying on their sides, which is theoretically impossible, but a little thing like that has never bothered the Eagles. At the climax of their act, the three planes fly low and straight at the audience, in tight formation with the two outer planes on their sides—and then the two outer planes cross in front of the middle one! Even though I have seen it before, and know that it is partly an illusion, I still get a brief cardiac arrest.

There is only one other thing in the whole of the California air-show culture that rivals the Eagles, and that is at Moffett Field and usually the *most* compelling reason for going to the Moffett show, which tends to be too deep into canopy-related rhetoric to be tolerable. The *second* most compelling reason for going to Moffett is that, besides being a naval aviation base, it also houses NASA's Ames Research facility, so that a fair number of genuinely exotic aircraft are to be seen, all turned out in innocent white livery.

But Moffett, when it was young, was the main west coast base for the U.S. Navy's big rigid airships, and from that period survives the most compelling reason for going there: this vast and unbelievable hangar, big enough to shelter one of those enormous dirigibles, and therefore over 800-foot long and 190-something high—you could put Centre Pompidou inside it and have room to tuck in a half-dozen of your favourite Wren churches around the ends.

What makes it the main attraction, though, is not only its sheer size—on public days full-size passenger-carrying balloons give joy rides *inside* it—but even more its sheer authority as a building. Over the elaborately latticed internal frame, its metal-clad sides slope inwards at about 20-degrees and merge into the rounded roof; its ends are sloped and rounded too, because they are gigantic doors that roll back on curved railroad tracks, opening to the full height of the building, like the maw of some enormous worm. It is awesome to contemplate; 55 years old, it is still overwhelmingly the best high-tech building in Silicon Valley, the ultimate shrine of the aviation culture of middle California.

One other fabulous memory I shall take away from the airshows: twice, at Salinas, after the Christen Eagles have drawn their perfect circle and the canopy relatives have dangled through it, every one has started pointing and ooo-ing back at the supposedly empty sky, and there, in the very centre of the fading smoke-ring and possessing it as if it was a giant halo, was the real master of the mild California skies, a golden eagle (*Aquila Chrysaetos*) soaring imperiously on motionless wings. *Once* could have been a happy accident, but *twice* makes you wonder who is in charge up there.

Actual Monuments

The time is 1952, the place Stokesay Court, the occasion a visit by the Second At-
tingham Park Summer School on the Great Houses of England. The house deserves
visitation for any number of reasons—as the Victorian counterpart of the famous medieval Stokesay Castle in the valley below, as a characteristic design by Thomas "Victorian" Harris, who first applied the term "Victorian" to architecture, and as the first
house in England to be specifically designed for electric lighting, as we know from the
construction photographs in the album which Harris presented to the Royal Institute
of British Architects.

But at this moment, none of the above is at issue. Together with the rest of the
party I am standing in the middle of the great flying landing halfway up the opulently
carved and carpeted main staircase, a space about 20 by 18 feet, hung about with
ancestral portraits and tapestries, which seems to impel some of the visitors to start
doing detective-novel routines. Feeling that some kind of ambiguously smart-ass observation is called for, I launch one: "Hey, I wonder if Hitchcock has seen this?" The

Originally appeared in *Art in America* 76 (October 1988): 173–177, 213, 215.

ambiguity is immediately taken up—and slapped down—by James van der Pool: "I take it you mean *Alfred* Hitchcock, *Russell* assuredly has."

I should have known. Henry-Russell Hitchcock was just coming into his period of maximum impact in England. His imposing figure and rasping voice seemed to be everywhere; he had seen everything, seemed to know everything and constantly inquired after the things he did not know. His sustained visibility was due chiefly to the fact that he was seeing *Early Victorian Architecture* through the proof stage for the Architectural Press, where I was then employed; he was also hard at work on his volume of the Pelican History of Art, whose editor was of course Nikolaus Pevsner, who was also the director of studies for my dissertation. Our points of closest encounter were a couple of very long evenings that we spent swapping sources, dates and attributions, for his Pelican and my dissertation. And if this produced any mistakes in either, it was probably because—as was usual on such occasions—we killed a whole bottle of Gordon's Dry Gin.

But never then, in those days of scholarly intimacy, nor later, when we had drifted somewhat apart, did it occur to me that I would one day find myself effectively stepping into Hitchcock's shoes here at the Institute of Fine Arts. Indeed, my gratitude to the Institute for inviting me to the post, and to the Solow Foundation for endowing the chair, will always be tinged with disbelief that this should be the crown of my career in architectural history. And between us, Russell and I have covered the whole life span of modern—and postmodern!—architectural history, from *Modern Architecture, Romanticism and Regeneration,* his first foray into the field in 1929, to *Making Architecture: The Paradoxes of High Tech,* on which I am working at present.[1] And we have both contributed to the postmodern phase, since Colin Rowe, the true founder of postmodernist thinking in the field, was Russell's student, and Charles Jencks, the most fluent exponent of the approach, was mine.

Now postmodernist history and criticism were never meant to be purely academic; they were applied to the training of architects and to public debate, they were meant to go out into the world and change things, and their success can be seen all over Manhattan. Hitchcock and Philip Johnson's *The International Style* was also meant to go out into the world and change things, and its success—with a little help from the zeitgeist—has been global. This remarkable book, published in 1932, will be the main topic of the course which I am to teach here this semester—indeed, this talk was to be an introduction to the course. But since it has now become an inaugural lecture, a time for declarations of faith, assaults on reputations, the laying out of theoretical frameworks, I intend to enrich my discourse with reflections on Hitchcock himself.

As a working historian Hitchcock has always seemed one of those who beats back against the tides of time—his earliest writings were mostly about architects who were of his own generation, his last were about the 17th century. This was not necessarily a systematic regression, but it did acquire something of the air of a grand design, as if each step backwards gave him the intellectual equipment—the courage, perhaps— to take a step farther back into the littered abyss of the past.

Part of his scholarly security in doing so came from the fact that he knew his build- ings—he *had* seen everything and his powers of recall could be amazing. He was, as they say, an "observational" historian, like my master Nikolaus Pevsner and—I hope—myself. I know from having seen the preparations for the field trips that pre- ceded each county volume of *The Buildings of England* that Pevsner certainly *intended* to see every single building of architectural note in that country, and usually suc- ceeded, since he would come back from the field trips completely exhausted—the life of a hands-on historian can be rewarding but very tough, and actually dangerous if, like me, you have to explore ancient pipes and ducts, or clamber about on the roofs of crumbling grain elevators. This kind of history of architecture has been called, by Rob- ert Maxwell of Princeton, a "Rhetoric of Presence": I have been there and seen for myself, and that is my license to speak.

So it was for Pevsner and Hitchcock, but they were different kinds of hands-on histo- rians. The preparations for a Pevsner county raid consisted chiefly of a monster card index of buildings that were already in the literature, already in the canon, and by the time he had worked through all the canonical buildings, there wasn't much time and space left for serendipity. Hitchcock, contrariwise, was much more free form, and had good peripheral or extra-canonical vision. He *noticed* things. Of all the historians and critics who wrote about the Larkin Company buildings in Buffalo, N.Y., he was the first and only one to draw attention to the high quality of any of the buildings that were not by Frank Lloyd Wright. The others visited the canonical office block and brushed off the rest as "just factories." And in another place, having mentioned the canonical airship hangars at Orly outside Paris, he also mentioned the Goodyear hangars outside Akron, Ohio, which have never attained canonical status, in spite of their very high quality.

Finding buildings was a sort of sport for Russell. In London in the early '50s, he was notorious for riding around on the upper decks of buses in order to command a better view, and then stamping on the floor above the driver's head and shouting, "Stop the bus, stop the bus!" because he thought he had spotted a forgotten Philip Hardwick or whatever. Indeed, it is said that the revived reputation of London's now madly fashionable Michelin Building, built in 1910 by François Espinasse, goes back to a Hitchcock sighting of this kind. He loved buildings—that was transparent to any- one who ever exchanged more than two words with him. And next to buildings, he loved gossip, which is the other essential for a good architectural historian.

However, he was a good architectural historian in a particular way that is now some- what out of fashion, but needs to be examined for the effect it had on the writing of *The International Style.* As Paul Goldberger put it in the obituary in the *New York Times,*

Hitchcock viewed buildings as "discrete aesthetic objects," and tended to avoid theory and ideology. Clearly, that will not serve in these deconstructivist times, but for *his* times I think it was a serviceably modernist attitude, not unlike Gertrude Stein's attitude to roses. And in insisting that a building is a building is a building he was not—I submit—being mulish or insensitive, but as modernist as Stein was, or as Marcel Duchamp was in insisting on the irreducible "thingishness" of things like urinals and bottle racks.

The formulation of this as an historian's standpoint is the celebrated phrase from *The International Style* about "a set of actual monuments." Or, in full: "For the international style already exists in the present, it is not merely something the future may hold in store. Architecture is always a set of actual monuments, not a vague corpus of theory." The language may be gentlemanly, but that's fighting talk, and would have been so just as much in 1932 as it is now. It also establishes the basic points of reference to which the argument of the book is anchored, and accounts for much of its persuasiveness.

Nowadays, I suppose, it would be the real or pretended indifference to theory and ideology that would attract attention: "not a vague corpus of theory" is the sort of phrase that would be guaranteed a hostile reception today, and not without good reason, since there is no ideologue as ideological as one who claims he isn't. Yet if we "historicize" the phrase(ology) and put it back in the historical and ideological context of its time, the matter begins to look different.

"Actual monuments" is the key phrase; it is what the book is about. *The International Style* (as far as I can ascertain) is the first book of propaganda for modern architecture which contains no visionary projects or renderings of uncompleted works. Every building is represented by photographs and plans; what you see is what you get. Even Bruno Taut's influential *Modern Architecture* of two years before includes, besides drawings of utopian visions, few photos or plans of real buildings, though these could have been found. Modern architecture, previously presented as an architecture *in potential,* is presented by Hitchcock and Johnson as a body of achieved monuments.

The power this must have given to the book, and to the exhibition it accompanied at the Museum of Modern Art, is worth reflection. The "actual monuments," represented in excellent photographs, were solid proof that the style existed, and would ward off the sneers of so-called "practical men" demanding to know "how're you going to make all that stand up." Furthermore, the book's documentation showed how widespread and all-pervading the style had become: 13 nations were included, besides Germany, still the most heavily represented, and the U.S. itself, with six examples. Not only was the geographical range broad—from France, Italy and Switzerland to Sweden, Czechoslovakia, the U.S.S.R., even Japan—but so was the range of building types— old people's homes and housing developments at one extreme, villas de luxe and expensive apartments at the other. Hospitals and schools, clubs for students and artists, filling stations and department stores, exhibition structures, two yacht clubs, factories, office towers and warehouses—and a drastically simplified hotel for leading a drastically simplified life on the Mediterranean, which must be the world's earliest warning of Club Med!

"The international style is broad and elastic" claims the text, and the illustrations prove it in a way that text alone never could, and this proof of universality warms up the argument for the proposition that *the* International Style is also *an* international style like those exemplary international styles of the past, the Gothic and the Baroque. This is heavy stuff—though some of Hitchcock and Johnson's contemporaries, Pevsner for instance, certainly shared the thought. But by presenting this claim without ideological or theoretical support, the authors seem to me to be implying that it was also a *finished* style waiting to be imported from Europe, a situation with which North Americans would be familiar after 40 years or so of the Beaux Arts.

However, what Hitchcock and Johnson gained in immediate persuasiveness by this device (unwitting, I believe), they lost in the longer term because they set aside the utopianism, the zeal for social reform, the messianic claims that drove the style in Europe, and without which most of us would have great difficulty in understanding what the movement was about. To put it bluntly, Hitchcock and Johnson presented a salable product, but not a driving vision, and risked finishing up as the proprietors of yet another Manhattan fashion, a fate from which they were rescued by events elsewhere and beyond their knowledge and control.

Now it is the well-known hypothesis of my California colleague David Gebhardt that what Hitchcock and Johnson did to the International Style would have happened to it anyway because "as each new style came across the Atlantic to America, its ideology fell into the ocean and was never seen or heard from again." But in the case of Hitchcock and Johnson we can see pretty well what they were up to. The suppression of theoretical or ideological context occurs at various levels throughout the book, but it is most clearly visible in Chapter II, titled "History," and in the concluding chapter on the *Siedlungen*—in their definition, state-sponsored modern community housing projects.

"History" takes a good, old-fashioned "materials and methods" view of architectural development, derived from the great line of 19th-century historians that runs from Gottfried Semper through Viollet-le-Duc to Auguste Choisy and H. P. Berlage. This view was still widely held at the time that *The International Style* was being written, especially in Germany. It had power among the "practical men," of course, but it did enormous damage: on my first teaching trip to the States an intelligent student said to me, "All that stuff you are telling us about Cubism and Paul Klee is really fascinating, but what *really* caused modern architecture is the steel frame and the electric elevator, right?"

In point of fact, this approach was already losing its charm in Europe. Books like Pevsner's *Pioneers of the Modern Movement* and Sigfried Giedion's *Space, Time and*

Architecture would bury it under broad masses of *Kulturgeschichte* by the time the decade was out. The process probably began with an almost forgotten document—a hurriedly commissioned and hurriedly written set of four articles by the eccentric British wine merchant and architecture buff Philip Morton Shand, which appeared in *The Architectural Review* in 1934–35. Perceptive and well-informed, Shand saw no reason to be bound too closely by the rules of argument or chronology, and the result is one of the most readable accounts of the rise of modern architecture that we have. It was published under the title "Scenario for a Human Drama."

No part of *The International Style* could be called that! In spite of the fact that a few personalities are admitted towards the end of the historical chapter—the heroes, like Gropius, Mies, Le Corbusier, J. J. P. Oud, had to be introduced somehow—and with them something about esthetic influences on their personal styles, this remains a very restricted account of history. I am almost tempted to call it "coy" because that is what the concluding chapter on *Siedlungen* really is, to the point where it enrages and baffles younger historians everywhere.

It was in the *Siedlungen,* perhaps more than anywhere else, that Shand's "human drama" scenario was being enacted. Rather than being simply a field of design where handsome groupings of housing and community buildings gave proof of the architects' ability to work on a larger than domestic scale, which is about all that Hitchcock and Johnson will allow, the *Siedlungen* brought together a complex of forces, ranging from social reform to trade-union activism, beliefs in communal property holding, self-help, mutual help, egalitarianism (no *Siedlung* was exclusively working class), make-work municipal investment and gigantic public mortgages, all with a distinctly utopian gleam in the eye!

The results were often a travesty (though not always) of these high ambitions, but they got built—and they got built in the International Style by architects with whom Hitchcock and Johnson were well acquainted. So they had to go in the book, where they are presented with a distinct coolness and avoidance of the key issues, or their reduction to an almost meaningless level of generality. Thus, as against all the forces I listed above which were galvanizing Dutch, German and Austrian cities to one of the greatest municipal rehousing efforts ever, our two authors merely offer "an increasing intervention of the political authorities" or "[the State] has itself become a patron of architecture in fields previously left to the individual" and "public and semi-public agencies are concerning themselves with inexpensive housing." So much for the Human Drama! This really is very flat beer, but why?

The answer, if one thinks about the times and the context, is surely politics, in the most narrow and the most general terms. Bluntly, Hitchcock and Johnson would have had to talk about Socialism, and that might not have been a smart thing to do in the dying years of the Hoover administration and in consideration of the network of Rockefellers, Goodyears and other very rich persons with whom they were involved in getting the fledgling Museum of Modern Art off the ground. I am prepared to allow that more study may be needed, but I believe that the case really was that the New Architecture would be presented without the Socialist fire in its belly, or it might not get presented at all! Or, at least, it would be presented in a carefully sanitized form in which only the most distant echoes of ideology might be discerned in phrases like "sociologically correct." The chapter ends in generalities and so does the book.

Yet there was to ensue a monstrous historical irony—more than one, in fact—that would fatally compromise the rather cavalier assumptions of Hitchcock and Johnson. Within two or three years of the publication of *The International Style,* it began to appear that the ideological baggage had not fallen in the Atlantic after all, but had merely been delayed in transit or—worse—been shipped on ahead and been waiting at the dockside. The former case is the better known—the arrival of the Hitler refugees, most notably the Silver Prince, Walter Gropius himself. Looking at the Museum of Modern Art's *Bauhaus* catalogue, which celebrated Gropius's installation at Harvard, it is very difficult to believe that only six years had elapsed since the publication of *The International Style,* which now looks a bit cozy and provincial.

But more important, I suspect, is the ideological baggage that had arrived earlier. There are, after all, six International Style buildings from North America in the book which, by definition, must already have been completed: a filling station in Cleveland by Alfred Clauss and George Daub, for example, and an experimental house in Syosset, Long Island, by A. Lawrence Kocher and Albert Frey, as well as the McGraw-Hill Building on 42nd Street by Hood and Fouilhoux, and Howe and Lescaze's brand-new Philadelphia Savings Fund Society skyscraper. Who had designed them? Earlier European immigrants with only one exception. These architects were Europeans acting either as their own principals—as with Neutra in California—or as design partners with an American office—as with William Lescaze at Howe and Lescaze in Philadelphia. Yet the most consequential of these earlier arrivals, I would submit, and the one who most effectively subverted the non-ideological view, was the long-forgotten Roland Wank.

Wank was here in New York in 1922, and by the end of the '20s was designing major railroad stations. At the beginning of the '30s he designed some trade-union housing down on Grand Street, and being thus proven to be ideologically sound, was invited by the Roosevelt administration to lay out some workers' housing in the depressed South in the opening year of the New Deal. While he was doing that, he was asked to comment on the designs of a new dam by the Army Corps of Engineers, and produced an alternative so radical that the choice between the two went to outside arbitration. Wank's was preferred: the result was Norris Dam and the adoption of the International Style as the house style of the Tennessee Valley Authority.

The TVA's version of the International Style was not always very pure, but it was near enough, very well made, and intended to have an impact on the public. And the public generally regarded the aims and actions of the TVA as Socialism of some sort, even though its organization was more like Mussolini's corporate state. In the vastly changed atmosphere of the Roosevelt epoch, the pure, abstract constructive forms of Hitchcock and Johnson were definitively reunited with their political origins and ideological sources. Even if you call it "The Welfare Style," as Bob Venturi used to do, the political connection is still there.

But enough of the book's chief failing. Let us now look at the two great strengths it possesses—one half-hidden, the other overt. As early as 1951 Hitchcock was complaining, in conversation and in print, that the book was being used as a style manual—"How to do International Style in ten easy chapters, profusely illustrated." And yet he and Johnson had, in a far more subtle way, produced a body of instruction that, if followed with understanding, would lead to International Style buildings. I repeat that this was never their intention. The intention was rigorous description of the style, word by word and canonical illustration by illustration, proceeding to the demonstration of its right to be considered a style in the grand historical sense.

To some extent the International Style's success under this heading may be attributed to the vulgarizing hand of Alfred H. Barr, Jr., the moving spirit behind the exhibition and the book, the book's editor and the author of its introduction. In that introduction, Barr reduced much of the subtler argument of the book to pulp, but he did produce three "distinguishing aesthetic principles of the International Style" which are so succinctly phrased that many students can still remember them after their midterms. They read as follows:

> » Emphasis upon volume—space enclosed by thin planes or surfaces as opposed to the suggestion of mass and solidity.
> » Regularity as opposed to symmetry or other kinds of obvious balance.
> » Lastly, dependence upon the intrinsic elegance of materials, technical perfection, and fine proportions, as opposed to applied ornament.

These three neat, binary clusters can stand exegesis on a number of counts, including the amount of modern movement mythology that is packaged into them, but what I want to concentrate on here is what they imply and the way they work together. For instance, volume rather than mass, as of 1932, still required steel or concrete-framed construction, and the skin would be applied in the form of a standard window-frame system, whose mechanical parts often did come close to perfection, and whose regular panes seemed to imply that proportion was all. Furthermore, the economics of standard systems effectively ruled out applied ornamentation that would be big enough to register visually, because of the costs of special installation (except in the case of traditional symmetrical compositions, which were anathema under clause 2 anyhow). The regularity rule could only be made explicit by the use of large repeating units, such as room-sized window openings, and the organization of such regularities in asymmetrical elevations would really need some help from the current state of abstract art, as did the idea of relying on technical perfection. And so the propositions curl back on one another until in the end we realize that we are confronted with a kind of minimal—but definitive, integrated and irreducible—description of building in the modern style. Following the hints and categories contained in the body of the book, Barr set out the whole business of the International Style in 50 words—everything except the reason for doing it in the first place.

Now, we have had to accept many of the great styles of the past with almost as little qualification. One of the great achievements of the Rationalist historians of the 19th century had been in offering explanations of the great styles that were "value free," and thus proof against romantic or religious interpretations (Ruskin being an obvious exponent of the latter, in spite of his many other virtues). The sort of blanket definition of a Great International Style that one would derive from the Rationalist attitude could be formulated as: the immanence of a coherent set of structural procedures and esthetic ambitions in an orderly sequence of monuments.

That is how Hitchcock and Johnson present their style—albeit in very cramped form—and that, in the end, is the shining virtue of their book in its time and its generation. It talks about *style.* From almost the beginning of the century "style" had been a dirty word in advanced architectural writing because it had been so abused and misused in the second half of the Victorian era. Early modern writers like W. R. Lethaby and H. P. Berlage looked forward to style as something we might have in the future. Auguste Perret declared that "Style is a word that has no plural," and both Walter Gropius and Le Corbusier would have nothing to do with it, Le Corbusier's anathema being "Architecture has nothing to do with the styles!"

Perret's version, "Style is a word that has no plural," always sounded to me like a deliberate conversation stopper, and the conversation *had* virtually stopped. And then along came Hitchcock and Johnson who, by tackling the style problem head on—and tackling practically nothing else—broke the intellectual logjam, got the conversation started again, and in such a comparatively calm tone of voice that it has taken more than 40 years to reach its current shrill tones of academic bad temper, particularly among British pundits. The book for all its persistent shortcomings must therefore stand as an achievement to be saluted. Unique among the modernist literature of the early '30s, it successfully reintroduced the concept of style into the arguments of its day, while for us latecomers, it provides a balanced view of a period we would otherwise know only through the eyes of the ideologues of the other camp.

So, when this year's instructor for Modern Architecture 101, or whatever it's called on any particular campus, sits down to compile the book list, *The International Style* will be there, along with Pevsner and Giedion and Banham and Frampton and even Tom

Wolfe. It is established in the canon, as it deserves to be. Indeed, published as it was in 1932, it is the most senior of the canonical texts in general use, and that again is a matter for congratulation and humble reflection, because the durable texts of modernism are so rare.

Yet, before I pay my closing respects to Henry-Russell Hitchcock, I have to say something about what the elevation to canonical status can do to a good book. Only in my last few observations here did I call *The International Style* a "text"; elsewhere I have been scrupulous to call it a "book," and I would like to explain why, because the difference is rather special in architecture, and takes visible form in the case of Hitchcock and Johnson. The version that will go onto the book list will, inevitably, be the Norton Library paperback of 1966, which is already different textually from the original, in that it has a new foreword and a discursive tailpiece by Hitchcock himself which—without any evil intent, we may be sure—makes it much more obviously a Hitchcock production. Also, certain words have disappeared from the title material: *The International Style: Architecture since 1922* has been shortened to simply *The International Style,* thus giving it a slightly spurious generality as against its original topical urgency.

More important, however, are the changes in the layout. As originally published, the book was one of the real pioneers of the Museum of Modern Art Style—printed on shiny coated stock to enhance the quality of its black-and-white illustrations, with plenty of white paper all around, and even an occasional blank page to assist the logical distribution of the pictures. It's not a big book, but it is a generous and striking book that sits well in the hand.

The Norton Library edition is smaller in its page format, though not very much, and tremendous ingenuity has been deployed to ensure that, in spite of the new text matter, every sentence and every illustration of the original shall fall on the same page number in the Norton Library edition—indeed, the text pages are reproduced exactly from the originals as far as I can see. *Except* that most of the original photographs were of so-called "landscape" format, wider than they are high, as is often the case in architectural illustration. These could not be fitted into the narrower paperback format of the Library edition without shrinking them so drastically that they would become almost illegible, so the publishers did the other thing and rotated them through 90 degrees—which means that on practically every other page, the reader has to rotate the book through 90 degrees as well! The result is not only awkward, but it totally changes the meaning of the object in the reader's hand. What had been an instrument of high impact architectural propaganda, every page opening clean and patent, has now become a text to be pored over. What had been an object to be handled with pleasure is now just another academic paperback with the usual muddy illustrations on dull paper stock. And a travesty of the original.

Great architecture books don't operate like that. From the very beginnings of the printed literature on architecture, the great books have brought text and illustrations together with great cunning, so much so that it is not the same book if the illustrations are even slightly rearranged. Put an original of Palladio's *Quattro Libri* alongside one of those 18th-century editions where the arrangement of the illustrations has been rationalized, and you will see at once that the latter is a deception, because the immediate, facing-page rapport between word and image has been lost. Equally, put the Palladio with its calm expanses of clear paper alongside a Serlio, with words and images so jigsawed together that hardly any paper can be seen at all, and you will know at once which of these great masters is offering insights into the high abstract principles of the noble art, and which is offering the first useful crib book of architectural details!

The physical, the visual nature of the book in the hand has been crucial, from the *Quattro Libri* to Le Corbusier's *Oeuvre complète* or the *Notebooks* of Paolo Soleri, or even Venturi's *Learning from Las Vegas*—indeed, the last two have been "miniaturized," and have lost almost everything in the process. But *The International Style* seems to me to remain the unfortunate classic of this kind of bowdlerization. It may not matter what a purely literary text actually looks like—even poetry seems to survive some murderous visual ill treatment. But "texts" are just words, whereas books are much more complex organisms.

And that matters to me as a hands-on historian. I seek that first edition in order to find out what the masters—and their publishers!—thought they were about. And wherever possible, I like my students at least to get their hands on good facsimile editions. For not only does architecture consist of a set of actual monuments, its history also consists of a set of actual books; and, of course, a set of actual historians, one of whom it has been my pleasure to salute tonight.

NOTE   1. The text of Banham's *Making Architecture* remained incomplete at his death.

A Black Box

The Secret Profession of Architecture

The difference between Wren and Hawksmoor, I have finally decided, is that Hawksmoor was an architect and Wren was not. This judgment may seem foolhardy, but it is not deliberately perverse. It has been forced on me by some months of visiting the Lloyd's building *chantier,* which gave me a chance to revisit St Paul's and sundry City churches I had not seen since student days. And it struck me that even when Wren was being as clever as he was in widening the central bay in each arcade at St Mary-le-Bow, or as inventive as he was in the upper parts of St Stephen Walbrook, he still was not doing whatever it was that Hawksmoor had done to make great architecture out of as humdrum a concept as the interior of St Mary Woolnoth.

The distinction I am making is not between different temperaments or levels of creative genius, but between fundamental modes of designing. Nor are the consequences of the architectural mode necessarily beautiful. Some pretty ugly stuff happens in the lantern of the mausoleum of the Dulwich Art Gallery, for instance, yet the result leaves us in no doubt that Sir John Soane was an absolute architect.

Whatever this mode, attitude or presence may be, one can recognise it—in the bot-

Originally appeared in *New Statesman and Society*, 12 October 1990, pp. 22–25.

tom of Philip Johnson's AT&T building, for example, but not in its middle or its top, nor in most other works of programmatic postmodernism. Its absence from Charles Jenck's own house in London, in spite of all its erudition *about* architecture, seems to confirm what the recent work of Robert Stern (but not, I think, of Robert Venturi) had been strongly suggesting. That reliance on erudition alone leaves postmodernism in the same relation to architecture as female impersonation to femininity. It is not architecture, but building in drag.

I propose to treat the architectural mode or presence as a classic "black box", recognised by its output though unknown in its contents. It is not to be mistaken for "good design", since architecture is often conspicuously present—in the work of Lutyens for instance—in buildings that are pretty dumb designs from other points of view. To separate architecture from good design in this way may unsettle those who do not question the mythologies by which architecture has operated for some six centuries now, but it does not imply that the two are incompatible; simply that one can have either without the other.

The situation has been much muddled by the tendency of the modern movement, since the time of William Morris, to gather up all decent buildings into the rubric of "architecture". This was a warm, friendly and egalitarian thing to do, but it must now seem as historically crude and as perniciously confusing as Nikolaus Pevsner's proposition that Lincoln Cathedral is architecture and a bicycle shed is not. The distinction was made on the basis that Lincoln Cathedral had aesthetic pretensions and bike sheds don't.

This was not only a piece of academic snobbery that can only offend a committed cyclist like myself, but also involves a supposition about sheds that is so sweeping as to be almost racist. How can he know that any particular bicycle shed, or even the whole typology of "bicycle shed" in general, was conceived without aesthetic intention? What one can know by practised observation, however (and what Pevsner may even have meant), is that cathedrals (including ugly ones) are generally designed *modo architectorum,* and bicycle sheds (even handsome ones) are more commonly done in one of the numerous other modes of designing buildings available.

Such is the cultural prestige of the purely architectural mode, however, within the protected area of "western civilisation", that most of us get brainwashed into believing that it is synonymous with "good design" or even "the design of buildings". The modern movement has done itself little good in promoting this muddle, because it thereby undermines one of its own most useful polemical devices. For, in spite of this inclusivist approach, there has been a long tradition—from before Adolf Loos to after Cedric Price—of using comparisons with certifiably non-architectural objects, from peasant crafts to advanced electronics, to reveal how bad regular architectural designing had become. Quite a lot of these paragons were indeed buildings, and good ones at that, but once they, in their turn, had become incorporated into the architectural canon, they lost their critical power and left the body of architecture confused rather than reformed.

Let us then re-divorce what should never have been joined together in this opportunistic marriage-of-convenience. Throw out all the Zulu kraals, grain-elevators, hogans, lunar excursion modules, cruck-houses, Farman biplanes and so forth, and look again at "this thing called architecture" in its own right, as one of a number of thinkable modes of design which, for some reason, has come to occupy a position of cultural privilege in relation to the construction industry.

What then would distinguish the products of this black box from those of other thinkable modes? Functional or environmental performance? Beauty of form or deftness of space? Truth to materials or structural efficiency? These are all qualities for which the architectural profession habitually congratulates itself, but a Buckminster Fuller dome or an Eskimo igloo can usually beat architecture on all six counts, and so can a lot of other buildings, ships, air liners, inflatables and animal lairs. So why do we not admit that what distinguishes architecture is not *what* is done—since, on their good days, all the world and his wife can apparently do it better—but *how* it is done.

We can distinguish that "how" in two crucial ways in the actual behaviour of architects as they perform their allotted tasks as building designers. The first is that architects—almost uniquely among modern design professionals—propose to assume responsibility for all of those six aspects of good building set out above, and to be legally answerable to the client for their proper delivery. Other professions (such as electrical and mechanical engineering) notoriously avoid such overall responsibilities, preferring to remain at one remove from the wrath of clients as "consultants"; hired guns who, like minor war criminals, "were only carrying out orders". Or, to be less offensive to engineers, a body of men who are too prone to say, for instance, "You design your concert hall any old shape you like, and I'll try and sort out the acoustics," rather than "That's a stupid shape for a concert hall, this will work a lot better."

However, this willingness to assume responsibility is only what makes architects a noble profession. It is not what makes them architects, as Lethaby seems to have perceived in his arguments against professionalisation at the beginning of the century. What makes them architects, and recognisable as such, is usually easiest to demonstrate anecdotally, beginning with that oft-repeated story of the architect who, when asked for a pencil that could be used to tighten the tourniquet on the limb of a person bleeding to death in the street, carefully enquired "Will a 2B do?"

The point of such stories is that they unconsciously reveal not only the fundamental value-system on which architects operate, but the narrowness of that system, and the unspoken—or unspeakable—assumptions on which it rests. The more revealing of these stories tend to originate from that crucial attitude-forming situation, the design crit in the architectural school studio.

In a telling example from my own experience, I once found myself defending point by point a student design for a penthouse apartment that had been failed by my academic colleagues. I secured their agreement that it fulfilled all the requirements of the programme, was convenient in its spatial dispositions, well lit, buildable on the roof-structure in question and that all this could be seen in the drawing pinned up for judgment. But the drawing was scratchily done in ball-point on one sheet of what appeared to be institutional toilet paper; an "insult to architecture", the year master announced, thus making it clear that, for him, the effective design of buildings was apparently something other than "architecture".

One could easily multiply such instances where, it seems, some secret value system applies, often at variance with the verbal expressions used in explanation. Everyone around architecture schools knows students who are convinced (rightly, in about one case in five) that they have been failed "because I don't draw in the right style", in spite of faculty assurances to the contrary. And most of us can remember crits that finished with the pronouncement, "Sorry. . . . It's very clever/beautiful/sensitive, but it isn't architecture, you know!"

These instances are no less weighty for being "only about school". That is where architects are socialised into the profession (as the great Jane Abercrombie used to phrase it) and they acquire attitudes, work-habits and values that will stay with them for life. Their persistence is neatly shown in the current modes of "engineering" high-tech buildings: the types of visible structures preferred by architects and the ways in which they detail them, neither of which would ever occur to engineers left to their own devices as "problem solvers". Admittedly, there are structural engineers like Peter Rice and Tony Hunt, who seem to glory in their complicity in architects' scheming; and the doyen of the profession in Britain at the moment, Frank Newby, did say to me recently that if architects want to "indulge in this kind of structural exhibitionism, then I can help them!"

The key phrase there is *this kind*. Engineers also enjoy structural exhibitionism, but architects have their own version, both in the choice and organisation of the larger forms and—even more intensely—in the marshalling and profiling of the smaller ones. The Lloyd's building, to pick an obvious instance—but Norman Foster's Renault Centre or Hopkins's Schlumberger labs at Cambridge would serve equally well—exhibits preferences and scruples, not to say obsessions, that one does not commonly find in regular engineering design. Compare forms and details of the structure of the Pompidou Centre with what it is so often jokingly compared with—an oil refinery—and you will see that there is *no* comparison, except at the level of a joke. There is, above all, a kind of pickiness over details that shows up in regular engineering only when a total stranger wanders in from another field, as did Henry Royce or Ettore Bugatti in the early days of the automobile.

For the sources of these differences of professional behaviour, one need look no further than the place where architects are socialised into their profession, the studio. Anthropologists have been known to compare the teaching studio to a tribal longhouse; the place and the rituals pursued there are almost unique in the annals of western education. One of the things that sustains this uniqueness is the frequency with which students are discouraged from pursuing modes of design that come from outside the studio. Usually, the discouragement need be no more than veiled or oblique, but when schools were under radical pressure in the early seventies, many students will have heard something which I personally heard at that time, the blunt directive: "Don't bother with all that environmental stuff, just get on with the architecture!"

How does one "get on with the architecture", forsaking all other modes? What is it, in other words, that architects uniquely do? The answer, alas, is that they do "architecture", and we are thus back at the black box with which we began. But we have recently been vouchsafed an accidental view of what the contents of that black box might be, because of an interesting story that has emerged from recent writing by, and about, Christopher Alexander and his "timeless way of building". Looking back on the early days of his "pattern language", he revealed one of its apparent failures to his biographer, Stephen Grabow:

> Bootleg copies of the pattern language were floating up and down the west coast, and people would come and show me the projects they had done, and I began to be more and more amazed that, although it worked, all these projects looked like any other buildings of our time . . . still belonged perfectly within the canons of mid-century architecture.

Now, if one hoped that the pattern language would be a revolutionary way of designing buildings, a new paradigm in architecture comparable with the Copernican revolution in cosmology, then clearly the project had failed and further research was indeed needed. But, in another light, the failure of the pattern language to change the nature of architectural design could be seen as something of a triumph: an unwitting first-approximation description of what architects actually do when they do architecture. It certainly does not tally with what architects normally claim that they do (explicit and implicit procedures are at variance in many professions), but it may still provide at least an analogy with the mental sets that students subliminally acquire in the studio long-house.

The heart of Alexander's matter is the concept of a "pattern", which is a sort of package of ideas and forms which can be subsumed under a label as commonplace as "comfortable window-seat" or "threshold" or "light on two sides of a room", or as abstract as "intimacy gradient". Such a labelled pattern contains not only the knowledge of the form and how to make it, but "there is an imperative aspect to the pattern . . . it is desirable pattern . . . [the architect] must create this pattern in order to maintain a stable and healthy world."

In other words, each such pattern will have moral force, will be the only right way of doing that particular piece of designing—at least in the eyes of those who have been correctly socialised into the profession. I seem to hear an echo here of Ernesto Rogers claiming long ago: "There is no such thing as bad architecture; only good architecture and non-architecture." And in general, as an outsider who was never socialised in the tribal long-house, it seems to me that Alexander's patterns are very like the kind of packages in which architects can often be seen to be doing their thinking, particularly at the sort of second sketch stage when they are re-using some of what was sketched out in the first version.

Such patterns—perhaps even a finite set of patterns—and their imperatives seem to be shared by all architects, and are, in some sense, what we recognise in Hawksmoor and do not find in Wren. This is not to say that Alexander's accidental revelation exhausts the topic. Far from it; for a start, it is still much too crude to explain anything really subtle. Being cast in a prescriptive, rather than descriptive, format, it avoids such questions as how such patterns are formed, and where, and cannot support the kind of anthropological investigation that has revealed the workings of other secret cultures to us in the past. It cannot yet open the black box, but it can give hints about the contents.

While we await their eventual revelation, what are we to make of architecture? No longer seen as the mother of the arts, or the dominant mode of rational design, it appears as the exercise of an arcane and privileged aesthetic code. We could, perhaps, treat it as one of the humanities, trivial or quadrivial, since its traditions are of the same antiquity and classicist derivation as the others (it even has a part share in a muse, Melpomene). We could stop pretending that it is "a blend of art and science", but is a discipline in its own right that happens to overlap some of the territory of painting, sculpture, statics, acoustics and so on. And we could halt the vulgar cultural imperialism that leads the writers of general histories of architecture to co-opt absolutely everything built upon the earth's crust into their subject matter.

To do so is to try to cram the world's wonderful variety of building arts into the procrustean mould of a set of rules of thumb derived from, and entirely proper to, the building arts of the Mediterranean basin alone, and whose master-discipline, design, is simply *disegno,* a style of draughtsmanship once practised only in central Italy. I am increasingly doubtful that the timber buildings of northern Europe, for instance, or the triumphs of Gothic construction, really belong under the rubric of architecture at all. Le Corbusier felt that Gothic cathedrals were "not very beautiful", not architecture even, because they were not made of the pure geometrical forms that he found in the buildings of classical Greece and imperial Rome. Current misgivings about high-tech, with its exposed structures and services, seem to derive from a similar classicist sentiment: that architecture is from masonry, held together by gravity, and its volumes effectively closed.

Recognising the very straitened boundaries of architecture as an academically teachable subject, we might deceive and confuse ourselves less if we stopped trying to cram the whole globe into its intellectual portfolio. We could recognise that the history of architecture is no more, but emphatically no less, than what we used to believe it was: the progression of those styles and monuments of the European mainstream, from Stonehenge to the Staatsgalerie, that define the modest building art that is ours alone.

We might then have a better view of the true value and splendours of the building arts and design methods of other cultures, avoiding the kind of sentimentality with which Charles Eames, for instance, sugar-coated the design arts of the Orient. We might also be more securely placed to study the mysteries of our own building art, beginning with the persistence of drawing—*disegno*—as a kind of meta-pattern that subsumes all other patterns and shelters them from rational scrutiny. Even before architectural drawings achieved the kind of commercial value they can claim nowadays, they had such crucial value for architects that being unable to think without drawing became the true mark of one fully socialised into the profession of architecture.

Recall the alarm, disguised as contempt, that greeted Michael Keyte's claim in the early sixties that, with the CLASP system, one could design buildings without making drawings at all, just a typewritten schedule of components and procedures. If that sounds suspiciously like a computer programme, let us acknowledge that Keyte was only anticipating the probably fatal blow that computer-aided design may have dealt the mystique of drawing, and thus to architecture too. Not by mechanising the act of drawing itself, but by rendering it unnecessary. Computers can indeed make drawings, copy them, and turn them in and out of perspective or isometric, and—most crucially—they can remember drawings. But they do not remember them in imagery that the eye can read.

Rather, they remember them in the usual bytes of bits of binary information that is the common content of all computer memories. And that kind of information can be punched in and out of the memory by means of an ordinary alphanumeric keyboard, without any draughtsmanship at all. And if draughtsmanship thus becomes unnecessary even for the making of drawings, then to persist in the act of drawing and in setting store by that act, becomes either an act of cultural defiance—"resistance" in the self-righteous cant of New York academe represented by Kenneth Frampton—or a conscious submission to the unspoken codes of a secret society.

To a certain kind of old-timer, this could be good news: confirmation that they were right all along and that we should have stuck to the orders and the theory of composition and ignored all that technology and modern stuff. To other interests, however, such as those of the rest of a world increasingly desperate for better buildings and a more habitable environment, architecture's proud but unadmitted acceptance of this parochial rule book can only seem a crippling limitation on building's power to serve humanity.

If architecture could "to its own self be true", accepting that it is not the whole art of building everywhere, but just the making of drawings for buildings in the manner practised in Europe since the Renaissance, it could be recognised as something that belongs as valuably at the heart of western culture as do the Latin language, Christian liturgy, Magna Carta or—precisely—the Masonic mysteries of *Die Zauberflöte.* And it could then get out of some of its more egregious perceptual and intellectual muddles, like those over Christopher Wren and Mies van der Rohe.

Wren could be seen as a master-builder of talent bordering on genius who tried to teach himself architecture out of books, like a postmodernist, but never gained entry to the inner *sancta* of its art or mystery. The west front of St Paul's remains the finest piece of urban scenography that a rational mind could have placed at the top of narrow old Ludgate Hill, but please don't call it architecture.

Mies, on the other hand, could be recognised as a true insider of the *arcana* of architecture, whose achievement has been largely obscured by the rhetoric of pure rationality that has come from his followers and explainers. Indeed, he is a very good case in counterpoint to Wren, an absolute architect whose building was so open to rational explanation that few noticed that these explanations had almost nothing to say about his architecture—until various good grey men had to try to explain his architecture in public at the planning inquiry into the proposed Mansion House Square development.

The egg left on the face of the modernist establishment by that enquiry does not mean that it is necessarily impossible to find language to discuss what is currently ineffable, but valuable, in the work of Mies and in the subculture of architecture in general. Not only have Christopher Alexander's confused gropings suggested one possible conceptual basis for deeper enquiry, but the bafflement of the general public in the face of the behaviour of architects might provoke some psychologist or anthropologist to try to break through the glass wall of inscrutability that surrounds the topic. Anthropologists have already gone a long way in penetrating the inner workings of societies far more remote than the tribe of architecture.

But the tribe would almost certainly have to resist the intrusion on its privacy if it were to preserve its integrity as a social grouping. It might well decide to defend the contents of the black box at whatever cost, as if it were the ark of its covenant. What else could architects do? The threat of ultimate revelation, of demystification or even deconstruction, would surely deliver architecture to yet another of the seemingly endless series of crossroads of decision that have confronted it since the first quarrel of the Ancients and the Moderns.

It could permit itself to be opened up to the understandings of the profane and the vulgar, at the risk of destroying itself as an art in the process. Or it could close ranks and continue as a conspiracy of secrecy, immune from scrutiny, but perpetually open to the suspicion, among the general public, that there may be nothing at all inside the black box except a mystery for its own sake.

Bibliography

BOOKS *Theory and Design in the First Machine Age.* London: Architectural Press; New York: Praeger, 1960.

Guide to Modern Architecture. London: Architectural Press; Princeton, N.J.: Van Nostrand, 1962.

The New Brutalism: Ethic or Aesthetic? London: Architectural Press; New York: Reinhold, 1966.

The Architecture of the Well-Tempered Environment. London: Architectural Press, 1969; Chicago: University of Chicago Press, 1984.

Los Angeles: The Architecture of Four Ecologies. London: Allen Lane; New York: Harper & Row, 1971.

The Aspen Papers: Twenty Years of Design Theory from the International Design Conference in Aspen. Edited volume. London: Pall Mall; New York: Praeger, 1974.

Critique Architecturale. Paris: Institut de l'Environment, 1975.

Mechanical Services A305: History of Architecture & Design 1890–1939, Unit 21. Milton Keynes: Open University Press, 1975.

Age of the Masters: A Personal View of Modern Architecture. Revised edition of *Guide to Modern Architecture.* London: Architectural Press; New York: Harper & Row, 1975.

Megastructure: Urban Futures of the Recent Past. London: Thames & Hudson; New York: Harper & Row, 1976.

'Introduction.' In *Design by Choice/Reyner Banham.* Edited by Penny Sparke. London: Academy Editions; New York: Rizzoli, 1981.

'Introduction,' and entries on industrial buildings. In *Buffalo Architecture: A Guide.* Cambridge, Mass.: MIT Press, 1981.

Scenes in American Deserta. Salt Lake City: Gibbs M. Smith; London: Thames and Hudson, 1982.

Contemporary Architecture of Japan, 1958–1984. With Hiroyuki Suzuki and Katsuhiro Kobayashi. New York: Rizzoli, 1985.

A Concrete Atlantis: U.S. Industrial Building and European Modern Architecture, 1900–1925. Cambridge, Mass.: MIT Press, 1986.

Visions of Ron Herron. London: Academy Editions, 1994 (completed summer 1987).

ARTICLES

1950 *Art News and Review*

25 March 1950, vol. 2, no. 4: 6, 'Gregorio Prieto.'

6 May 1950, vol. 2, no. 7: 6, 'Paintings by Archibald Ziegler'; and 'Cartoons and Caricatures by Jewish Artists.'

20 May 1950, vol. 2, no. 8: 4, 'Pic and Potwarowski.'

17 June 1950, vol. 2, no. 10: 4, 'Jo Jones.'

1 July 1950, vol. 2, no. 11: 4, 'Society of Marine Artists.'

15 July 1950, vol. 2, no. 12: 4, 5, 'Humbert, Sager and Young Contemporaries'; and 'Nineteenth-Century French Masters.'

13 August 1950, vol. 2, no. 14: 3, 'American Symbolic Realists.'

18 November 1950, vol. 2, no. 21: 6, 8, 'The Shape of Things'; and 'Alexander Hodgkinson.'

2 December 1950, vol. 2, no. 22: 6, 'Royal Society of Portrait Painters.'

1951 *Art News and Review*

13 January 1951, vol. 2, no. 25: 5, 'Eighteenth-Century Venice.'

10 February 1951, vol. 3, no. 1: 6, review of *Alfred Stevens,* by Kenneth Rommey Towndraw.

24 February 1951, vol. 3, no. 2: 6, 'The Shape of Things.'

24 March 1951, vol. 3, no. 4: 5, 'Realists and Visionaries.'

21 April 1951, vol. 3, no. 6: 7, 'Young Social Realists.'

5 May 1951, vol. 3, no. 7: 7, 'Les Roi Des Cieux.'

19 May 1951, vol. 3, no. 8: 1, 8, 'Pavilion'd in Splendour.'

14 July 1951, vol. 3, no. 12: 2, 'The Shape of Everything.'

11 August 1951, vol. 3, no. 14: 7, review of *Ubu Roi,* by Alfred Jarry.

25 August 1951, vol. 3, no. 15: 3, 'Ranelagh Resurrected.'

5 October 1951, vol. 3, no. 18: 4, 'Two Originals.'

20 October 1951, vol. 3, no. 19: 4, 'English Elysiums.'

17 November 1951, vol. 3, no. 21: 5, 10, 'Sunday Decorations'; and review of *Florentine Drawings,* by Andre Chastel; *English Drawings,* by Anne Carlisle; *Drawings in France,* by Gaston Diehl.

1952 *Architectural Review*

October 1952, vol. 112: 215–217, 'Italian Eclectic.'

December 1952, vol. 112: 366–371, 410, 'The Voysey Inheritance'; and 'UNESCO Headquarters.'

Art News and Review

12 January 1952, vol. 3, no. 25: 5, 'A Man and His Objects.'

26 January 1952, vol. 3, no. 26: 5, 'The Next Step.'

23 February 1952, vol. 4, no. 2: 4, 'Fashions in Fashion.'

8 March 1952, vol. 4, no. 3: 3, 'Pictures of the Passing World.'

5 April 1952, vol. 4, no. 5: 4, 'Catacomb Cities.'

12 July 1952, vol. 4, no. 12: 3, review of exhibition, Institute of Contemporary Art Gallery and Agnews.

26 July 1952, vol. 4, no. 13: 3, 5, review of exhibition, Marlborough Gallery, Royal College of Art and Architectural Association.

23 August 1952, vol. 4, no. 15: 4, review of exhibition, Royal Institute Galleries, Mathiesens.

6 September 1952, vol. 4, no. 16: 4, review of exhibition, Institute of Contemporary Art and Imperial Institute.

20 September 1952, vol. 4, no. 17: 2, review of exhibition, Archer Gallery.

18 October 1952, vol. 4, no. 19: 4–5, review of exhibition, Lefevre Gallery.

15 November 1952, vol. 4, no. 21: 3, 'Here's Richness,' review of *Persian Painting of the Fourteenth Century,* by Douglas Barrett.

27 December 1952, vol. 4, no. 24: 3, 'Inigo Jones.'

1953   *Architects' Journal*

15 January 1953, vol. 117: 108–110, 'Books of 1952,' review of *Modern Architectural Design,* by Howard Robertson; *Art and the Nature of Architecture,* by Bruce Allsopp; *The Heart of the City,* 8th Ciam Congress Report; *Elizabethan and Jacobean Architecture,* by Marcus Whiffen; *English Renaissance Architecture,* by Dr. Margaret Whinney; *Sir John Soane,* by John Summerson; *Greater London,* by Nikolaus Pevsner; *Goths and Vandals,* by Martin S. Briggs; *Indoor Plants and Gardens,* by H. F. Clark and Margaret Jones.

Architectural Review

February 1953, vol. 113: 73–77, 'Casa del Girasole.'

June 1953, vol. 113: 401–403, 'Painting and Sculpture of Le Corbusier.'

September 1953, vol. 114: 160–168, 199–202, 'Howard Robertson'; and 'Simplified Vaulting Practices.'

November 1953, vol. 114: 285–288, 'Pelican History in 48 Volumes.'

Art News and Review

24 January 1953, vol. 4, no. 26: 3, 'Two Sculptors.'

21 March 1953, vol. 5, no. 4: 6, review of exhibition, Guildhall Gallery.

4 April 1953, vol. 5, no. 5: 2, review of *The Drawings of Parmigianino,* by A. E. Popham.

2 May 1953, vol. 5, no. 7: 2, 8, 'Corbusier at the I.C.A.,' review of *Taliesin Drawings,* edited by Edgar Kaufmann, Jr.

25 July 1953, vol. 5, no. 13: 1, 7, 'High Brazil.'

3 October 1953, vol. 5, no. 18: 2, 'John Martin at the Whitechapel.'

28 November 1953, vol. 5, no. 22: 3, 'On Abstract Theory.'

1954   *Architects' Journal*

8 July 1954, vol. 120: 36, letter, 'Astragal at the Bartlett.'

Architectural Review

June 1954, vol. 115: 403–406, 'Object Lesson.'

August 1954, vol. 116: 84–93, 'Mendelsohn.'

September 1954, vol. 116: 153–158, 193–194, 'School at Hunstanton Norfolk'; and 'Encyclical,' review of *Form,* by Max Bill.

November 1954, vol. 116: 302–307, 'Facade, Elevational Treatment of the Hallfield Estate Paddington.'

Art News and Review

6 March 1954, vol. 6, no. 3: 1, 3, 'Venetian Villas.'

17 April 1954, vol. 6, no. 6: 2, 'Paris-Londres.'

2 October 1954, vol. 6, no. 18: 6, 'X.T.'

16 October 1954, vol. 6, no. 19: 1, 'The Last Old Master.'

1955 *Architects' Journal*

18 August 1955, vol. 122: 225, letter, 'Cybernetics.'

29 December 1955, vol. 122: 864, letter, 'A Reply to Llewellyn Davies.'

Architectural Review

April 1955, vol. 117: 224–228, 'The Machine Aesthetic.'

May 1955, vol. 117: 295–301, 339, 'Sant' Elia'; and 'Wren: Short and Long,' review of *Sir Christopher Wren,* by John Summerson; *Wren, The Incomparable,* by Martin S. Briggs.

July 1955, vol. 118: 51–53, 54, 'Man, Machine and Motion'; and 'Isokon Flats.'

September 1955, vol. 118: 194, 'Standard Histories,' review of *Art and Architecture in France, 1500–1700,* by Anthony Blunt; *Architecture in Britain,* by John Summerson.

December 1955, vol. 118: 354–361, 'The New Brutalism.'

Art

5 January 1955, p. 3, 'Vision in Motion.'

1 September 1955, p. 3, 'Vehicles of Desire.'

Art News and Review

30 April 1955, vol. 7, no. 7: 3, 'Mexican Architecture.'

19 July 1955, vol. 7, no. 12: 5, 'Lost Innocence.'

12 November 1955, vol. 7, no. 21: 6, 'Sir Herbert's Creed,' review of *Icon and Idea,* by Herbert Read.

26 November 1955, vol. 7, no. 22: 3, 'Art in British Advertising.'

Civiltà delle Machine

November/December 1955, 'Industrial Design and Popular Art' (in Italian, precis in English, p. 81).

Design

July 1955, no. 19: 24–25, 'A Rejoinder.'

The Listener

1 September 1955, vol. 54: 332–333, 'Where Man Meets Machine.'

1956   ### Architects' Journal

10 May 1956, vol. 123: 83–85, 477, '1, 2, 3, 4 . . . Green! Last Saturday's International Trophy
    Race at Silverstone'; and review, 'Two Masters of Our Time.'

12 July 1956, vol. 124: 37–39, 'High, Wide and Homeric.' Film review of *Threshold of Space.*

16 August 1956, vol. 124: 215–217, Not Quite Architecture: 'Not Quite Painting or Sculpture
    Either.'

13 September 1956, vol. 124: 361–363, Not Quite Architecture: 'Farnborough News-Letter:
    Close, Transonic Harmonies.'

4 October 1956, vol. 124: 469–471, Not Quite Architecture: 'Hair-cut, You!'

25 October 1956, vol. 124: 577–579, Not Quite Architecture: 'In Lotus Land.'

15 November 1956, vol. 124: 685–687, Not Quite Architecture: 'Above My Belt.'

27 December 1956, vol. 124: 917–919, Not Quite Architecture: 'Kirk Douglas—R.A.'

Architectural Review

June 1956, vol. 119: 343–344, 'Footnotes to Sant'Elia.'

August 1956, vol. 120: 75–83; 'Ateliers d'artistes: Paris Studio Houses and the Modern
    Movement.'

September 1956, vol. 120: 186–188, 'This Is Tomorrow.'

October 1956, vol. 120: 264, 'Wright Anthology,' review of *An American Architecture,* by Frank
    Lloyd Wright, edited by Edgar Kaufmann.

Ark

Spring 1956, no. 16: 44–47, 'New Look in Cruiserweights.'

Design

June 1956, no. 90: 24–28, 'Things to Come? Architects and Industry Look into the Future.'

July 1956, no. 91: 45, 'Sales Van for Seedsmen.'

The Listener

3 May 1956, vol. 55: 550–551, 'Industrial Design and the Common User.'

24 May 1956, vol. 55: 685, letter, 'Industrial Design and the Common User.'

7 June 1956, vol. 55: 76, letter, 'Industrial Design and the Common User.'

28 June 1956, vol. 55: 895, letter, 'Modern Italian Architecture.'

1957   ### Architects' Journal

17 January 1957, vol. 125: 119–126, 'Futurism and Modern Architecture.'

14 February 1957, vol. 125: 235–237, Not Quite Architecture: 'The Dad-Trap.'

21 March 1957, vol. 125: 415–417, 638, Not Quite Architecture: 'The Caliph'; and 'Architecture
    of the New Establishment,' review of *English Country Houses: Mid-Georgian,* by Christopher
    Hussey.

23 May 1957, vol. 125: 759–761, Not Quite Architecture: 'Spirit of St. Louis.' Film review of *The Spirit of St. Louis.*

1 August 1957, vol. 126: 161–162, Not Quite Architecture: 'Last Sight of an Oldish Master.'

15 August 1957, vol. 126: 233–235, Not Quite Architecture: 'Ungrab that Gondola.'

29 August 1957, vol. 126: 305–307, Not Quite Architecture: 'Pyke's Past,' review of *Nothing Like Science,* by Magnus Pyke.

26 September 1957, vol. 126: 456–461, 'Le Corbusier, 65 to 70,' review of *Oeuvre Complete,* vol. 6: *1952–1957.*

31 October 1957, vol. 126: 645–647, Not Quite Architecture: 'Up the Who? A Plea from the Beet-belt.'

28 November 1957, vol. 126: 802, letter, 'Rushbrooke Housing.'

5 December 1957, vol. 126: 833–835, Not Quite Architecture: 'Drop Dead Drophead.'

26 December 1957, vol. 126: 941–943, Not Quite Architecture: 'Alloway and After.'

Architectural Review

February 1957, vol. 121: 85–88, 'Ornament and Crime: The Decisive Contribution of Adolf Loos.'
April 1957, vol. 121: 243–248, 'The One and the Few: The Rise of Modern Architecture in Finland.'
October 1957, vol. 122: 227–229, 'Mondrian and the Philosophy of Modern Design.'

Builder

11 January 1957, pp. 89–90, 'Futurism and Modern Architecture.'

Design

September 1957, no. 105: 22–23, 'Executive Pilot Plant: New Bata Offices in London.'

RIBA Journal

February 1956, vol. 64: 129–138, 'Futurism and Modern Architecture.' Paper given before the RIBA on 8 January 1957.

1958   ### Architects' Journal

20 February 1958, vol. 127: 269–271, 279–282, Not Quite Architecture: 'Top Pop Boffin'; and review, 'White of Perspective.'
13 March 1958, vol. 127: 377–379, Not Quite Architecture: 'Author! Author! Ph.D.'
17 April 1958, vol. 127: 557–579, Not Quite Architecture: 'Space Fiction and Architecture.'
19 June 1958, vol. 127: 921–923, Not Quite Architecture: 'Don't Be a Square, Bo T.'
26 June 1958, vol. 127: 962, letter, 'Is Banham a Square?'
31 July 1958, vol. 127: 145–147, 'Hoist Yourself Petard Kit.'

Architectural Review

March 1958, vol. 123: 207–208, 210, 'Ideal Interiors'; and 'Half an Idea,' review of *The Idea of Louis Sullivan,* by John Szarkowski.
April 1958, vol. 123: 229–231, 'Tridon.'

The Listener

13 November 1958, vol. 60: 775–776, 'Without Mercy or Metaphor.'

New Statesman

29 March 1958, vol. 54: 404–405, 'The Cool Young Men.'

26 April 1958, vol. 54: 529–530, 'Frames for Big Business.'

7 June 1958, vol. 54: 728–730, 'Eiffelmanship.'

2 June 1958, vol. 54: 804, 'The Jet Jetty.'

19 July 1958, vol. 55: 83–84, 'Plucky Jims.'

16 August 1958, vol. 55: 192–193, 'Machine Aesthetes.'

30 August 1958, vol. 55: 255, 'Questions of Proportion,' review of *Modulor 2,* by Le Corbusier; *The Theory of Proportion in Architecture,* by P. H. Scholfield.

11 October 1958, vol. 55: 488, 'Home of Taste.'

1 November 1958, vol. 55: 589–590, 'Legislate for Life.'

8 November 1958, vol. 55: 628–630, 'The Partisan.'

6 December 1958, vol. 55: 802, 'Unesco House.'

20 December 1958, vol. 55: 882, 'Corb Goes to Liverpool.'

27 December 1958, vol. 55: 913–914, 'The Triumph of Style,' review of *The Functional Tradition in Early Industrial Buildings,* by J. M. Richards; *The Building of TVA,* by John H. Kyle.

1959 *Architects' Journal*

12 February 1959, vol. 129: 247–249, 'Back Home in Nadaville.'

5 March 1959, vol. 129: 362, letter, 'Corb and Banham.'

16 April 1959, vol. 129: 587, 'Lecturing at Ulm.'

23 April 1959, vol. 129: 607–609, 640, Not Quite Architecture: 'Rhein-Ruhr Rundschau'; and 'The Value of History to Students of Architecture.'

18 June 1959, vol. 129: 895–897, Not Quite Architecture: 'Hope Deferred.' Review of *The Golden City,* by Henry Hope Reed, Jr.

27 August 1959, vol. 130: 73–75, Not Quite Architecture: 'The Descent of F3.'

22 October 1959, vol. 130: 373–375, Not Quite Architecture: 'Thus Spake Finagle.'

17 December 1959, vol. 130: 697–699, Not Quite Architecture: 'First Time on Any Stage.'

Architectural Review

February 1959, vol. 125: 87–89, 143, 'The Glass Paradise'; and 'Elementarist,' review of *The Work of G. Rietveld, Architect,* by Theodore M. Brown.

April 1959, vol. 125: 230–235, 'Neoliberty: The Italian Retreat from Modern Architecture.'

August 1959, vol. 126: 77–80, 'Futurist Manifesto.'

Burlington Magazine

September 1959, vol. 101: 354–357, The Literature of Art: 'Architecture from 1800–1950.'

The Listener

21 May 1959, vol. 61: 884–885, 'Cool on the Kuhberg.'

3 December 1959, vol. 62: 974–975, 'Primitives of a Mechanized Art.'

New Statesman

10 January 1959, vol. 57: 41–42, 'Counter-attack in Aberdare.'

7 February 1959, vol. 57: 184–185, 'New Model Parliament.'

14 February 1959, vol. 57: 232, 'Architectural Wit,' review of *Here of All Places*, by Osbert Lancaster.

7 March 1959, vol. 57: 330–331, 'Well-detailed Dane.'

4 April 1959, vol. 57: 474–475, 'Dream Houses.'

18 April 1959, vol. 57: 543–544, 'Master of Freedom.'

16 May 1959, vol. 57: 686, 'Return to Pimlico.'

30 May 1959, vol. 57: 767, 'About Perret,' review of *Concrete: The Vision of a New Architecture*, by Peter Collins.

18 July 1959, vol. 58: 79, 'China Sea Less Salt.'

15 August 1959, vol. 58: 188–190, 'Thought Is Comprehensive.'

19 September 1959, vol. 58: 354, 'On Tair Carn Isaf.'

17 October 1959, vol. 58: 503–504, 'The Small Revolution.'

28 November 1959, vol. 58: 770, 'From AA to Zucalli,' review of *Everyman's Concise Encyclopaedia of Architecture*, by Martin S. Briggs.

5 December 1959, vol. 58: 793–794, 'The Double-Headed Monster.'

12 December 1959, vol. 58: 834–836, 'The Centre of London's Common Life.'

1960 *Architects' Journal*

7 January 1960, vol. 131: 1–3, Not Quite Architecture: 'So This Is FJ?'

14 January 1960, vol. 131: 37–39, Not Quite Architecture: 'Eighteen Thousand Marbleheads?'

7 April 1960, vol. 131: 527–529, Not Quite Architecture: 'I'd Crawl a Mile for . . . Playboy.'

5 May 1960, vol. 131: 671–673, Not Quite Architecture: 'The Medium.'

4 August 1960, vol. 132: 161–163, Not Quite Architecture: 'Cose Aint What They Use T'Essere.'

22 September 1960, vol. 132: 413–415, Not Quite Architecture: 'Fold, Like the Arab.'

27 October 1960, vol. 132: 593–595, Not Quite Architecture: 'Too Brief Chronicle.'

8 December 1960, vol. 132: 809–811, Not Quite Architecture: 'WORLD, the; book to change, a.'

Architectural Association Journal

February 1960, vol. 75, no. 839: 146–156, 'Vitruvius Go Home!'

Architectural Review

January 1960, vol. 127: 9–10, 'Architecture after 1960.'

February 1960, vol. 127: 93–100, '1960—Stocktaking of the Impact of Traditions and Technology on Architecture Today.'

March 1960, vol. 127: 183–190, 'The Science Side.'

April 1960, vol. 127: 253–260, 'The Future of Universal Man Symposium.'

May 1960, vol. 127: 325–332, 'History under Revision.'

June 1960, vol. 127: 373–375, 381–388, 'Perret Ascendancy'; and 'Propositions: The Editors, J. M. Richards, Nikolaus Pevsner, Hugh Casson, and H. de C. Hastings, Review the Trend of the Series.'

Arts

December 1960, vol. 35: 33–39, 'Futurism for Keeps.'

Design

June 1960, no. 138: 55, 'Persuading Image: A Symposium, A World Made Safe for Designers.'

Domus

December 1960, vol. 373: 9–10, 'Casa, Scuola, Palazzo dell'Arte.'

Industrial Design

March 1960, vol. 7: 45–58, Epitaph 'Machine Esthetic.'

The Listener

18 August 1960, vol. 64: 253–255, 'Schools for Today—Homes of Yesterday.'
25 August 1960, vol. 64: 289–290, 'A Train that Belongs to the Sixties.'
1 September 1960, vol. 64: 338–340, 'Milan: The Polemical Skyline.'

New Statesman

23 January 1960, vol. 59: 98–100, 'Cluster at Bethnal Green.'
20 February 1960, vol. 59: 260, 'Drayneflete-on-Cam,' review of *Inventory of the City of Cam-bridge,* HMSO for the Royal Commission on Historical Monuments.
27 February 1960, vol. 59: 288–289, 'Pocket Piazza.'
5 March 1960, vol. 59: 331–332, 'Alienation of Parts.'
30 April 1960, vol. 59: 639, 'Ears and Eyes,' review of *Experiencing Architecture,* by Steen Eiler.
28 May 1960, vol. 59: 784–786, 'The Road to Ubiquopolis.'
23 July 1960, vol. 60: 116–118, 'The Church Stimulant.'
29 August 1960, vol. 60: 240, 'Venezia-Incurabili 401.'
29 October 1960, vol. 60: 644–646, 'The End of Insolence.'
5 November 1960, vol. 60: 695, 'St. Catherine's College, Oxford.'
10 December 1960, vol. 60: 918–920, 'Monument with Frills.'
24 December 1960, vol. 60: 1004–1005, 'House and Land.'
31 December 1960, vol. 60: 1044, 'The Form-Givers,' review of *The Master Builders,* by Peter Blake.

1961   *Architects' Journal*

16 February 1961, vol. 133: 233–235, Not Quite Architecture: 'A Genuine Shambles.'
9 March 1961, vol. 133: 347, letter, 'Architecture on TV.'
23 March 1961, vol. 133: 413–415, Not Quite Architecture: 'A Model Essay upon the Varieties of Anticipation as Exemplified in the Works of Fred Hoyle, Genius.'
4 May 1961, vol. 133: 629–631, Not Quite Architecture: 'Counter-Attack, N.Y.'
25 May 1961, vol. 133: 753–755, Not Quite Architecture: '"Loco" Means Mad.'
26 July 1961, vol. 133: 109–111, Not Quite Architecture: 'On First Looking into Warshawsky.'

23 August 1961, vol. 134: 253–255, Not Quite Architecture: 'The Urbanistic Pitch.'
20 September 1961, vol. 134: 397–399, Not Quite Architecture: 'Not Even One More Time.'
29 November 1961, vol. 134: 1020–1022, Not Quite Architecture: 'Night, Mrs Jagbag.'

Architectural Forum

June 1961, vol. 114: 87, 'Architecture—Fitting and Befitting.'

Architectural Review

March 1961, vol. 129: 194–200, 'Criticism: Pirelli Building, Milan, Ponti, Nervi and Assoc., Architects.'
July 1961, vol. 130: 43–48, 'Design by Choice: 1951–1961.'
November 1961, vol. 130: 303–305, 'Urbanism USA.'
December 1961, vol. 130: 402–410, 'Park Hill Housing, Sheffield.'

Arquitectura (Madrid)

February 1961, vol. 3: 2–17, 'Balance 1960' (in Spanish).

Arts

September 1961, vol. 35: 65–66, review of Walter Gropius, by James Marston Fitch.

Builder

17 February 1961, pp. 321–323, 'A History of the Immediate Future.' Extracts from a lecture given at RIBA on 7 February 1961.

The Listener

23 February 1961, vol. 65: 347–349, 'History of the Immediate Future.'
9 March 1961, vol. 65: 437–438, letter, 'School Building in Britain.'

New Statesman

6 January 1961, vol. 61: 26–27, 'A Gong for the Welfare State.'
27 January 1961, vol. 61: 151–152, 'H.M. Fashion House.'
10 February 1961, vol. 61: 228, 'Furnex 61.'
3 March 1961, vol. 61: 356, 'Ravished Groves of Academe.'
24 March 1961, vol. 61: 482, 'Ego-Image Adjuster.'
7 April 1961, vol. 61: 556–557, 'The Last of the Goths.'
19 May 1961, vol. 61: 806, 'Handsome Doesn't.'
2 June 1961, vol. 61: 889, 'Black and White Magazine Show.'
30 June 1961, vol. 61: 1056, 'The Vertical Community.'
21 July 1961, vol. 62: 95, 'Rude Barn.'
28 July 1961, vol. 62: 126, 'Snaps,' review of Diaries 1922–1939, by Cecil Beaton.
1 September 1961, vol. 62: 281–282, 'Transistorama.'
8 September 1961, vol. 62: 317–318, 'Apropos the Smithsons.'

17 November 1961, vol. 62: 755–756, 'The Cult.'

8 December 1961, vol. 62: 896, 'Homage to Sir Edward Robertson.'

22 December 1961, vol. 62: 965, 'Europe on the Coffee Table,' review of *Great Houses of Europe,* edited by Sacheverell Sitwell; *Art and Architecture in Europe,* by Antonin Matejcek; *Regency Furniture: 1800 to 1830,* by Clifford Musgrave; *The Architecture of Sir John Soane,* by Dorothy Stroud.

RIBA Journal

May 1961, vol. 68: 252–260, 269, 'History of the Immediate Future.' Paper given before RIBA on 7 February 1961.

1962   ### Architects' Journal

24 January 1962, vol. 135: 169, letter, 'Dog Returns to Own Doggerel.'

31 January 1962, vol. 135: 219–221, Not Quite Architecture: 'Joke Tap.'

14 February 1962, vol. 135: 343, letter, 'Short on Doggerel.'

7 March 1962, vol. 135: 497–499, Not Quite Architecture: 'Aimez-vous Marienbad?'

27 June 1962, vol. 135: 1435–1437, Not Quite Architecture: 'Rapid Transit Pioneers.'

1 August 1962, vol. 136: 251–253, 'Big Doug, Small Piece.'

5 September 1962, vol. 136: 571–573, 'Festival Site to Let.'

10 October 1962, vol. 136: 841–843, Not Quite Architecture: 'A Thought for Your Pfennig.'

14 November 1962, vol. 136: 1091–1093, 'The Mysterious Affair of the Baronet's Reputation.'

Architectural Forum

August 1962, vol. 117: 118–119, 'Coventry Cathedral—Strictly "Trad, Dad".'

December 1962, vol. 117: 110–111, 'Report on the Design of Morse and Stiles Dormitories for Yale University.'

Architectural Review

January 1962, vol. 131: 7, 'Premature Monument,' review of *CIAM '59 in Otterlo,* compiled by Oscar Newman.

February 1962, vol. 131: 97–99, On Trial 1: 'The Situation: What Architecture of Technology?'

March 1962, vol. 131: 203–206, On Trial 2: 'Louis Kahn: The Buttery-Hatch Aesthetic.'

April 1962, vol. 131: 232–233, 249–252, 'What Is America?,' review of *Architecture and the Aesthetics of Plenty,* by James Martson Fitch; and On Trial 3: 'Jean Prouve: The Thin, Bent Detail.'

May 1962, vol. 131: 349–352, On Trial 4: 'Clasp: Ill-Met by Clipjoint.'

July 1962, vol. 132: 43–46, On Trial 5: 'The Spec-Builders: Towards a Pop Architecture.'

August 1962, vol. 132: 124–128, 134–135, On Trial 6: 'Mies van der Rohe: Almost Nothing Is Too Much Seattle World's Fair.'

October 1962, vol. 132: 251–260, 'Obsolescent Airport.'

Arts

February 1962, vol. 36: 70–73, 'The Fear of Eero's Mania.'

Industrial Design

April 1962, vol. 9: 48–49, 'The Unspeakable KG Factor.'

The Listener

4 January 1962, vol. 67: 15–16, 'On Criticizing Architecture.'
19 April 1962, vol. 67: 679–680, 'Painters of the Bauhaus.'
15 November 1962, vol. 68: 805–806, 'Come over to Paddo.'

New Statesman

12 January 1962, vol. 63: 61–62, 'Seed of Daedalus.'
9 February 1962, vol. 63: 200–201, 'Coronation Street, Hoggartsborough.'
23 February 1962, vol. 63: 275–276, 'Leeds Leading?'
23 March 1962, vol. 63: 425, 'Coffin-nails in Handy Packs.'
6 April 1962, vol. 63: 492, 'Master of Taliesin,' review of *Frank Lloyd Wright,* by Finis Farr.
4 May 1962, vol. 63: 655, 'Carbonorific.'
25 May 1962, vol. 63: 768–769, 'Coventry Cathedral.'
29 June 1962, vol. 63: 944, 'Kidder Smith's Conspectus,' review of *The New Architecture of Europe,* by G. E. Kidder Smith.
13 July 1962, vol. 64: 45–55, 'Morse and Stiles.'
3 August 1962, vol. 64: 152, 'Old Number One.'
24 August 1962, vol. 64: 233, 'The First Prodigy,' review of *The Quest for Nonsuch,* by John Dent.
28 September 1962, vol. 64: 427, 'England His England.'
28 October 1962, vol. 64: 590, 'Sons of the Cardinal.'
2 November 1962, vol. 64: 630–631, 'Underdone Underpass.'
23 November 1962, vol. 64: 745–746, 'The Trouble with Eero,' review of *Eero Saarinen on His Work,* edited by Aline Saarinen; *Saarinen,* by Allen Temko.
7 December 1962, vol. 64: 842–843, 'Kent and Capability.'
14 December 1962, vol. 64: 878, 'On the Gore.'

Program

Spring 1962, pp. 57–64, 'The Environmentalist.'

1963 ### Architects' Journal

9 January 1963, vol. 137: 57–59, Not Quite Architecture: 'How to Sneer at Cripples for Fun and Profit.'
6 February 1963, vol. 137: 275–277, Not Quite Architecture: 'Cyanide and After.'
6 March 1963, vol. 137: 499–500, 'British Railways: Are Beeching's Priorities Right?'
17 April 1963, vol. 137: 785–787, Not Quite Architecture: 'Remove Corb-Coloured Spectacles.'
22 May 1963, vol. 137: 1051–1053, Not Quite Architecture: 'Think Kieft, Think Fast.'
3 July 1963, vol. 138: 1–3, Not Quite Architecture: 'The Urban Scene—A Call for Action.'
14 August 1963, vol. 138: 301–303, Not Quite Architecture: 'Don't just stand there trembling . . .'
25 September 1963, vol. 138: 623–625, Not Quite Architecture: 'The Chairs.'
6 November 1963, vol. 138: 927–929, Not Quite Architecture: 'Back in the Saddle.'

Architectural Review

May 1963, vol. 133: 312–316, 'Europe—The Relevant Continent.' *AR Euromart,* special issue edited by R. Banham.

July 1963, vol. 134: 7, 'The Starting Place of Sprawl,' review of *Street Car Suburbs,* by Sam B. Warner.

Arts

October 1963, vol. 38: 66–69, 'Dymaxicrat.'

Design

September 1963, no. 177: 58–59, 'At Aspen—On the American Image Abroad.'

Industrial Design

August 1963, vol. 10: 76–78, 'Home Thoughts from Abroad.'

The Listener

31 January 1963, vol. 69: 200–202, 'The Stones of New York.'

27 June 1963, vol. 69: 1080–1081, 'First Master the Mass Media.'

Motif

1963, vol. 10: 3–13, 'Who Is This "Pop"?'

New Statesman

8 March 1963, vol. 65: 350–351, 'The Reputation of William Morris.'

12 April 1963, vol. 65: 528–530, 'The Embalmed City.'

3 May 1963, vol. 65: 687, 'Department of Visual Uproar.'

14 May 1963, vol. 65: 805, 'Six-Legged Dragon.'

12 July 1963, vol. 66: 51, 'Thunderbox.'

2 August 1963, vol. 66: 145, 'The Conformist Union,' review of *Fantastic Architecture,* by Ulrich Conrads and Hans Sperlich, translated, edited, and expanded by Christine Collins and George Collins; *SOM: Architecture of Skidmore, Owings and Merrill, 1950–1962,* with introduction by Henry Russell Hitchcock, text by Ernst Danz.

16 August 1963, vol. 66: 203–204, 'Shalimar in Walden.'

11 October 1963, vol. 66: 501–502, '(Think): Think!'

1 November 1963, vol. 66: 626, 'A Grid on Two Farthings.'

8 November 1963, vol. 66: 657, 'Harvesting,' review of *Great Gardens,* by Peter Coats; *Architecture: Frank Lloyd Wright,* by Jovanna Lloyd Wright; *World Architecture,* edited by Trewin Copplestone; *The Architecture of England,* by Doreen Yarwood; *The Art of the West,* vols. I and II: *Romanesque and Gothic,* by Henri Focillion; *Gothic Architecture,* by Paul Frankl.

15 November 1963, vol. 66: 714–715, 'No Dave.'

27 December 1963, vol. 66: 949, 'FO.'

The Observer Weekend Review

17 November 1963, p. 21, 'A Flourish of Symbols.'

1964 ### American Institute of Architects' Journal

November 1964, vol. 42: 37–39, 'History, Theory and Criticism: The 1964 AIA ACSA Teacher Seminar at Cranbook.'

Architects' Journal

8 January 1964, vol. 139: 57–59, Not Quite Architecture: 'Multijoke.'
3 January 1964, vol. 139: 1–3, Not Quite Architecture: 'Slum 2000.'
19 February 1964, vol. 139: 393–395, Not Quite Architecture: 'Norway on the Raw: 1.'
26 February 1964, vol. 139: 447–449, Not Quite Architecture: 'Norway on the Raw: 2.'
29 April 1964, vol. 139: 949–951, Not Quite Architecture: 'Dr. Doomsday.'
10 June 1964, vol. 139: 1283–1285, Not Quite Architecture: 'Farewell Old Column.'
2 December 1964, vol. 140: 1285–1287, Not Quite Architecture: 'Colonial thru' Greek.'

Architectural Forum

August–September 1964, vol. 119: 118–125, 'The Word in Britain: "Character".'

Architectural Review

March 1964, vol. 135: 163, 'Living in Europe,' review of *Une Tradition europeene dans l'habitation,* by Gianni Pirrone.
June 1964, vol. 135: 395, 'Industrial Patronage,' review of *Figini e Pollini,* by Cesare Blast.
August 1964, vol. 136: 85, 102–108, 'Historic Documents,' review of *Programme und Manifeste zur Architektur des 20 Jahrhunderts,* edited by Ulrich Conrads; and 'Speed and the Citizen: Urban Rapid Transit and the Future Cities.'
September 1964, vol. 136: 174–195, 'Criticism: St. Catherine's College, Oxford, and Churchill College, Cambridge.'

Ark

September 1964, no. 36: 3–9, 'Conversation on Design Education.'

Arts

October 1964, vol. 39: 44–47, 'Condit's Chicago.'

Design

January 1964, no. 181: 59, letter, 'Easy Rider.'

Industrial Design

August 1964, vol. 11: 60–61, 'Aspen Papers.'

The Listener

27 August 1964, vol. 72: 300–302, 'A Designers' Pugwash?'

Living Arts

1964, no. 3: 91–97, 'The Atavism of the Short-Distance Mini-Cyclist.'

New Statesman

7 February 1964, vol. 67: 216, 'Earth-Movers,' review of *The Master Builders,* by Robert Middle-
    mas; *James Lithgow, Master of Work,* by J. M. Reid.
14 February 1964, vol. 67: 261, 'The Style for the Job.'
6 March 1964, vol. 67: 372–373, 'How I Learnt to Live with the Norwich Union.'
10 April 1964, vol. 67: 574, 'The Rule of Lore.'
15 May 1964, vol. 67: 769–770, 'On the Road on the Scene,' review of *An Architectural Journey
    in Japan,* by J. M. Richards; *The Italian Townscape,* by Ivor De Wolfe; *The Highway and the City,*
    by Lewis Mumford.
22 May 1964, vol. 67: 819–820, 'At Swiss.'
5 June 1964, vol. 67: 885, 'Let Them Eat Steak.'
26 June 1964, vol. 67: 1006, 'All the Fun of the Flop.'
17 July 1964, vol. 68: 97–98, 'Brands Hatch.'
7 August 1964, vol. 68: 191–192, 'Peoples' Palaces.'
18 September 1964, vol. 68: 412, 'Tall Classic.'
2 October 1964, vol. 68: 502–503, 'Gesamptflanzweik,' review of *The Tropical Gardens of Burle
    Marx,* by P. M. Bardi; *The English Garden,* by Edward Hyams.
6 November 1964, vol. 68: 708–710, 'Clean Paul.'
4 December 1964, vol. 68: 889, 'Hot Houses.'

1965   ***Architects' Journal***

28 April 1965, vol. 141: 994–996, 'BOAC at JFK.'

Architectural Design

November 1965, vol. 35: 534–535, 'A Clip-on Architecture.' Reprint from *Design Quarterly,*
    no. 63, 1963, 3–30.

Architectural Review

September 1965, vol. 138: 186, 'Aviary, London Zoological Gardens.'

Art in America

April 1965, vol. 53: 70–79, 'A Home Is Not a House.'

Bartlett Society Transactions

1965/1966, vol. 4: 27–46, 'A Marginal Redefinition of Modern.'

Design Quarterly

1965, no. 63, 'A Clip-on Architecture.'

Industrial Design

August 1965, vol. 12: 38–41, 'Chill Dawn in Colorado.'
September 1965, vol. 12: 48–59, 'The Great Gizmo.'

Landscape

Winter 1965, vol. 15, no. 2: 4–6, 'Unrecognized American Architecture: The Missing Motel.'

The Listener

5 August 1965, vol. 74: 191–194, 'The Missing Motel.'

New Society

13 May 1965, vol. 5, no. 137: 29, 'The Man Who Watched the Arts Go By,' review of *The Irresponsible Arts,* by William Snaith.

19 August 1965, vol. 6, no. 151: 25–26, 'Kandy Kulture Kiterone,' review of *Kandy Kulture Kiterone,* by Tom Wolfe.

2 September 1965, vol. 6, no. 153, 'Nobly Savage Non-Architects,' review of *Architecture without Architects,* by Bernard Rudofsky.

9 September 1965, vol. 6, no. 154: 26–27, Arts in Society: 'Fiscal pursuivant, proceed.'

7 October 1965, vol. 6, no. 158: 28, Arts in Society: 'Homo Serendipitans.'

21 October 1965, vol. 6, no. 160: 26–27, 'A Particularly Soft English Hardback,' review of *Private View,* by Bryan Robertson, John Russell, and Lord Snowdon.

4 November 1965, vol. 6, no. 162: 26–27, Arts in Society: 'Corbolatry at County Hall.'

11 November 1965, vol. 6, no. 163: 34, letter, 'Models for Whom?'

16 December 1965, vol. 6, no. 168: 25, 'Pop and the Body Critical,' review of *Pop as Art,* by Mario Amaya; *Pop Art,* by John Rublowsky; *Nuovi Riti, Nuovi Miti,* by Gillo Dorfles.

New Statesman

8 January 1965, vol. 69: 49, 'Boss Span.'
15 January 1965, vol. 69: 83–84, 'Crowther's Acropolis.'
12 February 1965, vol. 69: 255–256, 'Extreme Environment.'
12 March 1965, vol. 69: 411, 'Zoo à la Mode.'
16 April 1965, vol. 69: 620, 'Liverpool Leading,' review of *Tyneside Classical,* by Lyall Wilkes and Gordon Dodds; *Seaport,* by Quentin Hughes.
23 April 1965, vol. 69: 656, 'Form Fuddles Function.'
28 May 1965, vol. 69: 858–859, 'La Kermesse Mecanique.'
25 June 1965, vol. 69: 1020, 'Missing Persons.'
30 July 1965, vol. 70: 145–146, 'Replanning Britain—2: New Look for Westminster.'
20 August 1965, vol. 70: 261, 'Carry on Gatters!'

Ulm: Zeitschrift der Hochschule für Gestaltung

December 1965, nos. 14–16: 2–7, 'Servants of the Public Will.'

1966 *American Institute of Architects' Journal*

September 1966, vol. 46: 64, 'Technology, A Boon and a Danger: Commentary and Discussion on the Opening Address by I. I. Rabi.'

Architects' Journal

2 February 1966, vol. 143: 317–319, Not Quite Architecture: 'Coronado: Or, Don't Smoke in Bed.'
31 August 1966, vol. 144: 503–505, Not Quite Architecture: 'Old Futuropolis.'
21 December 1966, vol. 144: 1527–1529, Not Quite Architecture: 'Unlovable at Any Speed.'

Architectural Review

March 1966, vol. 139: 173, 'Modern Mecca,' review of *Chicago's Famous Buildings,* edited by Arthur Siegel.
July 1966, vol. 140: 6–7, 59–62, 'Italian Idea,' review of *L'idea di Architettura,* by Renato de Fusco; and 'Motherwell and Others.'
August 1966, vol. 140: 97–108, 'The Last Formgiver.'
November 1966, vol. 140: 319, 'Honest Guide,' review of *A Guide to the Architecture of Washington, D.C.*

Art in America

September 1966, vol. 54: 76–79, 'Notes toward a Definition of U.S. Automobile Painting as a Significant Branch of Mobile Modern Heraldry.'

Arts and Architecture

September 1966, vol. 83: 26–30, 'Frank Lloyd Wright as Environmentalist.'

New Society

6 January 1966, vol. 7, no. 171: 22, Arts in Society: 'Architecture in Freedomland.'
20 January 1966, vol. 7, no. 173: 29, 'The Men Who Built Chicago,' review of *Culture and Democracy,* by Hugh Dalziel Duncan.
3 February 1966, vol. 7, no. 175: 21–22, U.S. Report: 'Grudge Racing Tonite.'
3 March 1966, vol. 7, no. 179: 21, Arts in Society: 'Zoom Wave Hits Architecture.'
17 March 1966, vol. 7, no. 181: 24–25, 'In—Architecture Illustrated,' review of *British Buildings, 1960–1964,* by Douglas Stephen, Kenneth Frampton, and Michael Carapetian.
24 March 1966, vol. 7, no. 182: 20–21, Arts in Society: 'The Gadget People.'
28 April 1966, vol. 7, no. 187: 19–20, Arts in Society: 'An Added Modern Pleasantness.'
26 May 1966, vol. 7, no. 191: 21, Arts in Society: 'Lair of Soane.'
16 June 1966, vol. 7, no. 194: 28, 'Growing Up in Architecture,' review of *Educreation,* by Paul Ritter.
30 June 1966, vol. 7, no. 196: 22, 'No More Plain Wrappers.'

14 July 1966, vol. 8, no. 198: 65, 'Accolades for a One-Answer Man,' review of *Aesthetics and Technology in Building,* by Pier Luigi Nervi, translated by Robert Einaudi.

4 August 1966, vol. 8, no. 201: 198–199, World Report: 'Brown Angels a Go-Go.'

18 August 1966, vol. 8, no. 271: 271, Arts in Society: 'Aesthetics of the Yellow Pages.'

29 September 1966, vol. 8, no. 209: 503–504, 'Looking and Seeing Cross-eyed,' review of *Looking and Seeing,* 1: *Pattern and Shape;* 2: *The Development of Shape;* 3: *The Shapes We Need;* 4: *The Shape of Towns,* by Kurt Rowland.

6 October 1966, vol. 8, no. 210: 546–547, Arts in Society: 'The Outhouses of Academe.'

13 October 1966, vol. 8, no. 211: 588, 'The Urban Transport Expert Problem,' review of *New Movement in Cities,* by Brian Richards.

3 November 1966, vol. 8, no. 214: 689, Arts in Society: 'Wuthering Archaeology.'

24 November 1966, vol. 8, no. 217: 805, 'Facts in Suspension,' review of *Victorian Architecture,* by Robert Furneaux Jordan.

1 December 1966, vol. 8, no. 218: 838–839, Arts in Society: 'Vinyl Deviations.'

22 December 1966, vol. 8, no. 221: 951, Arts in Society: 'Ghoultide Greetings.'

Print

September 1966, vol. 20: 40, 'Aspen, Quote, Unquote.'

1967 *Architectural Design*

April 1967, vol. 37: 174–177, 'Frank Lloyd Wright as Environmentalist.' Published courtesy of *Arts and Architecture.*

June 1967, vol. 37: 351–352, 'All that Glitters Is Not Stainless,' adapted from an address given at the Aspen Conference, Summer 1966, and review of *Architecture: Action and Plan,* by Peter Cook.

December 1967, vol. 37: 578–579, 'Rudolph Schindler: Pioneering without Tears.'

Architectural Review

May 1967, vol. 141: 331–335, 'Towards a Million-Volt Light and Sound Culture.'

Bauen and Wohnen

May 1967, vol. 22, no. 5: 166–173, 'Clip-on "Architektur" ' (in German).

Casabella

November 1967, no. 320: 48–51, 'L'Uomo all'Expo' (in Italian).

Ford Times

October 1966, vol. 44, no. 10: 10–12, 'Cumbernauld: Our First Successful Motor Town.'

Interior Design

May 1967, 'The Electric Environment.'

The Listener

9 February 1967, vol. 77: 196–197, 'The Architecture Below.'
9 March 1967, vol. 77: 317–318, 'The Fourth Monument.'
7 September 1967, vol. 78: 292–293, 'Beyond Expo 67.'

New Society

26 January 1967, vol. 9, no. 226: 135, Arts in Society: 'Erno Meets the Munsters.'
23 February 1967, vol. 9, no. 230: 284, Arts in Society: 'Message Is a Monkee.'
23 March 1967, vol. 9, no. 234: 436, World Report: 'Norse, but Not Coarse.'
20 April 1967, vol. 9, no. 238: 566–568, 'Chairs as Art.'
4 May 1967, vol. 9, no. 240: 645, Transport Now: 'Anti-technology.'
1 June 1967, vol. 9, no. 244: 811–813, Arts in Society: 'L'Homme a L'Expo.'
29 June 1967, vol. 9, no. 248: 959, Arts in Society: 'Shades of Summer.'
17 August 1967, vol. 10, no. 255: 231–232, Arts in Society: 'Flatscape with Containers.'
7 September 1967, vol. 10, no. 258: 338, letter, 'Flatscape with Containers.'
14 September 1967, vol. 10, no. 259: 353–355, 'Le Corbusier—Gurus of Our Time.'
28 September 1967, vol. 10, no. 261: 438, Arts in Society: 'On a distant prospect . . .'
12 October 1967, vol. 10, no. 263: 524, Arts in Society: 'Eheu, Carnabia.'
2 November 1967, vol. 10, no. 266: 636–637, Arts in Society: 'Horse of a Different Colour.'
7 December 1967, vol. 10, no. 271: 827–828, Arts in Society: 'Vitruvius over Manhattan.'
14 December 1967, vol. 10, no. 272: 869, 'Design for Living,' review of *Private Houses: An International Survey,* by Werner Weidert.

New York Review

12 October 1967, pp. 30–33, 'This Property Is Condemned,' review of *Modern Architecture and Expressionism,* by Dennis Sharp; *Architects on Architecture,* by Paul Heyer.

Studio International

June 1967, vol. 173, no. 890: 280–282, 'Future of Art from the Other Side.'

1968   *Architects' Journal*

11 December 1968, vol. 148: 1378–1379, 'Pevsner De Luxe Model,' review of *Studies in Art, Architecture and Design,* by Nikolaus Pevsner.

Architectural Design

November 1968, vol. 38: 310–311, 'Flatscape with Containers.' Originally appeared in *New Society,* 17 August 1966.

Architectural Review

October 1968, vol. 144: 257–260, 'Dark Satanic Century.' Excerpt from *The Architecture of the Well-Tempered Environment.*
November 1968, vol. 144: 328–341, 'History Faculty, Cambridge.'

Design

February 1968, no. 230: 23–24, 'Reyner Banham's Grand Festival.'
November 1968, no. 239: 50–55, 'Environment of the Machine Aesthetic.' Chapter from *The Architecture of the Well-Tempered Environment.*

Ford Times

July 1968, vol. 45, no. 5: 16–20, 'On Secret Service.'

The Guardian

4 November 1968, p. 7, 'Freewheeling the LA Way.'

The Listener

22 August 1968, vol. 80: 235–236, 'Encounter with Sunset Boulevard.'
29 August 1968, vol. 80: 267–268, 'Roadscape with Rusting Rails.'
5 September 1968, vol. 80: 296–298, 'Beverly Hills, Too, Is a Ghetto.'
12 September 1968, vol. 80: 330–331, 'The Art of Doing Your Thing.'
26 September 1968, vol. 80: 390–392, 'The Bauhaus Gospel.'

New Society

7 March 1968, vol. 11, no. 284: 348–349, World Report: 'Not a Young-Mobile.'
28 March 1968, vol. 11, no. 287: 446–447, 'Somewhere Totally Else.'
18 April 1968, vol. 11, no. 290: 569–570, Arts in Society: 'Monumental Wind-Bags.'
23 May 1968, vol. 11, no. 295: 762–763, Arts in Society: 'Disservice Areas.'
6 June 1968, vol. 11, no. 297: 846, 'Flower Power Mark 1,' review of *The Sources of Modern Architecture and Design,* by Nikolaus Pevsner.
1 August 1968, vol. 12, no. 305: 164, Out of the Way: 'College of Aspen '68.'
22 August 1968, vol. 12, no. 308: 275–276, Arts in Society: 'Cap'n Kustow's Toolshed.'
5 September 1968, vol. 12, no. 310: 343–344, Arts in Society: 'Bus-Pop.'
26 September 1968, vol. 12, no. 313: 454–455, Arts in Society: 'Cambridge—Mark II.'
31 October 1968, vol. 12, no. 318: 629–630, 'Triumph of Software.'
5 December 1968, vol. 12, no. 323: 846–847, Arts in Society: 'Pub-Shape and Landlubber-Fashion.'
12 December 1968, vol. 12, no. 324: 883–884, Arts in Society: 'First Bus to Psychedelia.'

Zodiac

1968, no. 18: 43–44, 'English Brutalism—Selection of Writings.'

1969 ### Architects' Journal

16 April 1969, vol. 149: 1028–1029, News: 'RIBA Discourse, Irony on Main Street.'

Architectural Design

January 1969, vol. 39: 45–48, 'A Home Is Not a House.' Reprint from *Art in America,* April 1965.

Architecture in Canada

December 1969, vol. 46: 11, 'Bauhaus Era: Architecture between Art and Technology.'

Ark

1969, vol. 44 (Summer): 2–11, 'Softer Hardware.'

Ford Times

July 1969, vol. 46, no. 7: 35–40, 'Involvement Is the Key.'

New Society

9 January 1969, vol. 13, no. 328: 41–42, 'Natural Gasworks.'

20 March 1969, vol. 13, no. 338: 435–443, 'Non-Plan: An Experiment in Freedom'; and in collaboration with Paul Barker, Peter Hall, and Cedric Price, 'Spontaneity and Space'; and Arts in Society: 'Californian Livery.'

17 April 1969, vol. 13, no. 342: 599–600, 'Out of the Way: Beyond Sir's Ken.'

8 May 1969, vol. 13, no. 345: 717–718, Arts in Society: 'Representations in Protest.'

19 June 1969, vol. 13, no. 351: 961–962, Arts in Society: 'On Victorian Lines.'

10 July 1969, vol. 14, no. 354: 63, Arts in Society: 'The Gutenberg Backlash.'

14 August 1969, vol. 14, no. 359: 256–257, Arts in Society: 'Folie de grandeur.'

28 August 1969, vol. 14, no. 361: 327–328, Arts in Society: 'Dunesaga.'

18 September 1969, vol. 14, no. 364: 446, Arts in Society: 'Unavoidable Options.'

6 November 1969, vol. 14, no. 371: 734–735, Arts in Society: 'Joe Levy's Contemporary City.'

18 December 1969, vol. 14, no. 377: 986–987, Arts in Society: 'The Last Professional.'

RIBA Journal

December 1969, vol. 76: 512–519, 'Wilderness Years of Frank Lloyd Wright.'

1970 ### Architects' Journal

3 June 1970, vol. 151: 1370, 'Scully Sees It Whole,' review of *American Architecture and Urbanism,* by Vincent Scully.

29 July 1970, vol. 152: 260, 'Brown Studies,' review of *The Necessary Monument,* by Theo Crosby.

2 September 1970, vol. 152: 506–509, 'Monaco Underground.'

Building Design

17 April 1970, no. 7: 8, 'HEVAC: Shop Window for Better Comfort Control.'

Ford Times

June 1970, no. 16: 13, 'New Skills.'

New Society

15 January 1970, vol. 15, no. 381: 100–101, Arts in Society: 'Household Godjets.'

12 February 1970, vol. 15, no. 385: 273–274, 'The Thoughts of Global Man,' review of *The Buckminster Fuller Reader,* by James Meller.

26 March 1970, vol. 15, no. 391: 531–532, 'Heroic Age,' review of *Victorian Engineering,* by L. T. C. Rolt.

2 April 1970, vol. 15, no. 392: 566–567, Arts in Society: 'Journals to the Trade.'

30 April 1970, vol. 15, no. 396: 739, Arts in Society: 'In the Van of Progress.'

14 May 1970, vol. 15, no. 398: 835–836, 'In the Stacks,' review of *Libraries: Architecture and Equipment,* by Michael Brawne.

28 May 1970, vol. 15, no. 400: 926–927, Arts in Society: 'Power of Trent and Aire.'

18 June 1970, vol. 15, no. 403: 1068, 'Stand: Sing Me to the White House.'

9 July 1970, vol. 16, no. 406: 77, Arts in Society: 'The Crisp at the Crossroads.'

13 August 1970, vol. 16, no. 411: 294, Arts in Society: 'A Hole in the Ground.'

27 August 1970, vol. 16, no. 413: 377, 'Listen: Bucky at Work,' review of *Utopia or Oblivion,* by R. Buckminster Fuller.

1 October 1970, vol. 16, no. 418: 592–593, Arts in Society: 'Put Out More Towers.'

8 October 1970, vol. 16, no. 419: 640, 'El Appleseedski,' review of *Russia: An Architecture for World Revolution,* by El Lissitsky, translated by Eric Dluhosch.

5 November 1970, vol. 16, no. 423: 827–828, 832–833, Arts in Society: 'Sailflyer's Rest'; and 'Pere Corbu and Tange San,' review of *Oeuvre Complete,* vol. 8, by Le Corbusier; *Kenzo Tange, 1946–69,* edited by Udo Kultermann.

26 November 1970, vol. 16, no. 426: 958–959, Arts in Society: 'Nature Morte Lives!'

1971 *Architects' Journal*

18 August 1971, vol. 154: 373, 'Old Time Religion,' review of *The Pentagon of Power,* by Lewis Mumford.

Architectural Design

April 1971, vol. 41: 227–230, 'LA: The Structure Behind the Scene.'

June 1971, vol. 41: 350–352, 'A & PhoT: Big Sig in the Roman Underground,' review of *Discussion of Architecture and the Phenomena of Transition,* by Sigfried Giedion.

Architectural Forum

July/August 1971, vol. 135: 10, review of *Beyond Habitat,* by Moshe Safdie.

Architectural Review

July 1971, vol. 150: 64, Obituary: 'Sibyl Moholy-Nagy.'

Architettura

16 March 1971, p. 769, 'Architettura della prima eta della macchina' (in Italian).

New Society

7 January 1971, vol. 17, no. 432: 26–27, 'Play Power,' review of *Programmes and Manifestos on Twentieth-Century Architecture,* edited by Ulrich Conrads.

14 January 1971, vol. 17, no. 433: 66–67, Arts in Society: 'The Historian on the Pier.'

4 February 1971, vol. 17, no. 436: 200, Arts in Society: 'A Fur-Out Trip.'

25 February 1971, vol. 17, no. 439: 323–324, 'Wig and Pencil,' review of *Architectural Judgement,* by Peter Collins.

8 April 1971, vol. 17, no. 445: 594–595, Arts in Society: 'Bennett's Leviathan.'

20 May 1971, vol. 17, no. 451: 834–835, 'A Proper Shambles?'

27 May 1971, vol. 17, no. 452: 922–923, 'No Book for Barnsberries,' review of *The Uses of Disorder,* by Richard Sennett.

24 June 1971, vol. 17, no. 456: 1100–1101, Arts in Society: 'Floreat Ballspondia.'

8 July 1971, vol. 18, no. 458: 76, letter, 'Floreat Ballspondia.'

5 August 1971, vol. 18, no. 462: 251–252, 'Great Builder,' review of *Thomas Cubitt: Master Builder,* by Hermione Hobhouse.

12 August 1971, vol. 18, no. 463: 282–283, 302, 'Had I the Wheels of an Angel'; and letter, 'Great Builder.'

9 September 1971, vol. 18, no. 467: 470–471, Arts in Society: 'The Glass of Fashion.'

30 September 1971, vol. 18, no. 470: 624–625, Arts in Society: 'Demon Tweak: Motor Racing Mechanics.'

9 December 1971, vol. 18, no. 480: 1154–1155, 1164, Arts in Society: 'Hermann in Eden'; and 'Review in Brief,' review of *History of Modern Architecture,* by Leonardo Benevolo.

Sunday Times Colour Supplement

8 August 1971, pp. 19–27, "The Master Builders: 5."

1972   Architectural Design

March 1972, vol. 43: 186–187, Review of *Schindler,* by David Gebhard.

April 1972, vol. 43: 227–228, 'Floreat Ballspondia.' First published in *New Society,* 24 June 1971.

Architectural Review

February 1972, vol. 151: 130, 'The Parts of Prouve,' review of *Jean Prouve, Prefabrication: Structures and Elements,* edited by Benediki Huber and Jean Claude Steinegger.

Casabella

August/September 1972, nos. 368–369: 8–9, 'Monaco Underground' (in Italian).

New Society

20 January 1972, vol. 19, no. 486: 128–129, Arts in Society: 'Prevento mori.'

10 February 1972, vol. 19, no. 489: 300–301, 'Cuttings Job,' review of *Design in Miniature,* by David Gentleman.

24 February 1972, vol. 19, no. 491: 405–406, Arts in Society: 'Immoral Uplift.'

23 March 1972, vol. 19, no. 495: 608–609, 'Shack Game,' review of *Supports: An Alternative to Mass-Housing,* by N. J. Habraken, translated by B. Valkenberg.

4 May 1972, vol. 20, no. 501: 241–243, Arts in Society: 'New Way North.'

25 May 1972, vol. 20, no. 504: 419–420, Arts in Society: 'Treasure House.'

13 July 1972, vol. 21, no. 511: 84–85, Arts in Society: 'Big Brum Artwork.'

27 July 1972, vol. 21, no. 513: 197–198, 'Past Perfect,' review of *In the Future Now,* by Michael Davie.

17 August 1972, vol. 21, no. 516: 352–353, Arts in Society: 'See It Their Way.'

14 September 1972, vol. 21, no. 519: 510–511, Arts in Society: 'Rank Values.'

5 October 1972, vol. 22, no. 522: 50, letter, 'Rank Values.'

9 November 1972, vol. 22, no. 527: 344–345, Arts in Society: 'LL/LF/LE v Foster.'

21 December 1972, vol. 22, no. 533: 702, 'Big Shed Syndrome.'

RIBA Journal

August 1972, vol. 79: 336–339, 'What's the Point of Architectural History'; and 'Only an Academic Flywheel?'

1973   *Architects' Journal*

14 February 1973, vol. 157: 401, 'Retro Colonisation,' review of *American Architecture Comes of Age,* by Leonard K. Eaton.

31 October 1973, vol. 158: 1014–1015, review of *Architecture of Aggression,* by Keith Mallory.

Architectural Design

September 1973, vol. 44: 601–603, 'Fitch—Viewed from Marlboro/Indian Country.'

Architectural Review

January 1973, vol. 153: 79, 'Proof of Baillie Scott,' review of *M. H. Baillie Scott and the Arts and Crafts Movement,* by James D. Kornwolf.

August 1973, vol. 154: 99–101, 'Death and Life of the Prairie School.'

Casabella

March 1973, no. 375: 2, 'La Megastruttura e morta' (in Italian).

New Society

1 February 1973, vol. 23, no. 539: 248–249, Arts in Society: 'Nostalgia for Style.'

15 February 1973, vol. 23, no. 541: 374, 'Review in Brief,' review of *Nine Chains to the Moon,* by R. Buckminster Fuller.

22 February 1973, vol. 23, no. 542: 426, Arts in Society: 'Paleface Trash.'

15 March 1973, vol. 23, no. 545: 576–577, 'A Quiet Bridge.'

10 May 1973, vol. 24, no. 553: 310–311, Arts in Society: 'Force of Example.'

31 May 1973, vol. 24, no. 556: 504–505, Arts in Society: 'Redbrick by Mail.'

28 June 1973, vol. 24, no. 560: 762, Arts in Society: 'Power Plank.'

26 July 1973, vol. 25, no. 564: 229, 'Review in Brief,' review of *Design in Architecture,* by Geoffrey Broadbent.

23 August 1973, vol. 25, no. 568: 450–453, 'Monuments to Modernity: 2. The Late 20th-century Hotel'; and 'A Case of samples.'

6 September 1973, vol. 25, no. 570: 587–588, Arts in Society: 'Iron Bridge Embalmed.'

18 October 1973, vol. 26, no. 576: 154–156, Arts in Society: 'The Parkhill Victory.'

15 November 1973, vol. 26, no. 580: 410–411, Arts in Society: 'Mythology Afoot.'

13 December 1973, vol. 26, no. 584: 666–667, Arts in Society: 'A Real Golden Oldie.'

The Observer Magazine

21 October 1973, p. 15, 'Preserve Us from Paranoid Preservers.'

RIBA Journal

May 1973, vol. 80: 247, letter, 'Dreaded Revival.'

1974 **Architects' Journal**

24 April 1974, vol. 159: 894, 'For a Moulded Environment,' review of *The Plastics Architect,* by Arthur Quarmby.

Architectural Review

April 1974, vol. 155: 197–198, 'Problem X 3 = Olivetti; Criticism.'

Architecture Plus

May–June 1974, vol. 2, no. 3: 108–115, 'Parkhill Revisited: English Public Housing that Broke the Rules (but Works Anyway).'

New Society

7 February 1974, vol. 27, no. 592: 330–331, Arts in Society: 'Old Wheels for New.'

7 March 1974, vol. 27, no. 596: 588–589, Arts in Society: 'Troglodyte Metropolis.'

11 April 1974, vol. 28, no. 601: 82–83, Arts in Society: 'Sundae Painters.'

9 May 1974, vol. 28, no. 605: 328, Arts in Society: 'Signs Municipal.'

13 June 1974, vol. 28, no. 610: 646–647, Arts in Society: 'Barnsbury-sur-Mer.'

4 July 1974, vol. 29, no. 613: 31–32, 'For Namesake,' review of *Watching My Name Go By,* by Mervyn Kurlansky, Jon Naar, and Norman Mailer.

11 July 1974, vol. 29, no. 614: 96, 'Model Failure,' review of *Model Estate: Planned Housing at Quarry Hill, Leeds,* by Alison Ravetz.

18 July 1974, vol. 29, no. 615: 160–161, Arts in Society: 'Nice, Modern and British.'

22 August 1974, vol. 29, no. 622: 494, Arts in Society: 'Radio Machismo.'

19 September 1974, vol. 29, no. 624: 748, Arts in Society: 'Godzilla in Halifax.'

24 October 1974, vol. 30, no. 629: 222–223, 'A Walled City.'

7 November 1974, vol. 30, no. 631: 372, review of *Psychology for Architects,* by David Cater.

14 November 1974, vol. 30, no. 632: 435, 'True Pioneers,' review of *The British Architect in Industry,* by H. A. N. Brockman.

28 November 1974, vol. 30, no. 634: 555–556, Arts in Society: 'Gentri-Mini Mania.'

19 December 1974, vol. 30, no. 637: 763–764, 'Out of the Way: Sex and the Single Lens.'

Society of Architectural Historians' Journal

May 1974, vol. 33, no. 2: 170–171, 'Megastructure—Civic Design at Bay.' Abstract of a paper presented at the joint meeting of the SAH (U.S.A.) and SAH (G.B.), 16–19 August 1973, Cambridge, England.

October 1974, vol. 33, no. 3: 260–261, review of *Le Corbusier, the Athens Charter,* translated by
Anthony Eardley.

1975 *Architects' Journal*

21 May 1975, vol. 161: 1066–1067, 'Towering Babel.'

29 October 1974, vol. 162: 891, 'When you've seen one glazed slab . . . ,' review of *HPP bauten
und entwurfe* (Buildings and Projects), Hentrich-Petschnigg & Partners.

Architectural Design

July 1975, vol. 45: 400–401, 'Megastructure.'

Architectural Review

November 1975, vol. 158: 322, 'College City: Rowe Replies.' Letters on the College City issue of
AR, August 1975; a reply to Nathan Silver by the authors Fred Koetter and Colin Rowe; a letter
by Charles Jencks; and a letter by Reyner Banham titled 'De Wolfe the Author.'

Casabella

November 1975, no. 407: 50–51, 'Age of the Masters: A Personal View of Modern Architecture.'
Excerpt from *A Personal View of Modern Architecture,* in Italian.

New Society

6 February 1975, vol. 31, no. 644: 330–331, Arts in Society: 'The Great Wall of Tyne.'

20 March 1975, vol. 31, no. 645: 733–734, Arts in Society: 'Les trous de Paris.'

24 April 1975, vol. 32, no. 655: 212, Arts in Society: 'Money into Form.'

22 May 1975, vol. 32, no. 659: 486–487, Arts in Society: 'Ovaltine and Oake.'

26 June 1975, vol. 32, no. 664: 787–788, Arts in Society: 'The Purified Aesthetic.'

7 August 1975, vol. 33, no. 670: 312–313, Arts in Society: 'A Dead Liberty.'

4 September 1975, vol. 33, no. 674: 529–530, Arts in Society: 'Up at Sybil's Place.'

2 October 1975, vol. 34, no. 678: 26–27, 'On the Sixth Day.'

30 October 1975, vol. 34, no. 682: 278, 'Ghost Dancing,' review of *Garbage Housing,* by Martin
Pawley.

20 November 1975, vol. 34, no. 685: 436–437, Arts in Society: 'Arnolfini Mk III.'

Times Literary Supplement

17 January 1975, pp. 57–58, 'The City Moses Made,' review of *Robert Moses and the Fall of
New York,* by Albert A. Caro.

13 June 1975, pp. 652, 660, 'The Great Good Windy City,' review of *Burnham of Chicago: Architect and Planner,* by Thomas S. Hines; and 'Urban Counsels.'

19 September 1975, p. 1046, 'Establishing the Precedents,' review of *George Howe: Toward a
Modern American Architecture,* by Robert A. M. Stern.

17 October 1975, p. 1236, letter, 'The American Landscape.'

1976 *Architects' Journal*

14 July 1976, vol. 164: 89, 92–94, 'The Rally of Art Net.'

Architecture

23 January 1976, p. 83, 'A Question of Magic.'

Architecture and Urbanism

June 1976, vol. 6, no. 6: 63–122, 'Piano & Rogers.'

The Listener

23 September 1976, vol. 96: 359–360, 'The Open City and Its Enemies.'

New Society

8 January 1976, vol. 35, no. 692: 62–63, Arts in Society: 'Come in 2001.'
12 February 1976, vol. 35, no. 697: 341, 347, Arts in Society: 'Repro Time Is Here'; and letter, 'Come in 2001.'
18 March 1976, vol. 35, no. 702: 618–619, Arts in Society: 'National Monument.'
6 May 1976, vol. 36, no. 709: 306–307, Arts in Society: 'The Mesa Messiah.'
1 July 1976, vol. 37, no. 717: 25–26, Arts in Society: 'Bricologues a la Lanterne.'
22 July 1976, vol. 37, no. 720: 195, letter, 'Bricologues.'
12 August 1976, vol. 37, no. 723: 352–353, Arts in Society: 'Ground Scraping.'
28 October 1976, vol. 38, no. 734: 202–203, Arts in Society: 'Castle on a Mall.'
2 December 1976, vol. 38, no. 739: 473, Arts in Society: 'The True False Front.'
9 December 1976, vol. 38, no. 740: 524–525, 'News of Nowhere,' review of *Seven American Utopias: The Architecture of Communitarian Socialism, 1790–1975,* by Dolores Hayden; *Architecture and Utopia,* by Manfredo Tafuri.

RIBA Journal

July 1976, vol. 83: 295, 'Where Are You, Universal Man, Now that We Need You?'

Times Literary Supplement

23 January 1976, pp. 83–84, 'A Question of Magic,' review of *Pueblo: Mountain, Village, Dance,* by Vincent Scully; *Energy and Form: An Ecological Approach to Urban Growth,* by Ralph L. Knowles.
23 July 1976, p. 907, 'The Tear-Drop Express,' review of *The Streamlined Decade,* by Donald J. Bush.

1977 *Architectural Review*

May 1977, vol. 161: 270–294, 'Centre Pompidou'; and a reply by R. Bird.
November 1977, vol. 162: 316, 'Living in Britain, 1952–1977.'

Data

October/December 1977, nos. 28/29: 18–39, 'L'architettura a stablie qual movimento' (in Italian).

New Society

13 January 1977, vol. 39, no. 745: 72–73, Arts in Society: 'Goat Island Story.'

3 March 1977, vol. 39, no. 752: 454, Arts in Society: 'Euston Arch of the Air.'

10 March 1977, vol. 39, no. 753: 485, 'Zapped-in in Buffalo.'

5 May 1977, vol. 40, no. 761: 238, Arts in Society: 'Lair of the Looter.'

23 June 1977, vol. 40, no. 768: 615, Arts in Society: 'County and Wet Bed.'

21 July 1977, vol. 41, no. 772: 138–139, Arts in Society: 'Valley of the Dams.'

18 August 1977, vol. 41, no. 776: 350–351, Arts in Society: 'The Four-Wheel Life.'

29 September 1977, vol. 41, no. 782: 673, letter, 'The Fen Tigers.'

6 October 1977, vol. 42, no. 783: 22–23, Arts in Society: 'Grass Above, Glass Around.'

27 October 1977, vol. 42, no. 786: 190–191, 'Summa Galactica.'

22/29 December 1977, vol. 42, nos. 794/795: viii–ix, 628–629, 'Good Time Charley's'; and 'Eupepsia, Tex.'

Society of Architectural Historians' Journal

December 1977, vol. 36, no. 4: 263–264, review of *A Language and a Theme: The Architecture of Denys Lasdun and Partners,* by William Curtis; *James Sterling Buildings and Projects, 1950–1974,* introduction by John Jacobas.

Times Literary Supplement

12 August 1977, p. 985, 'A Suburb in the Sea,' review of *Metabolism in Architecture,* by Kisho Kurokawa.

1978   *New Society*

9 February 1978, vol. 43, no. 801: 322–323, Arts in Society: 'Faces of Time.'

2 March 1978, vol. 43, no. 804: 501, 'Lack of History,' review of *Urban Utopias in the Twentieth Century,* by Robert Fishman.

23 March 1978, vol. 43, no. 819: 676–677, Arts in Society: 'Desert Hacienda.'

15 June 1978, vol. 44, no. 826: 608–609, Arts in Society: 'Collect $2,000,000.'

3 August 1978, vol. 45, no. 826: 252–253, Arts in Society: 'Taking It with You.'

21 September 1978, vol. 45, no. 833: 634–635, Arts in Society: 'Hanging Gardens, NW.'

9 November 1978, vol. 46, no. 840: 346–347, Arts in Society: 'The Last Cigar Store.'

21/28 December 1978, vol. 46, nos. 846/847: 712–713, 'Alternative Wheels?'

Society of Architectural Historians' Journal

October 1978, vol. 37, no. 3: 195–197, 'The Service of the Larkin "A" Building.'

October 1978, vol. 37, no. 3: 213–214, review of *A Guide to Architecture in Los Angeles and Southern California,* by David Gebhard and Robert Winter.

Student Publication of the School of Design: North Carolina State University

In *Great Models: Digressions on the Architectural Model,* 1978, pp. 17–20, 'Iso! Axo! (All Fall Down?).'

Times Literary Supplement

17 February 1978, pp. 191–192, 'Pevsner's Progress'; and review of *Morality and Architecture: The Development of a Theme in Architectural History and Theory from the Gothic Revival to the Modern Movement,* by David Watkin.

14 April 1978, p. 417, letter, 'Morality and Architecture.'

15 September 1978, p. 1013, 'The Geist in the Machine,' review of *The German Werkbund: The Politics of Reform in the Applied Arts,* by Joan Campbell.

17 November 1978, p. 1337, 'The Writing on the Walls,' review of *The Language of Post-Modern Architecture,* by Charles A. Jencks.

1979   **Little Journal/Western New York Chapter of the Society of Architectural Historians**

February 1979, vol. 3, no. 1: 2–19, 'Buffalo Industrial.'

Modulus: University of Virginia School of Architecture Review

1979, pp. 14–20, 'Culture, Ideology and Architecture: A Crisis of Style.'

New Society

1 March 1979, vol. 47, no. 856: 473–474, 'Schlock Horror Sensation.'

5 April 1979, vol. 48, no. 861: 26–27, Arts in Society: 'Hotel Deja-Quoi?'

12 April 1979, vol. 48, no. 862: 98–99, 'Manhattaglia,' review of *Delirious New York,* by Rem Koolhas.

31 May 1979, vol. 48, no. 869: 524–525, Arts in Society: 'Ecotopiary.'

12 July 1979, vol. 49, no. 875: 86–87, Arts in Society: 'Valentino: Simply Filed Away.'

2 August 1979, vol. 49, no. 878: 252–253, 'Rubbish: It's as Easy as Falling Off a Cusp,' review of *Rubbish Theory: The Creation and Destruction of Value,* by Michael Thompson.

9 August 1979, vol. 49, no. 879: 304–305, Arts in Society: 'Corn Is as High.'

1 November 1979, vol. 50, no. 891: 267–268, Arts in Society: 'New Kelmscott, NY.'

6 December 1979, vol. 50, no. 896: 555–556, Arts in Society: 'Woman of the House.'

RIBA Journal

March 1979, vol. 86: 132, obituary, 'John McHale.' Written in conjunction with Mary Banham.

Society of Architectural Historians' Journal

October 1979, vol. 38, no. 3: 300, review of *Amerika Bilderbuch Eines Architekten,* by Erich Mendelsohn.

1980   *AIA Journal: Architecture*

Mid-May 1980, vol. 69: 190, 'What's Next?'

June 1980, vol. 69: 56–57, 'MOMA's Architectural Mystery Tour.'

December 1980, vol. 69: 50, 'Two by Jencks: The Tough Life of the Enfant Terrible,' review of *Late Modern Architecture and Other Essays* and *Skyscrapers—Skycities,* by Charles A. Jencks.

Archetype

Winter 1980, vol. 1, no. 4: 43–47, 'Catacombs of the Modern Movement: Grain Elevators in Myth and Reality.'

Architectural Review

February 1980, vol. 167: 88–93, 'Buffalo Archaeological.'

March 1980, vol. 167: 192, 'Guess Whose Utopia,' review of *Collage City,* by Colin Rowe and Fred Koetter.

September 1980, vol. 168: 192, 'Revisionist Roth,' review of *A Concise History of American Architecture,* by Leland M. Roth.

Architecture Nebraska

1980, vol. 3: 6–11, 'The Arts of Ineloquence.'

Casabella

November/December 1980, nos. 463/464: 107, 'Critiche e interrogativi (al Movimento Moderno)' (in Italian).

New Society

3 January 1980, vol. 51, no. 900: 24–25, Arts in Society: 'Expo Relics.'

21 February 1980, vol. 51, no. 907: 400–401, Arts in Society: 'Marbled Perspectives.'

28 February 1980, vol. 51, no. 908: 464, 'Coming Clean,' review of *Propre en ordre,* by Genevieve Heller.

19 June 1980, vol. 52, no. 918: 297–299, Arts in Society: 'The Haunted Highway.'

17 July 1980, vol. 53, no. 922: 136–137, Arts in Society: 'The Widow's Might (Is Right).'

28 August 1980, vol. 53, no. 928: 414–415, Arts in Society: 'Rubber-gub-gub.'

2 October 1980, vol. 54, no. 933: 26–27, Arts in Society: 'Low and Cholo.'

23 October 1980, vol. 54, no. 936: 178, 'Drop-out Dottiness,' review of *Paper Heroes: A Review of Appropriate Technology,* by Witold Rybczynski.

18/25 December 1980, vol. 54, no. 944/945: 572–573, 'Masonic Moderns and the Soho Connection,' review of *The First Moderns: The Architects of the Eighteenth Century,* by Joseph Rykwert.

Society of Architectural Historians' Journal

May 1980, vol. 39, no. 2: 152, 'Voyeurs des ponts Chaussees,' review of *Robert Maillart's Bridges: The Art of Engineering,* by David P. Billington; *Iron Bridge to Crystal Palace: Impact and Images of the Industrial Revolution,* by Asa Briggs; *Arch Bridges and Their Builders, 1735–1855,* by

Ted Ruddock; *The Eads Bridge,* photographic essay by Quinta Scott and historical appraisal by Howard S. Miller; *Bridges and Aqueducts,* by Anthony Sealey; *Brooklyn Bridge: Fact and Symbol,* by Alan Trachtenburg.

1981 *Architects' Journal*

12 August 1981, vol. 174: 285, 'RIBA Conference Bags Banham.'
4 November 1981, vol. 174: 880, 'Design Freedom.'

Architectural Design

A.D. Profile 32, 1981, vol. 51, nos. 1/2: 35–38, 'Antonio Sant'Elia.'
A.D. Profile 35, 1981, vol. 51, nos. 6/7: 1–104, 'On Methodology of Architectural History.'

Architectural Review

January 1981, vol. 169: 64, 'Not a Movement,' review of *Late Modern Architecture,* by Charles Jencks.
May 1981, vol. 169: 283–290, 'Silicion Style.'

New Society

8 January 1981, vol. 55, no. 947: 60–61, Arts in Society: 'Garden Walls of Old Mexico.'
2 April 1981, vol. 56, no. 959: 23–24, Arts in Society: 'Preservation Adobe.'
25 June 1981, vol. 56, no. 971: 532–533, Arts in Society: 'Down the Vale of Chips.'
20 August 1981, vol. 57, no. 979: 314–315, Arts in Society: 'Not the Take-out Eucharist.'
27 August 1981, vol. 57, no. 980: 362–363, 'The Ism Count,' review of *American Architecture, 1607–1976,* by Marcus Whiffen and Frederick Koeper; *Robert Stern,* edited by Vincent Scully.
10 September 1981, vol. 57, no. 982: 436–437, Arts in Society: 'The NatWest Money-Warren.'
12 November 1981, vol. 58, no. 996: 284–285, Arts in Society: 'King Lut's Navy.'
17 December 1981, vol. 58, no. 996: 505–507, Arts in Society: 'Slight Agony in the Garden.'

Society of Architectural Historians' Journal

October 1981, vol. 40, no. 3: 257, review of *Chicago Tribune Tower Competition,* by Stanley Tigerman, introduction by Stuart Cohen.

1982 *Architectural Review*

December 1982, vol. 172: 34–41, 93–100, 'Art and Necessity: Inmos and the Persistence of Functionalism.'

New Society

25 February 1982, vol. 59, no. 1006: 318–319, 'The Isle of Vertical,' review of *The Skyscraper* and *The City Observed: New York,* by Paul Goldberger.
25 March 1982, vol. 59, no. 1010: 482–483, Arts in Society: 'Night-crawler to LA.'
13 May 1982, vol. 60, no. 1017: 264–265, Arts in Society: 'The Last Boom-Town.'
17 June 1982, vol. 60, no. 1022: 476–477, Arts in Society: 'Tolmers Cenotaph.'
1 July 1982, vol. 61, no. 1024: 22–23, Arts in Society: 'Brideshead Reviolated.'

19 August 1982, vol. 61, no. 1031: 304–305, Arts in Society: 'Great Barrier Grief.'

11 November 1982, vol. 62, no. 1043: 263–264, Arts in Society: 'Bertel's British Valhalla.'

18 November 1982, vol. 62, no. 1044: 307–308, Arts in Society: 'Kahn's Warehouse of Art.'

RIBA Journal

1982, vol. 1, no. 1: 33–38, 'The Architect as Gentleman and the Architect as Hustler' (transcript).

Society of Architectural Historians' Journal

March 1982, vol. 41, no. 1: 81–82, review of *Perspecta 16* and *Perspecta 17.*

1983   Architectural Review

May 1983, vol. 173: 34–38, 'Santa Cruz Shingle Style.'

New Society

3 February 1983, vol. 63, no. 1055: 187–188, Arts in Society: 'Dead on the Fault.'

17 February 1983, vol. 63, no. 1057: 271, 'Changing Spaces,' review of *The Politics of Park Design: A History of Urban Parks in America,* by Galen Cranz.

17 March 1983, vol. 63, no. 1061: 430–431, Arts in Society: 'The Sage of Corrales.'

5 May 1983, vol. 64, no. 1068: 188–189, Arts in Society: 'O, bright star . . .'

19 May 1983, vol. 64, no. 1070: 274, 'Old Designers' Tales,' review of *By Design,* by Ralph Caplan.

14 July 1983, vol. 65, no. 1078: 60–61, Arts in Society: 'Insider's Eye in Florida.'

28 July 1983, vol. 65, no. 1080: 138–139, Arts in Society: 'The Thing in the Forecourt.'

11 August 1983, vol. 65, no. 1082: 222, 'Anaffemas,' review of *The Complete Naff Guide,* by Kit Bryson, Selina FitzHerbert, and Jean-Luc Legris.

13 October 1983, vol. 66, no. 1091: 59–60, Arts in Society: 'What a Wonderful Bird.'

23 November 1983, vol. 66, no. 1094: 319–320, Arts in Society: 'Foyer! Foyer!'

Society of Architectural Historians' Journal

May 1983, vol. 42, no. 2: 194–195, review of *Richard Neutra and the Search for Modern Architecture: A Biography of a History,* by Thomas S. Hines.

December 1983, vol. 42, no. 4: 383–387, 'Ransome at Bayonne.'

Times Literary Supplement

7 January 1983, p. 19, 'Supplying the Geist,' review of *Bruno Taut and the Architecture of Activism,* by Iain Boyd Whyte.

25 March 1983, p. 306, 'Drop-Dead Effects,' review of *Exterior Decoration: Hollywood's Inside Out Houses,* by John Chase.

18 November 1983, p. 1265, 'Conspicuous Formalism,' review of *New American Art Museums,* by Helen Searing.

1984   AIA Journal: Architecture

March 1984, vol. 73: 143–149, 'Mountains of Modern Icons: The Exhilarating Experience of Kitt Peak.'

August 1984, vol. 73: 79–81, 'The Academic Arrival of Postmodernism.'

Architects' Journal

27 June 1984, vol. 179: 102, 'Not Quite Architecture.'

Architectural Review

August 1984, vol. 176: 22–29, 'AT&T: The Post-Deco Skyscraper.'
December 1984, vol. 176: 32–34, 'Celebration of the City.' With Emilio Ambasz and Oriol Bohigas.

Casabella

April 1984, no. 501: 34–35, 'Lingotto: Un punto di vista transatlantico' (in Italian).

New Society

13 January 1984, vol. 67, no. 1103: 54–55, 'Auto Dreamer,' review of *Harley Earl and the Dream Machine,* by Stephen Bayley.
26 January 1984, vol. 67, no. 1105: 131–132, Arts in Society: 'O Canberra!'
23 February 1984, vol. 67, no. 1109: 289–290, Arts in Society: 'Dinosaurs of San Francisco.'
19 April 1984, vol. 68, no. 1117: 101–102, Arts in Society: 'Reason's Skull and Dome.'
9 August 1984, vol. 69, no. 1129: 95–96, Arts in Society: 'The Great Wine Stand-Off.'
4 October 1984, vol. 70, no. 1137: 15–16, Arts in Society: 'Stirling Escapes the Hobbits.'
8 November 1984, vol. 70, no. 1142: 214–215, 'My Father's House,' review of *The Bungalow: The Production of a Global Culture,* by Anthony D. King.
20/27 December 1984, vol. 70, no. 1148: 459–461, Arts in Society: 'Big D Seeks Cultureplex.'

Society of Architectural Historians' Journal

March 1984, vol. 43: 33–37, 91, 'The Plot against Bernard Maybeck,' review of *The English Terraced House,* by Stefan Muthesius.
October 1984, vol. 43: 277, 'Industry, the Machine, Technology and Now Production,' review of *Avant Garde and Industrie,* edited by Stanislaus Von Moos and Chris Smeek; *Architecture of the Industrial Age, 1789–1914,* by Francois Loyer; *Archaeologia Industriale,* edited by Rosella Bigi.

Times Literary Supplement

17 February 1984, p. 171, 'Frozen Facets,' review of *Ice Palaces,* by Fred Anderes and Ann Agranoff.
3 August 1984, p. 876, 'Potlatch Ceremonies,' review of *The Anthropology of World's Fairs: San Francisco's Panama Pacific International Exposition of 1915,* edited by Burton Benedict.

UIA International Architect

1984, no. 5: 34–35, 'The State of the Art: A Cultural History of British Architecture'; and 'The Well-Tempered Environment Revisited,' abridged from the revised edition of the author's *The Well-Tempered Environment.*

1985   *A.A. Files*

Spring 1985, no. 8: 103–106, exhibition review, 'Cycles of the Price-Mechanism.'

AIA Journal: Architecture

March 1985, vol. 74: 110–119, special issue, 'San Francisco and Its Regions: The Greening of High Tech in Silicon Valley.'

Design Book Review (DBR)

Summer 1985, no. 7: 8–11, 'The Wright Stuff,' review of *Frank Lloyd Wright's Hanna House: The Client's Report,* by Paul R. Hanna and Jean S. Hanna; *The Pope-Leighey House,* edited by Terry B. Morton; *The Robie House of Frank Lloyd Wright,* by Joseph Connors; *Frank Lloyd Wright's Robie House,* by Donald Hoffmann; *Frank Lloyd Wright at the Metropolitan Museum of Art,* by Edgar Kaufmann.

New Society

18 April 1985, vol. 72, no. 1164: 86–88, Arts in Society: 'Fiat: The Phantom of Order.'
21 June 1985, vol. 72, no. 1173: 440–441, Arts in Society: 'A Classic of the Air.'
9 August 1985, vol. 73, no. 1180: 197–198, Arts in Society: 'Adrip in Sidgwick Avenue.'
20 September 1985, vol. 73, no. 1186: 418–419, Arts in Society: 'BIBA in Pittsburgh.'

Space Design

January 1985, no. 244: 126–130, 'Art and Necessity' (Japanese text).

Times Literary Supplement

11 January 1985, p. 30, 'Post-Modernist Predecessors,' review of *On the Edge of the World: Four Architects in San Francisco at the Turn of the Century,* by Richard Longstreth.
26 April 1985, p. 476, 'Stateside Styles,' review of *American Shelter: An Illustrated Encyclopedia of the American Home,* by Lester Walker.

1986   *AIA Journal: Architecture*

September 1986, vol. 75: 47–51, 'Glazed 'Plant House' Atop a Cascade of Silver Cylinders.'

Architectural Review

October 1986, vol. 180: 54–56, 'The Quality of Modernism.'
December 1986, vol. 180: 31–39, ' "Luxe, calme et technicite", Cite des Sciences La Villette.'

Architecture Plus

August 1986, no. 86: 12–14, 'Wechselnde Richtungen auf dem zeitlosen Weg,' review of *The Production of Houses,* by Christopher Alexander; *Christopher Alexander,* by Stephen Grabow (in German, based on article first published in *Times Literary Supplement,* 1 March 1986, pp. 15–16).

Casabella

March 1986, no. 522: 33, 'L'eterno modo di cambiare rotta Reyner Banham analizza Christopher Alexander' (in Italian).

September 1986, no. 527: 28–29, 'I complessi della prefabricazione,' review of *The Dream of the Factory-made House: Walter Gropius and Konrad Wachsmann,* by Gilbert Herbert (in Italian).

Design Book Review (DBR)

1986, no. 8: 18–20, review of *The Dream of the Factory-made House: Walter Gropius and Konrad Wachsmann,* by Gilbert Herbert.

1986, no. 9: 30–33, 'James Stirling: The Epiphany of the Failed Avant-Gardes,' review of *James Stirling: Buildings and Projects,* by James Stirling.

New Society

24 January 1986, vol. 75, no. 1204: 152–153, Arts in Society: 'Art-Space Angst.'

7 March 1986, vol. 75, no. 1210: 413–414, 'Stretch City.'

3 July 1986, vol. 77, no. 1227: 16–17, 'The Villages of AcronymiNY (SoHo).'

14 November 1986, vol. 78, no. 1246: 12–14, 'Modern Monuments.'

12 December 1986, vol. 78, no. 1250: 26–27, 'Arches that Flash in the Night,' review of *Orange Roofs, Golden Arches: The Architecture of American Chain Restaurants,* by Philip Langdon.

Times Literary Supplement

3 January 1986, pp. 15–16, 'Changing Tack the On Timeless Way,' review of *The Production of Houses,* by Christopher Alexander with Howard Davis, Julio Marinez, Ron Corner; *Christopher Alexander: The Search for a New Paradigm in Architecture,* by Stephen Grabow.

30 June 1986, p. 673, 'That Interesting Play,' review of *The Secret Life of Buildings: An American Mythology for Modern Architecture,* by Gavin Macrae-Gibson.

1987   *AIA Journal: Architecture*

March 1987, vol. 76: 120, 'A Proper, Old-Fashioned Biography,' review of *Richard Rogers: A Biography,* by Brian Appleyard.

June 1987, vol. 76: 84, 'Looking from the Future to the Immediate Past II.'

Architects' Journal

11 March 1987, vol. 185: 56–59, 'Corb's Morning's Work: Painting and Sculpture of Le Corbusier.'

Architectural Review

July 1987, vol. 181: 10, 'Ship Shape,' review of *Googie: Fifties Coffee Shop Architecture,* by Alan Hess; *Orange Roofs, Golden Arches: The Architecture of American Chain Restaurants,* by Philip Langdon.

Architecture and Urbanism

November 1987, vol. 11, no. 206: 82–86, 'Recent Works of Renzo Piano'; and 'In the Neighborhood of Art.'

Art in America

June 1987, vol. 75: 124–129, 'In the Neighborhood of Art.'

Casabella

March 1987, no. 533: 42–43, 'Musei per tutti' (in Italian).
October 1987, no. 539: 42–43, 'La fine della Silicon Valley' (in Italian).

New Society

24 July 1987, vol. 81, no. 1282: 11–13, 'Building Inside Out.'
16 October 1987, vol. 82, no. 1294: 18–20, 'On the Wings of Wonder.'

Society of Architectural Historians' Journal

December 1987, vol. 46: 429–430, review of *Imagining Tomorrow: History, Technology and the American Future,* edited by Joseph J. Corn.

Times Literary Supplement

18–24 September 1987, p. 1013, 'Prefabricated Virtues,' review of *The Comfortable House: North American Suburban Architecture, 1890–1930,* by Alan Gowans.

1988 *Art in America*

October 1988, vol. 76: 172–177, 'Actual Monuments.'

Casabella

January/February 1988, nos. 542/543: 74–81, 'TVA: L'ingegneria dell'utopia' (in Italian).
September 1988, no. 549: 28–29, 'La visione dei Becher secondo Reyner Banham: Ritratti compassati' (in Italian).
October 1988, no. 550: 32–33, 'Australia: Verso un 'architettura modestamente "galvo"' ' (in Italian).

New Society

22 January 1988, vol. 83, no. 1308: 20, 'Riders of the Empurpled Page.'

1989 *Architectural Review*

April 1989, vol. 185: 89–92, 'A Set of Actual Monuments' (inaugural lecture, Professor of Architectural History, New York University).

Architecture and Urbanism

March 1989, no. 3 Supplement, pp. 152–158, 'Making Architecture: The High Craft of Renzo Piano.'

1990 *New Statesman and Society*

12 October 1990, pp. 22–25, 'A Black Box: The Secret Profession of Architecture.'

'After the Hype, the Hustle: Did Reyner Banham Justify His Big Buildup for Last Week's RIBA Conference?' *Building Design,* no. 559 (28 August 1981): 3.

'Agents Provocateurs.' *Architectural Design* 38 (January 1968): 51. Review of the International Symposium on Architectural Theory in the Technishe Universitat, Berlin.

'An Interview with Reyner Banham.' *Architecture Australia* 72, no. 6 (November 1983): 40–41.

Anderson, S. 'Polemica con Reyner Banham architettura e tradizione vera.' *Architettura* 10 (April 1965): 831–833.

Angrisani, Marcello. 'Architettura: Forma o Fusions? Reyner Banham e l'environmentalism.' *Casabella* 34, no. 350–351 (1970): 41–46.

Angrisani, Marcello. 'Reyner Banham e l'environmentalism: La componente techologica nell'arcitettura.' *Casabella* 34 (July-August 1970): 67–74.

'Architecture of the Well-Tempered Environment.' Review by H. Faulkner Brown, *RIBA Journal* 76 (May 1969): 208; reply by R. Banham, *RIBA Journal* 76 (July 1969): 263; review by M. Pawley, *Architectural Design* 39 (April 1969): 184; review by H. Wright, *Architectural Forum* 131 (November 1969): 63; review by N. Taylor, *Design,* no. 243 (March 1969): 88–90; review by C. W. Condit, *Art Quarterly* 33, no. 2 (Summer 1970): 179–180; review by J. M. Fitch, *Society of Architectural Historians' Journal* 29 (October 1970): 282–284; review by K. Frampton, *Oppositions* (Winter 1976/1977).

Barnett, Jonathan. 'Art and Life at Aspen Meadows.' *Architectural Record* 140, no. 2 (August 1966): 121–122.

Boles, Daralice, and Susan Doubilet. 'Interview with Reyner Banham.' *Progressive Architecture* 67 (March 1986): 67–109.

Bottero, M. 'The Architectural Querelle: Design in the United States Today.' *Abitare,* no. 223 (April 1984): 91–95.

Boyarsky, Alvin, editor. 'IID Summer Session 71.' *Architectural Design* 43 (April 1972): 220–243.

Boyd, Robin. 'The Sad End of New Brutalism.' *Architectural Review* 142 (July 1967): 9–11.

'Building for Tomorrow.' *Times Literary Supplement,* 6 January 1961, p. 9.

'Concrete Atlantis: U.S. Industrial Building and European Modern Architecture, 1902–1925.' Review by R. Kimball, *Architectural Record* 174, no. 9 (August 1986): 71; review by M. Pawley, *Architects' Journal* 184, no. 36 (3 September 1986): 76; review by B. Hatton, *Building Design,* no. 8111, 7 November 1986, 36–37; review by N. Adams, *Times Literary Supplement,* 10 October 1986; review by A. Saint, *AA Files,* no. 14 (Spring 1987): 106–108; review by J. Masheck, *Art in America* 75, no. 1 (January 1987): 13–14; review by E. C. Cromley, *Society of Architectural Historians' Journal* 46, no. 3 (September 1987): 301–302.

'Contemporary Architecture of Japan, 1958–1984.' Review by M. Treib, *Journal of Architectural Education* 40, no. 1 (Fall 1986): 30–31; review by W. H. Coaldrake, AIA Journal: *Architecture* 75, no. 9 (September 1986): 107–108.

'Gold Medal Jury Decides on Seven Honorary Fellowships.' *RIBA Journal* 90, no. 4 (April 1983): 90.

'Guide to Modern Architecture.' Review by D. E. D., *RIBA Journal* 70, no. 3 (March 1963): 116; review in *Times Literary Supplement,* 5 April 1963, p. 228; review by Linda Biser, *AIA Journal* 41 (January 1964): 55–56.

'Institute Honors Nine for "Distinguished Achievements": 11 Foreign Architects Named as Honorary AIA Fellows.' *Architecture* (AIA) 72, no. 2 (February 1984): 14, 16, 21, 24.

'Interview with Reyner Banham.' *Jano/Arquitectura and Humanities,* no. 29 (July/August 1975): 57–61 (in Spanish).

Jackson, Neil. 'Thoughts of the Well-Tempered Reyner Banham: Interview in Santa Cruz.' *Building Design,* no. 495 (9 May 1980): 20–21.

Jackson, Neil. 'Californian Revolution: Reyner Banham of California 101 Conference.' *Building Design,* no. 496 (16 May 1980): 16–17.

Jencks, Charles A. 'In Undisguised Taste.' *Building Design,* no. 250 (16 May 1975): 12–13.

Jencks, Charles A. 'Post-Modernism,' letter to the editor. *Times Literary Supplement,* 1 December 1978, p. 1402.

Los Angeles: The Architecture of Four Ecologies. Review by A. Best, *Design,* no. 268 (April 1971): 92; review by P. French, *Times,* 5 April 1971, p. 11; review by J. Donat, *RIBA Journal* 78 (May 1971): 218; review by T. S. Hines, *Society of Architectural Historians' Journal* 31 (March 1972): 75–77; review by E. McCoy, *Progressive Architecture* 52 (October 1971): 50; review by A. McNab, *Architectural Digest* 43 (February 1972): 121; review by J. S. Margolies, *Architectural Forum* 135 (November 1971): 10; review by P. Plagens, *Artforum* 115 (December 1972): 67–76; review by R. Saxon, *Town Planning Institute Journal* 57 (June 1971): 291–292; review by P. Self, *Town and Country Planning* 40 (March 1972): 173–175; review by J. F. H. Sergeant, *Town Planning Review* 42 (July 1971): 314–316; review by E. L. Wemple, *Historic Preservation* 24 (April 1972): 46; review by G. Wickham, *Art and Artist* 7 (May 1972): 57.

Lyall, Sutherland. 'Banham's Background.' *RIBA Journal,* Conference Supplement, 88, no. 10 (October 1981): 3–5.

Mallory, Keith, and Ottar Arvid. 'Architecture of Aggression.' *Architects' Journal* 158, no. 44 (October 1973): 1015.

Maxwell, R. 'Reyner Banham: The Plenitude of Presence.' *Architectural Design* 51, no. 6 (1981): 52–57, Profile.

McKean, John Maule. 'The Last of England? A Profile of Reyner Banham: 1&2.' *Building Design,* no. 311 (13 August 1976): 8–9; *Building Design,* no. 312 (27 August 1976): 26–27.

Megastructures: Urban Futures of the Recent Past. Review: *Building* 232 (11 March 1977): 60–61.

Middleton, Robin. 'The New Brutalism, Or a Clean, Well-Lighted Place.' *Architectural Design* 37 (January 1967): 7–8.

The New Brutalism: Ethic or Aesthetic. Review by D. Gebhard, *Arts and Architecture* 84 (April 1967): 6; review, *Times Literary Supplement,* 27 April 1967, p. 352; review by P. Collins, *Progressive Architecture* 48 (March 1967): 198; review by F. Jenkins, *RIBA Journal* 74 (May 1967): 205–206; review by J. Rykwert, *Domus* (German edition), no. 451 (June 1967): 1; review, *AIA Journal* 48 (October 1967): 102.

Norman, Barry. 'One Pair of Eyes,' BBC 2. *Times,* 13 March 1972, p. 9.

Pawley, Martin. 'Connoisseur of the Contemporary.' Review of *Design by Choice,* edited by Penny Sparke, *Times Literary Supplement,* 5 March 1982, p. 249.

Pawley, Martin. 'The Last of the Piston Engine Men.' *Building Design,* no. 71 (1 October 1971).

'Quotes from Reyner Banham in Melbourne.' *Architecture* 7, no. 4 (August/September 1983): 14.

'RIBA Conference Bags Banham.' *Architects' Journal* 174, no. 32 (12 August 1981): 285.

Rogers, Ernesto. 'L'evoluzione dell'architettura.' *Casabella Continuita,* no. 228 (June 1959): 2–4.

Rowden, Ian. 'Megastructures: Dinosaurs of the Design Age.' *Building* 232, no. 6976 (11 March 1977): 60–61.

Scenes in American Deserta. Review by C. Vita-Finzi, *Times Literary Supplement,* 18 February 1983, p. 150; review by J. Ryle, *Sunday Times,* 20 February 1983, p. 46; review by G. Goulden, *Times,* 14 April 1984, p. 16; review by B. Polk, *Triglyph,* no. 9 (Winter 1989–1990): 48–49.

'Seven Just Fellows: Nominations of Seven New Honorary RIBA Fellowships.' *Architects' Journal* 177, no. 13 (March 1983): 21.

'Shoo-Fly Landings.' Review of Reyner Banham's inaugural lecture as Professor of History of Architecture at University College London, *Architectural Design* 41 (January 1971): 60.

Spade, Robert. 'Invincible Destroyer of Form.' *Architectural Design* 39 (June 1969): 297.

Sparke, Penny. 'The Machine Stops.' Interview and article, *Design* (London), no. 384 (December 1980): 31.

Sudjic, Deyan. 'California Snowflake.' *Building Design,* no. 594 (14 May 1982): 2.

'The Aspen Papers.' Review by Hilary Gelson, *Design,* no. 307 (July 1974): 72; review in *Times Educational Supplement,* 24 May 1974.

'The Experimental Architecture Dialogue at Folkestone.' *Domus* 442 (September 1966).

'The Great Debate that Never Was.' *Building Design,* no. 559 (28 August 1981): 2.

Theory and Design in the First Machine Age. Review by J. Barnett, *Architectural Record* 128 (August 1960): 84; review by G. Dorfles, *Domus,* no. 372 (November 1960): 40; review by R. Gardner-Medwin, *Town Planning Review* 31 (January 1961): 315–316; review by P. Goodman, *Arts* 35 (January 1961): 20–21; review by H. H. Hilberry, *Society of Architectural Historians' Journal,* 22 December 1963, p. 241; review by P. Johnson, *Architectural Review* 128 (September 1960): 173–175; review by S. Moholy-Nagy, *Progressive Architecture* 42 (April 1961): 200; review by F. Tentori, *Casabella,* no. 247 (January 1961): 23–25; review: *Industrial Design,* 7 December 1960, p. 10.

'This Is Tomorrow.' Review: *Architectural Design,* September 1956, p. 186.

Thorpe, J. N. Letter in response to 'Where Are You, Universal Man, Now that We Need You?' *RIBA Journal* (September 1976): 368.

Tournikiotis, P. 'Reyner Banham (1922–1988): A Historian of the Immediate Future.' *Architektonika Themata—Architecture in Greece,* no. 23 (1989): 28–31.

Tulloch, John. 'Reports on a Talk about Megastructures by Reyner Banham,' *Building Design,* no. 222 (18 October 1974): 9.

Tulloch, John. 'Megastructures—Just Like an Educational Toy.' *Building Design,* no. 226 (15 November 1974): 5.

Tulloch, John. 'Megastructures—Not So Much of a Revolution.' *Building Design,* no. 227 (22 November 1974): 7.

Tulloch, John. 'Urbanism, USA.' *Architectural Review* 130 (November 1961): 303–305.

Von Dijk, Hans. 'Acceptance as a Strategy: Reyner Banham's Articles Brought Together.' *Wonen—TA/BK,* no. 9 (May 1982): 26–31.

Watkin, D. J. 'Morality and Architecture,' letter to the editor. *Times Literary Supplement,* 3 March 1978, p. 256.

West, Anthony. 'Morality and Architecture,' letter to the editor. *Times Literary Supplement,* 28 April 1978, p. 475.

Whiteley, Nigel. '"Banham and Otherness": Reyner Banham (1922–1988) and His Quest for an Architectural Autre.' *Architectural History* 33 (1990): 188–221.

Wilkins, Louis. 'Dinosaurs of the Modern Movement.' *Building Design,* no. 327 (10 December 1976): 14–15.

Zevi, Bruno. 'L'andropausa degli architetti moderni italiani.' *L'Architettura* 5, no. 47 (August 1959): 223 (answer to Reyner Banham's article, 'Neoliberty: The Italian Retreat from Modern Architecture,' in *Architectural Review* 7125 [April 1959]: 230–255).

Index

Sponsoring Editor: Edward Dimendberg
Designer: Barbara Jellow
Compositor: G&S Typesetters, Inc.
Text: Franklin Gothic Book
Display: Frutiger Black
Printer: Data Reproductions
Binder: Data Reproductions